THE WESTERN READER'S GUIDE

The
Western Reader's Guide

A Selected Bibliography of Nonfiction Magazines, 1953–91

By JAMES A. BROWNING

Stillwater, Oklahoma

Library of Congress Cataloging-in-Publication Data

Browning, James A.
   The western reader's guide: a selected bibliography of nonfiction maga-
zines, 1953–91 / by James A. Browning.
      p.   cm.
   ISBN 0-935269-09-6
   1. West (U.S.)—History—Bibliography. 2. West (U.S.)—Biography—
Bibliography. I. Title.
Z1251.W5B87   1992
[F591]
016.978—dc20   92-35419
                                                                          CIP
Cover and book design by L.A. Smith

Published by Barbed Wire Press, P.O. Box 2107, Stillwater, OK 74076
Manufactured in the United States of America. First edition.

Introduction

When the first issue of *True West* rolled off the presses in 1953, it spawned a magazine genre that multiplied and flourished through the 1960s and '70s. In its wake more than two dozen nonfiction western magazine titles were introduced. Some lasted but a single issue. Others enjoyed long lives. As the western craze of the sixties and seventies waned, however, readership of the nonfiction western magazines declined to a smaller, dedicated group of Old West aficionados. The number of titles published fell off as well, and today, only three—*True West, Old West,* and *Wild West*—remain in publication.

The thousands of issues under all those western titles are an invaluable resource for anyone interested in the history of the Old West. Many books have been written about the more famous men and women of the Old West, yet much information about those individuals remains available exclusively in article form. Likewise, thousands of lesser-known individuals whose lives for one reason or another do not merit book-length biographies appear only in magazines.

Until now much of that information has effectively been locked away from the average researcher, simply because most of the western magazines have never been thoroughly indexed. Researchers have been forced either to rummage blindly through back issues or to simply neglect a vital source of information. Hence the need for a comprehensive bibliography of the western history magazines.

In 1990 Larry J. Walker, of El Paso, Texas, laid the foundation for such a bibliography by publishing a little book entitled *Catalog of Western Magazines Based on Years Since 1950*. In it he lists the title and facts of publication of every nonfiction western magazine published since that first issue of *True West* started it all in 1953. As I already owned several hundred of the issues listed, I set out to complete my set. Two years later, with the help of several individuals to whom I am greatly indebted, I had reached my goal.

In the meantime, in conducting my own research over the years, I had maintained a running file of notecards on articles in which specific individuals figured prominently. Because it was *people* who made the West and because it is *people* that I find the most interesting aspect of the West, that biographical approach seemed to me the most practical alternative to the impossibility of keeping index cards on every topic of every article ever published. As I filled in my magazine collection, I continued to update my card file, and my selected bibliography became as complete as any such listing can possibly be. Only then did it occur to me that the information I had compiled would be invaluable to other western history buffs and should be shared with them. So *The Western Reader's Guide* was born.

Individuals are listed alphabetically by their real last name, when it is known. Those individuals with only one name or with only an alias are alphabetized accordingly, and I have attempted to include cross-references where needed. The entries are in standard bibliographical form, though the labyrinthine reprint histories of many articles required some improvising. Articles are listed by the first publication in which they appeared; a chronological listing of reprints then follows in the main entry. Some of the quirks of the so-called "popular press" also defy the manuals for writing bibliographies. In such cases, I have included as much information as necessary to identify the specific issue of a publication.

In addition to my complete set of western history magazines, the bibliography also lists articles from complete files of the journals of the National Association of Outlaw and Lawman History, the Western Outlaw and Lawman History Association, and the Outlaw Trail History Association. I have also included listings from an incomplete set of Westerners Brand Books, many of which are very rare and difficult to find. Because the scholarly journals published by professional historians are thoroughly indexed elsewhere, I have not included them here. Obviously, any serious student of the Old West should also consult those publications. Nor have I included the random article about western history that occasionally shows up in the general interest periodicals.

Most of the back issues of those periodicals that are still in print are available from the publishers. Back issues of out-of-publication periodicals are more difficult to locate, but collectors would do well to consult the classified ads of the current western magazines. Flea markets, garage sales, and used book dealers are also good sources for back issues.

I would like to thank all of those people who have helped make this work possible. Among them are Jim Dullenty, of Hamilton, Montana; Chuck Parsons, of South Wayne, Wisconsin; Larry J. Walker, of El Paso, Texas; C. Felton Cochran, of Lubbock, Texas; and Gregg Davis, of Tempe, Arizona.

James A. Browning
Charleston, South Carolina

THE WESTERN READER'S GUIDE

Selected Bibliography of Westerners

Abernathy, John "Jack"

Gordon, Bill. "The Bare-Handed Coyote Catcher." *True Frontier,* June 1967, p. 8. Rpt. *True Frontier,* Dec. 1972, p. 20; and *True Frontier,* Special Issue No. 15, Summer 1976, p. 38.

Holding, Vera. "He Bagged 'em Bare-Handed." *Golden West,* Jan. 1965, p. 20. Rpt. *Western Frontier,* Summer 1979, p. 12.

Schuessler, Raymond. "He Caught Wolves With His Bare Hands." *Real West,* Sept. 1971, p. 6.

Waida, Marilyn. "Jack Abernathy—Oklahoma Legend." *Old West,* Summer 1969, p. 34.

Adams, Charlie

Phillips, Lanny. "Hell Gold of the Gila." *Real West,* Oct. 1957, p. 60.

Adams, J.H.

Archer, Myrtle. "California Stagecoach Skirmish." *True West,* May 1988, p. 44.

Adams, Jake

O'Neal, Bill. "George Flatt vs. George Wood and Jake Adams" ("Great Western Gunfights" column). *True West,* May 1988, p. 59.

Adams, John "Grizzly"

Baldwin, Carey. "Man and Beast On A Crash Course." *Old West,* Spring 1975, p. 16.

Coleman, J. Knowles. "Grizzly Adams and His Bears." *The West,* March 1964, p. 22. Rpt. *Western Frontier,* Nov. 1976, p. 33.

1

Fleming, Gerry. "A Man Called Grizzly." *True Frontier,* Special Issue No. 3, 1972, p. 28.

————. "Grizzly Fighter." *Pioneer West,* Sept. 1974, p. 26.

McCracken, Harold, and Gene Caesar. "Damndest Bear Hunter of Them All." *True Western Adventures,* Aug. 1960, p. 10.

Adamson, Carl

Parsons, Chuck. "Involved in Garrett Murder" ("Answer Man" column). *Frontier Times,* Oct. 1984, p. 41.

Weisner, Herman B. "Garrett's Death—Conspiracy or Doublecross?" *True West,* Dec. 1979, p. 6.

Adobe Walls Combatants, 1874

Sufrin, Mark. "The Massacre at Adobe Walls." *Frontier West,* Oct. 1972, p. 12.

Aldridge Brothers

Silva, Lee. "Attack on Wells Fargo." *Westerner,* Sept.-Oct. 1974, p. 29.

————. "Hold-Up: They Robbed Wells Fargo—Almost." *Westerner,* Feb. 1971, p.10.

Ali, Hadji ("Hi Jolly")

Bloom, Sam. "The Fantastic Camel Corps That Patrolled the West." *Frontier West,* April 1973, p. 44.

Farnsworth, Harriett. "Hi Jolly, Hero of the Camel Trails." *Real West,* Nov. 1969, p. 13.

Roensch, Dell. "Hi Jolly and the Camels." *True Western Adventures,* Oct. 1958, p. 30.

Sandell, Jay. "Hi Jolly's Camel Brigade." *Real West,* Sept. 1960, p. 26. Rpt. *Real West,* Annual, Spring 1968, p. 47.

Allee Family

Parsons, Chuck. "Four Generations of Texas Rangers" ("Answer Man" column). *True West,* July 1984, p. 31.

————. "Killed In A Barroom Brawl" ("Answer Man" column). *True West,* April 1988, p. 12.

Allemand, Joe

Nelson, Andre. "The Last Sheepman-Cattleman War." *True West,* May 1988, p. 14.

Allen, Jack
Repp, Ed Earl. "The Man They Couldn't Kill." *True Frontier*, Dec. 1975, p. 10. Rpt. *True Frontier*, Oct. 1977, p. 14.

Allison, Art (cousin of Clay Allison)
Bailey, Tom. "Showdown In Skeleton Canyon." *True Western Adventures*, Oct. 1959, p. 28.

Allison, Charles
Rasch, Philip J. "The Other Allison." *NOLA Quarterly*, Vol. V, No. 1, Oct. 1979, p. 14.

Allison, Clay
Barstow, Graig. "Wild Wolf Allison." *Big West*, Oct. 1967, p. 12.

Breihan, Carl W. "Clay Allison, Badman." *Oldtimers Wild West*, Feb. 1978, p. 14.

_____. "Clay Allison: Fantastic Gunslinger." *The West*, Dec. 1967, p. 10. Rpt. *Western Frontier*, Stagecoach Series, Fall 1974, p. 26; *Western Frontier*, May 1978, p. 26; and *Western Frontier*, Jan. 1983, p. 26.

_____. "Clay Allison: Gunfighter." *Westerner*, Nov. 1970, p. 10.

_____. "Clay Allison: Psychopathic Killer." *Golden West*, June 1972, p. 26. Rpt. *Western Frontier*, Annual No. 1, 1975, p. 40; and *Western Frontier*, July 1983, p. 34.

Carson, John. "Clay Allison." *True West*, Dec. 1961, p. 23.

DeMattos, Jack. "Clay Allison" ("Gunfighters of the Real West" column). *Real West*, March 1979, p. 18.

Dobie, J. Frank. "Gentleman Killer." *Frontier Times*, Winter 1957-58, p. 12.

_____. "The West's Most Eccentric Gunman." *True West*, Oct. 1968, p. 17.

France, Jay. "Life of Hell Raising Clay Allison." *Western Action*, Sept. 1960, p. 12.

Holben, Richard E. "Wild Man of Cimarron." *True Frontier*, April 1977, p. 18.

Kutz, Jack. "The Corpsemaker." *Great West*, Aug. 1973, p. 18. Rpt. *Great West*, Fall 1981, p. 20.

Mannings, Johnson. "'Blue Belly' Hating Gunslinger." *Wild West*, March 1970, p. 58.

Otero, Miguel Antonio. "Clay Allison of the Washita." *Old West*, Winter 1975, p. 21.

Parsons, Chuck. "Clay Allison: Vigilante." *Real West*, Aug. 1982, p. 15. Rpt. *Real West*, Special Issue, Spring 1983, p. 62.

_____. "An Editor's Humorous Look at Clay Allison." *Old West,* Fall 1987, p. 60.

Rasch, Philip J. "Chunk Colbert, Clay Allison Dined, Chunk Died." *NOLA Quarterly,* Vol. II, No. 4, Winter 1976, p. 8.

_____. "Sudden Death in Cimarron." *NOLA Quarterly,* Vol. X, No. 4, Spring 1986, p. 6.

Redding, Stan. "Clay Allison and Mr. Pecos." *True West,* Feb. 1977, p. 6.

Schoenberger, Dale. "Clay Allison: Cowboy Gunfighter." *Frontier Times,* Nov. 1966, p. 6.

Sufrin, Mark. "Cimarron's Fantastic Death Dance Duel." *Frontier West,* June 1974, p. 6.

Wiltsey, Norman B. "Clay Allison, Laughing Killer." *True West,* Aug. 1956, p. 22. Rpt. *Real West,* Jan. 1974, p. 32.

Allman, John
Bundy, Rex. "Outlaw Exterminators Helped With Arizona Law." *NOLA Quarterly,* Vol. I, No. 3, Autumn 1975, p. 11.

Almer, "Red Jack"
Gray, Morton. "The Petticoat Bandit." *Western Tales,* June 1960, p.10.

Long, J.A. "How Red Jack Almer Died." *The West,* Oct. 1964, p. 46.

Alvord, Burt
Dillon, Richard. "Arizona's Last Train Robbery." *Real West,* Sept. 1977, p. 50.

Harrison, John H. "Lawman's Loot." *Westerner,* Summer 1975, p. 22.

Hartley William B. "Turncoat From Tombstone." *True Western Adventures,* Dec. 1959, p. 30.

Ames Brothers (Oakes, Oliver)
Carroll, Murray L. "Pyramid on the Plains." *True West,* May 1991, p. 32.

Anderson, Annie
Roberts, Gary L. "Queen of the Cowtowns." *Frontier Times,* May 1964, p. 33.

Anderson, David L. (see Wilson, Billy)

Anderson, Hugh
Allegro. "The West's Bloodiest Duel." Rpt. Ed. Colin Rickards. *Old West,* Summer 1965, p. 25.

Compagnon, Frank D. "Mike's Mad Shadow." *True Western Adventures*, 1957, p. 23.

O'Neal, Bill. "McCluskie vs. Anderson" ("Great Western Gunfights" column). *True West*, Feb. 1988, p. 41.

_____. "The Newton General Massacre" ("Great Western Gunfights" column). *True West*, Jan. 1988, p. 47.

Anderson, Jack "White Eye"
Thorp, Raymond W. "White Eye: Last of the Old-Time Plainsmen." *True West*, April 1965, p. 6.

Anderson, William "Bloody Bill"
Breihan, Carl W. "The Battle of Centralia." *Real West*, Dec. 1980, p. 28. Rpt. *Real West*, Annual, 1981, p. 54.

_____. "Bloody Bill Anderson." *Real West*, July 1961, p. 26.

Hart, George. "Irvin Walley: The Murderer of Cole Younger's Father." *NOLA Quarterly*, Vol. XV, No. 1, 1991, p.4.

Morris, Roy, Jr. "Gunfighters and Lawmen" column. *Wild West*, Feb. 1989, p. 10.

McCarter, M.W. "Cord of Death." *Frontier Times*, Winter, 1961, p. 7. Rpt. *Old West*, Winter 1978, p. 6.

Parsons, Chuck. "Bloody Bill Anderson: Civil War Terror" ("Answer Man" column). *True West*, Oct. 1991, p. 12.

Thorp, Raymond W. "Death Rode the Brunswick Road." *Frontier Times*, Nov. 1965, p. 18.

Angus, William "Red"
Cortesi, Lawrence J. "The Johnson County War." *Pioneer West*, March 1979, p. 6.

Hawthorne, Roger. "New Insights to Johnson County War." *NOLA Quarterly*, Vol. IX, No. 1, Autumn 1984, p. 16.

Vail, Jason. "Hired Assassins Dreaded." *Wild West*, June 1988, p. 26.

Anthony Brothers (Gus and Aldo)
DeNevi, Don. "Derail the Gold Car!" *Westerner*, Summer 1975, p. 8.

Anthony, Leonel Ross (Polly Pry)
Hayden, Peter V. "The Incredible Polly Pry." *Frontier Times*, Jan. 1977, p. 16.

Antonio, Juan
McDonald, Russ. "Juan Antonio: Chief of All the Cahuillas." *True West,* Nov.
1991, p. 49.

Antrim, Catherine (Mrs. William H.)
Carson, Kit. "Who Was the Kid's Mother?" *Real West,* Sept. 1964, p. 14.

Antrim, Joe (see McCarty, Joe)

Apache Jack (Matt Longley)
Kevin, Glen. "The 'White Apache' Who Terrorized New Mexico." *Frontier West,*
Dec. 1972, p. 38.

Apache Kid
Cortesi, Lawrence. "How They Turned the Apache Kid Into A Desperate
Renegade." *Frontier West,* Aug. 1974, p. 12.

Dillon, Richard. "Al Sieber's War With the Apache Kid." *Westerner,* Sept.-Oct.
1974, p. 50.

Gaddis, Bob. "The Apache Kid: Meanest Killer in the West." *True Frontier,* Jan.
1969, p. 34. Rpt. *True Frontier,* Special Issue No. 9, 1974, p. 6; *True Frontier,*
Aug. 1976, p. 30; and *True Frontier,* April 1978, p. 20.

Guttman, Jon. "Warriors and Chiefs" column. *Wild West,* April 1991, p. 8.

Hayes, Jess G. "Apache Vengeance." *Frontier Times,* Sept. 1969, p. 6.

Hopson, William. "The Apache Kid: Arizona Terror." *True West,* Jan. 1955, p.
20. Rpt. *Old West,* Winter 1965, p. 48; and *Badman,* Summer 1971, p. 16.

Kemp, Ben W. "Ma-Si...Alias Apache Kid." *True West,* Feb. 1980, p. 20.

Kutz, Jack. "How White Man's Justice Turned the Apache Kid into a Renegade."
The West, Aug. 1973, p. 34. Rpt. *Western Frontier,* Jan. 1977, p. 34.

Long, James. "Legend of the Apache Kid." *Real West,* March 1966, p. 36.

Parsons, Chuck. "The Apache Kid: Renegade Scout" ("Answer Man" column).
True West, Dec. 1990, p. 14.

Sandell, Jay. "Betrayal of the Apache Kid." *Real West,* May 1959, p. 38.

Stanley, Samuel. "The Apache Kid." *Real West,* March 1981, p. 32. Rpt. *Real
West,* Yearbook, 1981, p. 32.

Apache Scouts
Bourke, John. "The Apaches: Greatest Scouts of Them All." *Western Frontier,*
Special Issue, March 1975, p. 38.

Chambers, Harold V. "The Apache Renegades." *Wild West,* July 1972, p. 14.

Apley, George W.
Kildare, Maurice. "Horror of Arizona's Wholesale Killer." *Westerner,* April 1971, p. 26.

Applegate, Jesse
Copeland, Edwin R. "The Wagon Train of 1848." *True Frontier,* March 1974, p. 26.

Fitzgerald, Arlene J. "He Pioneered the Applegate Trail." *The West,* Jan. 1967, p. 24. Rpt. *The West,* May 1974, p. 14; *Western Frontier,* Annual, 1977, p. 32; and *Western Frontier,* July 1984, p. 32.

Harrison, John H. "The South Road: Jesse Applegate's Infamous Emigrant Trail." *Real West,* Jan. 1982, p. 30. Rpt. *Real West,* Yearbook, Fall 1982, p. 25.

"Appleseed, Johnny" (Henderson Luelling)
Hall, Patrick A. "Oregon's Johnny Appleseed." *Frontier Times,* July 1967, p. 26.

Arbuckle, Henry "Hank"
Sanford, Jules. "Hank Arbuckle and Little Emma." *Real West,* Jan. 1961, p. 24.

Archeveque, Sostenes
Connant, Laura. "The Story of Sostenes Archeveque." *Pioneer West,* May 1969, p. 26.

Arizona Rangers
Dodge, Matt. "Saga of the Arizona Rangers." *Oldtimers Wild West,* Dec. 1977, p. 10.

Armijo, Manuel
Duncan, Gra'Delle. "New Mexico's Game of Death." *Golden West,* May 1966, p. 28. Rpt. *Golden West,* July 1974, p. 10.

Arnold, Philip
Hill, Leonard. "The Great Diamond Hoax" ("Treasure" column). *True Frontier,* Special Issue No. 12, 1975, p. 38. Rpt. *True Frontier,* Special Issue No. 20, Winter 1977, p. 8.

Scullin, George. "They Salted the Desert With Diamonds." *True Western Adventures,* June 1960, p. 30.

Sufrin, Mark. "The Fantastic Table Rock Swindle." *Frontier West,* June 1972, p. 12

Arrington, George W.
Qualey, Jake. "Island of the Dead." *Real West,* Jan. 1962, p. 14.

Walker, Wayne T. "Captain George Arrington: Iron Handed Ranger." *Real West,* June 1981, p. 29.

————. "G.W. Arrington: The Ranger Who Tamed the Panhandle." *Golden West,* Feb. 1973, p. 30.

Ash, Ben
Koller, Joe. "Ben Ash: Dakota Trailblazer." *Goldest West,* Jan. 1965, p. 10. Rpt. *Western Frontier,* Fall 1981, p. 33.

Ashley, William H.
Hurdy, John Major. "Great Fur Explosion." *Wild West,* June 1970, p. 44.

————. "Missouri Giant." *Pioneer West,* Nov. 1967, p. 34.

Astor, John Jacob
Malsbary, George. "King of the Fur Trade." *Great West,* June 1974, p. 18.

Aten, Ira
Hawkins, Rafe W. "Blood Bath in Texas." *Real West,* Oct. 1957, p. 4.

Morando, B. "Ira Aten." *Real West,* Americana Series, Fall 1965, p. 18.

Preece, Harold. "'I Fought These Masked Rustlers.'" *Real West,* May 1963, p. 20.

Shannon, Ted. "Ira Aten and the Disappearing Killer." *The West,* Feb. 1965, p. 16. Rpt. *The West,* May 1972, p. 20; and *Western Frontier,* May 1986, p. 20.

Stanley, Samuel. "The Fence Cutters War." *Real West,* Aug. 1985, p. 18.

Stilwell, Hart. "Dinamite [sic] Aten and His Big Boom." *True Western Adventures,* Oct. 1959, p. 22.

Webb, Walter Prescott. "The Fence Cutters." *True West,* June 1963, p. 12.

Whitehead, Ruth. "That Bloody Fence-Cutting War." *The West,* Nov. 1973, p. 32.

Atkinson, Henry
Cortesi, Lawrence. "Showdown at Bad Axe." *Frontier West,* June 1975, p. 26.

Aubry, Francois Xavier
Auer, L.C. "Fabulous Ride of Little Aubry." *The West,* Aug. 1965, p. 39. Rpt. *The West,* Annual, 1971, p. 21.

Bird, Roy. "Francois Aubry's Ride for Glory." *Real West,* Nov. 1979, p. 25.

Carpenter, Clinton. "The Fastest Ride in the Old West." *Real West,* April 1958, p. 45.

Dobie, J. Frank. "The West's Greatest Ride." *True Western Adventures*, Aug. 1959, p. 22.

Sheldon, Roger. "Plainsman in A Hurry." *True West*, Nov. 1954, p. 19.

Thomas, Kevin. "Ride With the Wind." *Pioneer West*, Sept. 1974, p. 16.

Walker, Wayne T. "Horses Flew for the Mighty Mite." *The West*, Dec. 1968, p. 18. Rpt. *Golden West*, Aug. 1973, p. 10.

Augustino, Giovanni Marie

Simpson, Audrey. "Hermit of the Organs." *True West*, Oct. 1963, p. 48.

White, Marjorie. "Hermit's Peak Legend." *Old West*, Spring 1988, p. 48.

Austin, Stephen F.

Ehly, Jean. "Stephen Austin: Father of Texas." *The West*, Sept. 1970, p. 28. Rpt. *Western Frontier*, Annual, 1977, p. 14.

Roebuck, Field. "Fifteen Years to a Republic." Part I, *True West*, March 1986, p. 14; Part II, *True West*, April 1986, p. 14.

Averill, James "Jim"

Anderson, Pete. "The Hanging of Cattle Kate." *True Western Adventures*, Dec. 1960, p. 28.

Boucher, Leonard H. "The Wyoming Invaders." *Great West*, Sept. 1969, p. 16.

Hines, Lawrence. "Horror Lynching of the Petticoat Rustler." *Frontier West*, Feb. 1973, p. 36.

"The Sweetwater Rustlers." *Great West*, Aug. 1970, p. 29.

Axelby, George

Engebretson, Doug. "The George Axelby Gang and the Stoneville Battle." *Real West*, April 1983, p. 22.

Koller, Joe. "Montana's Bloodiest Day." *The West*, Oct. 1964, p. 24. Rpt. *The West*, Annual, 1971, p. 38; and *Golden West*, June 1974, p. 9.

Baca Brothers (Enofre and Abran)
Edwards, Harold L. "Trouble in Socorro." *Old West,* Winter 1990, p. 42.

Baca, Cipriano
Hornung, Chuck. "Cipriano Baca, New Mexico Lawman." *Real West,* Dec. 1981, p. 8. Rpt. *Real West,* Yearbook, Fall 1982, p. 15.

Baca, Elfego
Clough, Bob. "The Odds Were Eighty to One." *Golden West,* Sept. 1969, p. 17.

DeMattos, Jack. "Elfego Baca" ("Gunfighters of the Real West" column). *Real West,* Jan. 1978, p. 32.

Epic, Norman. "The 33-Hour Gunfight." *Westerner,* July-Aug. 1973, p. 50.

Harnin, William. "Slaughter Odds, 80 to 1." *True West,* Feb. 1958, p. 18.

Hayes, Mike. "Elfego Baca and the Frisco Shootout." *Old West,* Spring 1990, p. 30.

Kutz, Jack. "Elfego Baca, Lawman." *Great West,* April 1973, p. 6. Rpt. "Elfeyo [sic] Baca, Lawman." *Great West,* Fall 1981, p. 60.

Lenz, M. Taylor. "Shoot-Out: 80 to 1." *Westerner,* Sept.-Oct. 1969, p. 16.

O'Neal, Bill. "Elfego Baca vs. Eighty Cowboys" ("Great Western Gunfights" column). *True West,* June 1988, p. 59.

Reiss, Malcolm. "Elfego Baca: the Courteous Gunfighter." *True Western Adventures,* April 1961, p. 10.

Baggett, Thomas "Tom"
Walker, Wayne T. "Gunsmoke at the Courthouse." *Goldest West,* Aug. 1974, p. 22.

Bailey, Mollie
Racker, John F. "The Glorious Mollie Bailey." *Golden West,* Nov. 1973, p. 26.

Baker, Cullen
Breihan, Carl W. "Cullen Baker: First of the Gunfighters." *The West,* July 1967, p. 16. Rpt. *The West,* May 1972, p. 8; and *Western Frontier,* Jan. 1983, p. 14.

Eason, Al. "Cullen Baker: Purveyor of Death." *Frontier Times,* Sept. 1966, p. 6.

Hayes, Frederick. "Grandaddy of the Six Gun." *Real West,* May 1960, p. 30.

Smallwood, James. "Swamp Fox of the Sulphur." Part I, *True West,* Oct. 1991, p. 20; Part II, *True West,* Nov. 1991, p. 38.

Winfield, Craig. "Cullen Baker, Texas Gunfighter." *Oldtimers Wild West,* June 1979, p. 10.

Baker, "Doc"

Bartholomew, F.L. "The Rawhide Railroad." *Real West,* Nov. 1966, p. 24.

Baker, Frank

Reynolds, William D. "Frank Baker: Forgotten Gunman of the Lincoln County War." *NOLA Quarterly,* Vol. XV, No. 3, July-Sept. 1991, p. 15.

Baker, James "Jim"

Carson, John. "Jim Baker: Man of the Mountians." *Real West,* May 1965, p. 24.

Gray-Shaffner, Char. "Jim Baker and the Struggles of a Mountain Man." *Old West,* Winter 1983, p. 21.

Pickering, Lillian. "Jim Baker: Mountain Man." *Real West,* Sept. 1976, p. 42. Rpt. *Real West,* Annual, Winter 1977-78, p. 26.

Reinhart Henry. "Forgotten Plainsman." *True West,* Dec. 1964, p. 9.

Baker, Pearl

Baker, Pearl. "Robbers Roost Recollections." *True West,* Aug. 1983, p. 22.

Baldwin, Elias Jackson "Lucky"

Barney, L.C. "Lucky Baldwin." *True West,* Aug. 1963, p. 30.

Starnes, Luke F. "Baldwin's Big Bonanza." *True Frontier,* May 1970, p. 30.

Washburn, Ned. "Hated Lucky Baldwin Died In Bed." *America's Frontier West,* n.d., Issue No. 1, p. 40.

Baldwin, Frank D.

Kurtz, Henry I. "General Baldwin's Fantastic Expedition." *Real West,* July 1965, p. 48.

Winslowe, John R. "Charge of the Wagon Train." *True Frontier,* July 1969, p. 42. Rpt. *True Frontier,* Special Issue No. 6, 1973, p. 26.

Baldwin, Theodore A.

Vebell, Ed. "The Man Who Took Custer's Place." Part I, *Real West,* Dec. 1971, p. 16; Part II, *Real West,* Jan. 1972, p. 25; Part III, *Real West,* Feb. 1972, p. 46.

Ballard, Charles Littlepage
Ball, Eve. "Charles Ballard: Lawman of the Pecos." *The English Westerners' Brand Book,* Vol. VII, No. 4, July 1965, p. 1.

_____. "Lawman of the Pecos." *True West,* June 1967, p. 20.

Ballew, Bud
Dickey, E.M. Letter. *True West,* Oct. 1970, p. 4.

Riotte, Louise. "Marshal Braziel and Bud Ballew." *Frontier Times,* Nov. 1980, p. 36.

_____. "Shoot-Out at the California Cafe." *Golden West,* March 1971, p. 28. Rpt. *The West,* Jan. 1974, p. 32; and *Western Frontier,* July 1983, p. 32.

Banks, Charles Wells
Cheney, Louise. "The Royal Embezzler." *Golden West,* Jan. 1967, p. 38. Rpt. *Western Frontier ,* Special Issue, Fall, 1974, p. 30.

Coe, Clint. "The Vengeance of Wells Fargo." *True Western Adventures,* Aug. 1961, p. 26.

Dillon, Richard H. "Wells, Fargo's Jekyll and Hyde." *The American West,* March 1971, p. 28.

Banta, Charles Albert Franklin "Charlie"
McKelvey, Nat. "Arizona Giant." *Frontier Times,* Winter 1959-60, p. 14.

Banta, O.W. "Tex"
Banta, OW. "Tex Banta: Mountain Man." Ed. Wayne Spiller. *Old West,* Spring 1966, p. 2.

Banta, William
Banta, William, and J.W. Caldwell, Jr. "Twenty-Seven Years on the Frontier." Part I, *Old West,* Summer 1970, p. 77; Part II, *Old West,* Fall 1970, p. 77.

Barber Brothers (Bill and Ike)
Speer, Lonnie R. "On the Trail of the Barefoot Outlaws." *True West,* July 1989, p. 44.

Barcelo, Dona Gertrude "La Tules" ("Dona Tula")
Cerveri, Doris. "La Tules: Gambling Lady." *Real West,* March 1973, p. 20.

Cheney, Louise. "La Tules of Old Santa Fe." *Golden West,* Jan. 1967, p. 8.

Moore, Jean M. "The Gambling Lady of Santa Fe." *True Western Adventures,* April 1961, p. 28.

Robbins, Lance. "La Tules, the Notorious Redhead." *Real West,* June 1968, p. 34.

Shields, Bob. "Dona Tula: The First of the Double Agents." *Frontier West,* April 1971, p. 38.

Bare, Delinda

Robertson, Dorothy. "Delinda Bare...One Hundred Pounds of Pure Courage." *True Frontier,* Special Issue No. 15, Summer 1976, p. 18.

Barker, Billy

Ives, Arthur. "The Redoubtable Billy Barker." *Old West,* Fall 1985, p. 28.

Martin, Cy. "Bill Barker of Barkersville." *Real West,* March 1970, p. 54.

Barlow, Samuel K.

Betts, William J. "They Built the Barlow Road." *Oldtimers Wild West,* Aug. 1979, p. 21.

Barnard, Kate

Shirley, Glenn. "Oklahoma Kate: Woman of Destiny." *The West,* March 1968, p. 18.

Barnes, Jane

Fitzgerald, A. "The Incredible Jane Barnes." *The West,* June 1966, p. 16.

Herberg, Ruth M. "The Only White Woman For A Thousand Miles." *Real Frontier,* April 1971, p. 26.

Barnes, William Croft "Will"

Barnes, Will C. "Will C. Barnes and the Apaches." Rpt. *Frontier Times,* July 1977, p. 12.

Fink, Clarence M. "Will Croft Barnes: Horatio Alger of Arizona." *Real West,* Nov. 1972, p. 52.

Koller, Joe. "Telegrapher Barnes Volunteers." *Golden West,* March 1968, p. 16.

Barrow, Samuel B.

Parsons, Chuck. "A Texas Sheriff" ("Answer Man" column). *True West,* Dec. 1988, p. 13.

Barter, Dick "Rattlesnake Dick"

Delmar, Josephine. "Rattlesnake Dick Barter." *Old West,* Spring 1987, p. 40.

Fink, Clarence M. "Rattlesnake Dick, Land Pirate of the Placers." *Real West,* Sept. 1974, p. 58.

Harrison, John H. "Too Much Gold." *True Frontier,* Special Issue No. 8, 1973, p. 34.

Millard, Joseph. "Vengeance of Rattlesnake Dick." *True Western Adventures,* Oct. 1960, p. 27.

Reese, Richard. "The Poet and the Pirate." *Old West,* Spring 1982, p. 38.

Roe, Kenn Sherwood. "Rattlesnake Dick." *The West,* May 1967, p. 22. Rpt. *The West,* Sept. 1972, p. 14; and *Western Frontier,* Sept. 1976, p. 28.

Stimmel, Thomas. "Rendezvous With Rattlesnake Dick." *True West,* April 1962, p. 23.

Bartlett, Polly

Arlandson, Leone. "Polly Bartlett: The Devil's Daughter." *Pioneer West,* Nov. 1973, p. 25.

Ballenger, Dean W. "Polly Bartlett, Wyoming's Amazing Poisoner." *Real West,* July 1963, p. 22.

_____. "Wyoming's Money-Mad Poisoner." *Golden West,* July 1965, p. 36. Rpt. *Western Frontier,* Annual, Winter 1977, p. 3.

Barton, Jerry

Rasch, Philip J. "Jerry Barton: A Noted Desperado." *Real West,* Feb. 1986, p. 37.

Bascom, George Nicholas

Mason, John. "The Blunder of Lieutenant Bascom." *Real West,* March 1960, p. 24.

Sacks, Benjamin H. "New Evidence on the Bascom Affair." *Arizona and the West,* Vol. IV, No. 3, Autumn 1962, p. 261.

Utley, Robert M. "The Bascom Affair: A Reconstruction." *Arizona and the West,* Vol. III, No. 1, Spring 1961, p. 59.

Yarbrough, Leroy. "The Apache and the Sioux." *Real West,* Special Issue, Winter 1970, p. 26.

Bascom, Sam

Henderson, Sam. "Sam Bascom: Fighting Preacher." *The West,* Feb. 1967, p. 28.

Bass, Lorenzo "Lon"

Kildare, Maurice. "Ranger Shoot-Out at the Cowboy Saloon." *The West,* Jan. 1973, p. 24.

O'Neal, Bill. "Arizona Rangers vs. Lon Bass" ("Great Western Gunfights" column). *True West,* Nov. 1990, p. 58.

Rasch, Philip J. "The Life and Death of Lon Bass." *NOLA Quarterly,* Vol. XIV, Nos. 3 and 4 (combined issue), 1990, p. 8.

Bass, Sam

"Ask Your Questions" column. *Real West,* May 1964, p. 6.

Breihan, Carl W. "The Day Outlaw Sam Bass Was Killed." *Real West,* May 1975, p. 46.

_____. "The Incredible Sam Bass." *Real West,* July 1960, p. 16. Rpt. *Real West,* Americana Series, Fall 1964, p. 44.

_____. "The Last Raid of Outlaw Sam Bass." *Pioneer West,* Jan. 1979, p. 18.

_____. "Sam Bass' First Brush With the Law." *Golden West,* July 1969, p. 34. Rpt. *Western Frontier,* Jan. 1978, p. 40.

_____. "Sam Bass's Last Train Robbery." *Real West,* July 1977, p. 30.

Caperton, Benjamin Franklin. "Sam Bass Robbed My Train." *True West,* June 1964, p. 28.

Dary, David. "Entangled Legends About Lost Treasure in Ellis County." *True West,* Sept. 1987, p. 26.

Dobie, J. Frank. "The Robinhooding of Sam Bass." *True West,* Aug. 1958, p. 8.

Glen, Calvin. "The Ghost of Sam Bass." *Frontier Times,* Sept. 1978, p. 12.

Hartley, William B. "They Don't Sing the Truth About Sam." *True Western Adventures,* Oct. 1958, p. 24.

Keller, Joe. "Sam Bass: Blundering Bandit." *Real West,* Nov. 1962, p. 42.

Lehman, M.P. "Sam Bass and the Round Rock Massacre." *True Frontier,* Nov. 1967, p. 48.

O'Neal, Bill. "The Sam Bass Gang in Round Rock" ("Great Western Gunfights" column). *True West,* Feb. 1989, p. 61.

Parker, Jerry A. "Twenty-Seven Years to Hell." *Great West,* Oct. 1968, p. 58.

Pearce, Bennett R. "Night of Terror at Big Springs." *The West,* May 1971, p. 18. Rpt. *Western Frontier,* Jan. 1981, p. 20.

Powers, Mark. "Sam Bass." *Great West,* Dec. 1972, p. 26.

Preece, Harold. "Who Killed Sam Bass?" *The West,* Jan. 1972, p. 39. Rpt. *Western Frontier,* March 1976, p. 5; *Western Frontier,* May 1979, p. 31; and *Western Frontier,* Nov. 1982, p. 19.

Robbins, Lance. "Young Man from Indiana." *Real West,* Aug. 1968, p. 39.

"Sam Bass: Texas Train Robber." *Gunslingers of the West,* Winter 1966, p. 32.

Scherer, Leo. "Nebraska's Great Train Robbery." *Golden West,* Jan. 1965, p. 14. Rpt. *Golden West,* Feb. 1972, p. 14; and *Western Frontier,* Special Issue, Summer 1974, p. 38.

Shannon, Dan. "My Cousin, Sam Bass." *Real West,* Nov. 1973, p. 40.

Shirley, Glenn. "How Heck Thomas Outwitted Sam Bass." *Real West,* Sept. 1968, p. 42.

Stillwell, Hart. "I Saw Them Kill Sam Bass." *True West,* Nov. 1954, p. 14. Rpt. *Badman,* Summer 1971, p. 32.

Thede, Marion, and Harold Preece. "The Story Behind the Song: The Ballad of Sam Bass." *Real West,* Nov. 1973, p. 14.

Winters, Jerry. "Sam Bass' Nerve." *Westerner,* Nov.-Dec. 1973, p. 38.

Wukovits, John F. "Big Score at Big Springs." *Wild West,* Dec. 1989, p. 27.

Bassett, Charlie

DeMattos, Jack. "Whatever Became of the Dodge City Peace Commission?" *Real West,* Jan. 1977, p. 38. Rpt. *Real West,* Yearbook, Summer 1978, p. 50.

Mays, Carelton. "Quiet Marshal, Quiet Town." *Real West,* July 1960, p. 8.

Walker, Wayne T. "Charlie Bassett: Dodge City Lawman." *Golden West,* July 1971, p. 14. Rpt. *The West,* Oct. 1974, p. 26; *Western Frontier,* May 1979, p. 20; *Western Frontier,* April 1983, p. 26.

Bassett Family (of Brown's Park)

Kelly, Charles. "Queen Ann of Brown's Hole." *Old West,* Winter 1969, p. 24.

Norwood, John. "Brown's Hole: Historic Border Hideout." *Frontier Times,* Feb. 1985, p. 43.

Bates, Alfred Elliott

Delo, David M. "The Battle of Snake Mountain." *True West,* Nov. 1987, p. 26.

Battey, Thomas C.

Frasier, Thomas A. "A Quaker Missionary Among the Kiowas." *Real West,* Dec. 1970, p. 19.

Baugh, "Lev" P.

Holt, Roy D. "Ordeals of A Fence Cutting Detective." *Westerner,* March-April 1974, p. 15.

Whitehead, Ruth. "That Bloody Fence-Cutting War." *The West,* Nov. 1973, p. 32.

Baylor, George Wythe

Baylor, W.K. "Pioneer Vengeance." *Vanishing Texas,* July 1981, p. 15.

Jameson, W.C. "Last Stand of the Mescalero Apaches." *True West,* Dec. 1991, p. 14.

Baylor, John R.

Baylor, W.K. "Pioneer Vengeance." *Vanishing Texas,* July 1981, p. 15.

Roebuck, Field. "The True Story of the Brazos Indian Reservation Skirmish." *Old West,* Spring 1988, p. 12.

Beach, Charlie

Schmidt, R. Roland. "Charlie Beach: The Fightingest Western Editor of Them All." *Frontier West,* June 1972, p. 50.

Beachy, Hill

Agnew, Henry T. "Beachy's Murderous Dream." *Real West,* Jan. 1965, p. 38.

Cheney, Louise. "Hill Beachy's Nightmare." *Golden West,* May 1967, p. 36.

Ford, H.D. "Nightmare in the Bitterroots." *Frontier Times,* Spring 1960, p. 14.

Hansen, John. "They Murdered Magruder." *Great West,* Oct. 1973, p. 14.

Pratt, Grace Roffey. "Hill Beachy's Prophetic Dream." *True West,* Dec. 1962, p. 24.

Stanley, Samuel. "Hill Beachy's Journey for Justice." *Real West,* April 1981, p. 28.

Weddle, Ferris. "How Bitter Were the Roots." *Real West,* May 1959, p. 41.

Weddle, Ferris M. "Murder in the Bitterroots." *Old West,* Winter 1964, p. 21.

Beale, Edward Fitzgerald

Cole, Martin. "Lieutenant Beale's Camel Corps." *Old West,* Summer 1986, p. 36.

Johnson, Paul L. "The Ride That Started the Gold Rush." *Frontier Times,* Spring 1961, p. 18.

Long, Paul F. "Personality" column. *Wild West,* Dec. 1991, p. 8.

Reynolds, Jerry. "Monarch of All He Surveyed." *Real West,* July 1978, p. 16.

Secrest, William B. "Last Stand at Tule River." *Old West,* Winter 1981, p. 6.

Bean, Roy

Allenbaugh, Carl. "The Secret Life of Judge Roy Bean." *Westerner,* Dec. 1970, p. 14.

Cheney, Louise. "Judge Roy Bean's Lady Fair." *Real West,* Feb. 1974, p. 50.

Dary, David. "The Prize Fight Texas Didn't Want." *True Frontier,* Sept. 1973, p. 12.

Hanna, Wilma. "Lillie Langtry and the 'Law West of the Pecos.'" *The West,* March 1973, p. 38. Rpt. *Western Frontier,* May 1986, p. 38.

"Judge Roy Bean: Law West of the Pecos." *Great West,* July 1969, p. 18.

McDaniel, Ruel. "Love West of the Pecos." *Real West,* July 1960, p. 18.

————. "Roy Bean." *Real West,* Americana Series, Fall 1965, p. 26.

————. "Vinegaroon: The Saga of Judge Roy Bean." Part I, *True West,* Oct. 1965, p. 6; Part II, *True West,* Dec. 1965, p. 6.

Morris, Roy, Jr. "Gunfighters and Lawmen" column. *Wild West,* Oct. 1988, p. 8.

Parsons, Chuck. "Judge Roy Bean" ("Answer Man" column). *True West,* April 1990, p. 12.

Preece, Harold. "The Barroom Judge Who Was the Law West of the Pecos." *Frontier West,* June 1971, p. 42.

Repp, Ed Earl. "Law of the Chaparral." *True Frontier,* July 1971, p. 34.

Roensch, Dell. "Little Caesar of the Pecos." *True Western Adventures,* Aug. 1959, p. 32.

Starnes, Luke F. "Roy Bean: Law West of the Pecos." *True Frontier,* May 1969, p. 22. Rpt. *True Frontier,* June 1976, p. 28: and *True Frontier,* April 1978, p. 14.

Wallace, Jack. Letter. *True West,* April 1966, p. 4.

Wood, Lamont. "Wanted: Roy Bean." *True West,* Jan. 1984, p. 52.

Beatty, Chapo
Kuehlthau, Margaret. "Last of the Arizona Rangers." *True West,* June 1964, p. 37.

Beaver, Oscar
Edwards, Harold L. "Oscar Beaver: A Gritty Little Devil." *Real West,* Dec. 1986, p. 38.

Bebee, Hiram
Garman, Mary. "Was He the Sundance Kid?" *NOLA Quarterly,* Vol. V, No. 4, April 1980, p. 6.

Beckham, Joe
Warren, C. "Joe Beckham: The Outlaw Sheriff." *Real West,* Aug. 1983, p. 28. Rpt. *Real West,* Yearbook, Fall 1984, p. 6.

Becknell, William
Holding, Vera. "The Road to Santa Fe." *True Frontier,* May 1971, p. 19.

Beckwith Family
Rasch, Philip J., and Lee Myers. "The Tragedy of the Beckwiths." *English Westerners' Brand Book,* Vol. V, No. 4, July 1963, p. 1.

Beckwith, John M.

Lofton, Monk. "Bleeding Hills." *Real West*, May 1961, p. 33.

Beckwourth, James P. (also spelled "Beckworth")

Brown, Hamilton. "Jim Beckworth: Great Negro Frontiersman." *The West*, May 1967, p. 8. Rpt. *The West*, Aug. 1973, p. 23.

Diel, Emanuel. "Beckworth's Elusive Elisa." *Frontier Times*, Aug. 1985, p. 22.

Garrett, Russell. "The Slave Who Became An Indian Chief." *Frontier West*, Dec. 1971, p. 12.

Lipton, Dean. "Jim Beckwourth: Trapper, Scout, and Indian Chief." *Pioneer West*, June 1972, p. 62.

_____. "The Black Crow Chief." *Wild West*, Dec. 1969, p. 46. Rpt. *Pioneer West*, Sept. 1974, p. 40.

Morgan, Charles. "A Mountain Man Writes A Book." *Frontier Times*, May 1963, p. 22. Rpt. *Old West*, Summer 1980, p. 34.

Parsons, Chuck. "Jim Beckwourth" ("Answer Man" column). *True West*, June 1991, p 12.

Repp, Ed Earl. "Jim Beckworth: Saint or Sinner?" *The West*, March 1969, p. 10. Rpt. *Western Frontier*, May 1976, p. 14.

_____. "Jim Beckwourth: Mountain Whirlwind." *Real Frontier*, Aug. 1971, p. 8. Rpt. *True Frontier*, Special Issue No. 19, Fall 1977, p. 37.

Ross, Thomas. "A Man to Match the Mountains." *Old West*, Fall 1987, p. 56.

Secrest, William B. "Dark Deed at San Miguel." *True West*, July 1982, p. 10.

Beeson, Chalkley McCarty "Chalk"

Bird, Roy. "The Wild Bunch Robbed the Spearville Bank." *Real West*, April 1987, p. 14.

Huston, Louise. "The Cowboy Band of Dodge City." *Real Frontier*, Aug. 1970, p. 39.

_____. "He Knew His Way Around." *The West*, Sept. 1970, p. 22.

Rozar, Lily-B. "An Old-Time Cowboy Band" ("Wild Old Days" column). *True West*, May 1988, p. 62.

Behan, John "Johnny"

Boyer, Glenn G. "Johnny Behan: Assistant Folk Hero." *Real West*, Part I, April 1981, p. 12; Part II, *Real West*, June 1981, p. 36. Rpt. as one-part article, *Real West*, Annual, Spring 1983, p. 6.

_____. "Johnny Behan of Tombstone." *Frontier Times*, July 1976, p. 6.

Traywick, Ben T. "The Lost Grave of Johnny Behan." *True West*, July 1991, p. 48.

Beidler, John Xavier "X"

Cantey, Emery, Jr. "John X. Beidler, Petitioner." *NOLA Quarterly,* Vol. IV, No. 1, Summer 1978, p. 13.

Kildare, Maurice. "Hangman From Hell." *Great West,* Nov. 1967, p. 22.

_____. "Hell Gate Hanging Bee." *Real West,* March 1967, p. 27.

McGonigle, Chris. "X. Beidler's Christmas Ambush." *True West,* Dec. 1987, p. 20.

O'Neal, Bill. "100 Years Ago In The West" column. *Old West,* Spring 1990, p. 14.

Randall, Gay. "You Can Have the Turkey." *Frontier Times,* Summer 1960, p. 22.

Randall, Richard. "Bannack Had A Christmas." *True Western Adventures,* Dec. 1959, p. 20.

Reed, James. "Red Butcher of the Vigilantes." *Real West,* Nov. 1958, p. 20. Rpt. *Real West,* Annual, Summer 1966, p. 70.

Thane, Eric. "The Hangman Named X." *True Frontier,* July 1969, p. 12. Rpt. *True Frontier,* Special Issue No. 7, Fall 1973, p. 20.

Walker, Wayne T. "Sand In His Craw." *Frontier Times,* Nov. 1963, p. 13.

Webb, Grayce R. "X. Beidler: Man Without Fear." *The West,* Sept. 1969, p. 16. Rpt. *The West,* Aug. 1974, p. 32.

Bell, Tom (Doc Hodges)

Arnold, Oren. "The West's First Stage Robbery." *True Western Adventures,* Issue No. 1, 1957, p. 10.

Rosenhouse, Leo. "California's Notorious Gun and Scalpel Bandit." *Real Frontier,* March 1970, p. 36. Rpt. *True Frontier,* Special Issue No. 1, 1971, p. 32.

_____. "The Cruel Doctor Who Plundered the West." *The West,* Sept. 1967, p. 32 Rpt. *The West,* Dec. 1973, p. 39; and *Western Frontier,* Annual No. 4, 1976, p. 13.

_____. "The Medic Who Terrorized the West." *Pioneer West,* Oct. 1970, p. 12.

Strunk, Gordon B. "Tom Bell: Greatest of the Road Agents." *Real West,* Feb. 1959, p. 34.

"Bella Rawhide"

"Hellcat Madam of Deadwood" (excerpts from her diary). *Man's Western,* Jan. 1960, p. 40.

Belmont, Cole
DeArment, R.K. "Cole Belmont: Barfly Witness." *NOLA Quarterly,* Vol XIV, No. 1, 1990, p. 4.

Bemis, Charlie (Charley)
Ryland, Lee. "Redemption of Charlie Bemis." *Real West,* March 1962, p. 12.

Timmen, Fritz. "The Poker Hand That Won A Wife." *True Frontier,* Special Issue No. 3, 1972, p. 30.

Bender Family (Katie, Pa, and Ma)
Archer, Jules. "The Girl With the Long Red Knife." *Western Tales,* June 1960, p. 24.

Ball, Eve. "The Bloody Benders." *Real West,* April 1984, p. 22.

Burkholder, Edwin V. "Those Murdering Benders." *True Western Adventures,* Feb. 1960, p. 36.

Cline, Don. "Strange Fate for the Bloody Benders." *NOLA Quarterly,* Vol. XI, No. 4, Spring 1987, p. 14.

Harrison, Fred. "The Red-Headed Witch of Labette County." *Real Frontier,* Oct. 1970, p. 8. Rpt. *True Frontier,* Special Issue No. 1, 1971, p. 28; *True Frontier,* June 1973, p. 8; and *True Frontier,* Fall 1977, p. 6.

Henderson, Mark. "Murder Tavern." *Great West,* May 1968, p. 11.

Holding, Vera. "The Goings on at the Bender Place." *Golden West,* Nov. 1968, p. 28. Rpt. *Golden West,* June 1972, p. 32.

Hunt, Greg. "Strange Mystery of the Frontier's Disappearing Devil Woman." *Frontier West,* Feb. 1975, p. 32.

Kuhn, Warren. "Cabin of Death." *True West,* Spring 1954, p. 10. Rpt. *Badman,* Summer 1971, p. 34.

Lehman, Leola. "The Butchering Benders." *Great West,* June 1971, p. 16.

Malocsay, Zoltan. "The Bloody Work of Katie Bender." *Westerner,* May-June 1974, p. 42.

Mays, Carelton. "The Truth About the Murdering Benders." *Real West,* April 1958, p. 12. Rpt. *Real West,* Annual, Summer 1966, p. 42.

Montgomery, Wayne. "Self-Styled Devil's Disciple." *True Frontier,* June 1972, p. 12. Rpt. *True Frontier,* Special Issue No. 11, Winter 1974-75, p. 16.

Offen, Charlotte M. "The Bloody Benders." *Big West,* Dec. 1969, p. 6.

Parsons, Chuck. "A Texas Gunfighter and the Kansas Murder Family." *Real West,* July 1980, p. 14. Rpt. *Real West,* Annual 1981, p. 14.

Richmond, Robert W. "Mementoes of Notoriety: John Brown and Kate Bender." *True West,* Oct. 1971, p. 26.

Robbins, Peggy. "Gunfighters and Lawmen" column. *Wild West,* Dec. 1988, p. 12.

Rozar, Lily-B. "Bloody Benders of Kansas." *Pioneer West,* April 1970, p. 22. Rpt. *Pioneer West,* Aug. 1972, p. 26; *Pioneer West,* June 1974, p. 22; and *Oldtimers Wild West,* Oct. 1976, p. 30.

Benham, Robert
Cameron, Caddo. "Buckskin to the Bone." *True West,* Winter 1953, p. 20.

Bennett, Charles
Jackson, John C. "The Pivotal Battle for Pacific Empire." *True West,* Sept. 1984, p. 24.

Reese, J.W. "Forgotten Man of Sutter's Mill." *Frontier Times,* Sept. 1973, p. 40.

Bennett, Polly
Mitchell, George. "The Day the Town Was Forced to Mourn Its Most Notorious Harlot." *Frontier West,* Feb. 1975, p. 14.

Benson, John W.
Thorp, Raymond W. "The Strange Story of Quantrill's Surgeon." *Old West,* Winter 1966, p. 10.

Bent Brothers
Egan, Ferol. "Bent's Old Fort-Castle In the Desert." *The American West,* Sept.-Oct. 1976, p. 10.

Grinnell, George Bird. "Bent's Old Fort and Its Builders." Part I, *The West,* Nov. 1965, p. 14; Part II, *The West,* Dec. 1965, p. 30. Rpt. Part I, *Western Frontier,* Aug. 1981, p. 14; Part II, *Western Frontier,* Jan. 1982, p. 28.

Holben, Richard E. "A Man to Match the Mountains." *Golden West,* Oct. 1974, p. 20.

Hutchinson, W.G. "Treasures Unearthed at Bent's Fort." *Frontier Times,* Sept. 1966, p. 42.

Bent, Charles
Carson, Phil. "Uneasy Peace Violated." *Wild West,* Oct. 1990, p. 43.

Carson, Xanthus. "Governor Charles Bent's Murder and Scalping." *True Frontier,* Nov. 1969, p. 26. Rpt. *True Frontier,* March 1974, p. 14; and *True Frontier,* April 1977, p. 28

Holben, Richard E. "The Avengers of St. Vrain." *Pioneer West,* May 1968, p. 39.

_____. "A Man to Match the Mountains." *The West,* March 1971, p. 40. Rpt. *Golden West,* Oct. 1974, p. 20.

Phillips, Chet. "The Cheyenne Brothers Lived Only to Avenge Their Tribe." *Frontier West,* Dec. 1971, p. 28.

Bent, George

Frazier, Thomas A. "George Bent: Owl Woman's Son." Part I, *Real West,* Sept. 1971, p. 52; Part II, *Real West,* Oct. 1971, p. 42. Rpt. as one-part article, *Real West,* Annual, 1972, p. 54.

Phillips, Chet. "The Cheyenne Brothers Lived Only to Avenge Their Tribe." *Frontier West,* Dec. 1971, p. 28.

Bent, William

Harrison, Fred. "William Bent's Vengeful Son." *Golden West,* July 1970, p. 22.

Koller, Joe. "Frontier Adventure of William Bent." *Golden West,* May 1968, p. 16. Rpt. *Western Frontier,* Jan. 1979, p. 16

Robinson, Max. "Frontier Entrepreneur." *Real West,* March 1976, p. 46.

Bergen, Tom

Lee, Hector H. "A Rope, A Gun and A Hank of Hair: John Wayne Should Have Been There!" *NOLA Quarterly,* Vol. IV, No. 2, Autumn 1978, p. 19.

Berry, Daniel

Walker, Wayne T. "The Short Grass Shoot-Out." *Great West,* June 1973, p. 6. Rpt. *Great West,* Summer 1981, p. 6.

Berry, Wiley

McAdams, Charles. "Sheep Camp Murders." *Frontier Times,* July 1970, p. 6.

Besler, Lloyd (Coup Cane)

Ballenger, Dean W. "Coup Cane's Revenge." *Oldtimers Wild West,* Feb. 1978, p. 29.

Bickerdyke, Mary A.

Kay, Jay F. "Mother of Kansas Colonists." *Golden West,* July 1965, p. 12. Rpt. *Golden West,* Nov. 1973, p. 22.

West, Bertha. "Mother Bickerdyke." *True Frontier,* Feb. 1972, p. 22.

Biddlecome, Joe

Baker, Pearl. "Robbers Roost Recollections." *True West,* Aug. 1983, p. 22.

Bidwell, John

Bidwell, John. "The First Emigrant Train to California." *The West,* April 1966, p. 34.

Simonds, A.J. "The Bartleson-Bidwell Party: First to California." *Real West,* Dec. 1969, p. 44. Rpt. *Real West,* Annual, Summer 1971, p. 40.

Bierce, Ambrose

Wingfield, William. "Ambrose Bierce: The Scribe of Satan." *Real West,* July 1974, p. 15.

Big Bow

Echols, Lee E. "The Kiowa Raiders of Rainy Mountain." *True West,* April 1978, p. 6.

Irons, Angie. "Big Bow: Terror of the Plains." *True West,* July 1987, p. 38.

Bigfoot (Sioux Chief)

Holding, Vera. "Wounded Knee: The Last Battle." *Pioneer West,* March 1969, p. 50.

Huntley, Allan. "Massacre at Wounded Knee." *Real West,* Americana Series No. 1, Winter 1963, p. 33.

Kildare, Maurice. "Death Danced at Wounded Knee." *Westerner,* March-April 1972, p. 34.

"The Last Battle, Wounded Knee." *Great West,* April 1971, p. 30.

Leroy, Edward. "Judgment Day at Wounded Knee." *Real West,* Oct. 1957, p. 44.

Mizrahi, Joseph. "Custer's Revenge." *Pioneer West,* Oct. 1971, p. 18. Rpt. *Pioneer West,* March 1974, p. 18.

Pinot, B. Hale. "The Tribe That Danced Itself to Death." *Westerner,* March-April 1969, p. 24.

Stanley, Samuel. "Big Foot's Death in the Cold Snow." *The West,* April 1969, p. 18. Rpt. *Western Frontier,* Jan. 1979, p. 2; and *Western Frontier,* May 1984, p. 2.

Wiltsey, Norman B. "Death on the North Plains." *True West,* June 1958, p. 24.

Bigfoot (Nampa, Nampuh, or Qualuck—Paiute Chief)

Friedman, Ralph. "Murdering Scourge of Snake River." *Real West,* Jan. 1963, p. 11.

Froman, Robert. "The Giant and the Gunslinger." *True Western Adventure,* Oct. 1960, p. 23.

Grimitt, R. "The Great Renegade, Qualuck." *Oldtimers Wild West,* May 1975, p. 32.

Kildare, Maurice. "Chief Bigfoot: Murdering Giant." *Westerner,* July-Aug. 1969, p. 11.

Richardson, Gladwell. "Bigfoot." *Westerner,* July-Aug. 1974, p. 8.

Bigford, George
Nolen, Oren Warden. "Saga of Ranger George Bigford." *The West,* May 1968, p. 28. Rpt. *Western Frontier,* April 1983, p. 38.

Big Mouth
Ball, Eve. "The Apache Comanche Fight." *Real West,* Special Issue, Winter 1970, p. 30.

Big Tree
Echols, Lee E. "The Kiowa Raiders of Rainy Mountain." *True West,* April 1978, p. 6.

Grove, Fred. "The Chiefs Must Die." *Golden West,* March 1970, p. 42.

Morgan, Ronald J. "The Warren Wagon Train Fight." *The West,* Oct. 1974, p. 8.

Billy Bowlegs
Walker, Wayne T. "Billy Bowlegs." *Great West,* Sept. 1974, p. 26.

_____. "Warpath of Billy Bowlegs." *Pioneer West,* Oct. 1971, p. 28. Rpt. *Pioneer West,* March 1974, p. 12; and *Oldtimers Wild West,* April 1977, p. 16.

Billy the Kid (Kid Antrim, Billy Bonney) (see McCarty, Patrick Henry)

Bisbee Hanging Victims (Dan Dowd, Red Sample, Tex Howard, Bill DeLaney, Dan Kelly)
Dodge, Matt. "Hanging: The Media Event." *Real West,* Annual, Spring 1982, p. 8.

Kildare, Maurice. "The Bisbee Massacre Hangings." *Real West,* Aug. 1971, p. 16.

Bissonette, Joseph
Austerman, Wayne R. "The Death Merchants of White River." *Real West,* Aug. 1986, p. 41.

Black Bart (see Bolton, Charles)

Black Beaver

Henderson, Sam. "The Incredible Story of the Blazing of the Chisholm Trail." *Frontier West,* Feb. 1973, p. 16.

Shirley, Glenn. "Captain Black Beaver." *Old West,* Spring 1970, p. 22.

Walker, Wayne T. "Captain Black Beaver: Forgotten Pathfinder to the Far West." *Real West,* June 1982, p. 30. Rpt. *Real West,* Special Issue, Spring 1983, p. 46.

_____. "The Great Captain Black Beaver." *Golden West,* Jan. 1971, p. 32.

Black Gray (Carl Enright)

King, Dale. "They Died in the Crater of the Moon." *Real West,* April 1958, p. 42.

Black Hawk

Cortesi, Lawrence. "Showdown at Bad Axe." *Frontier West,* June 1975, p. 26.

Black, James

Dobie, J. Frank. "Was James Black Inventor of the Bowie Knife?" *True West,* Dec. 1962, p. 47.

Phares, Ross. "He Created the Bowie Knife." *Frontier Times,* Spring 1958, p. 12.

Thorp, Raymond W. "The King and I and the Bowie Knife." *Frontier Times,* July 1964, p. 18.

Black Kettle

"Black Kettle." *Great West,* April 1970, p. 12.

Andre, Barbara E. "Custer of the Washita." *The West,* June 1968, p. 20. Rpt. *Western Frontier,* July 1979, p. 20.

Bailey, Tom. "The White Invaders." *True West,* Aug. 1963, p. 14.

Huston, Fred. "Night of the Red Moon." *Wild West,* Oct. 1969, p. 50. Rpt. *Pioneer West,* Dec. 1974, p. 48; and *Oldtimers Wild West,* Aug. 1979, p. 30.

Knudsen, Dean. "Sand Creek Avenged." *Wild West,* Oct. 1991, p. 22.

Mendoza, Robert. "Black Kettle and Col. Chivington." *Great West,* June 1972, p. 28. Rpt. *Authentic West,* Fall 1981, p. 32.

Sufrin, Mark. "The Massacre at Sand Creek." *Frontier West,* Feb. 1972, p. 18.

Swanson, Budington. "Massacre at Sand Creek." *True Frontier,* Sept. 1968, p. 18. Rpt. *True Frontier,* Special Issue No. 6, 1973, p. 10.

Turner, Don. "Prelude to Massacre." *True West,* Oct. 1968, p. 18.

"Black Kid," The

Secrest, William B. "The Black Kid's Big Hold-Up." *True Frontier,* Jan. 1970, p. 12. Rpt. *True Frontier,* Special Issue No. 5, 1973, p. 22.

Bland, John C.W.

Kildare, Maurice. "Murder the Witnesses." *Real West,* April 1973, p. 54.

Blevans, Henry

Winslowe, John R. "Buscadero Outlaw." *Westerner,* July-Aug. 1970, p. 14.

Blevins Clan

Bloom, Sam. "Shootout in Apache County's Hell Town." *Frontier West,* Dec. 1974, p. 34.

Combs, Richard. "War in the Tonto." *Real West,* Oct. 1986, p. 5.

O'Neal, Bill. "Commodore Perry Owens vs. the Blevins Clan" ("Great Western Gunfights" column). *True West,* Oct. 1989, p. 60.

Bligh, Delos Thurman ("Yankee Bligh")

Watson, Thomas Shelby. "The Day Jesse Turned Yankee Bligh Around." *Real West,* Jan. 1975, p. 26.

Bloody Knife

Hildreth, Reed C. "Arikara Scout Cemetery." *Frontier Times,* Jan. 1967, p. 45.

Reedstrom, Ernest Lisle. "Bloody Knife: Custer's Favorite Scout." *True West,* Feb. 1989, p. 20.

Blunt, James G.

Nieberding, Velma. "The General's Lady of Mystery." *The West,* May 1965, p. 26.

Swanson, Budington. "James Blunt: The General Who Would Never Retreat." *Golden West,* May 1972, p. 5.

Walker, Wayne T. "Massacre at Baxter Springs." *Old West,* Spring 1983, p. 18.

Bobbitt, Allen A. "Gus"

Breihan, Carl W. "Killing Jim Miller." *Real West,* July 1978, p. 50.

Katigan, Madelon B. "How the Beau Brummel Died." *Real West,* Sept. 1963, p. 36.

Bockius, James Monroe "Doc"
Parsons, Chuck. "Doc Bockius Survived Civil War, Texas Feud." *NOLA Quarterly*, Vol. II, No. 4, Spring 1977, p. 9.

Bodwin, William "Bill"
Durden, Victor. "The Counterfeiters of Shingle Creek." *True West*, Winter 1953, p. 22.

Bogan, Dan
DeArment, Robert K. "The Outlaw Trail of Dan Bogan." *True West*, Jan. 1984, p. 30.

Boggs, Thomas O.
Teal, Roleta. "Boggsville: The First Permanent Settlement in Southeastern Colorado." *Old West*, Summer 1985, p. 42.

"Bogus Charlie"
Neiberding, Velma. "The Conference of Death." *Golden West*, Aug. 1974, p. 16.

Walker, Wayne T. "A Modoc Called 'Bogus Charlie.'" *Great West*, April 1973, p. 22.

Bolin, Alfred "Alf"
Hartman, Viola R. "Alf Bolin's Reign of Terror." *Old West*, Summer 1983, p. 61.

Walker, Wayne T. "Bloody Alf Bolden [sic]." *Great West*, Dec. 1970, p. 18. Rpt. *Pioneer West*, Nov. 1979, p. 10.

Bolton, Charles E. "Black Bart"
Auer, L.C. "Black Bart, Ace of the Stage Coach Bandits." *Real West*, March 1969, p. 19.

Boswell, Charles. "Poet Laureate of the Highway." *True Western Adventures*, Oct. 1959, p. 24.

Breihan, Carl W. "Black Bart the PO 8." *Westerner*, May-June 1969, p. 12. Rpt. *Westerner*, Sept.-Oct. 1974, p. 32.

————. "Black Bart: Stage Robber." *Oldtimers Wild West*, June 1979, p. 24.

————. "Black Bart's Shotgun Was Empty." *Real West*, April 1973, p. 22.

————. "The Skittish Highwayman." *The West*, Feb. 1967, p. 16. Rpt. *The West*, Jan. 1973, p. 38; *Western Frontier*, July 1976, p. 42; and *Western Tales*, June 1960, p. 22.

Conant, Lora M. "The Walking Bandit." *Great West*, Feb. 1970, p. 30.

Hart, Richard. "Black Bart: Backpacking Robber Poet." *True West,* Oct. 1983, p. 35.

Mackay, Dean. "The Outlaw PO 8." *Frontier Times,* Fall 1958, p. 24.

Rosenhouse, Leo. "The Bandit Who Never Fired a Shot." *True Frontier,* Sept. 1969, p. 12. Rpt. *True Frontier,* Special Issue No. 5, 1973, p. 20.

_____. "Black Bart: Terror of Wells Fargo." *True Frontier,* July 1970, p. 8.

"When Wells Fargo Policed the West." *Authentic West,* Summer 1981, p. 16.

Wukovits, John F. "Gunfighters and Lawmen" column. *Wild West,* April 1991, p. 10.

Bonham, James

Von Kreisler, Max. "James Bonham: The Gallant Rebel." *The West,* June 1970, p. 18.

Bonneville, Benjamin L.E.

Spendlove, Earl. "Benjamin Bonneville: Buffoon or Hero?" *The West,* July 1967, p. 46. Rpt. *Golden West,* Aug. 1972, p. 10; and *Western Frontier,* May 1976, p 46.

_____. "Two Men for Twenty Horses." *True West,* Feb. 1963, p. 30.

Boone, Daniel

Thorp, Raymond D. "Colter's Boone." *Old West,* Summer 1966, p. 10.

Boone, Nathan

Walker, Wayne T. "Missouri's Greatest Hero: The Frontiersman Nobody Remembers." *Frontier West,* Oct. 1975, p. 18.

_____. "Nathan Boone: Distinguished Scout." *The West,* March 1970, p. 14.

Booth Brothers (Zack and John)

McAdams, Charles. "Sheep Camp Murders." *Frontier Times,* July 1970, p. 6.

Booth, John Wilkes

Edmond, Wilson. "Did John Wilkes Booth Really Escape?" *True Frontier,* Oct. 1967, p. 8.

James, Louise Boyd. "The Strange Legacy of John Wilkes Booth." *Old West,* Winter, 1983, p. 10.

Booth, Zack

Dodge, Matt. "Hanging: The Media Event." *Real West,* Annual, Spring 1982, p. 8.

Bordeaux, James "Jim"

Austerman, Wayne R. "The Death Merchants of White River." *Real West,* Aug. 1986, p. 41.

Legg, John. "Bordeaux's Trading Post." *Old West,* Fall 1989, p. 46.

Born, Henry "Dutch Henry"

Breihan, Carl W. "Horse Thief Deluxe." *Real West,* April 1975, p. 28.

Dary, David. "Dutch Henry, Horse Thief." *True West,* Nov. 1987, p. 40.

Walker, Wayne T. "Born and Ieuch: The Two Dutch Henrys." *Real West,* Oct. 1983, p. 46. Rpt. *Real West,* Special Issue, Spring 1984, p. 8.

_____. "Dutch Henry Born, Horsethief." *Oldtimers Wild West,* April 1979, p. 29.

_____. "Dutch Henry: The Outlaw Houdini." *Westerner,* May-June 1974, p. 22.

_____. "The Law vs. Dutch Henry." *Golden West,* Sept. 1966, p. 18. Rpt. *The West,* April 1972, p. 8; and *Western Frontier,* April 1983, p. 8.

Boswell, Nathaniel Kimball

Carroll, Murray L. "A Fatal Necktie Party: The Lynching of Si Partridge." *Old West,* Fall 1986, p. 22.

Carson, John. "Old Boz: Yankee With a Gun." *Old West,* Fall 1974, p.22.

Boucher, Francis

Austerman, Wayne R. "The Death Merchants of White River." *Real West,* Aug. 1986, p. 41.

Bourdon, Michael

Kildare, Maurice. "Michael Bourdon: Premier Mountain Man." *Real West,* June 1971, p. 6.

Bouyer, Mitchel "Mitch"

Murray, Bob. "Race With Death on the Bozeman Trail." *Old West,* Winter 1983, p. 52.

Bowdre, Charlie

Gehrman, B.L. "Charlie Bowdre's Wish." *Frontier Times,* Fall 1958, p. 19.

Parsons, Chuck. "Companion of Billy the Kid" ("Answer Man" column). *True West*, March 1988, p. 12.

_____. "Charlie Bowdre: Lincoln County Regulator" ("Answer Man" column). *True West*, Dec. 1991, p. 12.

Rasch, Philip J. Letter. *Frontier Times*, Summer 1959, p. 5.

Bowen, Brown

Parsons, Chuck. "The Death of Brown Bowen." *Real West*, Nov. 1976, p. 32. Rpt. *Real West*, Annual, Winter 1977-78, p. 31.

_____. "Postscript to the Death of Brown Bowen." *Real West*, Sept. 1979, p. 36.

Bowers, Eilley Orrum

Cheney, Louise. "Fabulous Eilley: The Washoe Seeress." *Real West*, May 1962, p. 36.

Gille, Marcia. "Lady Luck and the Peepstone Palace." *True West*, Jan. 1985, p. 42.

Sullivan, B.P. "Cinderella of the Comstock Lode." *True West*, Dec. 1956, p. 26.

Sullivan, Freyda. "The Curse of the Comstock." *Real West*, June 1981, p. 8.

Bowers, Milton J.

Majors, John. "Murder in Old San Francisco." *Real West*, March 1962, p. 44.

Bowers, Sandy

Gille, Marcia. "Lady Luck and the Peepstone Palace." *True West*, Jan. 1985, p. 42.

Sullivan, Freyda. "The Curse of the Comstock." *Real West*, June 1981, p. 8.

Bowie Brothers (Jim and Rezin)

Yarbrough, C.L. "In Search of Los Almagres." *Vanishing Texas*, May 1981, p. 12.

Bowie, James   "Jim"

Andrews, Harry. "Bowie: The Man and the Knife." *True West*, Feb. 1956, p. 29.

Breihan, Carl W. "Jim Bowie's Last Fight." *Frontier Times*, June-July 1963, p. 44.

Brown, Bob. "The Slashing Knife of Jim Bowie." *True Frontier*, July 1971, p. 30. Rpt. *True Frontier*, Special Issue No. 9, 1974, p. 14.

Cheney, Louise. "Jim Bowie's Lost Silver Mine." *Golden West*, July 1967, p. 26. Rpt. *Golden West*, July 1972, p. 40; and *Western Frontier*, May 1976, p. 32.

Derben, Jack. "Jim Bowie's Lost Mine." *Real West,* Sept. 1960, p. 17.

_____. "Jim Bowie's Secret Mine." *Real West,* Special Issue, Summer 1964, p. 19.

Dobie, J. Frank. "How Jim Bowie Got His Silver." *Frontier Times,* Summer 1958, p. 11.

Hart, George. "Strange Fate for Jim Bowie's Knife." *Real West,* Feb. 1972, p. 20. Rpt. *Real West,* Annual, Fall 1974, p. 50.

Hayes, Frederick. "Mexican File: What Happened at the Alamo?" *Real West,* July 1960, p. 28.

Jones, Julia. "Amazing Exploits of Jim Bowie." *The West,* Aug. 1968, p. 10. Rpt. *Golden West,* Jan. 1973, p. 21; *Western Frontier,* Annual No. 2, 1976, p. 34; and *Western Frontier,* Aug. 1985, p. 20.

Pike, Robert E. "He Didn't Want to Smoke." *True West,* June 1955, p. 29.

Wiltsey, Norman B. "Hot Blood and Cold Steel." *Real West,* June 1972, p. 46. Rpt. *Real West,* Yearbook, Spring 1974, p. 63.

_____. "Jim Bowie and the Deadly Knife." *Frontier Times,* Spring 1958, p. 10.

Winston, Stanley. "The Knife Wielding Scot From Texas." *Pioneer West,* May 1967, p. 14.

Bowl (Chief John Bowles)

Conley, Robert J. "Diwali: Chief of the Texas Cherokees." *True West,* March 1991, p. 37.

Johnson, Norman K. "Warriors and Chiefs" column. *Wild West ,* Aug. 1989, p. 12.

Walker, Wayne T. "Chief Bowl: Warlord of the Texas Cherokees." *Pioneer West,* March 1979, p. 14.

Bowman, Mason T. "Mace"

Parsons, Chuck. "Mace Bowman vs. Clay Allison?" ("Answer Man" column). *True West,* March 1991, p. 12.

Peters, James Steven. "The Strangulation of Damian Romero." *Old West,* Summer 1983, p. 18.

_____. "The Untimely Death of Mace Bowman." *Old West,* Fall 1984, p. 50.

Sufrin, Mark. "Cimarron's Fantastic Death Dance Duel." *Frontier West,* June 1974, p. 6.

Bowman, Sarah A. "The Great Western"

Convis, Charles L. "The Great Western." *True West,* Sept. 1989, p. 28.

Cheney, Louise. "The Great Western: Female Warrior." *The West,* July 1968, p. 34. Rpt. *The West,* Aug. 1974, p. 26.

Ferguson, Henry N. "Amazon of the Border." *True Western Adventures,* Oct. 1960, p. 28.

Rosson, Mary'n. "Sarah: The Great Western." *True Frontier,* July 1971, p. 18. Rpt. *True Frontier,* April 1976, p. 8.

Boyd, William

Stephenson, Peggy. "Those Busy Bogus Bond Boys." *True West,* May 1988, p. 40.

Boyett, John

Traywick, Ben T. "The Murder of Warren Baxter Earp." *Old West,* Winter 1990, p. 53.

Bozeman, John

Maxwell, George. "John Bozeman's Load of Potatoes." *Real West,* Nov. 1960, p. 28.

McKinnon, L.C. "Trail Blazing to Glory." *Real West,* Dec. 1982, p. 23. Rpt. *Real West,* Yearbook, Fall 1983, p.44.

Ryker, Lois. "A Wagon Road Through Crow Country." *Frontier Times,* June-July 1963, p. 42.

Brady, Jack

Robertson, Bill, and Russ Leadabrand. "The Great Southern Pacific Train Robbery." *Western Action,* Dec. 1960, p. 16.

Brannan, Samuel "Sam"

Fink, Clarence M. "All That Glittered Was Sam Brannan." *Real West,* April 1975, p. 42.

Hecox, Walter R. "Bar of Justice." *True Western Adventures,* April 1960, p. 29.

Jones, Julia. "Sam Brannan and Early California Justice." *Golden West,* Sept. 1966, p. 16. Rpt. *The West,* Sept. 1974, p. 14.

Pierce, Norman C. "A Curse Upon His Head." *Old West,* Fall 1967, p. 38.

Ray, John J. "The Amazing Sam Brannan." *The West,* March 1965, p. 10.

Rosenhouse, Leo. "Hang 'Em High." *Pioneer West,* Nov. 1973, p. 14.

_____. "Samuel Brannan: California's First Executioner." *Golden West,* May 1972, p. 12. Rpt. *Western Frontier,* Nov. 1980, p. 12.

_____. "When the Vigilantes Ruled San Francisco." *Frontier West,* Oct. 1974, p. 6.

Branton, Claude

Fitzgerald, A.J. "They're Hanging Claude Branton." *The West,* Dec. 1965, p. 38.

Brazel, Wayne

Carter, Jack. "Some Facts About Wayne Brazel." *Frontier Times,* July 1972, p. 10.

_____. Letter. *Golden West,* Sept. 1968, p. 50.

Miller, Lee. "He Killed Pat Garrett." *Real West,* Jan. 1960, p. 30.

Weisner, Herman B. "Garrett's Death: Conspiracy or Doublecross?" *True West,* Dec. 1979, p. 6.

Brazelton, William Whitney "Bill"

Bentz, Donald N. "The Bloody Mouth Stage Coach Bandit." *The West,* May 1969, p. 28. Rpt. *The West,* Jan. 1974, p. 22.

Kildare, Maurice. "Bob Brazelton, The One-Man Holdup Gang." *Real West,* Jan. 1970, p. 29. Rpt. *Real West,* Annual, Fall 1974, p. 37.

McCarthy, Donald. "Bill Brazelton: Stage Robber." *Frontier Times,* Jan. 1980, p. 31.

O'Dell, Roy. "Arizona's Flour-Sack Bandit." *True West,* Jan. 1989, p. 40.

Braziel, Dow

Riotte, Louise. "Marshal Braziel and Bud Ballew." *Frontier Times,* Nov. 1980, p. 36.

_____. "Shoot-Out at the California Cafe." *Golden West,* March 1971, p. 28. Rpt. *The West,* Jan. 1974, p. 32; and *Western Frontier,* July 1983, p. 32.

Breakenridge, William "Billy"

Carlson, Burfee. "Tombstone Deputy Sheriff Bill Breakenridge." *Golden West,* Nov. 1967, p. 20. Rpt. *Western Frontier,* April 1983, p. 14.

Earp, Josephine. "Sinister Shadow From the Past." Ed. Glenn Boyer. *True West,* Oct. 1975, p. 20.

Hane, Louis. "Deputy From Tombstone." *Westerner,* Oct. 1971, p. 20.

Harrison, John H. "Billy Breakenridge: The 'Tenderfoot' Deputy." *Real West,*

Jan. 1977, p. 18.

Kildare, Maurice. "The Wilcox Double Robbery." *Real West,* June 1968, p. 31.

O'Neal, Bill. "Deputy Sheriff Billy Breakenridge vs. Zweig Hunt and Billy Grounds" ("Great Western Gunfights" column). *True West,* July 1991, p. 59.

"True Western Hall of Fame." *True Western Adventures,* Feb. 1959, p. 59.

Brennan, Molly

Dittmos, Henry. "The Bat and the Rose." *True Western Adventures,* Issue No. 1, 1957, p. 16.

Harmon, John. "A Rose to Death." *Real West,* Aug. 1958, p. 28.

Brenner, Steve

Gunther, Ralph. "Hanging Pomeroy Had the Fastest Noose in the West." *Frontier West,* June 1971, p. 20.

Brewer, Richard M. "Dick"

Nolan, Frederick. "Dick Brewer: The Unlikely Gunfighter." *NOLA Quarterly,* Vol. XV, No. 3, July-Sept. 1991, p. 19.

Rasch, Philip J. "A Second Look at the Blazer's Mill Affair." *Frontier Times,* Jan. 1969, p. 30.

Rhodes, Alan. Letter. *Frontier Times,* Sept. 1963, p. 51.

Stratton, J.C. Letter. *Frontier Times,* Sept. 1963, p 51.

Bridger, James "Jim"

Harvey, Buck. "The Incredible Saga of Indian Scout Jim Bridger." *Frontier West,* Feb. 1972, p. 46.

Herberg, Ruth M. "'Old Gabe' In Armor." *The West,* March 1970, p. 10.

Hurdy, John Major. "The Grizzly That Talked Like a Man." *Pioneer West,* July 1969, p. 46.

Judge, Bill. "The Echo Canyon War." *Frontier Times,* Fall 1960, p. 10.

Legg, John. "Old Gabe: Man of the Wilderness." *True West,* Feb. 1988, p. 30.

Mallory, Joseph. "Jim Bridger and the Buffalo Skulls." *The West,* Feb. 1966, p. 13.

Ostrander, A.B. "Jim Bridger at Fort Kearny." *Frontier Times,* Nov. 1978, p. 18.

Stone, Kit. "Jim Bridger: The Blanket Chief." *Real Frontier,* Oct. 1970, p. 24. Rpt. *True Frontier,* June 1973, p. 16.

Wiltsey, Norman B. "Jim Bridger: King of Mountain Men." *Old West,* Winter 1964, p. 18.

_____. "Jim Bridger: Mr. Rocky Mountains." Part I, *Real West,* Oct. 1971, p. 12; Part II, *Real West,* Nov. 1971, p. 42.

_____. "King of Mountain Men." *True West,* Feb. 1959, p. 4.

Brighton, Jonas V.

Edwards, Harold L. "The Man Who Killed Ike Clanton." *True West,* Oct. 1991, p. 24.

Brink, LeRoy

Helson, Andre. "The Last Sheepman-Cattleman War." *True West,* May 1988, p. 14.

Brinster, Joseph

Parrish, Joe. "Crazy Hangings in El Paso." *Golden West,* Oct. 1974, p. 28.

Brocius, William "Curly Bill"

Boyer, Glenn G. "Curly Bill Has Been Killed at Last." *Real West,* June 1984, p. 32. Rpt. *Real West,* Yearbook, Winter 1986, p. 29.

Clanton, Chet. "The Skeleton Canyon Massacre." *Great West,* Sept. 1969, p. 12.

Knoles, Thelma. "Curly Bill." *Old West,* Summer 1980, p. 22.

Kubista, Robert. "Are These Curley Bill's Bones?" *The West,* Sept. 1965, p. 28.

Parsons, Chuck. "Curly Bill" ("Answer Man" column). *True West,* Dec. 1990, p. 14.

Qualey, J.S. "What Happened to Curly Bill's Head?" *Real West,* March 1960, p. 32.

Thomas, Robert L. "Gunfight at Iron Springs." *True West,* Feb. 1965, p. 38.

Broderick, David C.

Cox, Dick. "Duel At Dawn." *Real West,* Nov. 1968, p. 23.

Malsbary, George. "Guns, Gold and Politics." *Great West,* April 1973, p. 28.

Phipps, B.L. "The Last Great Duel." *Frontier Times,* Dec.-Jan. 1963, p. 44.

Rosenhouse, Leo. "The Duel That Rocked the Gold Coast." *Frontier West,* Oct. 1971, p. 10.

_____. "The Duel That Rocked the West." *True Frontier,* Oct. 1976, p. 16.

Ross, David R. "California's Gun-Toting Chief Justice." *Old West,* Summer 1989, p. 48.

Von Kreisler, Max. "Death in the Morning." *True Frontier,* July 1971, p. 8.

Young, Bob. "Terry, the Terrible." *Real West,* May 1961, p. 42.

Brooks, William L. "Billy"

DeMattos, Jack. "Billy Brooks" ("Gunfighters of the Real West" column). *Real West,* July 1980, p. 24.

Henderson, Sam. "Those Other Buffalo Bills." *Real West,* June 1975, p. 14.

Walker, Wayne T. "The Incredible Stage Coach War of Renegade Billy Brooks." *Frontier West,* Feb. 1975, p. 24.

_____. "Kansas' Incredible Stage Coach War." *Oldtimers Wild West,* April 1980, p. 6.

_____. "They Hung Billy Brooks, the Outlaw Marshal." *Great West,* April 1971, p. 12.

Brown, Baptiste

Kildare, Maurice. "How Baptiste Squawed Up." *True Frontier,* Special Issue No. 3, 1972, p. 6.

Brown, Clara

Lanza, Ruth Willett. "Aunt Clara Brown: The Black Angel of Central City." *True West,* April 1991, p. 38.

Brown, Henry (Hendry)

Breihan, Carl W. "Henry Brown: Gunfighter." *Westerner,* May-June 1970, p. 14.

_____. "Henry Brown, Hero and Villain." *Real West,* Jan. 1960, p. 34.

_____. "Henry Brown, Pseudo Lawman." *Real West,* April 1969, p. 23.

_____. "The Saga of Henry Brown, Gunman for Hire." *Oldtimers Wild West,* Oct. 1977, p. 10.

DeMattos, Jack. "Henry Brown" ("Gunfighters of the Real West" column). *Real West,* April 1980, p. 14.

"From Outlaw to Marshal to Corpse!" *Great West,* Nov. 1967, p. 35.

Huston, Fred. "The Bank Robbing Marshal." *Pioneer West,* April 1970, p. 50. Rpt. *Wild West,* Sept. 1972, p. 6; *Pioneer West,* June 1974, p. 58; and *Oldtimers Wild West,* June 1976, p. 44.

Keilman, Tom. Letter, "Henry Brown's Rifle." *Old West,* Spring 1977, p. 3.

O'Neal, Bill. "Henry Brown, Hired Gun in the Lincoln County War." *True West,* Feb. 1984, p. 17.

_____. "Medicine Lodge Bank Robbery." *True West,* Aug. 1983, p. 51.

_____. "The Medicine Lodge Bank Robbery, April 30, 1884" ("Great Western Gunfights" column). *True West,* July 1989, p. 58.

Parsons, Chuck. "Henry Newton Brown: Marshal and Badman" ("Answer Man" column). *True West,* Sept. 1991, p. 12.

Shirley, Glenn. "Killer With a Badge." *True Western Adventures,* June 1960, p. 8.

Walker, Wayne T. "The Backsliding Marshal of Caldwell." *The West,* May 1968, p. 16. Rpt. *Golden West,* June 1972, p. 8.

Brown, James "Jim"

Fisher, Eula Sue. "The Murder of Sam Sparks." *Frontier Times,* May 1979, p. 19.

Brown, John (of Oklahoma)

Poling, Frederick. "Mad Killer of the Cookson Hills." *Real West,* April 1958, p. 18.

Brown, John

Breihan, Carl W. "Incident at Harper's Ferry." *Oldtimers Wild West,* Dec. 1979, p. 6.

Harrison, Tom. "John Brown's Shadow." *Frontier Times,* Fall 1960, p. 24.

Mays, Carelton. "West's Bloodiest Killer." *Real West,* July 1962, p. 34.

Repp, Ed Earl. "Frontier Anarchy Paid Off." *Pioneer West,* Oct. 1970, p. 40.

Richmond, Robert W. "Mementoes of Notoriety: John Brown and Kate Bender." *True West,* Oct. 1971, p. 26.

Settle, Raymond W., and Mary Lund Settle. "John Brown's Vengeance." *True West,* June 1962, p. 42.

Whitt, W.C. "John Brown's Family." *True West,* Dec. 1975, p. 32.

Brown, "Kootenai"

Stevenson, John. "The Buffalo Hunter." *True West,* Jan. 1991, p. 48.

Brown, Molly

Cheney, Louise. "The Real Molly Brown." *Golden West,* May 1965, p. 10. Rpt. *The West,* March 1972, p. 41; and *Western Frontier,* Stagecoach Series, Dec. 1974, p. 29.

Brown, Neal

DeMattos, Jack. "Whatever Became of the Dodge City Peace Commission?" *Real West,* Jan. 1977, p. 38. Rpt. *Real West,* Yearbook, Summer 1978, p. 50.

Brown, Reuben "Rube"

Parsons, Chuck. "Rube Brown and the Atmosphere of Violence." *English Westerners' Brand Book,* Vol. XXIV, No. 1, Winter 1986, p. 13.

Brown, Sam
Parker, Will, Jr. "Killer Without Conscience." *True Western Adventures,* Issue No. 1, 1957, p. 15.

Pomplun, Ray. "Sam Brown: Dakota's Paul Revere." *Real West,* May 1973, p. 20.

Reardon, Daniel L. "The Despicable Sam Brown." *Frontier Times,* Oct.-Nov. 1965, p. 22.

Traywick, Ben T. "16 Notches to Doom." *Great West,* Feb. 1968, p. 4.

Brown, William H.
Strimike, Donald F. "Massacre at Salt River Canyon." *Great West,* Feb. 1970, p. 6.

Browning, John Moses
Perrins, Glen. "A Wizard With Guns." *Frontier Times,* Fall 1961, p. 10.

Browning, Sam
Robertson, Bill, and Russ Leadabrand. "The Great Southern Pacific Train Robbery." *Western Action,* Dec. 1960, p. 16.

Browns Park Bunch
Boren, Kerry Ross. "The Lost Ewing Mine." *The West,* Feb. 1971, p. 16.

Bruguier, John "Big Leggins"
Shannon, Dan. "Strange Curse of the Bruguier Brothers." *The West,* Nov. 1964, p. 12.

Brunckow, Frederick
Kubista, Arizona Bob. "The Fight at Brunckow's Cabin." *Frontier Times,* March 1968, p. 24.

Bruner, Hickman "Heck"
Bruner, James. "Gunfighters and Lawmen" column. *Wild West,* Oct. 1990, p. 12.

Holdzbauer, Dorothy E. "Robbers' Cave." *True West,* Dec. 1961, p. 36.

McKibben, Mike. "Siege of Rabbit Trap." *True Western Adventure,* Spring 1958, p. 16.

Pride, Joe. "The Battle of Tahlequah Canyon." *True West,* Oct. 1963, p. 18.

Rand, Phillip [sic]. "Blood In the Cookson Hills." *Real West,* Jan. 1958, p. 26.

Roy, Robert. "Oklahoma's Bandit Hideout." *Real West,* Nov. 1975, p. 32.

Turpin, Bob. "Bruner's Graveyard." *True West,* April 1977, p. 37.

Bryan, Electa Plummer

Parsons, Chuck. "Henry and Electa" ("Answer Man" column). *True West,* Oct. 1991, p. 13.

Bryant, Charley "Black Face Charley"

Kildare, Maurice. "Bullet Swapout in Oklahoma." *Real West,* Feb. 1973, p. 48. Rpt. *Real West,* Annual, Fall 1974, p. 62.

Shirley, Glenn. "One Hell-Firin' Minute to Death." *Golden West,* Sept. 1967, p. 16. Rpt. *Golden West,* Feb. 1972, p. 46; and *Western Frontier,* Special Issue, Fall 1974, p. 34.

Buck Gang

Cortesi, Lawrence. "Six Days of Terror for the Oklahoma Territory." *Frontier West,* June 1973, p. 26.

Glynn, Dean. "The Buck Gang's Thirteen Days of Terror." *Westerner,* March-April 1969, p. 52. Rpt. *Westerner,* Sept.-Oct. 1973, p. 44.

McKennon, C.H. "When the Buck Gang Rode." *True West,* Aug. 1976, p. 24.

Meyers, Olevia E. "Rufus Buck's Thirteen Days of Hell." *Real West,* July 1965, p. 34.

Powers, Mark. "Rob! Rape! Kill!" *Great West,* Oct. 1970, p. 12.

Buckskin Joe (see Hoyt, Edward Jonathan)

Buffalo Horn

Fitzgerald, Arlene. "Buffalo Horn's Revenge." *The West,* June 1965, p. 30.

Buffalo Hump

Derben, Jack. "Battle at Bird Creek." *Real West,* Aug. 1959, p. 18.

Buffalo Soldiers

Austerman, Wayne R. "Army's Unluckiest Regiment." *Wild West,* June 1991, p. 26.

Bulette, Julia

Aymar, John B. "New Slant on the Murder of Julia Bulette." *True West,* Feb. 1977, p. 20.

Cerveri, Doris. "The Lucrative Legend of Julia Bulette." *Old West,* Winter, 1985, p. 24.

_____. "Million Dollar Grave." *The West,* Feb. 1966, p. 30. Rpt. *The West* Jan. 1972, p. 24.

Cheney, Louise. "Tainted Queen of the Comstock." *Pioneer West,* July 1970, p. 32. Rpt. *Wild West,* Sept. 1972, p. 36; *Oldtimers Wild West,* April 1974, p. 52; and *Pioneer West,* May 1976, p. 46.

_____. "The Soiled Dove of Virginia City." *Big West,* Oct. 1967, p. 23.

Coriell, Marian M. "Virginia City Madam." *True Frontier,* May 1969, p. 40. Rpt. *True Frontier,* Nov. 1973, p. 38; and *True Frontier,* Feb. 1977, p. 18.

Hall, Milo. "Julia Bulette." *Frontier Times,* Summer, 1962, p. 35.

Hecox, Walter R. "The Story of Julia Bulette." *True Western Adventures,* Feb. 1960, p. 32.

Ketchum, E.D. "Julia Bulette." *Great West,* Oct. 1973, p. 20.

Schmidt, R. Roland. "The Sweetheart of Virginia City." *True Frontier,* July 1971, p. 38.

Wilson, William R. "Dastardly Murder of the Comstock Courtesan." *Golden West,* Jan. 1969, p. 12. Rpt. *Golden West,* April 1972, p. 22; and *Western Frontier,* Aug. 1982, p. 24.

Bull, John Edwin

DeArment, Robert K. "John Bull: Gunman, Gambler: A Frontier Odyssey." *True West,* March 1986, p. 32.

Bullion, Laura (Della Rose, Laura Casey, Clara Hays)

Grey, James L. "Laura Bullion: Outlaw's Sweetheart." *Westerner,* Nov.-Dec. 1973, p. 47.

_____. "Laura Bullion (Della Rose), Outlaw Sweetheart." *NOLA Quarterly,* Vol. II, No. 1, Spring 1975, p. 12.

Ripple, Sam. "Rose of the Wild Bunch." *Westerner,* March-April 1972, p. 41.

Bullis, John Lapham

Austerman, Wayne R. "The Black Scalp Hunters." *Real West,* June 1986, p. 32.

McCright, Grady E. "John Bullis: Chief Scout." *True West,* Oct. 1981, p. 12.

Robinson, Charles M. III. "The Whirlwind and His Scouts." *Old West,* Summer 1991, p. 28.

Bullock, Seth

Koller, Joe. "When Bullock's Cowboys Hoorahed the Potomac." *Old West,* Fall 1965, p. 16.

Bunch, Eugene Franklin

O'Dell, Roy. "Bunch and Hobgood: Partners in Crime." *English Westerners' Brand Book,* Vol. XXIII, No. 2, Summer 1985, p. 8.

Buntline, Ned (see Judson, Edward Z.C.)

Bunton, William "Bill"
Reimers, Henry. "Henry Plummer's Second in Command." *Frontier Times,* March 1972, p. 6.

Burke, E.R.
Johnston, Richard. "The Outlaw and the Jewel Thief." *NOLA Quarterly,* Vol. III, No. 3, Summer 1977, p. 1.

Burke, Steve
Freeman, Frank M. "The Preacher Wore Guns." *Great West,* June 1970, p. 20
Repp, Ed Earl. "Preacher Steve Burke: Six-Guns in the Pulpit." *True Frontier,* Oct. 1972, p. 17. Rpt. *True Frontier,* Special Issue No. 15, Summer 1976, p. 13.
_____. "The Six-gun Sky Pilot." *Golden West,* Jan. 1969, p. 22. Rpt. *The West,* Dec. 1972, p. 32.

Burnett, Samuel Burk
Walker, Wayne T. "Burk Burnett and the Four Sixes." *Real West,* Jan. 1981, p. 40. Rpt. *Real West,* Annual, 1981, p. 21.
_____. "Legend of the Four Sixes." *Golden West,* March 1971, p. 10. Rpt. *Golden West,* March 1974, p. 28, and *Western Frontier,* Feb. 1986, p. 10.
_____. "Where Burk Burnett Got the 6666 Brand." *The West,* June 1968, p. 14.

Burnett, James "Justice Jim"
Dodge, Matt. "Jim Burnett: The Law in Charleston." *Real West,* April 1982, p 16. Rpt. *Real West,* Annual, Spring 1983, p. 37.
Lake, Ivan C. "Instant Justice." *Real West,* Nov. 1966, p. 29.
Traywick, Ben T. "Copper King of Cananea." *Golden West,* Nov. 1970, p. 16.
_____. "The Czar of Charleston." *The West,* March 1970, p. 36.

Burns, Tom
Secrest, William B. "The Gunfight at Stone Corral." *True Frontier,* June 1973, p. 26.

Burrow, Reuben "Rube"
Agee, G.W. "Rube Burrow: King of Outlaws and His Band of Train Robbers." *Old*

West, Spring 1968, p. 67.

Albertson, Peter. "The Great Hates of Reuben Burrows [sic]." *Western Tales,* June 1960, p. 20.

Breihan, Carl W. "The Day Train Robber Rube Burrow Was Killed." *Real West,* Nov. 1973, p. 30.

_____. "Rube Burrow's Bold Stroke." *Real West,* Sept. 1981, p. 16. Rpt. *Real West,* Special Issue, Spring 1982, p. 33.

Carson, John. "Rube Burrow" ("Backgrounds of Famous Badmen" column). *True West,* Aug. 1961, p. 39.

Cortesi, Lawrence. "The Dude Who Conducted His Own War Against the Iron Horse." *Frontier West,* Dec. 1973, p. 12.

Hines, James. "Prince of Robbers." *Real West,* March 1961, p. 25.

Jacobsen, Bill. "Rube Burrow's Daring Plan." *Westerner,* Nov.-Dec. 1973, p. 41.

Larck, George. "The One-Man Hold Up." *Westerner,* Jan.-Feb. 1972, p. 32.

Neville, Fonville. "The Hound Who Ran Down Burrows [sic]." *The West,* April 1968, p. 30. Rpt. *Western Frontier,* Speical Issue, Summer 1974, p. 10.

"Rube Burrow." *Great West,* June 1970, p. 14.

Willingham, Jo. Letter, "Rube Burrow." *True West,* Feb. 1962, p. 47.

Winfield, Craig. "The Day Rube Burrow Died." *Oldtimers Wild West,* April 1979, p. 10.

Burt, Andrew H.
Thompson, George A. "Was It Justice...or Vengeance?" *Real West,* Aug. 1982, p. 26. Rpt. *Real West,* Special Issue, Spring 1985, p. 28.

Burts, Matt
Repp, Ed Earl. "Loot the Village: Kill the Males." *True Frontier,* Nov. 1969, p. 38.

Butler, David
Swanson, Budington. "The Great Seal Robbery." *Great West,* Oct. 1973, p. 24.

Butterfield, John
Pinkerton, Robert E. "Hell for Leather." *True Western Adventures,* Oct. 1958, p. 26.

Rosenhouse, Leo. "Butterfield's Truce With Cochise." *The West,* March 1970, p. 32. Rpt. *Western Frontier,* Nov. 1977, p. 28; and *Western Frontier,* May 1984, p. 28.

_____. "The Mail Stage the Apaches Wouldn't Attack." *True Frontier,* March

1968, p. 16. Rpt. *True Frontier,* Aug. 1972, p. 28; and *True Frontier,* Special Issue No. 11, Winter 1974-75, p. 20.

_____. "Stagecoach." *Great West,* Aug. 1973, p. 14. Rpt. *Great West,* Fall 1981, p. 16.

Byrne, Thomas
Stano, Mary G. "Camp Beale Springs Ordeal." *True West,* July 1989, p. 28.

Byrnes, William Wallace "Bill"
Secrest, William B. "Fast Guns in Old California." *Real West,* June 1980, p. 10. Rpt. *Real West,* Special Issue, 1981, p. 6.

Cafferal, Pete
Nelson, Andre. "The Last Sheepman-Cattleman War." *True West,* May 1988, p. 14.

Cahill, Francis (Frank) P. "Windy"
Radbourne, Allan, and Philip J. Rasch,. "The Story of 'Windy Cahill.'" *Real West,* Aug. 1985, p. 22. Rpt. *Real West,* Annual, Summer 1986, p. 28.

Cahill, T. Joe
Donoho, Ron. "He Hanged Tom Horn." *The West,* Sept. 1971, p. 28. Rpt. *The West,* July 1974, p. 18; and *Western Frontier,* May 1985, p. 28.

Calamity Jane (see Cannary, Martha Jane)

Campbell, B.H. "Barbeque"
Holding, Vera. "XIT...Five Million Acres in Two States." *Real Frontier,* Aug. 1971, p. 34.

Campbell, George
Metz, Leon C. "Four Dead in Ten Seconds." *Real West,* Annual , Summer 1973, p. 46.

Campbell, H.H.
Wallis, George A. "Cattle Kings." Part II, *True West*, June 1964, p. 6.

Canby, E.R.S.
Barkdull, Tom. "Modoc's Bloody Ground." *Wild West*, June 1970, p. 21.

Boucher, Leonard H. "The Battle of the No-Kissin' Kin." *The West*, Oct. 1969, p. 14.

Deac, Wilfred P. "Indian Fortress Assailed." *Wild West*, Feb. 1991, p. 34.

"The Deadly Squaw Soldiers." *Great West*, Dec. 1968, p. 30.

Gregg, Andy. "Sibley's Army of the Dead." *Real West*, Nov. 1964, p. 26.

Linscombe, Matt. "The Fantastic Alliance That Triggered the Civil War's Strangest Battle." *Frontier West*, June 1973, p. 30.

Rosenhouse, Leo. "The Last Stand of the Modocs." *Westerner*, July-Aug. 1969, p. 38.

_____. "The Rage of Captain Jack." *True Frontier*, March 1971, p. 8.

Stanley, Samuel. "The War the Army Would Like to Forget." *Real Frontier*, June 1970, p. 24. Rpt. *True Frontier*, Aug. 1972, p. 14.

Wiltsey, Norman B. "Hell With the Fires Out." *True West*, Nov. 1954, p. 6.

Zoltan, E.L. "Slaughter on the Lava Beds." *True Frontier*, March 1969, p. 38. Rpt. *True Frontier*, Special Issue No. 10, 1974, p. 24.

Candy, Sam
Ives, Nellin. "Back Trail of a Genial Gunman." *Western Frontier*, Nov. 1985, p. 2.

Cannary, Martha Jane "Calamity Jane"
Abrams, Cliff V. "Calamity Jane's Last Day." *True West*, Aug. 1964, p. 59.

"Autobiography of Calamity Jane." Rpt. *Gunslingers of the West*, Winter 1966, p. 55.

Brink, Elizabeth A. "Clothing Calamity Jane." *True West*, Nov. 1990, p. 20.

Burke, John. "The Wildest Woman in the West." *True Frontier*, June 1967, p. 12. Rpt. *True Frontier*, Special Issue No. 7, Fall 1973, p. 10.

"Calamity Jane." *Great West*, July 1969, p. 12.

Hart, George. "Who Was Calamity Jane?" *Real West*, Jan. 1974, p. 28.

Hiatt, Diane. "Calamity Jane's True Story." *True Frontier*, Feb. 1975, p. 11; and *True Frontier*, Dec. 1976, p. 45.

Holding, Vera. "Calamity Jane: The Cussing Canary." *Westerner*, May-June 1972, p. 22.

_____. "Calamity Jane: Wildcat's Kitten." *Westerner,* March-April 1969, p. 32.

Klock, Irma H. "Taps for Calamity Jane" ("Nuggets" column). *Frontier Times,* Nov. 1980, p. 60.

Mays, Carelton. "The True Calamity Jane." *Real West,* Jan. 1960, p. 27.

Nelson, D.J. "Calamity Jane's Last Ride." *The West,* May 1968, p. 40. Rpt. *The West,* Sept. 1973, p. 26; *Western Frontier,* Special Issue, Summer 1974, p. 12; and *Western Frontier,* May 1976, p. 44.

Repp, Ed Earl. "The Lady Was a Cavalryman." *Golden West,* June 1972, p. 12. *The West,* Jan. 1969, p. 22.

Secrest, William B. "The Last Days of Calamity Jane." *True Frontier,* March 1970, p. 8. Rpt. *True Frontier,* Special Issue No. 13, 1975, p. 14.

"True Western Hall of Fame" column. *True Western Adventures,* Oct. 1960, p. 43.

Wright, Kathryn. "The Real Calamity Jane." *True West,* Dec. 1957, p. 22. Rpt. *True West,* Special Issue 1978, p. 20.

Canton, Frank M. "Joe Horner"

Boyer, Glenn G. "Alias General Canton." *Real West,* Feb. 1985, p. 16. Rpt. *Real West,* Yearbook, Fall 1985, p. 14.

Carson, John. "Frank Canton: Gunfighter." *Frontier Times,* Sept. 1966, p. 34.

DeMattos, Jack. "Frank Canton" ("Gunfighters of the Real West" column). *Real West,* May 1979, p. 22.

Rescorla, Richard. "Frank M. Canton: Johnson County Raider." *Golden West,* Jan. 1971, p. 42. Rpt. *Golden West,* Feb. 1974, p. 32; and *Western Frontier,* Annual No. 4, 1976, p. 44.

Secrest, William B. "The Best of the Bad Men." *Real Frontier,* Nov. 1971, p. 32.

Captain Dutch

Walker, Wayne T. "Captain Dutch." *Real Frontier,* Nov. 1971, p. 36.

Captain Jack (Keintpoos)

Arthur, Jim. "Fifty Braves to Stand Off the US Cavalry: The Last Battle of the Modocs." *Frontier West,* Dec. 1971, p. 16.

Barkdull, Tom. "Modoc's Bloody Ground." *Wild West,* June 1970, p. 27.

Chatfield, Harry. "The Modocs Fought Back." *Real West,* March 1964, p. 22.

Cook, David C. "Captain Jack and the Modoc War." *True Western Adventures,* Dec. 1959, p. 16.

Deac, Wilfred P. "Indian Fortress Assailed." *Wild West,* Feb. 1991, p. 34.

"The Deadly 'Squaw Soldiers.'" *Great West,* Dec. 1968, p. 30.

Ewing, Norris. "Death in the Lava Beds." *Real West,* Special Issue, Winter 1963, p. 53.

Farfan, G.B. "War of the Burnt-Out Fires." *Frontier Times,* March 1967, p. 34.

Indrysek, Don. "The Long Winter of Captain Jack." *True Frontier,* Oct. 1976, p. 10.

Jones, Sherwood. "Captain Jack's Untold Story." *The West,* Jan. 1965, p. 47. Rpt. *Western Frontier,* Nov. 1978, p. 5.

Roe, Ken Sherwood. "Warcry at the Infernal Caves." *Great West,* Dec. 1973, p. 24. Rpt. *Authentic West,* Spring 1981, p. 24.

Rosenhouse, Leo. "The Last Stand of the Modocs." *Westerner,* July-Aug. 1969, p. 38.

_____ . "The Rage of Captain Jack." *True Frontier,* March 1971, p. 8.

Stanley, Samuel. "The War the Army Would Like to Forget." *Real Frontier,* June 1970, p. 24. Rpt. *True Frontier,* Aug. 1972, p. 14.

Walker, Wayne T. "War Drums of the Modocs." *Pioneer West,* Sept. 1974, p. 21.

Wiltsey, Norman B. "Hell With the Fires Out." *True West,* Nov. 1954, p. 6.

Zoltan, E.L. "Slaughter On the Lava Beds." *True Frontier,* March 1969, p 38 Rpt. *True Frontier.* Special Issue No. 10, 1974, p. 24.

Captain John
Paterson, T.W. "Captain John: Ill-Fated Indian Chief." *Real West,* Aug. 1973, p. 32.

Captain Pete
Cerveri, Doris. "Paiute Leaders." *Real West,* Special Issue, Spring 1972, p. 14.

Carey, Joseph Maull "Joe"
Koller, Joe. "Joseph Maull Carey: Mr. Wyoming." *Golden West,* May 1972, p. 38.

Carleton, James H.
Martin, Cy. "Col. Carleton Showed the Hostiles No Mercy." *Frontier West,* Feb. 1973, p. 44.

Carlisle, William "Bill"
Freeman, Frank M. "Robin Hood of the Rails." *The West,* March 1968, p. 8. Rpt. *Golden West,* Oct. 1973, p. 41; *Western Frontier,* Special Issue, Summer 1974, p. 15; and *Western Frontier,* May 1977, p. 23.

Latham, George J. "Railroad Bushwhacking Was a Loner's Game." *Frontier West,* Aug. 1972, p. 32.

McNair, H.M. "The Lone Bandit." *Frontier Times,* March 1963, p. 20.

Shipp, Cameron. "The Paragon of Train Robbers." *True Western Adventures,* Issue No. 1, 1957, p. 29.

Smetternik, Gene. "The One-Man Railroad Robber." *Westerner,* Jan.-Feb. 1974, p. 45.

Smith, Fay. Letter, "Bill Carlisle." *Frontier Times,* Sept. 1963, p. 4.

Carr, Eugene A.
Kildare, Maurice. "The General and the Medicine Man." *Westerner,* Sept. 1970, p. 36.

Carrington, Henry B.
Camp, Bernie. "Hell Is Forty Below." *Golden West,* Sept. 1968, p. 10. Rpt. *Western Frontier,* March 1978, p. 10.

Malsbary, George. "Warcry." *Great West,* Dec. 1972, p. 4.

Carrington, Margaret Irvin
Camp, Bernie. "Short Honeymoon of an Army Wife." *Western Frontier,* Special Issue, Dec. 1974, p. 34.

Carroll, Henry
O'Neal, Bill. "Captain Henry Carroll: Southwestern Indian Fighter." *Real West,* June 1982, p. 19. Rpt. *Real West,* Annual , Spring 1983, p. 55.

Carson, Christopher "Kit"
Auer, Louise. "Kit Carson's Strange Romance." *The West,* Feb. 1965, p. 14.

Boyer, Jack K. "Kit Carson, the Mountain Man." *La Gaceta* (El Corral de Santa Fe Westerners), Vol. V, No. 2, 1970, p. 3.

Carson, Charles. "The Real Story of Kit Carson." *Western Tales,* June 1960, p. 14.

Fink, Clarence M. "Young Kit Carson: His Early Talent for Adventure." *Real West,* Yearbook, Fall 1979, p. 37.

Frémont, Jessie Benton. "Jessie Benton Frémont Appraises Carson." *Frontier Times,* July 1970, p. 32.

Hall, Andrew. "Elusive Enemy Pursued." *Wild West,* Aug. 1989, p. 19.

Howe, Mark. "Green River Shindig." *True West,* Dec. 1957, p. 12.

Huff, H. Andy. "The Other Battle of Adobe Walls." *True Western Adventures,* Dec. 1959, p. 28.

Johnston, Langford, with Eve Ball,. "Long Walk Escapees." *True West,* May 1982, p. 20.

Malsbary, George. "Kit Carson's Bloody Detour." *Golden West,* Sept. 1972, p. 28. Rpt. *Western Frontier,* Sept. 1976, p. 14; and *Western Frontier,* May 1979, p. 6.

Marston, Russell. "Kit Carson's Phantom Scout." *Real West,* March 1960, p. 8.

Martin, Cy. "Kit Carson and the Utes." *Real West,* April 1968, p. 12.

Meketa, Jackie. "Kit Carson and Chief Ouray: Partners in Peace. *Real West,* Dec. 1986, p. 18.

Murphy, John F. "Personality" column. *Wild West,* Feb. 1991, p. 12.

Richmond, Robert W. "Jessie's Recollection of Kit Carson." *The West,* Nov. 1970, p. 10. Rpt. *The West,* Oct. 1974, p. 19.

Ross, Leonard. "When Death Stalked the Kit Carson Pass." *True Frontier,* Sept. 1969, p. 18.

Sassone, Richard. "Kit Carson, the Giant Killer." *Pioneer West,* Oct. 1971, p. 8. Rpt. *Oldtimers Wild West,* June 1979, p. 34.

Settle, Raymond W. "The Twilight Days of Kit Carson." *The West,* March 1969, p. 14. Rpt. *Golden West,* Aug. 1973, p. 20, and *Western Frontier,* May 1976, p. 26.

Settle, Raymond W., and Mary Lund Settle. "He Struck Terror to Apache Hearts." *True Frontier,* Special Issue No. 6, 1973, p. 24.

Spendlove, Earl. "Kit Carson's Navajo Round-Up." *The West,* Sept. 1968, p. 36. Rpt. *The West,* Jan. 1973, p. 20; and *Western Frontier,* Aug. 1985, p. 26.

_____. "The Monument Valley Slaughter." *Great West,* Oct. 1973, p. 26.

Carson, James "Jim"

Kildare, Maurice. "Gold On the Cottonwood." *Oldtimers Wild West,* April 1976, p. 36.

Carson, Kit, III

Cole, J.B., III. "Kit Carson Dies." *Frontier Times,* July 1975, p. 7.

Porter, Rufus L. "Kit Carson's Grandson." *Frontier Times,* Sept. 1974, p. 18.

Carson, Moses

Bentz, Donald N. "Kit's Brother: Moses Carson." *The West,* Aug. 1967, p. 24. Rpt. *The West,* May 1974, p. 22.

Carson, William "Kit"

Retort, Robert D. "William Kit Carson." *Real West,* Feb. 1984, p. 34. Rpt. *Real West,* Yearbook, Fall 1984, p. 44.

Carter, William H.
Thrapp, Dan L. "War on the Cibicu." *True West,* April 1964, p. 26.

Carver, W.F. "Doc"
Kay, Jay F. "Man of Destiny." *Golden West,* Nov. 1964, p. 37. Rpt. *Golden West,* Jan. 1972, p. 35.

Thorp, Raymond W. "Doc Carver vs. Buffalo Bill." Part I, *Real West,* March 1967, p. 18; Part II, *Real West,* May 1967, p. 30.

_____. "Rifle King." *Frontier Times,* March 1964, p. 10.

Carver, Will "Bill"
Holt, Roy D. "The End of Will Carver." *True West,* June 1970, p. 36.

Linn, William C. "Bill Carver Missed But Skunk Didn't." *NOLA Quarterly,* Vol. III, No. 1, Summer 1977, p. 11.

Sooner, Paul. "Will Carver's Last Showdown." *Westerner,* July-Aug. 1973, p. 26.

Casement, Jack
Williams, John Hoyt. "Purged by Six-Gun." *Wild West,* June 1990, p. 18.

Casey, Edward Wanton
Koller, Joseph. "Casey's Cheyenne Scouts." *Real West,* Americana Series, Winter 1964, p. 50.

_____. "Lieutenant Casey's Journey to Death." *Real West,* March 1964, p. 10.

Miller, Don. "Casey's Scouts." *Real West,* Special Issue, Spring 1984, p. 59.

Casey Gang
Ballenger, Dean W. "The Saga of the Great Tecumseh Bank Robbery." *Frontier West,* Oct. 1973, p. 30.

Lehman, Leola. "The Violent End of the Casey Gang." *True Frontier,* Nov. 1968, p. 42. Rpt. *True Frontier,* Special Issue No. 1, 1971, p. 36.

Lehman, M.P. "Bert Casey, Outlaw." *Great West,* Dec. 1970, p. 22.

Casey, Joseph "Joe"
Kildare, Maurice. "The Mysterious Gunman." *The West,* Dec. 1966, p. 21. Rpt. *The West,* Aug. 1972, p. 14; and *Western Frontier,* Annual, Winter 1977, p. 14.

O'Dell, Roy. "Arizona's Forgotten Escape Artist." *Old West,* Fall 1990, p. 14.

_____. "Joseph Casey: Arizona Escape Artist." *NOLA Quarterly,* Vol. XIII, No. 2, Fall 1989, p. 22.

Richardson, Gladwell. "Mystery Outlaw of the Border." *Westerner,* Nov.-Dec.
    1969, p. 22.

Casey, Patrick
Rezatto, Helen. "A Spectacular Suicide in Deadwood." *True West,* May 1991, p.
    62.

Casharoga, James W. (George Wilson)
Kelsey, Frederick W. "Judge Parker's Last Hanging." *The West,* June 1974, p. 23.

Cashman, Nellie
Barkdull, Tom. "Nellie Cashman." *Old West,* Summer 1980, p. 26.

Bentz, Donald N. "Frontier Angel." *Golden West,* March 1966, p. 28. Rpt. *The
    West,* July 1972, p. 6; and *Western Frontier,* Special Issue, Dec. 1974, p. 26.

Cheney, Louise. "Angel of the Gold Camps." *Wild West,* Sept. 1970, p. 20. Rpt.
    Oldtimers Wild West, May 1975, p. 20; and *Oldtimers Wild West,* Oct. 1979,
    p. 10.

Hogan, Charles. "Did Nellie Cashman Find Gold?" *The West,* May 1965, p. 17.
    Rpt. *Western Frontier,* Sept. 1980, p. 41.

Lake, Ivan C. "Nellie Cashman Blazed the Frontier Trails." *Real West,* Nov. 1965,
    p. 58.

Qualey, J.S. "Nellie Cashman's Secret Mine." *Real West,* Sept. 1962, p. 38.

Sandos, John. "The Angel of Tombstone." *Real West,* March 1960, p. 21.

Tidwell, Dewey. "Nellie Cashman, An Angel of Mercy." *Real West,* Oct. 1981,
    p. 32. Rpt. *Real West,* Yearbook, Fall 1982, p. 43.

Cassidy, Butch (see Parker, Robert Leroy)

"Catfish Kid" (see Gough, John B.)

Catron, Thomas "Tom"
Bates, L.T. Letter, "Thomas Catron." *True West,* Feb. 1962, p. 44.

"Cattle Kate" (see Watson, Ella)

Chacon, Augustine
Guttman, Jon. "Gunfighters and Lawmen" column. *Wild West,* April 1990, p. 10.

Hartley, William B. "Turncoat From Tombstone." *True Western Adventures,*
    Dec. 1959, p. 30.

Meyer, Dick. "Dick Meyer Ballad of Augustine Chacon." *NOLA Quarterly,* Vol. II, No. 2, Summer 1975, p. 10.

Rickards, Colin. "The Hairy One: Arizona's Deadly Bandit." *The West,* Dec. 1970, p. 30. Rpt. *Western Frontier,* Jan. 1983, p. 30.

Waltrip, Lela and Rufus. "Top Man of the Fearless Thirteen." *True West,* Dec. 1970, p. 22.

Chadwell, William "Bill"

Gehrman, B.L. "Hardened Criminal." *True West,* Dec. 1958, p. 21.

Repp, Ed Earl. "Who Was Bill Chadwell?" *Golden West,* Nov. 1973, p. 38. Rpt. *Western Frontier,* Sept. 1976, p. 2.

Sandell, Jay. "Whistling Bill: Nemesis of the Youngers." *Real West,* May 1960, p. 32.

Chambers, Annie

Albert, Anthony. "Queen of the Red Lights." *True Western Adventures,* Aug. 1959, p. 42.

Carroll, Lenore. "Matronly Madame Annie Chambers." *True West,* June 1987, p. 38.

Moffat, George Alan. "Madame Was a Lady." *Real West,* Jan. 1958, p. 18.

Chambers, William "Persimmon Bill"

Kildare, Maurice. "Persimmon Bill." *Big West,* April 1968, p. 30.

Champion, Nate

Anderson, Bryce W. "One Against An Army." *True West,* Dec. 1956, p. 22.

Christy, Mort. "King of the Rustlers." *Real West,* Aug. 1958, p. 16.

Hartley, William. "One Against Fifty-three." *True Western Adventures,* Summer 1958, p. 12.

Kelly, Bill. "The Death of Nate Champion and Nick Ray." *Real West,* Sept. 1979, p. 24.

Rickards, Colin. "Nate Champion Tells About the Wyoming Range War." *Real West,* March 1970, p. 58.

Vail, Jason. "Hired Assassins Dreaded." *Wild West,* June 1988, p. 20.

Wiltsey, Norman B. "The Saga of Nate Champion." Part I, *Real West,* April 1968, p. 22; Part II, *Real West,* May 1968, p. 48.

Winski, Norman. "Diary of a Cowboy About to Die." *Pioneer West,* Nov. 1967, p. 42.

Chapman, Amos

Bailey, Tena. "Amos Chapman and the Battle of Buffalo Wallow." *True West*, Jan. 1983, p. 50.

Cheney, Louise. "Battle at the Buffalo Wallow." *Wild West*, March 1970, p. 44.

Glynn, Dean. "Six Who Risked Death." *Westerner*, March-April 1970, p. 48.

Knox, William P. "Last Stand on a Texas Prairie." *Golden West*, July 1966, p. 36. Rpt. *The West*, April 1972, p. 12; and *Western Frontier*, May 1978, p. 12.

Lafferty, Jack. "Six Medals of Honor." *True West*, June 1960, p. 26.

Montgomery, Wayne. "Amos Chapman, Scout." *Frontier Times*, May 1972, p. 26.

Turpin, Robert F. "The Fight at Buffalo Wallow." *Great West*, Oct. 1970, p. 24.

Walker, Wayne T. "Fighting Army Scouts of the Indian Wars." *Great West*, June 1972, p. 14.

Chapman, Huston I.

Rasch, Philip J. "The Murder of Huston I. Chapman." *Los Angeles Westerners Brand Book* , Vol. VIII, 1959, p. 69.

Charbonneau, Baptiste

Dullenty, Jim. "Sacajawea's Son Buried in Oregon." *Old West*, Winter 1982, p. 30.

Howard, Helen Addison. "The Puzzle of Baptiste Charbonneau." *Frontier Times*, July 1970, p. 10.

Walker, Wayne T. "Baptiste Charbonneau: Mysterious Son of Bird Woman." *Real West*, April 1980, p. 7. Rpt. *Real West*, Special Issue, 1981, p. 42.

_____. "Pomp: Son of Sacajawea." *The West*, July 1970, p. 11.

Charlton, John B.

Blalock, Fred Frank. "John B. Charlton, Cavalryman by Choice." *Real West*, Sept. 1974, p. 22.

Charter, Bert

Emery, Olin E. Letter. *True West*, April 1980, p. 4.

Wright, Kathryn. "Dad Rode With the Wild Bunch." *True West*, Feb. 1979, p. 21.

Chase, Edward "Ed"

Peabody, Olive. "Denver's Gambling King." *Golden West*, Jan. 1971, p. 36.

Cheneworth, Otto

Ferguson, John F. "The Happy Horse Thief." *The West,* Sept. 1965, p. 22.

Smith, Wilson D. "Horsethief Caballero." *Real West,* Aug. 1959, p. 25.

"Cherokee Bill" (see Goldsby, Crawford)

Chiles, James J. "Jim Crow"

Hale, Donald R. "James Chiles: A Missouri Badman." *The West,* Oct. 1968, p. 14. Rpt. *Golden West,* April 1972, p. 6, and *Western Frontier,* July 1983, p. 12.

McRay, Bennett. "Fantastic Story of Missouri's Mad Cannibal." *Real West,* March 1966, p. 14.

Thorp, Raymond W. "How 'Jim Crow' Chiles Died." *Real West,* Jan. 1962, p. 32.

Chisholm, Jesse

Burkholder, Edwin V. "Blood on the Chisholm Trail." *True Western Adventures,* Oct. 1955, p. 20.

Henderson, Sam. "The Incredible Story of the Blazing of the Chisholm Trail." *Frontier West,* Feb. 1973, p. 16.

King, Dan. "Up the Chisholm Trail." *True West,* June 1961, p. 26.

Mooney, Charles W. "Prairie Jess Chisholm." *Great West,* Dec. 1970, p. 28.

Walker, Wayne T. "Jesse Chisholm: Saga of a Peacemaker." *Golden West,* Nov. 1970, p. 34. Rpt. *Golden West,* Oct. 1973, p. 29; and *Western Frontier,* Nov. 1986, p. 6.

Chisum, John Simpson (originally "Chisholm")

Brand, C.R. Letter. *Real West,* Jan 1964, p. 77.

Martin, Cy. "Cattle King John Chisum." *Golden West,* Sept. 1970, p. 22. Rpt. *Western Frontier,* Annual , Spring 1981, p. 42.

Mays, Carelton. "The Cattle Baron Who Wouldn't Fight." *Real West,* Aug. 1958, p. 6.

Taylor, T.V. "John Simpson Chisum." *Frontier Times,* July 1978, p. 12.

Wallace, George A. "Cattle Kings." *True West,* Feb. 1964, p. 66.

Waltrip, Rufus. "John Chisum, Empire Builder." *The West,* June 1972, p. 8. Rpt. *Western Frontier,* Oct. 1984, p. 8.

Chivington, John M.

Bailey, Tom. "The White Invaders." *True West,* Aug. 1963, p. 14.

Breihan, Carl W. "The Bloody Sand Creek Massacre." *Real West,* Annual, Summer 1971, p. 33.

_____. "The Sand Creek Massacre." *Real West,* Sept. 1979, p. 29.

Dunn, J.P., Jr. "The Shame of Sand Creek." *The West,* Sept. 1964, p. 32. Rpt. *The West,* May 1972, p. 14.

Knudson, Dean. "Sand Creek Avenged." *Wild West,* Oct. 1991, p. 22.

Mason, John. "Crime of Colonel Chivington." *Real West,* Nov. 1958, p. 9.

Mendoza, Robert. "Black Kettle and Col. Chivington." *Great West,* June 1972, p. 28. Rpt. *Authentic West,* Fall 1981, p. 32.

Secrest, Clark. "Horror of Sand Creek." *Real West,* Americana Series, Winter 1966, p. 66.

Strucinsky, Mitchell J. "Permission to Murder." *Frontier Times,* Winter 1960, p. 14.

Sufrin, Mark. "The Massacre at Sand Creek." *Frontier West,* Feb. 1972, p. 18.

Swanson, Budington. "Massacre at Sand Creek." *True Frontier,* Sept. 1968, p. 18. Rpt. *True Frontier,* Special Issue No. 6, 1973, p. 10.

Chouteau Family
Walker, Wayne T. "The Chouteaus: Vanguards of the Frontier." *Great West,* Feb. 1973, p. 22.

Christian, William T. "Black Jack"
Bentz, Donald N. "Alias 'Black Jack' Christian." *Old West,* Spring 1970, p. 52.

Boessenecker, John. "The Beginning and End of Black Jack Christian and His Train Robbers." *Golden West,* Sept. 1973, p. 34. Rpt. *Western Frontier,* Annual, Fall 1980, p. 34.

Burton, Jeff. "Bureaucracy, Blood Money and Black Jack's Gang." *English Westerners' Brand Book,* Vol. XXII, No. 1, Winter 1983, and No. 2, Summer 1984 (combined issue), p. 1.

Carter, Thomas G. "Who Was Black Jack?" *NOLA Quarterly,* Vol. XV, No. 2, April-June 1991, p. 11.

Kildare, Maurice. "Black Jack Christian: Two-Bit Outlaw." *Great West,* April 1970, p. 26.

Repp, Ed Earl. "Brothers of El Diablo." *True Frontier,* March 1970, p. 22. Rpt. *True Frontier,* Special Issue No. 5, 1973, p. 26.

Tidwell, Dewey. "The Demise of Black Jack Christian." *Real West,* April 1982, p. 26. Rpt. *Real West,* Special Issue, Spring 1983, p. 36.

Young, Bob. "Black Jack Christian, Murderer." *NOLA Quarterly,* Vol. IX, No. 2, Autumn 1984, p. 17.

Christie, Ned

Hart, George. "Ned Christie, Oklahoma's Mad Killer." *Real West,* Nov. 1970, p. 18.

McBee, Fred. "Wanted, Dead or Alive: Ned Christie." *Great West,* April 1971, p. 6.

McKibben, Mike. "Siege at Rabbit Trap." *True Western Adventures,* Spring 1958, p. 16.

O'Neal, Bill. "Ned Christie vs. Posse of Twenty-Five," ("Great Western Gunfights" column). *True West,* Jan. 1990, p. 60.

Powers, Mark. "Ned Christie's Vendetta." *Wild West,* March 1972, p. 38. Rpt. *Pioneer West,* Sept. 1975, p. 34.

Pride, Joe. "The Battle of Tahlequah Canyon." *True West,* Oct. 1963, p. 18.

Rand, Phillip [sic]. "Blood in the Cookson Hills." *Real West,* Jan. 1958, p. 26

Roy, Robert. "Oklahoma's Bandit Hideout." *Real West,* Nov. 1975, p. 32.

Speer, Bonnie. "Ned Christie: Wolf of Cookson Hills." *True West,* Jan. 1983, p. 26.

Turpin, Robert F. "The Posse Trap." *Pioneer West,* Jan. 1968, p. 8.

Walker, Wayne T. "Ned Christie: Terror of the Cookson Hills." *Real West,* Nov. 1978, p. 30.

Wallace, Hill. "The One-Man Army." *Westerner,* Jan.-Feb. 1974, p. 52.

Claiborne, William "Billy the Kid"

O'Neal, Bill. "Buckskin Frank Leslie vs. Billy the Kid Claiborne" ("Great Western Gunfights" column). *True West,* March 1991, p. 60.

Clanton Family (Newman Haynes "Old Man," Ike, Phin, Billy)

Deac, Wilfred P. "Two Minutes in Tombstone." *Wild West,* Aug. 1991, p. 42.

Kantor, Seth. "Time: Oct. 26, 1881—Place: OK Corral." *Western Action,* Dec. 1960, p. 30.

Malocsay, Zoltan. "OK Corral: 100 Years of Lies." *Westerner,* July-Aug. 1973, p. 34.

Mason, Frank. "What Really Happened at the O.K. Corral?" *True West,* Oct. 1960, p. 35.

Mays, Carelton. "What Really Happened at the OK Corral?" *Real West,* Jan. 1958, p. 14. Rpt. *Real West,* Annual, Summer 1966, p. 28.

Parsons, Chuck. "Phin Clanton's Demise" ("Answer Man" column). *True West,* April 1989, p. 12.

Rasch, Philip J. "Farewell to the Clantons." *New York Westerners' Brand Book,* Vol. V, 1958 p. 43.

Roberts, Gary L. "The Fight That Never Dies." *Frontier Times,* Nov. 1965, p. 6.
_____. "The Fremont Street Fiasco." *True West,* July 1988, p. 14.
Turner, Alford E. "The Clantons of Apache County." *Real West,* March 1979, p. 46.
Van Slyke, Sue C. "The Truth About the Clantons of Tombstone." *NOLA Quarterly,* Vol. II, No. 1, Spring 1975, p. 8.
_____. Letter ("Trails Grown Dim" column). *Old West,* Spring 1986, p. 60.
_____, and Dave Johnson. "Kin to the Clantons." *NOLA Quarterly,* Vol. XIV, No. 2, Summer 1990, p. 8.

Clanton, Ike
Edwards, Harold L. "The Man Who Killed Ike Clanton." *True West,* Oct. 1991, p. 24.

Clanton, Newman Haynes "Old Man"
Benay, Larry. "Old Man Clanton Cashes In." *The West,* Jan. 1971, p. 29. Rpt. *The West,* Jan. 1974, p. 31; and *Western Frontier,* July 1978, p. 41.

Clark, Ben
Lamb, Lucylle M. "Ben Clark: King of Scouts." *Wild West,* Dec. 1970, p. 38.
Thomas, Kevin. "Ben Clark: The Scout Who Defied Custer." *Oldtimers Wild West,* Feb. 1980, p. 22.
Walker, Wayne T. "Ben Clark." *Big West,* April 1970, p. 19.
_____. "Ben Clark: Chief of Scouts." *Real West,* May 1976, p. 8.
_____. "Ben Clark, the Scout Who Defied Custer." *Great West,* Feb. 1971, p. 6.

Clark, William
Gulick, Bill. "William Clark's Indian Love Child." *True West,* Feb. 1984, p. 12.
Hurdy, John Major. "The Impossible Mission of Lewis and Clark." *Pioneer West,* April 1971, p. 22.

Clark, William Andrew
Clark, Helen. "The Copper Kings." *Pioneer West,* Sept. 1969, p. 24. Rpt. *Pioneer West,* Aug. 1972, p. 36; *Oldtimers Wild West,* May 1975, p. 50; and *Pioneer West,* Nov. 1979, p. 38.
Fink, Clarence M. "W.A. Clark: Self-Made Westerner." *Real West,* March 1978, p. 56.
Grimmett, R.G. "The Richest Hill on Earth." *Golden West,* Oct. 1974, p. 11.

Clarke, James "Jim" (sometimes spelled "Clark")
Breihan, Carl W. "Quantrill's Last Man." *Westerner,* Sept.-Oct. 1973, p. 28.

Clarke, Marcellus Jerome "Sue Mundy"
Parsons, Chuck. "A Guerrilla Named Sue" ("Answer Man" column). *True West,* Nov. 1991, p. 12.

Clatworthy, Luke
Feldman, Max. "Bounty Hunter." *Great West,* Aug. 1971, p. 16.

Clay, Dannie
Nieberding, Velma. "Killing of Dannie Clay." *The West,* Sept. 1965, p. 16.

Clem, John
Grubb, R.L. "The Heartwarming Story of the Little Drummer Boy of Shiloh: From Ten-Year-Old Private to Major General." *The West,* Dec. 1973, p. 35.

Clement(s), Archibald J. "Arch"
Parsons, Chuck. "Civil War Guerrilla Arch Clements" ("Answer Man" column). *True West,* Nov. 1991, p. 12.

Clements Brothers (Mannen, Joe, Jim, John)
Parsons, Chuck. "A Texas Gunfighter and the Kansas Murder Family." *Real West,* Annual 1981, p. 14.

_____. "Mystery Photo: Joe Clements and Friends." *Real West,* July 1981, p. 22. Rpt. *Real West,* Special Issue, Spring 1984, p. 62.

Clements Family (Israel, "Slick," Eliza, Jim C., Amanda E.)
Treat, E.J. Letter. *Old West,* Spring 1967, p. 52.

Clements, James "Jim"
Parsons, Chuck. "James Clements, Peripheral Gunfighter." *English Westerners' 25th Anniversary Publication,* 1980, p. 82.

Clements, Joe
Parsons, Chuck. "Who Were Friends of Joe Clements....Mystery Photo?" *NOLA Quarterly,* Vol. III, No. 3, Winter 1978, p. 11.

Clements, Mannen (Manning, Emanuel)
Leftwich, Bill. "The Death of Mannen Clements." *True West,* April 1974, p. 15.

Mays, Carelton. "Mannen, the Great." *Real West,* May 1961, p. 8.

Clements, William T. "Slick"
Gillett, J.B. "Slick Clements: Dead Shot." Rpt. *Old West,* Summer 1966, p. 17.

Clendening, John
Archer, Myrtle. "California Stagecoach Skirmish." *True West,* May 1988, p. 44.

Clum, John
Bloom, Sam. "The Agent Who Tamed the Apaches." *Golden West,* March 1972, p. 10.

Boyer, Glenn. "John Clum and the Alaskan Postal Service." *True West,* May 1985, p. 10.

Carson, Xanthus. "The Man Who Tricked Geronimo." *True Frontier,* April 1977, p. 6.

DeMattos, Jack. "The Incredible John Philip Clum." *Real West,* May 1977, p. 8. Rpt. *Real West,* Annual, Winter 1979, p. 24.

Henderson, Sam. "Tombstone's Adventurous Journalist: John Clum." *Golden West,* Nov. 1969, p. 28. Rpt. *The West,* Dec. 1971, p. 22.

Repp, Ed Earl. "The School Teacher Who Arrested Geronimo." *Real Frontier,* March 1970, p. 25. Rpt. *True Frontier,* Aug. 1972, p. 21; and *True Frontier,* Aug. 1976, p. 21.

Woodson, Weldon D. "Indian Agent's Funny Bone" ("Wild Old Days" column). *True West,* Feb. 1988, p. 62.

Clyman, James
Fink, Clarence M. "Portrait of a Mountain Man! James Clyman." *Real West,* Feb. 1972, p. 6.

Cochise
Auer, L.C. "Cochise: Chief of the Apache Chiricahuas." *Golden West,* Jan. 1966, p. 18. Rpt. *Golden West,* Feb. 1972, p. 32; *Western Frontier,* Special Issue, March 1975, p. 26; *Western Frontier,* March 1979, p. 2; and *Western Frontier,* Jan 1981, p. 28.

Bloom, Sam. "Suicide Run Was Six Miles of Pure Hell." *Frontier West,* Aug. 1972, p. 28.

Fisher, Ralph A., Sr. "When Chief Cochise Doomed the Overland." *Real West,* March 1980, p. 36.

Lehman, Leola. "Massacre at Ramos." *True Frontier,* Special Issue No. 6, 1973, p. 38.

Lewis, Wendell. "Betrayal Led to Cochise's Vendetta of Slaughter." *Frontier West,* Aug. 1971, p. 32.

Rosenhouse, Leo. "Stagecoach." *Great West,* Aug. 1973, p. 14. Rpt. *Great West,* Fall 1981, p. 16.

Stanley, Samuel. "How the West Point Tenderfoot Turned the Peaceful Prairie Into a Deadly Battlefield." *Frontier West,* Oct. 1975, p. 22.

Tevis, James H. "Arizona in the Fifties." Rpt. *True West,* June 1968, p. 6.

"True Western Hall of Fame" column. *True Western Adventures,* Feb. 1961, p. 50.

White, Wilmer A. "Cochise." *Frontier Times,* March 1974, p. 40.

Wiltsey, Norman B. "Hawks of the Desert." *True West,* Dec. 1955, p. 19.

Yarbrough, Leroy. "The Apache and the Sioux." *Real West,* Special Issue, Winter 1970, p. 26.

Cockrell, James

Kildare, Maurice. "The First American Prospector: James Cockrell." *Real West,* April 1971, p. 11.

Cody, Isaac

Lehman, Leola. "Isaac Cody: Frontiersman." *Great West,* Feb. 1971, p. 24.

Cody, William F. "Buffalo Bill"

Beardsley, J.L. "Buffalo Bill Ends an Indian War." *Real West,* Jan. 1968, p. 28.

Breihan, Carl W. "The Killing of Yellow Hand." *Real West,* Aug. 1970, p. 14.

Copeland, Edwin R. "I Knew Buffalo Bill." *Real West,* May 1971, p. 24.

DeMarco, Mario A. "The Fabulous Buffalo Bill." *Real West,* March 1975, p. 42.

Dodge, Matt. "Buffalo Bill in Arizona." *Real West,* March 1982, p. 8. Rpt. *Real West,* Special Issue, Spring 1983, p. 40.

Frazier, Thomas A., Jr. "Buffalo Bill, The Man and the Legend." Part I, *Real West,* May 1969, p. 13; Part II, *Real West,* June 1969, p. 16; Part III, *Real West,* Aug. 1969, p. 20.

Gartman, Clarence. "Last Days of Buffalo Bill." *The West,* Dec. 1966, p. 40. Rpt. *Golden West,* Feb. 1973, p. 34; and *Western Frontier,* July 1976, p. 22.

Hart, George. "How the Wild West Went East." *Real West,* June 1970, p. 16.

Jones, Gene. "Buffalo Bill's Tragic Last Days." *Real West,* March 1966, p. 9.

"The Legacy of Buffalo Bill." *Westerner,* Sept.-Oct. 1969, p. 26.

Lehman, L.C. "Buffalo Bill's Great Hunt." *Real West,* May 1965, p. 23.

Lehman, Leo. "Buffalo Bill's Last Fox Hunt." *Westerner,* Jan. 1971, p. 48.

Lehman, Leola. "Willie Cody's School Room." *Real Frontier,* Aug. 1970, p. 8. Rpt. *True Frontier,* Nov. 1973, p. 34.

McCreight, M.I. "Buffalo Bill As I Knew Him." *True West,* Aug. 1957, p. 25.

Muller, Dan. "My Life With Buffalo Bill." Rpt. Part I, *Old West,* Winter 1981, p. 47; Part II, *Old West,* Spring 1982, p. 49; Part III, *Old West,* Summer 1982, p. 45; Part IV, *Old West,* Fall 1982, p. 51.

Nolan, Paul. "Buffalo Bill's Secret Life." *Real West,* Sept. 1966, p. 26.

Pearce, Bennett R. "The Day Denver Buried Buffalo Bill." *The West,* April 1973, p. 34. Rpt. *Western Frontier,* March 1976, p. 30.

Rand, Philip. "Buffalo Bill, The Lovable Rogue." *Real West,* April 1958, p. 24. Rpt. *Real West,* Annual, Summer 1966, p. 55.

Red Fox, Chief, and Lenore Sherman. "I Was With Buffalo Bill." *Real West,* April 1968, p. 26.

Riske, Milt. "Buffalo Bill and the Death of White Chief." *Pioneer West,* Nov. 1979, p. 22.

Schuessler, Raymond. "Buffalo Bill Rides Again." *Real West,* July 1974, p. 40.

Thorp, Raymond W. "Doc Carver vs Buffalo Bill." Part I, *Real West,* March 1967, p. 18; Part II, *Real West,* May 1967, p. 30.

"True Western Hall of Fame" column. *True Western Adventures,* April 1959, p. 59.

Webb, Harry E. "Buffalo Bill and Me." Part I, *Westerner,* June 1971, p. 14.; Part II, *Westerner,* Aug. 1971, p. 36.

_____. "Buffalo Bill As I Knew Him." *The West,* Nov. 1967, p. 34. Rpt. *Western Frontier,* Annual, Feb. 1980, p. 34.

_____. "Buffalo Bill Rides Again: Almost." *Westerner,* Jan.-Feb. 1972, p. 43.

_____. "My Years With Buffalo Bill's Wild West Show." Part I, *Real West,* Jan. 1970, p. 12; Part II, *Real West,* Feb. 1970, p. 40.

Yost, Nellie Snyder. "Buffalo Bill Cody: Outlaw, Lawman, Showman." *NOLA Quarterly,* Vol. VIII, No. 3, Winter 1982-83, p. 3.

_____. "Buffalo Bill's Bungled First Rehearsal." *True West,* May 1991, p. 44.

_____. "Why I Wrote the Book About Buffalo Bill." *True West,* Dec. 1983, p. 14.

Zachry, Juanita Daniel. "Mining Adventures of Buffalo Bill Cody." *True West,* April 1990, p. 37.

Coe, Frank
Ball, Eve. "Friend to Billy the Kid." *Westerner,* Spring 1975, p. 32.

Coe, Philip Houston, Jr. "Phil"
O'Neal, Bill. "Wild Bill vs. Phil Coe" ("Great Western Gunfights" column). *True West,* March 1988, p. 59.

Parsons, Chuck. "'Wild Bill' Hickok Killed Two Men in Abilene." *NOLA Quarterly,* Vol. I, No. 1, 1975, p. 9.

_____. "Phil Coe: Professional Gambler From Texas." *NOLA Quarterly,* Vol. IV, No. 1, Summer 1978, p. 12.

Coe, Wilbur

Coe, Louise H. "Some Personal Papers of Wilbur Coe." *True West,* Aug. 1974, p. 20.

Coe, William "Will," "Willie," "Billy"

Henderson, Sam. "The Hunt for Will Coe's Gold." *Pioneer West,* Nov. 1979, p. 28.

Holben, Richard. "The Private War of William Coe: Oklahoma's Most Vicious Rustler." *Frontier West,* Aug. 1974, p. 24.

Packer, C.L. "Coe's Castle on the Carrizo—1867." *True West,* Aug. 1967, p. 14.

Robbins, Lance. "Handsome Baron of Robbers Roost." *Real West,* Oct. 1968, p. 44.

Shirley, Glenn. "Wild Willie and His Terrible Forty." *Old West,* Winter 1988, p. 14.

Coffee, "Gib"

Ebert, Leonard. "Elgin Constables Led Short Lives." *Frontier Times,* July 1969, p. 65.

Coffee, Holland

McLeRoy, Sherrie S. "The Short Life and Hard Death of Holland Coffee." *True West,* Dec. 1989, p. 24.

Coit, Lillie

Jan, Bob. "Lillie Coit, the West's Bombshell." *Western Frontier,* Special Issue, Dec. 1974, p. 44.

Rosenhouse, Leo. "Lady Who Went to Blazes." *Western Round-Up,* Aug. 1970, p. 52.

Colcord, Charles Francis "Chuck," "Charlie"

Henderson, Sam. "The Incredible Saga of Oklahoma's Two-Gun Banker." *Frontier West,* Oct. 1975, p. 30.

Katigan, Madelon B. "Charles F. Colcord, Cowboy Who Made Good." *Real West,* Sept. 1967, p. 42.

Repp, Ed Earl. "Chuck Colcord: Scourge of the Cattle Rustlers." *Golden West,* July 1973, p. 26.

Coldwell, Neal
Sewell, A.J. "Neal Coldwell: Gallant Texas Ranger." *Old West,* Fall 1969, p. 18.

Coleman, William T.
Lipton, Dean. "The Vigilantes." *Great West,* June 1973, p. 14. Rpt. *Great West,* Summer 1981, p. 14.

McGuckin, Andrew J. "San Francisco's Vigilantes Versus the U.S. Navy." *The West,* Oct. 1974, p. 28.

Colgate, George
LeGresley, Roscoe. "Did George Colgate Have to Die?" *Old West,* Summer 1968, p. 30.

Collins, Caspar Weaver
Copeman, L. Berger. "Death at Platte River Bridge." *The West,* June 1965, p. 10. Rpt. *The West,* Sept. 1974, p. 8; and *Western Frontier,* Annual, Spring 1981, p. 16.

_____. "Terror of Platte Bridge Station." *Real West,* Americana Series, Fall 1966, p. 22.

Harrison, Fred. "Savage Fight at Platte Bridge." *Pioneer West,* Dec. 1971, p. 24.

Judge, Bill. "I Am No Coward." *Frontier Times,* Spring 1960, p. 28. Rpt. *Old West,* Summer 1979, p. 10.

Collins, James L.
Meketa, Jacqueline Dorgan. "Mystery Death in the Palace." *True West,* Dec. 1991, p. 44.

Colorow
Werner, Fred W. "Ute Fury at Milk Creek." *Real West,* Aug. 1985, p. 32. Rpt. *Real West,* Yearbook, Winter 1986, p. 51.

Colt, Samuel "Sam"
Peterson, Howard. "Frontier Life Insurance." *The West,* April 1974, p. 10. Rpt. *Western Frontier,* Jan. 1977, p. 11.

Qualey, J.S. "Sam Colt's Deadly Equalizers." *Real West,* Annual, Spring 1968, p. 12.

Strunk, Gordon F. "Boss Gun." *Real West,* Oct. 1957, p. 30.

Colter, John

Almada, Manuel. "Naked Man's Race Against Death." *True West,* Jan. 1955, p. 13.

Beckham, Joe. "Men With the Strength of Mountains." *True Frontier,* July 1970, p. 14.

Heald, Weldon F. "The Indians Couldn't Catch Him!" *Frontier Times,* Fall 1960, p. 26.

Lipton, Dean. "Colter's Hell." *Great West,* Oct. 1972, p. 14.

O'Hagen, Howard. "Bloody Ordeal of Trapper John." *True Western Adventures,* Aug. 1959, p. 14.

Peters, Donald L. "Run, White Crow, Run." *Real West,* July 1961, p. 34.

Thorp, Raymond W. "Colter's Boone." *Old West,* Summer 1966, p. 10.

Comcomly

Neill, Wilfred T. "The Wandering Skull of Chief Com-Comly." *Golden West,* Oct. 1974, p. 22.

Comstock, Henry P.T.

Bailey, Tom. "Henry Comstock: Monumental Liar." *True West,* April 1961, p. 15.

Noren, Evelyn. "Comstock! The Man Behind the Name." *Old West,* Summer 1986, p. 42.

Sharp, N. "Comstock's Sixty-Dollar Bride." *The West,* Oct. 1965, p. 26. Rpt. *Western Frontier,* March 1980, p. 24.

Sullivan, Freyda. "The Curse of the Comstock." *Real West,* June 1981, p. 8.

Comstock, William Averill "Billy" ("Medicine Bill")

Beardsley, J.L. "Billy Comstock: The Original Buffalo Bill." *Golden West,* April 1974, p. 31. Rpt. *Western Frontier,* March 1977, p. 5.

Bird, Roy. "Medicine Bill Comstock." *Real West,* April 1983, p. 32.

Gray, John S. "Will Comstock: The Natty Bumppo of Kansas." *Chicago Westerners' Brand Book,* Vol. XVIII, No. 12, Feb. 1962, p. 89.

Henderson, Sam. "Those Other Buffalo Bills." *Real West,* June 1975, p. 14.

Snell, Joseph W. "Messenger to the Indians." *Old West,* Fall 1969, p. 12.

Walker, Wayne T. "Fighting Army Scouts of the Indian Wars." *Great West,* June 1972, p. 14. Rpt. *Authentic West,* Fall 1981, p. 16.

Connell, Edward Fulton

Connell, Douglas H. "Gun Battle at Mesa Redonda" ("Wild Old Days" column). *True West,* Aug. 1968, p. 37.

Connell, Ira Aten. "Automobile Sheriff" ("Nuggets" column). *Frontier Times,* Jan. 1965, p. 34.

Connell, Sophia H. "Wife of a Panhandle Sheriff." *Old West,* Spring 1980, p. 22.

Trussell, Eddie Connell. "Four Years in the Deaf Smith County Jail." *Frontier Times,* May 1976, p. 38.

Connelly, C.T.
"The Way It Was at Coffeyville." *Western Frontier,* May 1985, p. 20.

Connor, Patrick Edward
Bundy, Rex. "The Powder River Expedition." *Western Frontier,* Oct. 1984, p. 12.

Chatfield, Harry E. "The Bloody Bannock Massacre." *Real West,* May 1968, p. 38.

Flagg, Stuart. "The Bear River Massacre." *Westerner,* March-April 1982, p. 13.

Judge, Bill. "Battle on Bear River." *True West,* Feb. 1961, p. 16.

Kildare, Maurice. "Massacre at Bear River." *Wild West,* June 1969, p. 10.

Mather, R.E. "Nevada's Phantom Outlaw Band." *NOLA Quarterly,* Vol. XV, No. 4, Oct.-Dec. 1991, p. 15.

Morgan, Joseph. "The Powder River Fiasco." *The West,* Jan. 1966, p. 37.

Schindler, Harold. "Blood for Blood." *True West,* Oct. 1965, p. 42.

Simmonds, A.J. "Battle on the Bear." *The West,* Nov. 1966, p. 16. Rpt. *Western Frontier,* March 1979, p. 16, and *Western Frontier,* May 1984, p. 16.

Smith, J. Greg. "Powder River Expedition." *True West,* April 1967, p. 32.

Spendlove, Earl. "Battle of Bear River." *Great West,* April 1973, p. 10.

Contant, George C. (see Sontag, George C.)

Contant, John (see Sontag, John)

Cook, Bill (Cook Gang)
Harrison, Fred. "A Slight Case of Double-Cross." *Western Frontier,* May 1986, p. 8.

Parsons, Chuck. "The Cook Gang" ("Answer Man" column). *True West,* Sept. 1991, p. 12.

Taylor, Walter. "The Last Marshal." *True West,* April 1962, p. 6.

Turpin, Robert F. "Saga of the Deadly Cook Gang." *True Frontier,* Nov. 1969, p. 8. Rpt. *True Frontier,* Special Issue No. 5, 1973, p. 17; and *True Frontier,* Special Issue No. 17, Winter 1976, p. 13.

Cook, Dave

Cook, D.J. "First Bullet Entered His Heart." *Westerner,* March-April 1974, p. 30.

_____. "When Outlaws Organized the West." *Westerner,* March-April 1974, p. 26.

McCarroll, Ralph. "The Bane of Thieves." *True West,* April 1967, p. 26.

Cook, George

Beery, Gladys B. "He Died Game." *Real West,* Yearbook, Fall 1984, p. 31.

Cooke, Philip St. George

Averett, Walter R. "Battle of the Bulls." *True West,* Dec. 1962, p. 34.

Kubista, Bob. "Keep 'Em Fed, Keep 'Em Marching." *Pioneer West,* May 1968, p. 26.

Cooley, Corydon Eliphalet

Kildare, Maurice. "The Trouble-Shooter." *True Frontier,* May 1971, p. 13. Rpt. *True Frontier,* Special Issue No. 11, Winter 1974-75, p. 39.

Cooley, Scott

Walker, Wayne T. "Vendetta." *Pioneer West,* Jan. 1979, p. 6.

White, Lucille. Letter, "Scott Cooley's Grave." *Frontier Times,* March 1976, p. 3.

Cooney, James C. "Jim"

Harnin, William. "Apache Siege at Alma." *True West,* June 1956, p. 8.

Lycons, James H. "Captain Cooney's Fate." Rpt. *Old West,* Summer 1970, p. 14.

Copeland, "Joe"

Holt, Roy D. "Ordeals of a Fence Cutting Detective." *Westerner,* March-April 1974, p. 15.

Corbett, Boston

Chesney, W.D. "The Mad Crusader." *True West,* Dec. 1961, p. 28.

Hunt, Burl. "Boston Corbett: The Mad Hatter." *Golden West,* May 1971, p. 40.

Spencer, G. "The Strange Little Man of Cloud County, Kansas." *Real West,* June 1986, p. 10.

Cormack, Charlie

Cormack, Thomas J. "Charlie Cormack: Forsyth Scout." *Frontier Times,* Nov. 1979, p. 24.

Cornett, Brack
Burton, Jeff. "The Most Surprised Man in Texas." *Frontier Times,* March 1973, p. 18.

Coronado, Francisco Vasquez de
Carson, Xanthus. "The Obsessed." *True Frontier,* Special Issue No. 16, Fall 1976, p. 19.

Cortez, Gregorio
Kildare, Maurice. "Hell on the Nueces." *True Frontier,* March 1971, p. 18.

Jameson, W.C. "The Flight of Gregorio Cortez." *Real West,* Aug. 1985, p. 10. Rpt. *Real West,* Yearbook 1986, p 47

Cortina, Juan Nepomucena (sometimes "Cortinas")
Cheney, Louise. "The Bandido Who Captured a City." *Big West,* Dec. 1967, p. 12.

_____. "Cortino's [sic] Vaqueros." *Pioneer West,* May 1969, p. 44.

_____. "Historic Fort Brown." *The West,* Sept. 1965, p. 32.

Lawton, Steve. "Juan Cortinas: The Badman Who Brought Texas to Her Knees." *Frontier West,* Feb. 1972, p. 10.

McDaniel, Ruel. "Juan Cortina: Hero or Bandit?" *True West,* Oct. 1956, p. 24.

Roebuck, Field. "Cheno Cortina: Red Robber of the Rio Grande." *True West,* Sept. 1989, p. 16.

Cottle, Albert R. "Al"
McKennon, C.H. "Oklahoma's Long-Time Marshal." *The West,* May 1969, p. 44.

Coulter, Charlie
Youngs, C. Daniel. "County Seat Blood." *Real West,* May 1960, p. 22.

Courtney, Morgan (Richard Moriarty)
Earl, Phillip I. "Violent Life of a Nevada Badman." *NOLA Quarterly,* Vol. XII, No. 3, Winter 1988, p. 9.

Hopkins, A.D. "Morgan Courtney, Gunfighter From Pioche." *Old West,* Spring 1981, p. 8.

Sasser, Charles W. "Pioche, Nevada: The Bloodiest Town in the Old West." *Old West,* Sumer 1984, p. 24.

Young, Jan. "Plunderers of Pioche." *Real West,* Nov. 1961, p. 38.

Courtright, James "Longhair Jim"

Breihan, Carl W. "Courtright's Last Gunfight." *Westerner,* March 1971, p. 10.

_____. "Luke Short's Mystery Gun Fight." *Real West,* March 1961, p. 32. Rpt. *Real West,* Annual, Spring 1968, p. 50.

Burton, Carl. "Shoot-Out That Shocked the West." *Westerner,* July-Aug. 1973, p. 18.

Cheney, Louise. "Longhair Jim Courtright: Fast Gun of Fort Worth." *Real West,* Nov. 1970, p. 26. Rpt. *Real West,* Special Issue, Fall 1973, p. 14.

Cunningham, Eugene. "Courtright the Longhaired." *True West,* June 1957, p. 12.

Kildare, Maurice. "American Valley Went Up in Smoke." *Frontier Times,* Nov. 1975, p. 8.

O'Neal, Bill. "Luke Short vs. Longhaired Jim Courtright" ("Great Western Gunfights" column). *True West,* Sept. 1989, p 55.

Scott, Jay. "Marshal of Fort Worth." *True Western Adventures,* Dec. 1959, p. 22.

Stanley, Samuel. "Jim Courtright, Gunfighter." *Real West,* June 1986, p. 14.

Walker, Wayne T. "Jim Courtright: Gunfighter." *Great West,* June 1970, p. 10.

_____. "Jim Courtright: Professional Gunfighter." *Pioneer West,* Nov. 1977, p. 8.

Cozens, William Z. "Bill"

Chatfield, Harry E. "Bill Cozens: Colorado's Forgotten Sheriff." *The West,* June 1968, p. 16. Rpt. *Western Frontier,* Nov. 1986, p. 30.

Tibbets, Robin. "Don't Cross That Line." *Frontier Times,* Nov. 1964, p. 41.

Crabtree, Lotta

Enright, Felton. "Lotta, the Untouchable." *Real West,* July 1960, p. 27.

Fink, Clarence M. "Lotta Crabtree: Wonderful Angel of the Miners." *Real West,* April 1970, p. 8.

Crandall, Prudence

Rozar, Lily-B. "Rebel Without a Cause." *Western Round-Up,* Aug. 1970, p. 8. Rpt. *Oldtimers Wild West,* Jan. 1975, p. 56.

Cravens, Benjamin Crede "Ben"

Hughes, F. Horace. "Friend to No Man." *Old West,* Fall 1966, p. 61.

Secrest, William B. "The Best of the Bad Men." *True Frontier,* Special Issue No. 9, 1974, p. 38.

Shirley, Glenn. "Ben Cravens, Lobo Killer." *Real West,* Aug. 1968, p. 26.

_____. "Killer With Two Faces." *True West,* June 1989, p. 14.

Turpin, Robert F. "A Bandit Named Cravens." *Great West,* Sept. 1969, p. 36.

Crawford Brothers (Wiley, Charlie, John)
"They Looted Stages." *Westerner,* Sept.-Oct. 1974, p. 26.

Crawford, Emmet
Bourke, John G. "An Apache Campaign." Part I, *Great West,* June 1967, p. 38; Part II, *Great West,* Sept. 1967, p. 20.

Harrison, Fred. "On the Trail of Geronimo." *Westerner,* March-April 1970, p. 21.

Malsbary, George. "Betrayal of the Chiricahua Scouts." *Wild West,* March 1972, p. 42. Rpt. *Pioneer West,* Sept. 1975, p. 44.

Nalty, Bernard C., and Truman B. Strobridge. "Death of a Brave Man." *Golden West,* Sept. 1966, p. 27. Rpt. *The West,* April 1973, p. 41.

Nebraska State Historical Society. "Emmet Crawford: Hero." *True West,* Dec. 1978, p. 54.

Norton, Hana Samek. "Kaytennae and the End of the Apache Wars." *True West,* June 1988, p. 14.

Swanson, Budington. "The Best Indian Fighter." *Real West,* Dec. 1984, p. 26. Rpt. *Real West,* Yearbook, Fall 1985, p. 38.

Crawford, Foster
Kelly, Bill. "The Odyssey of Kid Lewis." *Real West,* March 1977, p. 24.

McBee, Fred. "The Newspapers Called Him the Mysterious Kid." *Great West,* June 1971, p. 28.

Wilson, Steve. "How a Lynching Helped Open a Territory." *True Frontier,* Oct. 1967, p. 24.

Crawford, Henry "Hank"
Kildare, Maurice. "Sheriff Crawford Bushwhacked Henry Plummer." *Great West,* Oct. 1970, p. 26.

Crawford, Jack
Nolan, Paul T. "Captain Jack Crawford: Veteran and Western Hero." *Real West,* April 1970, p. 19.

_____. "Captain Jack, the Poet Scout." *Real West,* Jan. 1965, p. 22.

Crawford, Samuel J.
Bloom, Sam. "The Iron-Fisted Governor Who Ruled Kansas' Nine Million Bloody Acres." *Frontier West,* Feb. 1975, p. 34.

Crazy Horse

Arthur, Alton. "Warriors and Chiefs" column. *Wild West,* June 1991, p. 10.

Carroll, John M. "The Man Who Killed Crazy Horse." *Old West,* Summer 1991, p. 38.

Feraca, Steve. "Crazy Horse: The Enigmatic Sioux." *Frontier Times,* Jan. 1964, p. 14.

Lone Eagle. Letter, "The Death and Burial of Chief Crazy Horse." *Frontier Times,* July 1964, p. 39.

Nebraska State Historical Society. "Chief Crazy Horse." *Frontier Times,* Nov. 1974, p. 9.

Paul, Jan S. "Legend of Crazy Horse." *Golden West,* Sept. 1966, p. 8. Rpt. *Golden West,* March 1972, p. 37; *Western Frontier,* Special Issue, March 1975, p. 25; and *Western Frontier,* Jan. 1981, p. 41.

Smith, J.L. Letter, "Crazy Horse." *Frontier Times,* July 1964, p. 4.

Wiltsey, Norman B. "The Betrayal and Murder of Crazy Horse." *Real West,* Feb. 1973, p. 16. Rpt. *Real West,* Annual , Fall 1974, p. 8.

_____. "The Day Crazy Horse Got Whipped." *True West,* Oct. 1960, p. 18.

Wycoff, Roy A., Jr. Letter. *Real West,* Jan. 1962, p. 6.

Yarbrough, Leroy. "The Tragic Life of Crazy Horse." *Real West,* July 1963, p. 36. Rpt. *Real West,* Americana Series, Winter 1963, p. 22.

"Crazy Horse Lil"

Coriell, Marian M. "Crazy Horse Lil." *Pioneer West,* Aug. 1972, p. 6.

"Crazy Snake" (Chitto Harjo)

Brewington, E.H. "Crazy Snake: The Last Rebel." *True West,* Oct. 1972, p. 18.

Cerro, Samuel. "Crazy Snake: Redskin Spieler." *Golden West,* Sept. 1970, p. 20. Rpt. *The West,* April 1974, p. 20.

Hardcastle, Stoney. "Crazy Snake's Last Stand." *Real West,* Sept. 1978, p. 51. Rpt. *Real West,* Yearbook, Fall 1979, p. 26.

Rolling Cloud. "The Story of Crazy Snake." *Great West,* Feb. 1969, p. 50.

Creal, John

Archer, Myrtle. "California Stagecoach Skirmish." *True West,* May 1988, p. 44.

The Creede, Colorado, Gang

Bayworth, Jerome. "Creede, Sin City of Colorado." *The West,* Sept. 1965, p. 40.

Martin, Cy. "There Was No Night in Creede." *Real West,* Annual , Fall 1974, p. 14.

Creede, Nicholas C.
Gaddis, Robert. "Creede: Four Years of Glory." *True Frontier,* Nov. 1973, p. 40.

Creighton, Edward
Koller, Joe. "Edward Creighton: Singing Wire Chief." *Golden West,* Sept. 1965, p. 16.

Creighton Oscar (Rodney M. Merrick, Oscar M. Wheelock)
Rossen, M.N. "The Dynamiter." *Westerner,* Sept.-Oct. 1972, p. 42.

Crenshaw, George W. "Bud"
Stephens, Robert W. "Ambush in the Chaparral." *Frontier Times,* May 1967, p. 30.

Crittenden, Alexander Parker "Aleck"
Boswell, Charles. "The High Noon of Aleck Crittenden." *True Western Adventures,* Feb. 1961, p. 18.

Crockett, David "Davy"
Bishop, Curtis. "King of the Wild Frontier." *True West,* Aug. 1955, p. 12.

Brady, Cyrus T. "Davy Crockett and the Most Desperate Defense in American History." *Golden West,* Nov. 1965, p. 28. Rpt. *The West,* Oct. 1974, p. 16; and *Western Frontier,* Oct. 1984, p. 23.

Palmquist, Robert F. "David Crockett: The Young Backwoodsman 1786-1815." *Real West,* Sept. 1981, p. 6. Rpt. *Real West,* Yearbook, Fall 1982, p. 53.

_____. "'High Private' David Crockett at the Alamo." *Real West,* Dec. 1981, p. 12. Rpt. *Real West,* Special Issue, Spring 1983, p. 4.

_____. "Mr. Crockett Goes to Washington." *Real West,* Oct. 1981, p. 14. Rpt. *Real West,* Annual , Spring 1983, p. 18.

Shulsinger, Stephanie Cooper. "The Real Davy Crockett." *Real West,* Annual, Winter 1979, p. 56.

Crockett, Davy, II
Craig, Frank. "The Ill-Fated Revenge of Davy Crockett's Renegade Nephew." *Frontier West,* Jan. 1976, p. 36.

Hornung, Chuck. "The Forgotten Davy Crockett: Bad Boy of Cimarron, N.M." Part I, *NOLA Quarterly,* Vol XIII, No. 1, Spring 1988, p. 8; Part II, *NOLA Quarterly,* Vol. XIII, No. 2, Summer 1988, p. 14.

_____. "The 'Other' Davy Crockett." *The West,* Sept. 1972, p. 36. Rpt. *Western Frontier,* Jan. 1978, p. 24.

Robbins, Lance. "David Crockett's Unheroic Grandson." *Old West,* Winter 1974, p. 34.

Crook, George
Aranda, Daniel. "An Expedition Into the Sierra Madre." *Real West,* Annual 1981, p. 38.

Austerman, Wayne R. "Debacle on Powder River." *Wild West,* Dec. 1991, p. 22.

Barsness, John, and William Dickinson. "Hard Luck General." *True West,* April 1966, p. 26.

Bourke, John G. "An Apache Campaign." Rpt. Part I, *Great West,* June 1967, p. 38; Part II, *Great West,* Sept. 1967, p. 20.

Bourke, John J. [sic, John Gregory Bourke] "General Crook in the Indian Country." Rpt. *The West,* June 1966, p. 18; *The West,* Nov. 1971, p. 22, and *Western Frontier,* Annual, Fall 1980, p. 23.

Darlington, David. "Battle on the Redfork." *True West,* Nov. 1988, p. 14.

Doorley, Lawrence. "That Reckless Hibernian, Finerty of the Times." *True West,* May 1986, p. 14.

Holloway, W.L. "General Crook's Campaign." *Golden West,* Jan. 1965, p. 26. Rpt. *Western Frontier,* Jan. 1980, p. 2.

Judge, Bill. "Battle of the Mighty Three." *True West,* June 1963, p. 26.

Keenan, Jerry. "Command Tested Under Fire." *Wild West,* Aug. 1989, p. 42.

Kutac, C. "General Crook's Mules." *Real West,* July 1980, p. 6.

Malsbary, George. "Apache Exodus." *Real West,* Annual, Winter 1977-78, p. 44.

_____. "Betrayal of the Chiricahua Scouts." *Wild West,* March 1972, p. 42. Rpt. *Pioneer West,* Sept. 1975, p. 44.

_____. "The 'Last Stand' Avenged." *Real West,* April 1980, p. 11. Rpt. *Real West,* Special Issue, 1981, p. 22.

O'Neal, Bill. "100 Years Ago in the West" column. *Old West,* Spring 1990, p. 15.

Roe, Ken Sherwood. "War Cry at the Infernal Caves." *Great West,* Dec. 1973, p. 24. Rpt. *Authentic West,* Spring 1981, p. 24.

Stanley, Samuel. "Day the General Met His Match." *Pioneer West,* July 1970, p. 22.

_____. "General Crook's Private War With the Apaches." *Westerner,* Feb. 1971, p. 50.

Strimike, Donald F. "Massacre at Salt River Canyon." *Great West,* Feb. 1970, p. 6.

Crow Dog

McDermott, Burton. "How the Sioux Chief Taught the White Man the Real Meaning of Honor." *Frontier West,* Dec. 1973, p. 14.

Schott, Joseph. "The Word of Crow Dog." *True Western Adventures,* Dec. 1960, p. 11.

Spencer, G. "Murder Among the Sioux." *Real West,* Jan. 1988, p. 18.

Wiltsey, Norman B. "Warrior's Pledge." *Old West,* Spring 1966, p. 33. Rpt. *Western Frontier,* Special Issue, March 1975, p. 2.

Cruse, Thomas "Irish Tommy"

Darwin, Wayne. "The Mother Lode of 'Irish Tommy' Cruse." *The West,* June 1971, p. 38. Rpt. *Western Frontier,* July 1984, p. 6.

Moore, Jean-Michael. "Silver Creek Reminescences." *Old West,* Spring 1966, p. 16.

Cruse, Thomas

Perry, Samuel D. "Apache Fight at Big Dry Wash." *Pioneer West,* Jan. 1976, p. 6.

Cruz, Florentino

Turner, Alford E. "The Florentino-Earp Affair." *Real West,* Jan. 1979, p. 16.

Culbertson, Alexander

Ege, Robert J. "The Marias Massacre." *Real West,* Americana Series, Winter 1966, p. 71.

Taylor, Dabney. "The Major's Blackfoot Bride." *Frontier Times,* Jan. 1969, p. 26.

Cullinan, Tom Allen

Shannon, Dan. "Marshal Cullinan's Iron Fist." *Real West,* March 1965, p. 16.

Cummings, Mary K. ("Big Nose" Kate Elder)

Boyer, Glenn G. "On the Trail of Big Nosed Kate." *Real West,* March 1981, p. 14. Rpt. *Real West,* Yearbook, 1981, p. 24.

Kegley, Howard. "The Unpredictable Kate Elder." *True West,* Oct. 1960, p. 26.

Quale, J.L. "The Strange Love Affair of Big Nose Kate and Doc Holliday." *Real West,* Sept. 1964, p. 36.

Ripple, Sam. "Doc Holliday's Girl." *Westerner,* Nov.-Dec. 1971, p. 48.

Traywick, Ben T. "Big Nose Kate and Other Ladies of Tombstone." *True Frontier,* April 1972, p. 8.

Cummings, Sarah
Guthrie, Mark. "Sarah Cummings' Ladies-of-All-Nations Pleasure Parlor." *Frontier West,* Aug. 1971, p. 42.

Cummins, Jim
Hale, Donald H. "The James Gang's Last Survivor." *The West,* March 1969, p. 20. Rpt. *Golden West,* Jan. 1973, p. 18; *Western Frontier,* Nov. 1976, p. 34; and *Western Frontier,* March 1980, p. 34.

Pyles, Lida Wilson. "Gentle Jim Cummings [sic]." *Frontier Times,* Fall 1962, p. 16.

Curley
Chatfield, Harry. "The Truth About Curley, Custer Scout." *Real West,* May 1963, p. 42.

Currie, George Sutherland ("Flat Nose George")
Dullenty, Jim. "George Currie and the Curry Brothers." *NOLA Quarterly,* Vol. V, No. 1, Oct. 1979, p. 4.

Kirby, Edward M., and Mary C. Preece. "Billy Preece, Frontier Lawman." *Real West,* July 1979, p. 8.

Currie, James "Big Jim"
O'Neal, Bill. "Big Jim Currie vs Maurice Barrymore and Company" ("Great Western Gunfights" column). *True West,* Sept. 1990, p. 55.

Rasch, Philip J. "One Killed, One Wounded." *NOLA Quarterly,* Vol. IV, No. 2, Autumn 1978, p. 11.

Curry, Harvey "Kid Curry" (see Logan, Harvey)

Curry, John "Johnnie" (John Logan)
Coburn, Walt. "No Re-Ride." *True West,* Sept. 1954, p. 11.

Morin, Marvin M. "Two Graves in Montana." *True West,* March 1984, p. 48.

Cushing, Howard Bass
Bentz, Donald N. "Sword of Revenge." *Golden West,* Sept. 1965, p. 22.

Cushman, Pauline
Bentz, Donald N. "The Little Major Came a Cropper." *The West,* Oct. 1970, p. 38.

Cheney, Louise. "The Rise and Fall of Pauline Cushman." *Real West,* July 1967, p. 18.

Von Kreisler, Max. "Espionage Agent Pauline Cushman." *Old West*, Spring 1978, p. 18.

Custard, Amos J.
Copeman, L. Berger. "Massacre at Red Butte." *The West*, Sept. 1973, p. 32. Rpt. *Western Frontier*, Jan. 1977, p. 2.

Custer, George A.
Andre, Barbara E. "Custer at the Washita." *The West*, June 1968, p. 20. Rpt. *Western Frontier*, July 1979, p. 20.

Ballenger, Dean. "Custer's Stolen Gold." *Westerner*, Summer 1975, p. 25.

Barkdull, Tom. "Was Custer in Command or Dead?" *Pioneer West*, April 1972, p. 8.

Barnard, James W. "What Happened to the Seventh Cavalry at the Little Big Horn?" *Real West*, Oct. 1974, p. 40.

Beardsley, J.L. "The Invincible Seventh." *The West*, July 1974, p. 34. Rpt. *Western Frontier*, Annual, Feb. 1980, p. 30.

Breihan, Carl W. "Custer's Fatal Ride." *Oldtimers Wild West*, Annual 1979, p. 16.

_____. "Was It Only Custer's Folly?" *Golden West*, July 1968, p. 10.

_____. "Who Was the Woman With Custer?" *Real West*, Nov. 1958, p. 10.

Chatfield, Harry. "Custer's Last Message." *Real West*, July 1963, p. 26.

_____. "Custer's Secret Romance." *The West*, July 1964, p. 38. Rpt. *Western Frontier*, Summer 1978, p. 2.

_____. "He Saw Custer Die." *Real West*, Jan. 1964, p. 20.

Cooper, Ben. "The Day General Custer Went AWOL." *Great West*, Sept. 1967, p. 34.

Cunningham, Reba Pierce. "The Mysteries of Custer's Watch." *True West*, May 1984, p. 19.

Eastman, Charles Alexander. "Custer: The Massacre and the Truth." *Wild West*, March 1971, p. 54.

_____. "Custer Was Not Massacred." *Pioneer West*, March 1968, p. 27.

Forman, John Frederick. "Custer's Greatest Blunder." *Real West*, Sept. 1965, p. 26. Rpt. *Real West*, Annual, Spring 1968, p. 28.

Frazier, Thomas A. "Custer, the Man and the Legend." *Real West*, Aug. 1968, p. 18.

Fristad, Palma. "A Home for Custer's Seventh." *True West*, Dec. 1961, p. 38.

Frost, Lawrence A. "Custer and the Kidder Massacre." *Westerner*, Sept. 1970, p. 26.

_____. "Custer's Last Orders—Found." *Westerner*, March 1971, p. 20.

Godfrey, W.S. "Custer's Last Battle." Part I,*The West*, Aug. 1966, p. 14; Part II, *The West*, Sept. 1966, p. 18. Rpt. Part I, *Western Frontier*, May 1977, p. 14; and *Western Frontier*, Annual, Fall 1981, p. 14; Part II, *Western Frontier*, July 1977, p. 18; and *Western Frontier*, Jan. 1982, p. 18.

Gordon, Grant. "Lost Custer Treasure Cache." *Wild West*, Oct. 1969, p. 32. Rpt. *Pioneer West*, Aug. 1972, p. 32; and *Pioneer West*, Dec. 1974, p. 30.

Huston, Fred. "Night of the Red Moon." *Wild West*, Oct. 1969, p. 51. Rpt. *Pioneer West*, Dec. 1974, p. 48.

Judge, Bill. "The Custer Story." *True West*, Oct. 1963, p. 9.

Katigan, Madelon. "Was Custer the Villain at Washita?" Part I, *Real West*, March 1966, p. 26; Part II, *Real West*, May 1966, p. 36.

Kildare, Maurice. "Custer: Coward." *Westerner*, June 1968, p. 29.

Kraft, Louis. "Warrior's Fierce Battle." *Wild West*, Feb. 1990, p. 26.

Lamb, Lucylle M. "General Custer's Secret Son." *True Frontier*, March 1971, p. 36. Rpt. *True Frontier*, Special Issue No. 14, 1975, p. 60.

Masters, Al. "Missing Cash of Custer's Lost Command." *Real West*, April 1971, p. 43.

Mays, Carelton. "The Romping Custers." *Real West*, Feb. 1959, p. 28. Rpt. *Real West*, Annual, Summer 1966, p. 63.

McLaine, Bruce. "The Custer Massacre They Couldn't Glorify." *True Western Adventures*, Aug. 1961, p. 13.

Mizrahi, Joe. "Custer: Man and the Myth." *Big West*, Aug. 1967, p. 26.

Morris, Ralph. "Custer, Hero or Coward?" *Westerner*, March-April 1972, p. 32.

Perry, Milton F. "Come On! Be Quick!" *True West*, April 1957, p. 14.

Preece, Harold. "Custer's Insurance Policy." *Wild West*, Dec. 1970, p. 50.

Schneider-Wettengel, Georg Wenzel. "Did Custer Commit Suicide?" *Real West*, May 1973, p. 14.

_____. "Did Custer's Battalion Run Out of Ammunition?" *Real West*, Sept. 1973, p. 19.

_____. "Who Laid Out Custer?" *Real West*, Nov. 1973, p. 32.

Schoenberger, Dale T., ed. "Camp's Lost Account of Custer's Last Fight." *Old West*, Winter 1989, p. 40.

Shannon, Malone. "Those Bumptious Custers." *The West*, June 1965, p. 12. Rpt. *Golden West*, Nov. 1973, p. 10.

Shulsinger, Stephanie C. "Custer's Luck." *Real West,* July 1973, p. 12.

_____. "Did Custer Really Have It Coming?" *Real West,* March 1974, p. 42.

_____. "The Real General Custer." *Real West,* July 1976, p. 20.

_____. "The Unforgettable Custers." *Real West,* Sept. 1975, p. 38.

_____. "What Really Happened at Little Big Horn?" *Real West,* Aug. 1972, p. 46.

Turner, Don. "Prelude to Massacre." *True West,* Oct. 1968, p. 18.

Vangen, Roland Dean. "The Searchers." *Great West,* Sept. 1969, p. 22.

Wiltsey, Norman B. "We Killed Custer." *Real West,* June 1968, p. 25.

Wolfe, George D. "Which Indian Killed Custer?" *Frontier Times,* Winter 1959-60, p. 23.

Wright, Jim. "Custer: Hero." *Westerner,* June 1968, p. 28.

Custer, Thomas "Tom"

Bird, Roy. "The Custer-Hickok Shootout in Hays City." *Real West,* May 1979, p. 28.

Schoenberger, Dale T. "Tom Custer: The General's Brother." *Real West,* Jan. 1982, p. 23. Rpt. *Real West,* Special Issue, Spring 1985, p. 34.

Daily, Bradford
Austerman, Wayne R. "Bradford Daily: A Brave Man and a Good Shot." *Real West,* June 1987, p. 36.

Dalton, Adeline
Preece, Harold. "Adeline Dalton, Outlaw Mother." *Real West,* Sept. 1965, p. 10.

Dalton, Anthony
Edwards, Harold L. "Anthony Dalton, Not a Member of the Dalton Gang." *NOLA Quarterly,* Vol. XIII, No. 4, 1989, p. 16.

Dalton Brothers
Walker, Wayne T. "When the Dalton Brothers Wore the White Hats." *Real West,* Annual , Spring 1982, p. 28.

Dalton, Emmett
Charbo, Eileen. "Doc Outland and Emmett Dalton." *True West,* Aug. 1980, p. 43.

Dalton, Emmett. "Prison Delivery." Rpt. *Old West,* Spring 1971, p. 74.

Martin, Chuck. "Emmett Dalton's Six-Shooter." *True West,* Feb. 1956, p. 12. Rpt. *Badman,* Fall 1972, p. 34.

Mattis, Wil. "Emmett Dalton's Bold Stroke." *Westerner,* Nov.-Dec. 1973, p. 42.

Mulgannon, James H. "Aftermath at Coffeyville and San Fernando." *Real West,* Annual, Winter 1977-78, p. 22.

Pannill, Mark S. "Roy Dalton: The Son Emmett Never Had." *NOLA Quarterly,* Vol. XV, No. 2, April-June 1991, p. 13.

Preece, Harold. "The Truth About Emmett Dalton." *Real West,* March 1966, p. 30.

Repp, Ed Earl. "Last of the Old Time Outlaws." *True Frontier,* Jan. 1974, p. 24. Rpt. *True Frontier,* Special Issue No. 17, Winter 1976, p. 6.

Samuelson, Nancy B. "Emmett and Julia: A Dalton Myth." *NOLA Quarterly,* Vol. XIV, No. 2, Summer 1990, p. 6.

Dalton Family
Brant, Marley. "Outlaws' Inlaws in California." *Frontier Times,* Feb. 1985, p. 18.

Edwards, Harold L. "The Daltons in California." *NOLA Quarterly,* Vol. X, No. 1, Summer 1985, p. 18.

Noren, William. "The Daltons Were Our Neighbors in California." *True West,* Sept. 1983, p. 29.

Steele, Phillip W. "The Dalton Family Found in California." *NOLA Quarterly,* Vol. XII, No. 2, Fall 1987, p. 5.

_____. "The Daltons After Coffeyville." *NOLA Quarterly,* Vol. IX, No. 1, Summer 1984, p. 14.

Dalton, Frank

Mays, Carelton. "Greatest of the Daltons." *Real West,* March 1960, p. 18.

Rand, Philip. "Frank Dalton." *Real West,* Americana Series, Fall 1965, p. 22.

Morton, Arnold M. "That Good Dalton Boy." *The West,* Dec. 1965, p. 24. Rpt. *The West,* April 1974, p. 42; and *Western Frontier,* Annual No. 5, 1977, p. 26.

Dalton Gang

Breihan, Carl W. "The Daltons and Bill Doolin." *Western Frontier,* July 1979, p. 14.

Chesney, W.D. "I Saw the Daltons Die." *Real West,* May 1964, p. 18. Rpt. *Real West,* Americana Series, Fall 1964, p. 31.

Collins, Charles. "Bloody Coffeyville." *Great West,* May 1968, p. 34.

"The Dalton Brothers and Their Astounding Career of Crime." Part I, *Real West,* July 1962, p. 24; Part II, *Real West,* Sept. 1962, p. 24.

Deac, Wilfred P. "Outlaws' Deadliest Double-Dare." *Wild West,* April 1989, p. 35.

DeMattos, Jack. "The Daltons" ("Gunfighters of the Real West" column). *Real West,* Dec. 1983, p. 32. Rpt. *Real West,* Yearbook, Fall 1984, p. 48.

Hane, Louis. "Bloodbath at Coffeyville." *Westerner,* Jan.-Feb. 1972, p. 34.

McClelland, Marshall K. "The Day the Daltons Died." *True West,* Feb. 1956, p. 10. Rpt. *Badman,* Fall 1972, p. 32.

Nieberding, Velma, and Harold Preece. "The West's Outlaws Found No Peace Even in Death." *Frontier West,* Dec. 1971, p. 42.

Preece, Harold. "The Day the Daltons Died." *Frontier West,* April 1971, p. 10.

Rozar, Lily-B. "Inside the Dalton Legend." *The West,* Aug. 1972, p. 32. Rpt. *Western Frontier,* Special Issue, Sept. 1975, p. 8; *Western Frontier,* Special Issue, Nov. 1982, p. 22; and *Western Frontier,* July 1977, p 32.

Sailor, John Noble. "Untold Facts About the Daltons." *Real West,* Aug. 1958, p. 18.

St. George, Tim. "Were the Daltons Guilty?" *Real West,* Jan. 1962, p. 18.

Walker, Wayne T. "When the Dalton Brothers Wore the White Hats." *Real West,* July 1981, p. 32.

Whittlesey, D.H. "He Said 'Hell No' to the Daltons." *Golden West,* May 1974, p. 38.

Dalton, Grat

Boessenecker, John. "Grat Dalton's California Jailbreak." *Real West,* Aug. 1988, p. 14.

O'Neal, Harold. "The San Joaquin Train Holdups." *Golden West,* March 1966, p. 44.

Preece, Harold. "Grat Dalton's Fatal Looking Glass." *The West,* Dec. 1964, p. 14. Rpt. *Western Frontier,* Nov. 1982, p. 32.

Dalton, J. Frank

Breihan, Carl W. "Alias Jesse James." Part I *Real West,* Jan. 1971, p. 22; Part II, *Real West,* Feb. 1971, p. 46.

Dalton, Julia

Pannill, Mark S. "Roy Dalton: The Son Emmett Never Had." *NOLA Quarterly,* Vol. XV, No. 2, April-June 1991, p. 13.

Samuelson, Nancy B. "Emmett and Julia: A Dalton Myth." *NOLA Quarterly,* Vol. XIV, No. 2, Summer 1990, p. 6.

Dalton, Robert "Bob"

Carpen, George Blackwell. "Bob Dalton, Renegade Marshal." *True Western Adventures,* Oct. 1958, p. 8.

Lansdale, Joe R. "When Bob Dalton Hit the Longview Bank." *Old West,* Summer 1978, p. 6.

Dalton, Roy

Pannill, Mark S. "Roy Dalton: The Son Emmett Never Had." *NOLA Quarterly,* Vol. XV, No. 2, April-June 1991, p. 13.

Samuelson, Nancy B. Letter. *NOLA Quarterly,* Vol. XV, No. 3, July-Sept. 1991, p. 2.

Miller, Lora. Letter. *NOLA Quarterly,* Vol. XV, No. 3, July-Sept. 1991, p. 2.

Dalton, William "Bill"

Breihan, Carl W. "Exit: Bill Doolin and Bill Dalton." *Real West,* June 1975, p. 46.

O'Neal, Bill. "Bill Dalton's Last Raid." *Real West,* June 1983, p. 6. Rpt. *Real West,* Annual, Spring 1984, p. 10.

_____. "First National Bank Robbery" ("Great Western Gunfights" column).
    True West, Oct. 1991, p. 58.

Preece, Harold. "The Incredible Bill Dalton." *Real West,* Jan. 1964, p. 36.

Daly, Marcus

Clark, Helen. "The Copper Kings." *Pioneer West,* Sept. 1969, p. 24. Rpt. *Pioneer*
    West, Aug. 1972, p. 36; *Oldtimers Wild West,* May 1975, p. 50; and *Pioneer*
    West, Nov. 1979, p. 38.

_____. "King of the Western Turf." *Wild West,* March 1971, p. 34.

Grimmett, R.G. "The Richest Hill on Earth." *Golden West,* Oct. 1974, p. 11.

Dana, James T.

Rube, B. Johnny. "The Killing of Sheriff Dana." *Real West,* Aug. 1983, p. 16.

Daniels, Benjamin Franklin "Ben"

DeMattos, Jack. "Ben Daniels" ("Gunfighters of the Real West" column). *Real*
    West, Sept. 1979, p. 50.

Secrest, William B. "The Best of the Bad Men." *Real Frontier,* Nov. 1971, p. 32.

_____. "Fighting Man." *Frontier Times,* May 1969, p. 6.

Daniels, Edwin B.

Zink, Wilbur A. "Gunbattle at Roscoe." *Frontier Times,* March 1969, p. 6.

Daniels, Shelby

Martinson, Fred. "Shelby Daniels' Incredible Brine Barrel Justice." *Frontier*
    West, April 1973, p. 30.

Daniels, William

Ormes, Carl. "Blood at Bisbee." *Real West,* May 1959, p. 23.

Roensch, Dell. "Bisbee's Bath of Blood." *True Western Adventures,* Dec. 1959,
    p. 38.

Dansford, Rolly

Humbolt, Gary. "The Black Renegade Who Killed for the Law." *Frontier West,*
    Dec. 1973, p. 34.

Darlington, Brinton

Hover, L. "The Crises at the Cheyenne-Arapaho Reservation." *Golden West,* May
    1966, p. 40. Rpt. *Western Frontier,* July 1977, p. 10.

Dart, Isom (Ned Huddleston)

Ballenger, Dean W. "Isom Dart, the Ex-Slave Who Made Rustling a Fine Art." *Oldtimers Wild West,* June 1978, p. 24.

Isham, Dell. "Last of the Tip Gault Gang." *Real West,* Sept. 1978, p. 36.

Kildare, Maurice. "The Calico Cowboy." *Great West,* Aug. 1971, p. 26.

Daugherty, Roy "Arkansas Tom"

Castleman, Sean. "Arkansas Tom: Last of the Horseback Outlaws." *Oldtimers Wild West,* Aug. 1979, p. 10.

Gold, Alan. "Arkansas Tom." *Great West,* April 1967, p. 30.

Rickards, Colin. "Last of the Horseback Outlaws." *Frontier Times,* May 1971, p. 14.

Walker, Wayne T. "Arkansas Tom, Gunslinger." *Great West,* Dec. 1973, p. 10. Rpt. *Authentic West,* Spring 1981, p. 10.

D'Autremont Brothers (Roy, Ray, Hugh)

Williams, Gary. "The Case of the Siskiyou Slayings." *Frontier Times,* March 1973, p. 38.

Davis, Alice Brown

Hanna, Wilma. "Alice Brown Davis: Seminole Chief." *The West,* July 1971, p. 40.

Davis, A.J. "Big Jack"

Erberich, Gerry. "Here's Outlaw Treasure." *Westerner,* Aug. 1971, p. 40.

Harrison, John. "Big Jack Davis." *Great West,* Dec. 1974, p. 26.

Davis, "Gentleman Jack"

Scullin, George. "Stand and Deliver." *True Western Adventures,* Dec. 1959, p. 42.

Davis, Jackson Lee "Diamondfield Jack"

Hansen, John. "Alias Diamondfield Jack." *Great West,* Dec. 1973, p. 22. Rpt. *Authentic West,* Spring 1981, p. 22.

Spendlove, Earl. "The Legend of Diamondfield Jack: Was He Just a Cheap Killer Who Got Lucky?" *The West,* Nov. 1972, p. 34.

Stanley, Samuel. "Diamond Field Jack." *Real West,* Nov. 1976, p. 28. Rpt. *Real West,* Annual, Winter 1977, p. 28.

Taylor, Dabney. "He Hired Out...to Kill." *True West,* June 1966, p. 16.

Davis, John Monroe
Walker, Wayne T. "The Guns of J.M. Davis." *Great West,* June 1974, p. 28. Rpt. *Authentic West,* Summer 1981, p. 62.

Davis, R.S.
Holt, Roy D. "Ordeals of a Fence Cutting Detective." *Westerner,* March-April 1974, p. 15.

Davis, Scott "Quickshot"
Harrison, C. William. "Shotgun Messenger On Hell's Highway." *True Western Adventures,* April 1959, p. 16.

Koller, Joe. "Saga of Quickshot Davis." *The West,* March 1971, p. 30.

Dawson, Nickolas M.
Howell, Montie. "The Woods Clan and the Dawson Massacre." *True West,* June 1988, p. 52.

Day, John
Grant County Museum, Canyon City, Oregon. "Who Was John Day?" ("Wild Old Days" column) *True West,* Dec. 1964, p. 34.

Timmen, Fritz. "Mysterious John Day." *Old West,* Summer 1968, p. 20.

Deaver, Joseph J.
Nolen, Oren W. "The Young Buffalo Hunter of the Texas Plains." *Golden West,* Nov. 1967, p. 26. Rpt. *The West,* Nov. 1973, p. 14, and *Western Frontier,* Annual No. 4, 1976, p. 40.

De Cordova, Jacob
Coleman, N. "Texas' Pied Piper." *Wild West,* Nov. 1971, p. 55. Rpt. *Oldtimers Wild West,* July 1974, p. 56.

Deger, Larry
Ernst, Robert R. "Dodge City Sued." *True West ,* Nov. 1986, p. 32.

Huston, Fred. "Larry Deger, Dodge's One Man Posse." *True Frontier,* Dec. 1974, p. 42. Rpt. *True Frontier,* Feb. 1977, p. 20.

Delaney, William "Bill"
Carson, Xanthus. "The Bisbee Massacre." *Westerner,* Nov. 1970, p. 48.

Ormes, Carl. "Blood at Bisbee." *Real West,* May 1959, p. 23.

Roensch, Dell. "Bisbee's Bath of Blood." *True Western Adventures,* Dec. 1959, p. 38.

DeLong, Charles
Henderson, Sam. "Bulletins and Bullets." *Golden West,* Oct. 1974, p. 12.

DeLong, Sidney Randolph
Leavengood, Betty. "Mayor DeLong and the Camp Grant Massacre." *True West,* July 1989, p. 37.

Delony, Lewis S.
Delony, Lewis S. "Forty Years a Peace Officer." *Old West,* Winter 1970, p. 69.

DeMores, Antoine Amadee Marie Vincent Mance deVallambrosa
Jones, Jerry. "That Fabulous Frenchman." *The West,* Oct. 1965, p. 38.

Mays, Carelton. "That Crazy Frenchman." *Real West,* March 1963, p. 18.

Deno, Lottie (see Thurmond, Charlotte)

Densmore, John
Hascombe, Ralph S. "'Indian Scalping' Wagon Guide." *Pioneer West,* June 1972, p. 26.

Denton, Aimee
Whistler, Alfred. "Frontier Girl." *Real West,* Oct. 1957, p. 24.

De Remer, James "Jim"
Holben, Richard E. "Rock Forts and Iron Men." *Great West,* June 1974, p. 10. Rpt. *Authentic West,* Summer 1981, p. 56.

De Smet, Pierre Jean
Ege, Robert J. "Father de Smet, First Jesuit in Montana." *Real West,* Nov. 1971, p. 12.

Koller, Joe. "Father de Smet: Black Robe of the Rockies." *Golden West,* March 1969, p. 16.

LeBlanc, Pierre. "Pierre Jean de Smet: Father of Peace." *The West,* Feb. 1966, p. 8. Rpt. *Golden West,* Sept. 1972, p. 32.

De Vaca, Cabeza
Colin, Michael. "Red Bearded 'Rain God' of the New World." *Big West*, Aug. 1967, p. 38.

Comtois, Pierre. "Explorer's Awesome Journey." *Wild West*, Feb. 1991, p. 42.

Devine, John
Freeman, Olga. "A Cattle Empire Is Born." *Real West*, April 1973, p. 8.

Devine, Robert M. "Bob"
Conroy, George. "The Truth About the Battle at Hole-in-the-Wall." *The West*, June 1965, p. 26.

Dewey, Chauncey
Walker, Wayne T. "The Short Grass Shoot-Out." *Great West*, June 1973, p. 6. Rpt. *Great West*, Summer 1981, p. 6.

"Diamondfield Jack" (see Davis, Jackson Lee)

Dickinson, Susannah
Auer, L.C. "The Alamo's Messenger of Defeat." *The West*, Sept. 1965, p. 47. Rpt. *The West*, Annual 1971, p. 8.

McDonald, A.A. "Heroine of the Alamo." *Real West*, May 1974, p. 38.

Dilda, Dennis
Kutac, C. "The Last Days of Dennis Dilda." *Real West*, Annual, Summer 1986, p. 34.

Dimsdale, Thomas J.
Praast, Vera Lund. "Historian of the Vigilantes." *Old West*, Summer 1968, p. 28.

Dixon Brothers (Simp, Bud, and Tom)
Parsons, Chuck. "Answer Man" column. *True West*, Jan. 1983, p. 18.

Dixon, Thomas
Nelson, Andre. "The Last Sheepman-Cattleman War." *True West*, May 1988, p. 14.

Dixon, William "Billy"
Beardsley, J.L. "Boldest of the Buffalo Scouts." *Real Frontier*, April 1970, p. 16. Rpt. *True Frontier*, Special Issue No. 11, Winter 1974-75, p. 9.

Breihan, Carl W. "The Second Fight at Adobe Walls." *Big West,* April 1970, p. 50.

Chase, Bob. "Double Jeopardy: The Battles of Billy Dixon." *Old West,* Spring 1987, p. 56.

Cheney, Louise. "Battle at the Buffalo Wallow." *Wild West,* March 1970, p. 44.

Deac, Wilfred P. "Victory by a Long Shot." *Wild West,* Dec. 1989, p. 35.

Glynn, Dean. "Six Who Risked Death." *Westerner,* March-April 1970, p. 48.

Knox, William P. "Last Stand on a Texas Prairie." *Golden West,* July 1966, p. 36. Rpt. *The West,* April 1972, p. 12, and *Western Frontier,* May 1978, p. 12.

Lafferty, Jack. "Six Medals of Honor." *True West,* June 1960, p. 26.

Nobles, Pat. "Billy Dixon: Boy Scout." *Real West,* Feb. 1987, p. 26.

Turpin, Robert F. "The Fight at Buffalo Wallow." *Great West,* Oct. 1970, p. 24.

Walker, Wayne T. "Fighting Army Scouts of the Indian Wars." *Great West,* June 1972, p. 14.

Watson, James A. "The Battle of Adobe Walls." *True Western Adventures,* Issue No. 1, 1957, p. 6.

Doan Brothers (Jonathan and Calvin)

Irons, Angie. "Doan's Crossing." *True West,* Nov. 1989, p. 44.

Doan, Corvin

Burns, George R. "Corvin Doan's Ghost." *Real West,* Sept. 1960, p. 22.

Dodge, Fred

Dodge, Fred. "Undercover Agent for Wells Fargo." Ed. Carolyn Lake. Rpt. *True West,* April 1970, p. 6.

Dodge, Granville

"General Granville Dodge: Indian Fighter." *Great West,* April 1970, p. 20.

Malocsay, Zoltan. "Riding the Rails With General Dodge." *Westerner,* Oct. 1971, p. 32.

Moore, Lynn. "Discovery of Lone Tree Pass." *True West,* Dec. 1971, p 44.

Shannon, Dan. "The Frontier Railroading Dream Became a Nightmare." *Frontier West,* Oct. 1972, p. 46.

Doell, Henry

Johnson, Dave. "The Doell Killing: Feudal Vengeance or Private Murder?" *NOLA Quarterly,* Vol. XI, No. 1, Summer 1986, p. 8.

Dolan-Murphy Faction

Pryor, Rafaelita. "Siege of the McSween House." *Frontier Times,* May 1969, p. 24.

Rasch, Philip J. "How the Lincoln County War Started." *True West,* April 1962, p. 30.

Doniphan, Alexander William

Cortesi, Lawrence J. "The Battle of Sacramento." *Oldtimers Wild West,* Oct. 1979, p. 28.

_____. "Colonel Doniphan's Expedition." *True Frontier,* April 1972, p. 32.

Malsbary, George. "Doniphan's Ringtailed Roarers." *Great West,* Dec. 1974, p. 8.

Mason, John. "Los Goddamies." *Real West,* Sept. 1960, p. 30.

Smith, Robert. "Volunteer Forces Epic March." *Wild West,* June 1991, p. 42.

Traywick, Ben T. "Alexander William Doniphan: Fighting Missourian." *Golden West,* July 1968, p. 39. Rpt. *Golden West,* Aug. 1973, p. 33.

Donner Party

Croy, Homer, "The Ordeal of the Doomed Donners." *True Western Adventures,* Aug. 1960, p. 37.

Rosenhouse, Leo. "The Donner Trek." *True Frontier,* Special Issue No. 15, Summer 1976, p. 24.

Skaar, Sven. "The Donner Tragedy." *Frontier Times,* Winter 1957, p. 4. Rpt. *Old West,* Winter 1978, p. 16.

Donohue, Teresa Susan

Traywick, Ben T. "The Madam of O'Farrell Street." *Western Round-Up,* Aug. 1970, p. 28.

Doolin Gang

Breihan, Carl W. "The Daltons and Bill Doolin." *Western Frontier,* July 1979, p. 14.

Cortesi, Lawrence. "The Bloody Shootout at Murray's Saloon." *Frontier West,* Aug. 1972, p. 22.

Crane, Ray. "The Doolin Gang." *Great West,* Feb. 1970, p. 44.

Glynn, Dean. "The Last Fight of the Wild Bunch." *Westerner,* July-Aug. 1970, p. 42.

Kerr, William Ray. "In Defense of Ingalls, Oklahoma." *True West,* Oct. 1964, p. 6.

Kildare, Maurice. "Six-Gun Justice Took Strange Turns in Cimarron." *Frontier West,* Dec. 1973, p. 26.

Koller, Joe. "Bloody Ingalls Under Siege." *The West,* Aug. 1972, p. 38. Rpt. *Western Frontier,* July 1976, p. 6.

Powers, Mark. "The Doolin Gang's Last Shoot-Out." *True Frontier,* March 1968, p. 22. Rpt. *True Frontier,* Special Issue No. 1, 1971, p. 42.

Smith, Robert Barr. "No God West of Fort Smith." *Wild West,* Oct. 1991, p. 46.

Walker, Wayne T. "The Day the Outlaws Came to Town." *The West,* Nov. 1971, p. 30. Rpt. *Western Frontier,* Sept. 1979, p. 20.

Doolin, William "Bill"

Bird, Roy. "The Wild Bunch Robbed the Spearville Bank." *Real West,* April 1987, p. 14.

Breihan, Carl W. "Exit: Bill Doolin and Bill Dalton." *Real West,* June 1975, p. 46.

Lee, Paul. "Bill Doolin: King of Oklahoma Outlaws." *Pioneer West,* June 1972, p. 16.

O'Neal, Bill. "Bill Doolin vs Heck Thomas" ("Great Western Gunfights" column). *True West,* Sept. 1991, p. 60.

Osborne, Shy. "Gun With a Story to Tell." *Badman,* Fall 1972, p. 36.

Phelps, Barton K. "Who Killed Bill Doolin?" *Real West,* Jan. 1958, p. 40.

Winfield, Craig. "Bill Doolin's Bold Hold-Up." *Westerner,* Jan.-Feb. 1974, p. 43.

Dorion, Marie

Anderson, Lee. "Madonna of the Oregon Trail." *Wild West,* Dec. 1970, p. 29.

Freeman, Olga. "Oregon's First Woman Immigrant Was an Indian." *Real West,* March 1972, p. 18. Rpt. *Real West,* Americana Series, Summer 1973, p. 28.

Hardee, Jim. "The Ordeal of Marie Dorion." *True West,* Oct. 1991, p. 46.

Hicks, Flora Weed. "Madame Marie Dorion." *The West,* Jan. 1969, p. 30.

Pratt, Grace Roffey. "Daughters of Courage." *True West,* June 1964, p. 24.

Dorsey, Charles

Secrest, William B. "Dead Men and Desperadoes." *True West,* May 1989, p. 14.

Dorsey, Steven W.

Robinson, William H. "The Dorsey Mansion: New Mexico Chimera." *True West,* Nov. 1985, p. 44.

Turner, Don. "A Hard Man to Understand." *Old West,* Winter 1967, p. 42.

Douglass, Percy
Edwards, Harold L. "The Unpleasant Task." *True West*, March 1990, p. 20.

Dowd, Cleophas J.
Boren, Kerry Ross. "Cleophas J. Dowd, the Man Who Named the Sundance Kid." *Real West*, May 1978, p. 38.

_____. "The Mysterious Pinkerton." *True West*, Aug. 1977, p. 28.

_____. "The Violent, Tragic Life of Cleophas J. Dowd." *NOLA Quarterly*, Vol. II, No. 1, Spring 1975, p. 3.

Dowd, Daniel "Dan"
Carson, Xanthus. "The Bisbee Massacre." *Westerner*, Nov. 1970, p 48

Ormes, Carl. "Blood at Bisbee." *Real West*, May 1959, p. 23.

Roensch, Dell. "Bisbee's Bath of Blood." *True Western Adventures*, Dec. 1959, p. 38.

Dowler, Benjamin Franklin
Kelly, Bill. "End of the Line for Jim Klein." *Real West*, Jan. 1980, p. 22. Rpt. *Real West*, Yearbook, 1980, p. 27.

_____. "The Vendetta Against Violets." *Real West*, July 1978, p. 38.

Dowling, Richard W, "Dick"
Cheney, Louise. "Dick Dowling: Civil War Hero of Texas." *Real West*, May 1969, p. 32.

Downing, Bill (Bill Jackson)
Parsons, Chuck. "Bill Downing: Arizona Badman" ("Answer Man" column). *True West*, Jan. 1991, p. 12.

Repp, Ed Earl. "Loot the Village: Kill the Males." *True Frontier*, Nov. 1969, p 38.

Drannan, William F.
Chatfield, Harry E. "The Truth About William F. Drannan." *The West*, Aug. 1970, p. 14.

Snipes, Earl. "Will Drannan: Indian Scout." *Golden West*, May 1974, p. 10. Rpt. *The West*, July 1968, p. 8.

Dreban, Sam
Rosson, Mary'n. "The Incredible Texas Saga of Sam Dreban." *Frontier West*, June 1973, p. 20.

Drouillard, George
Underwood, Larry. "George Drouillard: Frontier Scout." *True West,* Nov. 1987, p. 50.

Drumheller, Daniel Montgomery "Uncle Dan"
Drumheller, Dan. "Uncle Dan Drumheller Tells Thrills of Western Trails in 1854." *Old West,* Fall 1968, p. 75.

Ducks and Hounds
Lipton, Dean. "The Vigilantes." *Great West,* Summer 1981, p. 14.

Rosenhouse, Leo. "Ducks and Hounds of the Mother Lode." *Oldtimers Wild West,* Aug. 1975, p. 28.

Dudley, Nathan A.M.
Best, J.C. "I Beg You, Colonel Dudley." *Real West,* Aug. 1988, p. 40.

Cline, Don. "Sue McSween and Colonel Dudley." *NOLA Quarterly,* Vol. XV, No. 1, 1991, p. 17.

Duesha, Charley
Kildare, Maurice. "Frontier Hellion." *Real West,* March 1970, p. 14.

Duffield, Milton B.
Kildare, Maurice. "Criminal Who Became a US Lawman." *The West,* March 1967, p. 10.

Lake, Ivan Clyde. "How Death Came to the Old Ruffian." *The West,* Nov. 1964, p. 28.

Duggan, Martin J. "Mart"
DeArment, Robert K. "Mart Duggan: Leadville Lawman." *Frontier Times,* Feb. 1985, p. 10.

Hines, Lawrence. "The Best Marshal Money Couldn't Buy." *Pioneer West,* May 1978, p. 6.

————. "The Colorado Marshal No Money Could Buy." *Frontier West,* June 1972, p. 46.

Duggan, Stanford S.C.
Cook, D.J. "The Noose Didn't Fit." *Westerner,* March-April 1974, p. 36.

Holben, Richard. "Everybody Danced at Stanford Duggan's Necktie Party." *Frontier West,* Dec. 1973, p. 40.

Dull Knife

Andre, Barbara E. "The Long March North." *Real Frontier,* Aug. 1970, p. 36.

Bailey, Tom. "The White Invaders." *True West,* Aug. 1963, p. 14.

Bloom, Sam. "Ambush! The Day the Fourth Cavalry Walked Into Hell." *Frontier West,* June 1974, p. 40.

Darlington, David. "Battle on the Redfork." *True West,* Nov. 1988, p. 14.

Guttman, Jon. "Warriors and Chiefs" column. *Wild West,* Oct. 1989, p. 10.

Kiewit, Fred. "Outrage at Oberlin." *Frontier Times,* Sept. 1965, p. 18.

Long, James. "Death Trail of the Cheyenne." *Real West,* Sept. 1964, p. 20.

Millard, Joseph. "The Reluctant Warriors." *True Western Adventures,* Feb. 1959, p. 40.

Smith, Ann M. "The Cheyenne Shadows." *Pioneer West,* June 1972, p. 48.

_____. "Let My People Go." *Western Round-Up,* May 1970, p. 40. Rpt. *Pioneer West,* Nov. 1973, p. 52; and *Oldtimers Wild West,* Dec. 1976, p. 16.

Stanley, Samuel. "Breakout at Fort Robinson: The Cheyennes Vowed No Stockade Would Hold Them." *Frontier West,* April 1975, p. 36.

_____. "Their Hearts Yearned for Home." *The West,* Aug. 1968, p. 36. Rpt. *Golden West,* April 1972, p. 8; and *Western Frontier,* Special Issue, March 1975, p. 28.

Swanson, Budington. "Winter War." *Real West,* Oct. 1970, p. 16.

Dunham, James

Meier, Gary. "The Mystery of Santa Clara Valley." Part I, *True West,* Oct. 1989, p. 28; Part II, *True West, Nov.* 1989, p. 28.

Duniway, Abigail Scott

Dunlap, Patricia Riley. "Abigail Scott Duniway: Pioneer Woman." *Old West,* Winter 1991, p. 51.

O'Neal, Harold. "Abigail Scott: Fighting Northwest Suffragette." *True Frontier,* Sept. 1973, p. 30.

Dunlap, Jack "3-Fingered Jack"

Qualey, J.S. "Jeff Milton, Nemesis of Three Fingered Jack." *Real West,* March 1962, p. 38.

Traywick, Ben T. "Jack Dunlap: Alias Three-Fingered Jack." *The West,* Jan. 1971, p. 14. Rpt. *Golden West,* Jan. 1974, p. 32; *Western Frontier,* Sept. 1975, p. 2; *Western Frontier,* Sept. 1977, p. 32; and *Western Frontier,* Jan. 1983, p. 38.

Dunn Brothers (Bill or "B," John, George, Dal, Calvin)

Kildare, Maurice. "Six-Gun Justice Took Strange Turns in the Cimarron." *Frontier West,* Dec. 1973, p. 26.

McBee, G. Fred. "Don't Wake the Neighbors!" *Golden West,* March 1971, p. 20.

Parsons, Chuck. "Dunn Brothers" ("Answer Man" column). *True West,* April 1988, p. 12.

_____. "Turncoats" ("Answer Man" column). *True West,* Jan. 1990, p. 14.

Dunn, John

Bundy, Rex. "John Dunn: An Old-Styled Lawman." *Golden West,* Nov. 1970, p. 28. Rpt. *Western Frontier,* April 1983, p. 12.

Owens, Harry J. "The Thrilling Capture of the Sundance Kid and Kid Curry." *NOLA Quarterly,* Vol. X, No. 4, Spring 1986, p. 9.

Dunn, Rose (Rosa) "Rose of the Cimarron"

Breihan, Carl W. "Rose of the Cimarron." *Real West,* Annual, Winter 1979, p. 18.

Kerr, William Ray. "In Defense of Ingalls, Oklahoma." *True West,* Oct. 1964, p. 6.

Tilghman, Zoe A. "I Knew Rose of the Cimarron." *True West,* June 1958, p. 20.

Dunning, George

Williams, Gary. "Dunning's Strange Confession: Five Dollars a Day to Ride, Fifty Dollars to Kill." *The West,* July 1964, p. 14. Rpt. *Golden West,* June 1974, p. 30.

Dupuy, Louis

Lord, John. "Monsieur Dupuy's Fabulous Hotel." *Real West,* Jan. 1962, p. 26.

Gray, Felton J. "The Amazing Monsieur Dupuy." *The West,* Nov. 1965, p. 18.

Rozar, Lily-B. "Colorado's Fabulous Frenchman." *Pioneer West,* Jan. 1970, p. 17. Rpt. *Pioneer West,* July 1973, p. 13.

Durand, Earl

Thane, Eric. "The Last Owl-Hoot." *Frontier Times,* Winter 1957-58, p. 24.

Durbin, J. Walter

Stephens, Robert W. "Ambush in the Chaparral." *Frontier Times,* May 1967, p. 30.

Durfey, Jeff
Burke, Emmett W. "Jeff Durfey, Buffalo Hunter." *True West,* Aug. 1975, p. 42.

Durgan, Millie
Cerveri, Doris. "Saga of Millie Durgan." *The West,* Oct. 1965. p. 24. Rpt. *The West,* July 1973, p. 14.

Dyer, John L.
Chatfield, Harry E. "Father Dyer: The Snowshoe Itinerant." *Golden West,* Nov. 1967, p. 22.
Sampson, Joanna. "Gold Rush Gospel on Skis." *True West,* March 1991, p. 48.

Eagleworth, William "Lizard Bill"
Kildare, Maurice. "Lizard Bill's Silver." *Westerner,* Oct. 1971, p. 44.

Earnest, Boney
Parsons, Chuck. "Boney Earnest" ("Answer Man" column). *True West,* June 1991, p. 12.

Earp Brothers
Boyer, Glenn G. "Those Marryin' Earp Men." *True West,* April 1976, p. 14.
Deac, Wilfred P. "Two Minutes in Tombstone." *Wild West,* Aug. 1991, p. 42.
DeMattos, Jack. "A Tour of Earp Country." *Real West,* Annual 1981, p. 12.
Kantor, Seth. "Time: Oct. 26, 1881—Place: OK Corral." *Western Action,* Dec. 1960, p. 30.
Malocsay, Zoltan. "OK Corral: 100 Years of Lies." *Westerner,* July-Aug. 1973, p. 34.
Mason, Frank. "What Really Happened at the O.K. Corral?" *True West,* Oct. 1960, p. 35.
Mays, Carelton. "What Really Happened at the OK Corral?" *Real West,* Jan. 1958, p. 14. Rpt. *Real West,* Annual, Summer 1966, p. 28.
O'Neal, Bill. "Aftermath of the O.K. Corral" ("Great Western Gunfights" column). *True West,* May 1991, p. 60.

Roberts, Gary L. "The Fight That Never Dies." *Frontier Times,* Nov. 1965, p. 6.
_____. "The Fremont Street Fiasco." *True West,* July 1988, p. 14.

Earp, George Washington
Harris, Richard W. "The Mayor of Ulysses." *Frontier Times,* Fall 1961, p. 22.

Earp, Morgan
Boyer, Glenn G. "Morgan Earp: Brother in the Shadow." *Old West,* Winter 1983, p. 16.

Earp, Nicholas
Urban, William. "Wyatt Earp's Father." *True West,* May 1989, p. 30.

Earp, Virgil
"Arizona Affairs: An Interview With Virgil W. Earp." *Real West,* Jan. 1982, p. 26.
DeMattos, Jack. "Virgil and Wyatt Earp" ("Gunfighters of the Real West" column.). Part I, *Real West,* Oct. 1981, p. 36; Part II, *Real West,* Dec. 1981, p. 30. Rpt. as one-part article, *Real West,* Special Issue, Spring 1985, p. 38.
Palmquist, Robert F. "A Busy Season: Virgil Earp in Prescott, 1877." *Real West,* Dec. 1980, p. 32. Rpt. *Real West,* Annual 1981, p. 60.
Turner, Alford E. "Colton's Marshal Earp." *Real West,* March 1981, p. 28. Rpt. *Real West,* Annual, Spring 1982, p. 52.

Earp, Warren
Rasch, Philip J. "The Violent Life of Warren Earp." *NOLA Quarterly,* Vol. XIV, No. 1, 1990, p. 3.
Traywick, Ben T. "The Murder of Warren Baxter Earp." *Old West,* Winter 1990, p. 53.

Earp, Wyatt
Bailey, Tom. "Wyatt Earp's Last Gun Fight." *True Western Adventures,* Issue No. 1, 1957, p. 2.
Bainright, Frank. "The Truth About Wyatt Earp's Mystery Marriage." *The West,* Jan. 1965, p. 42.
Ballenger, Dean W. "The Day Wyatt Earp Tamed 100 Men." *Pioneer West,* Nov. 1978, p. 36.
Becker, Bill. "Wyatt Earp's Own Vice Madam." *Man's Western,* Aug.-Sept. 1959, p. 10.
Boyer, Glenn G. "Curly Bill Has Been Killed at Last." *Real West,* Feb. 1984, p. 32. Rpt. *Real West,* Yearbook, Winter 1986, p. 29.

_____. "The Secret Wife of Wyatt Earp." *True West,* June 1983, p. 12.

_____. "Trailing an American Myth." *Real West,* Jan. 1981, p. 14. Rpt. *Real West,* Special Issue, Spring 1982, p. 10.

DeMattos, Jack. "Virgil and Wyatt Earp" ("Gunfighters of the Real West" column). Part I, *Real West,* Oct. 1981, p. 36; Part II, *Real West,* Dec. 1981, p. 30. Rpt. as one-part article, *Real West,* Special Issue, Spring 1985, p. 38.

Dullenty, Jim. "Was Wyatt Earp a Horsethief?" *NOLA Quarterly,* Vol. X, No. 2, Fall 1985, p. 8.

Earp Josephine. "The Earps In Tonopah." Ed. Glenn G. Boyer. *True West,* Aug. 1975, p. 14.

_____. "Sinister Shadow From the Past." Ed. Glenn G. Boyer. *True West,* Oct. 1975, p. 20.

Earp, Wyatt. "How Wyatt Earp Routed a Gang of Arizona Outlaws." Rpt. *Real West,* May 1978, p. 16. Rpt. *Real West,* Annual, Winter 1979, p. 8.

_____. "Wyatt Earp Tells Tales of the Shotgun Messenger Service." Rpt. *Real West,* July 1978, p. 46.

Edwards, Harold L. "Was Wyatt Earp Cowed?" *True West,* Sept. 1991, p. 51.

Hinkle, Milt. "The Earp and Masterson I Knew." *True West,* Dec. 1961, p. 25.

Kantor, Seth. "Time: Oct. 26, 1881—Place: OK Corral." *Western Action,* Dec. 1960, p. 30.

King, A.M. "The Last Man." *True West,* June 1959, p. 28.

_____. "Wyatt Earp's Million Dollar Shotgun Ride." *True West,* Aug. 1958, p. 16.

Malocsay, Zoltan. "OK Corral: 100 Years of Lies." *Westerner,* July-Aug. 1973, p. 34.

Mays, Carelton. "What Really Happened at the OK Corral?" *Real West,* Jan. 1958, p. 14.

Mays, George Carelton. "Wyatt Earp." *Real West,* Americana Series, Fall 1965, p. 6.

McCarty, Lea. "The Wyatt Earp Burial Secret." *True West,* Oct. 1957, p. 16.

_____. "Wyatt Earp's Grave Robbed." *True West,* Oct. 1957, p. 18.

McVey, William D. "Wyatt Earp At Ellsworth." *Chicago Westerners Brand Book,* Vol. X, No. 9, Nov. 1953, p. 1.

McVey, William D., and R.N. Mullin. "Wyatt Earp: Frontier Peace Officer." *Chicago Westerners Brand Book,* Vol. VI, No. 9, Nov. 1949, p. 1.

Moreau, Derek. "That Famous Gunfight Where?" *Real West,* Sept. 1981, p. 20. Rpt. *Real West,* Special Issue, Spring 1982, p. 58.

Murray, Tom G. "The Day Wyatt Earp Died." *Golden West,* May 1965, p. 48. Rpt. *The West,* June 1972, p. 18; and *Western Frontier,* March 1976, p. 46.

————. "The Town Named for Wyatt Earp." *Old West,* Winter 1977, p. 14.

————. "Wyatt Earp's Letters to Bill Hart." *True West,* June 1968, p. 20.

Nolen, Richard. "Gunfight in Gomorrah." *Westerner,* Sept.-Oct. 1972, p. 30.

Palmquist, Robert F. "Good Bye Old Friend." *Real West ,* May 1979, p. 24.

Rickards, Colin. "Wyatt Earp Tells About the Gunfight at the O.K. Corral." *Real West,* Feb. 1970, p. 36. Rpt. *Real West,* Americana Series, Fall 1973, p. 39.

Roberts, Gary L. "The Fight That Never Dies." *Frontier Times,* Nov. 1965, p. 6.

————. "The Night Wyatt Earp Almost KO'ed Boxing." *The West,* April 1966, p. 14. Rpt. *The West,* Nov. 1971, p. 10.

————. "Was Wyatt Earp Really a U.S. Deputy Marshal?" *True West,* Feb. 1961, p. 30.

Roemer, Joseph. "The Third Man: Wyatt Earp." *True Western Adventures,* Feb. 1960, p. 35.

Roy, Robert. "The True Story of Wyatt Earp." *Real West,* Yearbook, Summer 1977, p. 36.

St. John, Harvey. "Wyatt Earp As I Knew Him." *Real West,* Nov. 1965, p. 27.

Sooner, Paul. "Earp: The Man Who Invented His Own Legend." *Westerner,* Oct. 1971, p. 41.

Taylor, Paul. "Wyatt Earp's Town." *Old West,* Spring 1989, p. 60.

Thomas, Robert L. "Gunfight at Iron Springs." *True West,* Feb. 1965, p. 38.

————. "I Think Earp Took Johnny Ringo." *Old West,* Fall 1972, p. 13.

Thorp, Raymond W. "Wyatt Earp: A Triple Acquaintance." *Frontier Times,* March 1963, p. 24.

Turner, Alford E. "The Florentino-Earp Affair." *Real West,* Jan. 1979, p. 16. Rpt. *Real West,* Yearbook 1980, p. 44.

————. "Wyatt Earp's Unique Faro Game." *Real West,* June 1986, p. 48.

Virgines, George E. "The Weapons of Wyatt Earp." *Golden West,* Jan. 1970, p. 16. Rpt. *Western Frontier,* Annual, Winter 1977, p. 38.

Walker, Wayne T. "The Truth About the Dodge City War." *Real West,* March 1970, p. 28.

Williams, Jack. "Goldfield: and the Wyatt Earp I Knew." *Frontier Times,* Winter 1959-60, p. 16.

Winfield, Craig. "The Adventurous Saga of Wyatt Earp." *Pioneer West,* Sept. 1977, p. 6.

East, James H. "Jim"

Bundy, Rex. "Jim East: Western Lawman." *Real West,* June. 1971, p. 21.

Castleman, Sean. "Shootout at Tascosa." *Pioneer West,* Nov. 1978, p. 18.

Kildare, Maurice. "The Gut Fighter Who Made 'Hell Town' the Bloodiest Place in Texas." *Frontier West,* Dec. 1972, p. 28.

Shannon, Dan. "Taming Wild Tascosa." *The West,* March 1964, p. 12.

Walker, Wayne T. "The Incredible Saga of Jim East: The Tascosa Pacifier." *Frontier West,* Oct. 1974, p. 40.

Eaton, Ed
Nelson, Andre. "The Last Sheepman-Cattleman War." *True West,* May 1988, p. 14.

Eaton, Frank
Ross, Raymond J. "The Vengeance of Marshal Frank Eaton." *The West,* Oct. 1966, p. 24. Rpt. *Golden West,* Nov. 1972, p. 32; *Western Frontier,* May 1979, p. 44; and *Western Frontier,* May 1985, p. 44.

Shirley, Glenn. "Pistol Pete: Badmen's Nemesis." *Westerner,* May-June 1969, p. 44.

Turpin, Robert F. "'Pistol Pete' Eaton." *Pioneer West,* April 1972, p. 16.

Edgerton, Sidney
Bundy, Rex. "Sidney Edgerton: Forgotten Man of Montana." *Real West,* March 1972, p. 6.

Edmonds, Newton
Koller, Joe. "Newton Edmonds: Treaty Maker of Dakota." *Golden West,* May 1974, p. 24.

Edwards, Hayden
Scullin, George. "Dreamer In No Man's Land." *True Western Adventure,* Feb. 1961, p. 30.

Edwards, John Newman
Bell, Morris. "Editor Edwards and His Pardoning Pen." *Real West,* Aug. 1986, p. 37.

Egan, James R.
Vaughn, J.W. "Captain James Egan." *The New York Westerners' Brand Book*, Vol. 13, No. 1, 1966, p. 1.

Ehrenberg, Hermann
Brownell, Elizabeth R. Letter. *True West,* Aug. 1986, p. 6.

Von Schweinitz, Helga. "Herman Ehrenberg: Fighting for Texas." *True West,*
April 1986, p. 22.

Elder, "Big Nose" Kate (see Cummings, Mary K.)

Elder, James Bailey
Parsons, Chuck. "James Bailey Elder: Buffalo Hunter." *Real West,* May 1979, p.
12.

Eldridge Family
Chrisman, Harry E. "The Johnson-Eldridge Feud." *Golden West,* June 1974, p.
18.

Elkins, George M.
Hornung, Chuck. "The Cowboy Ranger." *Real West,* Yearbook, Winter 1986, p.
20.

Elliott, Elijah
Landes, Cheryl. "Eastern Oregon's Lost Wagon Train." *True West,* March 1991,
p. 50.

Elliott, Joel H.
Huston, Fred. "Night of the Red Moon." *Oldtimers Wild West,* Aug. 1979, p. 30.

Elliott, Joseph "Joe"
Hawthorne, Roger. "Conflict and Conspiracy." *True West,* June 1984, p. 12.

Ellis, Abraham "Bullet Hole Ellis"
Christopher, Mrs. O.H., Westport Historical Society, Kansas City, Missouri.
Letter. *Real West,* May 1969, p. 9.
Hart, George. "I Carried Quantrill's Bullet In My Brain." *Westerner,* May-June
1974, p. 8.

Ellis, Jennie
Clifford, Mike. "They Still Remember Jennie." *True West,* Aug. 1963, p. 34.

Ellwood, Isaac L.
Wallis, George A. "Cattle Kings." Part I, *True West,* April 1964, p. 8.

Emerson, Jason
Kester, Dan. "Laramie's Women Auctions." *Pioneer West,* April 1972, p. 10.

Emge, Joe
Nelson, Andre. "The Last Sheepman-Cattleman War." *True West,* May 1988, p. 14.

Emory, Tom
Smith, Joe H. "How 'Poker Tom' Got His Name." *Frontier Times,* May 1975, p. 27.

Engalitcheff, Susanna Bransford Emery Holmes Delitch
Thompson, George A. "Silver Queen." *Westerner,* July-Aug. 1974, p. 33.

English, Dave
Bayer, Jonas. "Outlaw Turned Hero." *Golden West,* Nov. 1964, p. 14. Rpt. *The West,* Dec. 1973, p. 22.

English, Lawrence Buchanan "Buck"
Chegwyn, Michael. "Finest Kind." *Old West,* Summer 1991, p. 21.

Eskiminzin
Danielson, Helga. "Over-Kill in Apache Land." *Frontier Times,* July 1971, p. 14.

Kutz, Jack. "Eskiminzin: Peacemaker!" *Great West,* June 1974, p. 14.

Schellie, Don. "Apache Vengeance." *Real West,* Americana Series, Winter 1964, p. 30.

————. "When Apache Vengeance Failed." *Real West,* May 1963, p. 10.

Espinosa Brothers
Burke, William. "Vendetta." *True Western Adventures,* Spring 1958, p. 40.

Carson, Kit. "Reward for Juan Espinosa's Head." *Real West,* Sept. 1962, p. 30.

Carson, Xanthus. "Rampage of the Espinosas." *Pioneer West,* July 1969, p. 12.

Kildare, Maurice. "The Killers." *Great West,* Dec. 1972, p. 20. Rpt. *Great West,* Summer 1981, p. 56; and *Authentic West,* Fall 1981, p. 61.

Evans, Chris
Boessenecker, John. "Buckshot for a Marshal." *Real West,* Feb. 1983, p. 35.

Edwards, Harold L. "Chris Evans: The Ready Killer." Part I; *NOLA Quarterly,*

Vol. XI, No. 1, Summer 1986, p. 5; Part II, *NOLA Quarterly,* Vol. XI, No. 2, Fall 1986, p. 14.

_____. "Hatred of Railroads Triggers Death." *NOLA Quarterly,* Vol. IX, No. 1, Summer 1984, p. 6.

_____. "The Man Who Killed Ike Clanton." *True West,* Oct. 1991, p. 24.

O'Neal, Harold. "The San Joaquin Train Holdups." *Golden West,* March 1966, p. 44. Rpt.*Western Frontier,* Aug. 1981, p. 36.

Parker, John L. "Chris Evans: The Questionable Outlaw." *True West,* April 1984, p. 48.

Secrest, William B. "The Fantastic Train Robbery Drama." *True Frontier,* May 1970, p. 38. Rpt. *True Frontier,* Special Issue No. 5, 1973, p. 29.

_____. "Four Lawmen Ambush Two California Outlaws." *NOLA Quarterly,* Vol. III, No. 1, Summer 1977, p. 1.

_____. "The Gunfight at Stone Corral." *True Frontier,* Special Issue No. 1, 1971, p. 18. Rpt. *True Frontier,* June 1973, p. 26; *Real Frontier,* June 1974, p. 8; and *True Frontier,* Aug. 1975, p. 36.

_____. "He Saw the Posse Die." *Frontier Times,* July 1966, p. 10.

Sullivan, Edward. "The Last of the West's Desperadoes." *Pioneer West,* May 1967, p. 11.

Young, Bob and Jan. "Tilt With the Iron Horse." *True West,* Dec. 1956, p. 18.

Evans, Jesse

Ball, Eve. "What Became of Jesse Evans?" *True West,* Feb. 1979, p. 14.

Parsons, Chuck. "Convict's Disappearance" ("Answer Man" column). *True West,* Oct. 1990, p. 12.

Walker, Wayne T. "Jesse Evans: Pistolero of the Pecos." *Oldtimers Wild West,* Annual 1979, p. 6.

Evans, John

Fink, Clarence M. "John Evans: Colorado's Pioneer Activist." *Real West,* Oct. 1974, p. 46.

Koller, Joe. "John Evans, Quaker Rebel Out West." *Golden West,* Sept. 1966, p. 10.

Evens, Laura

Jenkins, Nedra C. "Lively Lady from Leadville." *Western Frontier,* Special Issue, Dec. 1974, p. 8.

Everleigh Sisters (Ada and Minna)
Uhlarik, Carl. "The Sin Sisters Who Made Millions." *Real West,* Annual, Summer 1971, p. 15.

Ewing, Jesse
Boren, Kerry Ross. "The Lost Ewing Mine." *The West,* Feb. 1971, p. 16.
Isham, Dell. "An Odd Freak of Humanity." *Real West,* May 1977, p. 32.

Fair, Laura
Boswell, Charles. "The High Noon of Aleck Crittenden." *True Western Adventures,* Feb. 1961, p. 18.
Young, Bob. "The Lady Loved to Kill." *Real West,* Nov. 1961, p. 42.

Fairweather, William "Bill"
Darwin, Wayne. "Tobacco Money: One Hundred Million Dollars." *The West,* Dec. 1968, p. 24. Rpt *The West,* Nov. 1972, p. 14.
Henry, R.C. "Fairweather's Luck." *True West,* Dec. 1970, p. 26.
Ryan, Jack. "The Man Who Made Montana." *True Western Adventures,* Aug. 1960, p. 26.

Fall, Albert Bacon
Carson, Xanthus. "The Senator Who Brought Disgrace to New Mexico." *True Frontier,* Feb. 1973, p. 22. Rpt. *True Frontier,* Special Issue No. 11, Winter 1974-75, p. 29.
_____. "This Was Rangeland Justice: The Fantastic Courtroom Saga of the Lion of the West." *Frontier West,* Oct. 1972, p. 38.

Fallen Leaf (Ahoappa—also Falling Leaf)
Koller, Joe. "Tragic Sacrifice of Falling Leaf." *Real West,* Nov. 1963, p. 36.
McDermott, Burton. "The Entire Frontier Mourned the Indian Princess." *Frontier West,* Oct. 1973, p. 18.
Winslowe, John R. "Spotted Tail's Daughter." *Westerner,* Jan.-Feb. 1970, p. 26.

Fancher, Charles
Altman, Larry. "Mountain Meadows Massacre." *Real West,* Nov. 1958, p. 26.

Fannin, James W. "Jim"
Holding, Vera. "The Goliad Massacre." *Great West,* June 1972, p. 30. Rpt. *Authentic West,* Fall 1981, p. 36.

Teer, Louis B. "Colonel Fannin's Ghastly Blunder." *Real West,* Nov. 1964, p. 34.

Farr, Edward J. "Ed"
Burton, Jeff. "Suddenly in a Secluded and Rugged Place." Part I, *English Westerners' Brand Book,* Vol. XIV, No. 3, April 1972, p. 1; Part II, *English Westerners' Brand Book,* Vol. XIV, No. 4, July 1972, p. 1.

Titsworth, B.D. "Hole-in-the-Wall Gang." *True West,* Dec. 1956, p. 10.

Farwell, Charles B.
Wallace, George A. "Cattle Kings." *True West,* Feb. 1964, p. 12.

Farwell, John V.
Holding, Vera. "XIT: Five Million Acres in Two States." *Real Frontier,* Aug. 1971, p. 34.

Faucett, Miles
Cerveri, Doris. "Ghosts of Murders Past." *Big West,* April 1970, p. 14.

Faver, Don Milton
Scobee, Barry. "Don Milton Faver: Founder of a Kingdom." *True West,* June 1962, p. 18.

_____. Letter. *True West,* Aug. 1962, p. 60.

Fellows, Richard "Dick"
Cheney, Louise. "Dick Fellows, Highwayman." *Great West,* Sept. 1969, p. 27.

Cox, Dick. "The Bandit Dreamer." *Westerner,* April 1971, p. 16.

Hart, George. "Dick Fellows, Comic Opera Bandit." *Real West,* Dec. 1969, p. 42. Rpt. *Real West,* Annual, Summer 1971, p. 52.

Hartley, William B. "The Man the Broncs Busted." *True Western Adventures,* April 1960, p. 34.

Kelly, Bill. "California's Bungling Outlaw." *Real West,* Jan. 1982, p. 12. Rpt. *Real West,* Yearbook, Fall 1982, p. 21.

Malsbary, George. "The Road Agent Who Was Afraid of Horses." *True Frontier,* July 1971, p. 11.

Ryland, Lee. "The Outlaw Who Couldn't Ride a Horse." *True Frontier,* March 1969, p. 20. Rpt. *True Frontier,* Feb. 1973, p. 16; and *True Frontier,* Oct. 1976, p. 27.

Secrest, William B. "Dick Fellows: Hard Luck Outlaw." Part I, *True West,* Oct. 1990, p. 14; Part II, *True West,* Nov. 1990, p. 14.

Young, Jan. "Horseless Highwayman of the High Sierra." *The West,* May 1964, p. 38. Rpt. *The West,* July 1974, p. 14; and *Western Frontier,* May 1985, p. 14.

Ferge, Charles "Seldom Seen Slim"
Murray, Tom G. "Last of the Burromen: 'Seldom Seen Slim.'" *True West,* Dec. 1972, p. 20.

Ferris, Henry
Ballenger, Dean W. "Two-Gun Lawyer." *Pioneer West,* Jan. 1971, p. 38. Rpt. *Oldtimers Wild West,* Aug. 1975, p. 52.

Fetterman, William J.
Day, DeWitt F. "Massacre and Rescue at Fort Phil Kearney [sic]." *America's Frontier West,* Issue No. 1, n.d., p. 32.

Dunn, J.P., Jr. "Slaughter at Fort Phil Kearney [sic]." *Real West,* Sept. 1964, p. 10.

Judge, Bill. "The Battle of One Hundred Slain." *True West,* June 1962, p. 20.

Malsbaiy, George. "Warcry." *Great West,* Dec. 1972, p. 4.

McNellis, George. "Massacre in the Dakota Territory: Col. Fetterman's Ghastly Mistake." *Frontier West,* April 1971, p. 42.

Ficklin, Ben
Austerman, Wayne R. "Ben Ficklin: Master of the Concords." *Real West,* May 1988, p. 14.

_____. "Iron Concords on the Plains." *Real West,* June 1985, p. 20. Rpt. *Real West,* Special Issue, Spring 1986, p. 21.

Field, Stephen J.
Freeman, Frank M. "The Case of the Imperious Men." *Golden West,* Sept. 1968, p. 34.

Finerty, John F.
Doorley, Lawrence. "That Reckless Hibernian, Finerty of the Times." *True West,* May 1986, p. 14.

Fink, Mike

Hanser, Richard. "Mike the Mighty." *True Western Adventures,* Oct. 1959, p. 52.

Hurdy, John Major. "The Maverick River Baron." *Big West,* Oct. 1967, p. 30.

Hurdy, Major J. [sic]. "Old Ring-Tailed Roarer." *Wild West,* Aug. 1969, p. 48. Rpt. *Oldtimers Wild West,* Jan. 1975, p. 46.

Finkel, Frank

Ege, Robert J. "He Survived the Custer Massacre." *Real West,* Nov. 1966, p. 10.

Robertson, Ken. "Frank Finkel: Sole Survivor of Custer." *Old West,* Spring 1984, p. 10.

Finley, William "Bill"

Repp, Ed Earl. "Wagons Over the Sierras." *True Frontier,* June 1973, p. 12.

Finney, James Edwin "Ed"

Shoemaker, Arthur. "James Finney: Trader Among the Osages." *Old West,* Fall 1991, p. 37.

Fisher Family

Steele, Phillip W. "The Shannon-Fisher War." *Old West,* Fall 1985, p. 44.

Fisher, John King

Allen, Perry D. "Fancy Pants Killer." *Western Tales,* April 1960, p. 26.

Bishop, Curtis. "King Fisher's Road." *True West,* Feb. 1963, p. 35.

Breihan, Carl W. "The Day King Fisher and Ben Thompson Were Killed." *Oldtimers Wild West,* April 1977, p. 6.

————. "John Fisher, King of Texas." *Real West,* April 1968, p. 10.

————. "King Fisher: Texas Heller." *True Western Adventures,* Oct. 1960, p. 11.

————. "The Sadistic Pistoleer." *Pioneer West,* May 1969, p. 14.

————. "Wanted: King Fisher." *Westerner,* July-Aug. 1969, p. 48.

Coe, Clint. "Tiger Pants for a Killer." *True Western Adventures,* April 1961, p. 17.

DeMattos, Jack. "King Fisher" ("Gunfighters of the Real West" column). *Real West,* Sept. 1978, p. 12.

Harrison, Fred. "San Antonio's Greatest Murder Enigma." *Golden West,* May 1965, p. 34.

O'Neal, Bill. "Ben Thompson and King Fisher" ("Great Western Gunfights" column). *True West,* April 1990, p. 60.

Paxton, Fred. "King Fisher, Dude Desperado." *Real West,* Jan. 1961, p. 19.

"Reform Came Too Late to King Fisher." *Gunslingers of the West,* Winter 1966, p. 41.

Winfield, Craig. "The Outlaw Sheriff." *Westerner,* Nov.-Dec. 1972, p. 35.

Fitzpatrick, Thomas "Tom"

Mays, Carelton. "Broken-Hand Fitzpatrick, Mountain Man Extraordinary." *Real West,* May 1966, p. 9.

Thomas, Kevin. "The Saga of 'Broken-Hand' Fitzpatrick." *Oldtimers Wild West,* April 1980, p. 29.

Walker, Wayne T. "Saga of Thomas 'Broken-Hand' Fitzpatrick." *The West,* June 1969, p. 12.

Flatt, George

O'Neal, Bill. "George Flatt vs. George Wood and Jake Adams" ("Great Western Gunfights" column). *True West,* May 1988, p. 59.

Fletcher, Lizzie

Jones, Gene. "Tragic Mystery of Lizzie Fletcher." *The West,* July 1964, p. 10.

Flipper, Henry

Bentz, Donald. "Henry Flipper: West Point's First Black Graduate." *The West,* July 1972, p. 17.

Robinson, Charles M., III. "The Court Martial of Lt. Henry Flipper." *True West,* June 1989, p. 20.

Flores, Juan

Kennelly, Joe. "The Capture and Execution of Juan Flores." *Golden West,* July 1965, p. 10. Rpt. *Western Frontier,* Annual, Winter 1977, p. 20.

Fly, Camillus S.

Kelly, Joseph F. "He Captured Wicked Tombstone." *True West,* Feb. 1983, p. 10.

Leonard, Phillis G. "The Man Who Shot Geronimo." *True Frontier,* Aug. 1974, p. 36. Rpt. *True Frontier,* Summer 1977, p. 30.

Fontenelle, Logan

Koller, Joe. "Logan Fontenelle: White Chief." *Golden West,* Nov. 1971, p. 42. Rpt. *Western Frontier,* Annual, Fall 1981, p. 42.

Fontenelle, Lucien
Koller, Joe. "Logan Fontenelle: White Chief." *Golden West,* Nov. 1971, p. 42. Rpt. *Western Frontier,* Annual, Fall 1981, p. 42.

Foote, Robert
Koch, Anna Elaine. "Cowtown Merchant, Cattle War Santa Claus." *True West,* Jan. 1991, p. 20.

Carroll, Murray L. Letter. *True West,* March 1991, p. 6.

Ford, Barney L.
McIntyre, Gary L. "The Runaway Slave Who Became the Baron of Colorado." *Frontier West,* April 1973, p. 26.

Pearce, Bennett R. "Barney L. Ford: From Runaway Slave to Millionaire." *The West,* Feb. 1969, p. 16.

Sorensen, Russell. "Slave Who Became the Baron of Colorado." *Pioneer West,* Dec. 1971, p. 33.

Ford, Charles "Charley"
Bird, Roy. "Those Dirty Little Cowards." *Real West,* May 1988, p. 32.

Hart, George. "Stanley Waterloo Meets the Fords." *NOLA Quarterly,* Vol. XIV, No. 1, 1990, p. 1.

Ford, Charles P. "One-Armed Charlie"
Koop, W.E. "A Rope For One-Armed Charlie." *True West,* Feb. 1967, p. 22.

Ford, John Salmon "Rip"
Beck, Paul. "Palmito Ranch, Texas: The Last Battle in the Civil War." *Old West,* Summer 1985, p. 24.

Coleman, Neil. "When 'Ironshirt' Clashed With 'Old Rip.'" *Pioneer West,* Sept. 1967, p. 42.

Fried, Joseph. "Rip Ford, Lone Star Giant." Part I, *Real West,* Sept. 1966, p. 10.

Green, Ford. "Rip Ford's River Warriors." *Frontier Times,* Sept. 1980, p. 54.

Kurtz, Henry I. "Rip Ford, Lone Star Giant." Part II, *Real West,* Nov. 1966, p. 36.

Silke, Jesse R. "John Ford's Cavalry." *Big West,* Oct. 1968, p. 10.

Ford, Robert "Bob"
Balcombe, Stephen. "Bob Ford: The Man Who Killed Jesse James." *True West,* April 1955, p. 10. Rpt. *Badman,* Summer 1971, p. 18.

Bird, Roy. "Those Dirty Little Cowards." *Real West,* May 1988, p. 32.

Breihan, Carl W. "Bob Ford Did Kill Jesse James." *Real West,* May 1959, p. 28.

————. "Death of Bob Ford." *Real West,* March 1970, p. 20. Rpt. *Real West,* Nov. 1975, p. 24.

Gaddis, Robert. "Creede: Four Years of Glory." *True Frontier,* Sept. 1969, p. 38.

Hart, George. "Stanley Waterloo Meets the Fords." *NOLA Quarterly,* Vol. XIV, No. 1, 1990, p. 1.

Huston, Fred. "Death of the Coward Killer." *Real Frontier,* Aug. 1971, p. 19.

Jessen, Kenneth. "Chain of Death Ends in Creede." *NOLA Quarterly,* Vol. XI, No. 3, Fall 1987, p. 15.

Martin, Cy. "There Was No Night in Creede." *Real West,* Annual, Fall 1974, p. 14.

Rickards, Colin. "Bob Ford Tells 'How I Killed Jesse James.'" *Real West,* Jan. 1970, p. 15.

Thomason, Hugh. "The Dirty Little Coward Who Shot Mr. Howard." *True Western Adventures,* Summer 1958, p. 4.

Fornoff, Fred

Virgines, George E. "Fred Fornoff: New Mexico Badge Toter." *True West,* Aug. 1988, p. 46.

Forsyth, George A.

Dahl, Peter Andrew. "Battle at Beecher's Island." *Real West,* Jan. 1958, p. 6.

Indrysek, Don. "A Fight on the Arickaree Fork!" *True Frontier,* July 1970, p. 38.

Keenan, Jerry. "Cheyenne Island Siege." *Wild West,* June 1988, p. 35.

Settle, Raymond W., and Mary Lund Settle. "Thunder on the Arickaree." *Frontier Times,* Fall 1959, p. 10.

Raskop, Jack. "The U.S. Cavalry, Heroes in the Dust." *Real West,* Annual, Summer 1970, p. 8.

Ross, Arthur. "Fifty Mercenaries, One Thousand Braves." *Pioneer West,* May 1967, p. 30.

Sackett, S.J. "Arickaree!" *Frontier Times,* Summer 1962, p. 6.

Fossett, William D. "Big Bill"

Manigold, Burt V., and Joseph R. Rosenberger. "Last of the Gunfighters." *Golden West,* May 1968, p. 10. Rpt. *Western Frontier,* Annual 1980, p. 10.

Fountain, Albert Jennings

Carson, Xanthus. "Strange Murder of Colonel Fountain." *Pioneer West,* Oct. 1970, p. 48.

_____. "This Was Rangeland Justice: The Fantastic Courtroom Saga of the Lion of the West." *Frontier West,* Oct. 1972, p. 38.

Hicks, Flora Weed. "The Magic Fountain Trick: He Disappeared Forever." *Golden West,* March 1969, p. 14. Rpt. *Western Frontier,* March 1980, p. 14.

Lofton, Monk. "Who Killed Judge Fountain?" *True West,* April 1963, p. 40.

Myers, Lee. "Soldier's Hill, New Mexico." *English Westerners' Brand Book,* Vol. XXIV, No. 1, Winter 1986, p. 1.

Rodehaver, Gladys. "Tragic Deaths in the A.J. Fountain Family." *True West,* April 1977, p. 6.

Smith, William R. "Death in Dona Ana County." Part I, *English Westerners' Brand Book,* Vol. IX, No. 2, Jan. 1967, p. 12; Part II, *English Westerners' Brand Book,* Vol. IX, No. 3, April 1967, p. 1.

Williams, Gary. "Mystery in the White Sands." *The West,* April 1965, p. 20.

Fowler, Harry A. "Joel"

Cline, Don. "A Cold Night for Angels." *Real West,* Dec. 1984, p. 32. Rpt. *Real West,* Yearbook, Fall 1985, p. 48.

Cline, Donald. "Socorro Killer." *Frontier Times,* Feb.-March 1974, p. 26.

Fraeb, Henry

Schoenberger, Dale T. "Henry Fraeb, Mountain Man." *Frontier Times,* June 1985, p. 52.

Franc, Otto

Saban, Vera D. "Otto Franc: Riddle of the Pitchfork." *True West,* April 1974, p. 24.

France, George

Betts, James. "Get Off My Land or Die." *Golden West,* Nov. 1973, p. 40.

Francis, "Long George"

Cheney, Elizabeth M. "Robin Hood of the High-line." *Frontier Times,* Summer 1962, p. 57.

Coburn, Walt. "Goodhearted and Unlucky." *Old West,* Spring 1968, p. 8.

Franklin, Ed

Cook, D.J. "First Bullet Entered His Heart." *Westerner,* March-April 1974, p. 30.

Frazer, Robert A. "Bud"
O'Neal, Bill. "Killin' Jim Miller vs Sheriff Bud Frazer" ("Great Western Gunfights" column). *True West,* May 1989, p. 60.

Fredericks, William M.
Edwards, Harold L. "By the Rope Route." *Real West,* Nov. 1987, p. 22.

Secrest, William B. "A Folsom Graduate." *True West,* Oct. 1979, p. 6.

Free, Mickey
Cheney, Louise. "Strange Life of Mickey Free." *The West,* Aug. 1966, p. 10. Rpt. *Golden West,* Nov. 1971, p. 36.

Griffith, A. Kinney. "Mickey Free: Manhunter." Part I, *Old West,* Summer 1968, p. 2; Part II, *Old West,* Fall 1968, p. 2.

Harrison, John H. "Mickey Free: Cold-Blooded Killer or Apache Wars' Hero?" *Frontier West,* Oct. 1974, p. 14.

Freeman, George D.
Koop, W.E. "A Rope for One-Armed Charlie." *True West,* Feb. 1967, p. 22.

Freeman, Jay C.
Freeman, Olga. "Jay C. Freeman: Horse and Buggy Sheriff." *Real West,* Feb. 1971, p. 8.

Freeman, Leigh Richmond
Miller, Don. "Neutrality in Nothing." *Old West,* Winter 1981, p. 32.

Frémont, John C.
Breckenridge, Thomas E. "Survivor of Camp Desolation." *True West,* June 1966, p. 12.

Burke, Philip. "Frémont's Great Blunder." *The West,* Nov. 1964, p. 20. Rpt. *The West,* Annual 1971, p. 44, and *Western Frontier,* Feb. 1980, p. 20.

Copeland, E.R. "The Frontier Officer Who Wasn't Allowed to Fire a Gun." *Frontier West,* Aug. 1973, p. 16.

Egan, Ferol. "Frémont at Bent's Fort." *The American West,* Sept.-Oct. 1976, p. 18.

Griffiths, Mel. "Disaster in the San Juans." *Old West,* Summer 1986, p. 14.

Lewis, Ernest Allen. "The Strange Story of Frémont's Lost Cannon." *True West,* March 1983, p. 46.

Malsbary, George. "When the Pathfinder Got Lost." *Real West,* Sept. 1979, p. 46.

Martin, Bernice. "Christmas, 1848." *True West,* Dec. 1958, p. 24.

McGehee, Micajah. "Rough Times in Rough Places." *Golden West,* May 1966, p. 34. Rpt. *Western Frontier,* Jan. 1982, p. 14.

O'Neal, Harold. "Pea Soup and Dog Meat." *Big West,* Oct. 1969, p. 50.

Repp, Ed Earl. "Tale of the Disappearing Cannon." *The West,* Feb. 1974, p. 22.

Rosenhouse, Leo. "Frémont: a Very Stubborn Man." *Real Frontier.* Dec. 1970, p. 20.

_____. "He Raided the West to Set It Free." *The West,* Feb. 1973, p. 35.

_____. "The Bear Flag Revolt." *True Frontier,* March 1970, p. 32.

Scullin, George. "Death on the Fourth." *True Western Adventures,* Feb. 1960, p. 18.

Settle, Raymond W., and Mary Lund Settle. "The Bullheaded Pathfinder of the Rockies." *Pioneer West,* March 1968, p. 12. Rpt. *Wild West,* May 1972, p. 16.

Shulsinger, Stephanie Cooper. "A Bear Stands and Fights." *Real West,* March 1969, p. 31.

_____. "Frémont's Fabulous Folly." *Real West,* May 1969, p. 19.

Wiltsey, Norman B. "White Hell in the Rockies." *Real West,* July 1967, p. 35.

Wingfield, William. "Frémont: Triumph Between Tragedies." *Real West,* Feb. 1975, p. 28.

French, James "Jim"

Foutz, Jim. "I Saw Jim French Die." *Old West,* Spring 1967, p. 34.

McBee, Fred. "The Gunslingers." *Great West,* Oct. 1972, p. 8.

French, Peter

Arlandson, Leona. "Boss of the Blitzen." *Wild West,* Dec. 1969, p. 49. Rpt. *Pioneer West,* Sept. 1974, p. 21; and *Oldtimers Wild West,* April 1978, p. 22.

Freeman, Olga. "The Cattle Empire of Peter French." *Real West,* Jan. 1969, p. 44.

Friedman, Ralph. "Legend of the Amazing Pete French." *Real West,* May 1962, p. 43.

Landes, Cheryl. "The Valley of Death." *Old West,* Spring 1990, p. 41.

Ryland, Lee. "Being a Cattle Baron Was a Killing Job." *Frontier West,* Dec. 1972, p. 26.

Stanley, Samuel. "Peter French: Oregon Cattleman." *Real West,* Nov. 1978, p. 49.

Werner, Ben. "Death Comes to Oregon's Cattle King." *True West,* April 1969, p. 28.

Fritz, Emil
Vanderwerth, W.C. "Which Way Did They Go?" *Real West,* Yearbook, Summer 1978, p. 52.

Fry, Johnny
Howes, Nick. "Johnny Fry of the Pony Express." *Real West,* March 1976, p. 20.

Fusselman, Charley
Reynolds, Mrs. Charles G. Letter. *True West,* Oct. 1991, p. 6.

Gabriel, J.P. "Pete"
Auer, L.C. "Gun Grudge in Florence." *Pioneer West,* July 1967, p. 24.
Ford, I.M. "Shootout on Gunman's Walk." *The West,* June 1966, p. 24. Rpt. *Golden West,* Oct. 1973, p. 32; *Western Frontier,* Sept. 1977, p. 6; and *Western Frontier,* July 1983, p. 6.
McKelvey, Nat. "Death of an Angry Gun." *True Western Adventures,* June 1959, p. 28.
————. "Riddle of the Redfield Robbers." *True West,* Feb. 1958, p. 24.
Rickards, Colin. "Sheriff Pete Gabriel and Deputy Phy." *Golden West,* Sept. 1970, p. 32.
Wilkes, Homer. "Justice and Joe." *Old West,* Winter 1968, p. 31.

Galusha, Jandon R.
Hornung, Chuck. "They Called Him Chief: J.R. Galusha, New Mexico Lawman." *Real West,* Dec. 1984, p. 14. Rpt. *Real West,* Yearbook, Fall 1985, p. 60.

Gard, George
Secrest, William B. "The Gunfight at Stone Corral." *True Frontier,* June 1973, p. 26.

Gardner, Phillip "Big Phil" ("Cannibal Phil")
Freeman, Frank M. "Bizarre Big Phil." *Real West,* March 1982, p. 34.

_____. "Fabulous Cannibal Phil." *The West,* Nov. 1966, p. 22. Rpt. *The West,* Sept. 1973, p. 14.

Jenkins, Nedra C. "The Strange Appetite of Phil Gardner." *True Frontier,* July 1970, p. 22. Rpt. *True Frontier,* Special Issue No. 5, 1973, p. 32.

Gardner, Roy
Campbell, Barney. "Under the Fence Is Out." *Western Frontier,* Feb. 1980, p. 9.

Garfias, Henry
Kildare, Maurice. "Fastest Gun in Phoenix." *Frontier Times,* Jan. 1968, p. 16.

Garnier, Baptiste "Little Bat"
Bordigon, Maxine G. "Warriors and Chiefs" column. *Wild West,* Oct. 1991, p. 14.

Garreau, Pierre
Jones, Gene. "Fighting Devil of Fort Berthold." *The West,* July 1965, p. 20.

Garrett, Buck
Henderson, Sam. "The Many Careers of Sheriff Buck Garrett." *The West,* July 1968, p. 16. Rpt. *The West,* April 1972, p. 18.

Riotte, Louise. "Buck Garrett: Man and Legend." *True West,* Feb. 1970, p. 22.

_____. "Shoot-Out at the California Cafe." *Western Frontier,* July 1983, p. 32.

Garrett, Elizabeth
Adams, Clarence Siringo. "A Balancing of Opposites" ("Wild Old Days" column). *True West,* Aug. 1968, p. 36.

Garrett, Patrick Floyd "Pat"
Breihan, Carl W. "The Day Pat Garrett Was Killed." *Real West,* April 1975, p. 14.

_____. "Saga of Patrick Floyd Garrett." *Golden West,* Jan. 1968, p. 26. Rpt. *Golden West,* May 1974, p. 12; and *Western Frontier,* Sept. 1977, p. 12.

Carter, A.G. "Neighborhood Talk About Pat Garrett." *Old West,* Fall 1970, p. 20.

Cline, Don. "Pat Garrett's Tragic Lawsuit." *Old West,* Summer 1989, p. 18.

_____. "The Murder of Pat Garrett." *NOLA Quarterly,* Vol. XIII, No. 4, 1989, p. 19.

_____. "Turmoil at the Custom House." *NOLA Quarterly,* Vol. X, No. 1, Summer 1986, p. 13.

DeMattos, Jack. "Pat Garrett" ("Gunfighters of the Real West" column). *Real West,* Aug. 1982, p. 30.

Hervey, James Madison. "The Assassination of Pat Garrett." *True West,* April 1961, p. 16.

Judia, Bert. "The Real Pat Garrett." *Frontier Times,* March 1964, p. 31.

McCubbin, Robert G. "Pat Garrett at His Prime." *NOLA Quarterly,* Vol. XV, No. 2, April-June 1991, p. 1.

Metz, Leon. "The Last Days of Pat Garrett." *True West,* Sept. 1983, p. 12.

_____. "My Search for Pat Garrett and Billy the Kid." *True West,* Aug. 1983, p. 35.

_____. "The Pat Garrett Nobody Knew." *The West,* Oct. 1972, p. 32. Rpt. *Western Frontier,* July 1977, p. 6.

Miller, Lee. "He Killed Pat Garrett." *Real West,* Jan. 1960, p. 30.

Molthan, Ruth. "Battle at the Wildy Well." *Real Frontier,* Aug. 1970, p. 24. Rpt. *True Frontier,* Oct. 1974, p. 26; and *True Frontier,* Special Issue No. 17, Winter 1976, p. 26.

Murach, I.B. "Pat Garrett." *Real West,* Americana Series, Fall 1965, p. 16.

O'Neal, Bill. "Pat Garrett's Posse vs Oliver Lee and James Gilliland" ("Great Western Gunfights" column). *True West,* Nov. 1991, p. 60.

Raymond, Charles. "The Man Who Killed the Man Who Killed Billy the Kid." *Real West,* March 1969, p. 48.

Rickards, Colin. "Pat Garrett Tells 'How I Killed Billy the Kid.'" *Real West,* April 1971, p. 31. Rpt. *Real West,* Americana Series, Fall 1973, p. 30. Rpt. *Real West,* Annual. 1972, p. 32.

Rosson, Mary'n. "The Gun That Killed Billy the Kid." *Old West,* Winter 1977, p. 6.

Smith, Joe Heflin. "The Tragic Life of Pat Garrett." *Real West,* Jan. 1968, p. 10.

Smith, William R. "Death in Dona Ana County." Part I, *English Westerners' Brand Brook,* Vol. IX, No. 2, Jan. 1967, p. 12; Part II, *English Westerners' Brand Brook,* Vol. IX, No. 3, April. 1967, p. 1. Rpt. Part I, *Western Frontier,* Sept. 1977, p. 12; Part II, *Golden West,* May 1974, p. 12.

Sonnichsen, C.L. "Pat Garrett's Last Ride." *True West,* Dec. 1958, p. 4.

Weisner, Herman B. "Garrett's Death: Conspiracy or Doublecross?" *True West,* Dec. 1979, p. 6.

_____. "Pistol or Shotgun: Which Killed Billy?" *Old West,* Summer 1981, p. 12.

Garry, Spokan

Ryker, Lois. "Spokan Garry: Peaceful Indian Chief of the Northwest." *Real West,* Feb. 1974, p. 24.

Gass, Patrick
Spencer, G. "Patrick Gass of the Lewis and Clark Expedition." *Real West,* Oct. 1984, p. 46. Rpt. *Real West,* Special Issue, Spring 1986, p. 50.

Gates, John W. "Bet-A-Million"
Allan, Alfred K. "Last of the Great Gamblers." *Western Frontier,* Annual No. 1, 1975, p. 5.

Karolevitz, Bob. "'Bet-A-Million' Gates: Magician." *Old West,* Fall 1966, p. 48.

Rothman, Warren. "'Bob' Wire Changed the West." *Frontier West,* April 1971, p. 18.

Gatewood, Charles
Grady, Gwynn, and Ray Hogan. "Bitter Sunset." *True West,* Aug. 1955, p. 22. Rpt. *Old West,* Summer 1966. p. 24.

Chatfield, Harry. "Lt. Charles Gatewood, Arizona's Forgotten Hero." *Real West,* March 1966, p. 34.

Gay, Albert
Meketa, Jacqueline Dorgan. "Private Gay and the Battle That Shouldn't Have Been Fought." *True West,* May 1988, p. 20.

Gay, Sam
Lewis, Georgia. "Sam Gay: Las Vegas' Immortal Sheriff." *Wild West,* Jan. 1972, p. 56.

Gay, William "Bill"
Koller, Joe. "Hanging of Bill Gay." *The West,* Feb. 1965, p. 40.

Gentles, William
Carroll, John M. "The Man Who Killed Crazy Horse." *Old West,* Summer 1991, p. 38.

George, Joe
Kildare, Maurice. "The Wilcox Double Robbery." *Real West,* June 1968, p. 31.

Georges, "Sundown Slim"
Kildare, Maurice. "Sundown Slim's Golden Mirage." *Wild West,* Nov. 1971, p. 26.

Gerald, George Bruce
Conger, Roger N. "Last of the Fire Eaters." *True West*, Oct. 1962, p. 18.

Gerard, Frederic F.
Harrison, Fred. "The Terrible Vengeance of the Squaw Man." *Real Frontier*, April 1970, p. 36. Rpt. *True Frontier*, Oct. 1972, p. 26.

German Family (sometimes spelled "Germaine")
Greer, Thorwald. "Six Months of Terror." *Westerner*, May-June 1972, p. 36.

Hopper, John. "Death Trap at Smoky Hill." *Great West*, June 1967, p. 6.

Lee, Wayne C. "Death Hollow." *Old West*, Spring 1977, p. 30.

Mays, Carelton. "Bloody Tragedy of the Germaine Family." *Real West*, Sept. 1962, p. 8.

Wingo, Ella Mae. "Death and Abduction on the Panhandle." *Pioneer West*, April 1970, p. 28.

Geronimo
Ball, Eve. "On the Warpath With Geronimo." *The West*, Aug. 1971, p. 16. Rpt. *Western Frontier*, Jan. 1980, p. 6.

Betzinez, Jason. "I Rode With Geronimo." *Westerner*, June 1971, p. 13.

Bloom, Sam. "Suicide Run Was Six Miles of Pure Hell." *Frontier West*, Aug. 1972, p. 28.

Bourke, John G. "An Apache Campaign." Rpt. Part I, *Great West*, June 1967, p. 38.; Part II, *Great West*, Sept. 1967, p. 20.

Chambers, Howard V. "Geronimo's Last Battle." *Pioneer West*, March 1969, p. 6.

Chesney, W.D. "I Talked With Geronomo." *Real West*, Sept. 1967, p. 28.

Dahl, Peter Andrew. "Geronimo, Hero or Villain?" *Real West*, Aug. 1958, p. 12. Rpt. *Real West*, Annual, Summer 1966, p. 16.

Dominguez, Gil. "Geronimo in San Antonio." *True West*, Jan. 1989, p. 14.

Eherts, Walter. "Geronimo's Secret Weapon." *Real West*, Oct. 1985, p. 43.

Foster, Orville. "Geronimo's Bloody Calling Card." *Golden West*, June 1974, p. 37. Rpt. *Western Frontier*, Sept. 1977, p. 37.

Harrison, Fred. "On the Trail of Geronimo." *Westerner*, March-April 1970, p. 21.

Harriss, Jonathan. "The 'Devil Machine' That Whipped Geronimo." *Western Frontier*, Jan. 1981, p. 5.

Hart, George. "Geronimo's Last Fight." *Real West*, March 1971, p. 6. Rpt. *Real West*, Special Issue, Spring 1972, p. 24.

Henderson, Sam. "Were Geronimo's Bones Stolen?" *Western Frontier,* Nov. 1975, p. 34. Rpt. *Western Frontier,* Annual, Winter 1977, p. 26.

Jones, John Caldwell. "Secret of Geronimo's Gold." *Western Frontier,* Special Issue, Sept. 1978, p. 32.

Lehman, Leola. "Geronimo: Terrible Avenger." *Real Frontier,* April 1971, p. 8. Rpt. *True Frontier,* Special Issue No. 14, 1975, p. 16.

Lijon, Paul J., with Dell Roensch. "Geronimo's Last Raid." *True Western Adventures,* Summer 1958, p. 45.

McCright, Grady E. "Geronimo and the Talking Light." *True Frontier,* Oct. 1977, p. 22.

Mooney, Charles W. "Why Geronimo Killed." *Western Round-Up,* Nov. 1970, p. 18. Rpt. *Pioneer West,* Nov. 1973, p. 8; *Pioneer West,* Jan. 1976, p. 27; and *Oldtimers Wild West,* Oct. 1976, p. 14.

Reis, Judy R. "An Unlikely Power Struggle." *True West,* Feb. 1991, p. 26.

Roberts, Brigadier General Charles D. "I Met Geronomo." *Frontier Times,* Fall 1962, p. 18.

Rozar, Lily-B. "Taming of a Savage." *Pioneer West,* Feb. 1972, p. 38. Rpt. *Oldtimers Wild West,* May 1975, p. 60.

Sanchez, Lynda. "Geronimo's Wives." *Old West,* Summer 1978, p. 14.

Savage, G.L. "The Chief Who Collected Hats." *The West,* March 1969, p. 22. Rpt. *The West,* Dec. 1972, p. 23.

Sharrock, Thomas. "Geronimo: The Captive Warrior." *Real West,* Americana Series, Winter 1963, p. 46.

Skinner, Woody. Letter. *True West,* April 1989, p. 6.

Taylor, Blaine. "Warrior Tactics Adopted." *Wild West,* June 1988, p. 19.

Vanderwerth, W.C. "Geronimo: Justice of the Peace." *True Frontier,* Feb. 1973, p. 8.

Gholson, Sam
Bedingfield, John "Dub." "The Spikes-Gholson Feud." *Real West,* Dec. 1985, p. 18. Rpt. *Real West,* Annual , Summer 1986, p. 24.

Gibbon, John
Forrest, Earle R. "Big Hole Battlefield." *Frontier Times,* Sept. 1965, p. 6.

Spendlove, Earl. "Battle at Big Horn Basin." *Great West,* Dec. 1973, p. 6. Rpt. *Authentic West,* Spring 1981, p. 6.

Stanley, Samuel. "Joseph's Nez Percé: The Last Retreat." *The West,* Aug. 1973, p. 28.

Werner, Fred W. "Big Hole: Nez Percé Badge of Courage." *Real West,* Jan. 1981, p. 36.

Gibbons, Augustus
Rasch, Philip J. "Death Comes to Saint Johns." *NOLA Quarterly,* Vol. VII, No. 3, Autumn 1983, p. 1.

Gibbons, Charlie
Ekker, Barbara B. "Charlie Gibbons, Friend of the Wild Bunch." *NOLA Quarterly,* Vol. III, No. 2, Autumn 1977, p. 13.

Gibbs, Elijah
Rasch, Philip J. "The Lake County War." *Real West,* Yearbook, Fall 1984, p. 62.

Gilbert, William T. "Bill"
Gilles, Albert S., Sr. "Bill Gilbert and Al Jennings." *Western Frontier,* Fall 1974, p. 16.

Gildea, Augustine Montague "Gus"
Rasch, Philip J. "Gus Gildea: An Arizone Pioneer." *English Westerners' Brand Book,* Vol. XXIII, No. 2, Summer 1985, p. 1.

Giles, James J.
Jones, Calico. "The Jekyll-Hyde Killer." *Wild West,* Nov. 1971, p. 46.

Gillett, James B. "Jim"
Bloom, Sam. "The Christmas That Became a Nightmare." *The West,* Jan. 1973, p. 30.

Cunningham, Eugene. "The Fightin'est Ranger." *Frontier Times,* Winter 1957-58, p. 20. Rpt. *Old West,* Fall 1978, p. 26.

Edwards, Harold L. "Trouble in Socorro." *Old West,* Winter 1990, p. 42.

Gillespie, Thomas P. "Fight on the Concho Plains." *True West,* June 1963, p. 32.

Jones, Calico. "Guns at the Ready." *True Frontier,* July 1971, p. 24.

Metz, Leon C. "An Incident at Christmas." *NOLA Quarterly,* Vol. XIV, No. 1, 1990, p. 1.

_____, and Kenneth A. Goldblatt. "Murdered in Church." *Frontier Times,* Nov. 1969, p. 32.

"True Western Hall of Fame" column. *True Western Adventures,* Aug. 1959, p. 66.

Walker, Wayne T. "Jim Gillett: Ranger Diablo." *Real West,* June 1980, p. 18.

_____. "Jim Gillett: The Ranger They Called Diablo!" *Great West,* June 1971, p. 6.

_____. "Jim Gillett, 'Sergeant Diablo' of the Texas Rangers." *Oldtimers Wild West,* Feb. 1978, p. 6.

_____. "Ranger Gillett: Texas' Town Tamer." *The West,* Aug. 1974, p. 34.

Gilliam, Cornelius
Hall, Patrick. "Cornelius Gilliam: Born to Lead." *The West,* May 1967, p. 42.

Gilliland, James "Jim"
O'Neal, Bill. "Pat Garrett's Posse vs Oliver Lee and James Gilliland" ("Great Western Gunfights" column). *True West,* Nov. 1991, p. 60.

Gladden, George W.
Johnson, Dave. "G.W. Gladden: Hard Luck Warrior." *NOLA Quarterly,* Vol. XV, No. 3, July-Sept. 1991, p. 1.

Glanton, John
Lindermuth, J.R. "Gunfighters and Lawmen" column. *Wild West,* Feb. 1991, p. 8.

Glass, Charley
Kirkpatrick, J.R. "Charley Glass: Black Cowboy Man of Mystery." *Real West,* Dec. 1974, p. 22.

Glass, Hugh
Bailey, Tom. "The Man Who Wouldn't Die." *True Western Adventures,* Oct. 1958, p. 7.

Beardsley, J.L. "The Hunter Who Died Twice." *Pioneer West,* Feb. 1972, p. 19. Rpt. *Pioneer West,* June 1975, p. 19.

Bracewell, Rozella. "A Study in Bravery: Hugh Glass Crawled Two Hundred Miles From His Grave to Life." *Frontier West,* Feb. 1973, p. 30.

Covington, E. Gorton. "Alone and Left to Die." *True West,* Oct. 1962, p. 46.

du Bois, Charles G. "The Glass That Wouldn't Break." *Old West,* Winter 1987, p. 30.

Lewis, Emily H. "Hugh Glass: Mountain Man." *Great West,* Feb. 1969, p. 39.

Neffendorf, Roy C. "He Came Back to Life—and Hate." *Golden West,* Nov. 1973, p. 28.

Wiltsey, Norman B. "A Man Don't Quit." *Real West,* June 1968, p. 35.

Young, Bob. "Hugh Glass' Empty Revenge." *Real West,* May 1964, p. 14.

Glazier, Willard

Egan, William. "Capt. Willard Glazier: Forgotten Hero." *True West,* March 1991, p. 23.

Glispin, James

Parsons, Chuck. "James Glispin, Nineteenth Century Minnesota Sheriff." *Real West,* March 1981, p. 6. Rpt. *Real West,* Yearbook 1981, p. 35.

Gobles, Reese

Parsons, Chuck. "Reese Gobles: Predator." *NOLA Quarterly,* Vol. XIV, No. 2, Summer 1990, p. 3.

Godey, Alexis

Bartholomew, Virginia. "Alexis Godey's Kinship With Risk." *Frontier Times,* Nov. 1970, p. 24.

Upjohn, Carl. "Godey's Dance of Death." *The West,* Sept. 1965, p. 18. Rpt. *The West,* Nov. 1973, p. 10.

Godfrey, Holon

"The Child Killer of Julesburg Junction." *Westerner,* Jan.-Feb. 1973, p. 28.

Godfroy, Frederick

McCright, Grady E. "Death of an Indian Agency Clerk." *Real West,* May 1979, p. 41.

Goff, Thomas Jefferson "Tom"

Sparks, John E. "Tom Goff, Texas Ranger." *True West,* Dec. 1987, p. 14.

Goins, Archie

Sheller, Roscoe. "The Killing Needed Doing." *Golden West,* Oct. 1974, p. 26.

Gokliya

Grady, Gwynn, and Ray Hogan. "Bitter Sunset." *Old West,* Summer 1966, p. 24.

Goldsby, Clarence

Etter, Jim. "Cherokee Bill's Brother." *True West,* Oct. 1974, p. 14.

Goldsby, Crawford "Cherokee Bill"

Braun, Bill. "The Life and Hard Times of Crawford Goldsby." *True Frontier,* Oct. 1974, p. 20. Rpt. *True Frontier,* July 1977, p. 30.

Breihan, Carl W. "Cherokee Bill Goldsby." *Real West,* Jan. 1970, p. 42. Rpt. *Oldtimers Wild West,* Dec. 1978, p. 10.

_____. "Desperate Men, Desperate Guns." *Real West,* Annual, Winter 1977-78, p. 16.

"Cherokee Bill." *Gunslingers of the West,* Winter 1966, p. 19.

DeMattos, Jack. "Cherokee Bill" ("Gunfighters of the Real West" column). *Real West,* Sept. 1980, p. 16.

Gordon, Wes. "Cherokee Bill." *Man's Western,* Aug.-Sept. 1959, p. 28.

Havelock-Bailie, R. "Cherokee Bill's Last Stand." *True Western Adventures,* Spring 1958, p. 36.

Hayden, Lucas. "The Desperate Manhunt for Blood Killer Cherokee Bill." *Frontier West,* Dec. 1971, p. 38.

Lehman, M.P. "A Good Day for Dying." *The West,* Feb. 1972, p. 28.

Monan, Charles. "Unlucky Thirteen." *Real West,* July 1960, p. 43.

Penot, Barbara Hale. "The Hanging of Cherokee Bill." *True Frontier,* Jan. 1969, p. 12. Rpt. *True Frontier,* Special Issue No. 1, 1971, p. 48.

Winston, Morris. "A Murderer Is Loose On the Cherokee Strip." *Great West,* April 1967, p. 13.

Gooch, Benjamin

Polk, Stella Gibson. "Benjamin Gooch's Live Oaks." *True West,* Oct. 1976, p. 29.

Good, Harmon "Hi"

Repp, Ed Earl. "Massacre at Rock Creek." *Western Frontier,* Annual, Spring 1981, p. 38.

Good, Joseph "Joe"

Harvey, James E. "Joe Good of Brown's Park." *Frontier Times,* Dec. 1963, p. 30.

Goodall, John W.

Koller, Joe. "John W. Goodall: Dakota Badlander." *Golden West,* July 1969, p. 16.

Goodell, George

DeArment, R.K. "George 'Red' Goodell, Forgotten Gunfighter." *NOLA Quarterly,* Vol. XIII, No. 4, 1989, p. 8.

Goodfellow, George Emery

Shandorf, Peter. "'Man's Best Friend' Dr. George Goodfellow." *True West,* July 1987, p. 14.

Traywick, Ben T. "Tombstone's Dr. Goodfellow." *Real West,* Dec. 1983, p. 26. Rpt. *Real West,* Yearbook, Fall 1984, p. 36.

Goodnight, Charles "Charlie"

Baker, Glen. "The Fabulous Charlie Goodnight." *True West,* Dec. 1959, p. 20.

Haley, J. Evetts. "The Making of a Scout." *True West,* June 1966, p. 6.

Holding, Vera. "Charlie Goodnight, Trail Blazer." *Westerner,* May-June 1969, p. 8.

Kevin, Glen. "Fence Cutting Led to Slaughter." *Frontier West,* Oct. 1972, p. 52.

Stanley, Samuel. "'Colonel' Charles Goodnight, Trail-Blazing Cattleman of the Southwest." *Pioneer West,* Jan. 1978, p. 14.

Wallace, George A. "Cattle Kings." *True West,* Feb. 1964, p. 6.

Goodrich Brothers (Jake and Willie)

Nelson, Andre. "The Last Sheepman-Cattleman War." *True West,* May 1988, p. 14.

Gordon, Jack

Austerman, Wayne R. "Unholy Terror Cornered." *Wild West,* June 1990, p. 35.

Gordon, John. "Trouble at the Illegal Stockade." *The West,* Sept. 1973, p. 9.

Gore, Lou

Brand, George R. "The Amazing Lou Gore." *The West,* Jan. 1965, p. 34.

Stone, Fred R. "A Woman Called 'Lou.'" *Real West,* Aug. 1958, p. 36.

Gore, Sir St. George

Grabill, Minton R. "Bloody Gore and the Buffaloes." *The West,* Dec. 1965, p. 14.

Gotebo

Echols, Lee E. "The Kiowa Raiders of Rainy Mountain." *True West,* April 1978, p. 6.

Gough, John B. "Catfish Kid"

Kildare, Maurice. "Hellacious Catfish Kid." *Real West,* July 1974, p. 8.

Gould, George
Bloom, Sam. "The Railroad Scramble." *Real West,* April 1980, p. 32.

Gouyen
Ball, Eve. "The Vengeance of Gouyen." *Real West,* Americana Series, Winter 1966, p. 21.

Graham Clan.
Breihan, Carl W. "Death in Pleasant Valley." *The West,* Feb. 1970, p. 14.

Bruce, John. "When Death Came to Tonto Basin." *Real West,* Nov. 1960, p. 38.

Combs, Richard. "War in the Tonto." *Real West,* Oct. 1986, p. 5.

Forrest, Earle R. "The Old West's Bloodiest Feud." *NOLA Quarterly,* Vol. IX, No. 2, Autum 1984, p. 1.

Guttman, Jon. "Unpleasant Valley War." *Wild West,* Oct. 1990, p. 19.

Kildare, Maurice. "Cabin Bushwhack." *Real West,* Jan. 1969, p. 17.

————. "The Horrible Graham-Tewksbury Feud." *Real West,* Nov. 1967, p. 14.

————. "Long Remember." *True West,* Feb. 1969, p. 22.

————. "Posse Bushwhack." *Great West,* July 1968, p. 40.

Millard, Joseph. "Valley of Blood." *True Western Adventures,* Dec. 1959, p. 8.

O'Neal, Bill. "Graham War Party vs Tewksburys" ("Great Western Gunfights" column). *True West,* May 1990, p. 54.

Peterson, Marc. "The Tonto Basin War." *Old West,* Summer 1965, p. 38.

Smith, Richard C. "Arizona's Bloodiest Feud." *Pioneer West,* May 1968, p. 20.

Stanley, Samuel. "The Pleasant Valley War in Arizona." *Oldtimers Wild West,* Aug. 1977, p. 23.

Graham, Isaac
Repp, Ed Earl. "Buckskin Derby." *The West,* Dec. 1973, p. 12.

Graham, Tom
Smith, McDougal. "Horse Thieves Called Him 'The Bloodhound.'" *Real West,* Aug. 1983, p. 32. Rpt. *Real West,* Annual, Spring 1984, p. 31.

Graham, William Hicks "Will"
Secrest, William B. "Fast Guns in Old California." *Real West,* June 1980, p. 10. Rpt. *Real West,* Special Issue, 1981, p. 6.

————. "Fire Eater: The Saga of Will Hicks Graham." *True West,* May 1991, p. 14.

Grant, George
Hager, Jean. "When the British Colonized Kansas." *The West,* Sept. 1973, p. 34.

Grant, Ulysses Simpson "Sam"
Hoopes, Chad L. "The Unhappy Officer at Fort Humbolt." *The West,* Oct. 1967, p. 10.

Kyllo, Joan. "Sam Grant on the West Coast." *The West,* Feb. 1974, p. 16.

Lewis, Lloyd. "Capt. Sam Grant: The Dissolution of a Soldier." *True West,* June 1967, p. 12.

Rosenhouse, Leo. "When Ulysses S. Grant Resigned from the Army." *True Frontier,* May 1970, p. 8. Rpt. *True Frontier,* Aug. 1974, p. 25.

Wingfield, William. "Grant Before Greatness." *Real West,* June 1975, p. 8.

Grattan, John L.
Bailey, Tom. "The White Invaders." *True West,* Aug. 1963, p. 14.

Ballenger, Dean W. "How Joel Flader's Cow Caused a Sioux Massacre." *Frontier West,* Feb. 1973, p. 40.

Eastin, Stephen. "Grattan Massacre: The Battle of the Ten Dollar Cow." *Real West,* July 1973, p. 26.

Judge, Bill. "The Grattan Massacre." *True West,* April 1962, p. 27.

Graves, Charlie
McGurr, Marty. "Two Gun Vengeance." *Man's Western,* Jan. 1960, p. 18.

Graydon, James "Paddy"
Hicks, Flora. "The Passing of Paddy Graydon." *Frontier Times,* July 1969, p. 30.

Greathouse, James "Jim"
Robbins, Lance. "A Dream Gone Wrong." *Real West,* July 1968, p. 19.

Kildare, Maurice. "Whiskey Jim Greathouse." *Real West,* Aug. 1972, p. 54. Rpt. *Real West,* Yearbook, Spring 1974, p. 58.

"The Great Western" (see Bowman, Sarah A.)

Green, D.R. "Cannonball"
Shirley, Glenn. "Jehu of the Stage Lines." *Westerner,* March-April 1969, p. 8.

Greene, William C.
Dodge, Matt. "Jim Burnett: The Law in Charleston." *Real West,* April 1982, p.

16. Rpt. *Real West,* Annual, Spring 1983, p. 37.

Jones, George. "Fightingest Man of the West." *True West,* Oct. 1959, p. 14.

Mason, Frank. "The Baron of Cananea." *Frontier Times,* Dec.-Jan. 1963, p. 20. Rpt. *Old West,* Spring 1980, p. 8.

O'Neal, Bill. "The Cananea Riots of 1906." *Real West,* Aug. 1984, p. 34. Rpt. *Real West,* Annual, Spring 1985, p. 26.

Traywick, Ben T. "Copper King of Cananea." *Golden West,* Nov. 1970, p. 16. Rpt. *The West,* May 1974, p. 26.

Greenwood, Caleb

McCarroll, Ralph. "I Married a Crow." *True West,* April 1965, p. 24.

O'Neal, Harold. "Gold Lake Liar." *The West,* Jan. 1974, p. 20.

Repp, Ed Earl. "Wagons Over the Sierras." *True Frontier,* June 1973, p. 12.

Greer Brothers (Nat, Dick, Harris)

Kildare, Maurice. "Arizona's Fighting Greers." *Real West,* Nov. 1966, p. 32.

Greer, Edward W. "Ed"

Ernst, Robert R., and Angie Greer Berkstresser. "Ed Greer: Small Town Marshall." *NOLA Quarterly,* Vol. XIV, No. 1, 1990, p. 6.

Gregg, Josiah

Kyllo, Joan. "Santa Fe Trader." *Frontier Times,* Jan. 1965, p. 20.

Von Kreider, Max. "Josiah Gregg: Frontier Scientist." Part I, *The West,* Sept. 1969, p. 18; Part II, *The West,* Oct. 1969, p. 26.

Gregory, John

Meaders, Margaret. "Mystery Man of the Colorado Goldfields." *Frontier Times,* March 1975, p. 20.

Grey, Zane

Early, Eleanor. "He Made the West Famous." *True West,* April 1969, p. 20.

Farley, G.M. "Zane Grey: Man of the West." *Real West,* Sept. 1972, p. 26.

Lazaru, Leon. "Zane Grey." *Man's Western,* Jan. 1960, p. 36.

Gridley, Reuel Colt

Auer, Louise. "Nevada's Sack of Golden Flour." *Real West,* Sept. 1963, p. 41.

Grubb, Bob. "The Double-Barrelled Election." *True Frontier,* Feb. 1975, p. 25.

Rpt. *True Frontier,* Feb. 1977, p. 33.

Noren, Evelyn. "Reuel Gridley: Civil War Hero Without a Gun." *True West,* May 1987, p. 44.

"The Quarter Million Dollar Sack of Flour." Rpt. *Great West,* Feb. 1968, p. 30.

Smith, Alson J. "The Strange Pay-Off." *Frontier Times,* Sept. 1965, p. 13.

Griego, Francisco "Pancho"

Rasch, Philip J. "Sudden Death in Cimarron." *NOLA Quarterly,* Vol. X, No. 4, Spring 1986, p. 6.

Rasch, Philip J. "Taking a Closer Look at Cimarron Murders." *NOLA Quarterly,* Vol. III, No. 3, Winter 1978, p. 8.

Grierson, Benjamin H.

Miles, Bob. "Nine Against a Hundred." *Old West,* Fall 1971, p. 20.

Robb, Berniece. "Parched Horror on the Staked Plains." *Golden West,* April 1974, p. 40.

Underwood, Larry. "Colonel Grierson and the Buffalo Soldiers." *True West,* May 1989, p. 46.

Wiltsey, Norman B. "Hawks of the Desert." *True West,* Dec. 1955, p. 19.

Grijalva, Merejildo

Bentz, Donald N. "El Chivero of Arizona." *Golden West,* May 1972, p. 30.

Meketa, Jacqueline. "Grijalva's Apache Revenge." *Old West,* Fall 1986, p. 14.

Grimes, Absalom Carlisle

Breihan, Carl W. "No Prison Could Hold HIm." *The West,* Jan. 1974, p. 38. Rpt. *Western Frontier,* Annual, Winter 1977, p. 32.

Stephens, Robert W. "Ambush in the Chaparral." *Frontier Times,* May 1967, p. 30.

Grosch Brothers (Hosea and Allen)

Kaltenbach, Peter J. "The Secret of the Grosches." *True West,* Feb. 1975, p. 8.

Grouard, Frank (sometimes spelled "Gruard")

"The Cavalry Troop Sitting Bull Couldn't Massacre." *Western Frontier,* Jan. 1977, p. 8.

Kutac, C. "The Loyalty of Frank Grouard." *Real West,* Sept. 1981, p. 40. Rpt. *Real West,* Yearbook, Fall 1982, p. 63.

Malden, George R. "Saga of a Great Scout." *The West,* Aug. 1965, p. 44. Rpt. *The West,* April 1974, p. 38.

Qualey, J.H. "Gruard's Amazing Retreat." *Real West,* July 1962, p. 28.

Stanley, Samuel. "Milk River Run Was a Trail Straight from Hell." *Frontier West,* Feb. 1973, p. 32.

Steed, Jack. "The Sibley Scout: Frank Grouard's Greatest Challenge." *Old West,* Fall 1988, p. 16.

Grounds, William F. "Billy"

Bailey, Tom. "Arizona's Buried Treasure Mystery." *True Western Adventures,* Summer 1958, p. 8.

Boyer, Glenn G. "Murder at Millville." *Real West,* April 1983, p. 10.

Hill, Janaloo. "Yours Until Death, William Grounds." *True West,* April 1973, p. 14.

Kildare, Maurice. "The Desperado Kids." *Real West,* Dec. 1968, p. 11.

O'Neal, Bill. "Deputy Sheriff Billy Breakenridge vs Zweig Hunt and Billy Grounds" ("Great Western Gunfights" column). *True West,* July 1991, p. 59.

Rasch, Philip J. "The Brief Careers of Billy Grounds and Zwing Hunt." *Real West,* Feb. 1985, p. 12. Rpt. *Real West,* Yearbook, Winter 1986, p. 57.

Grover, Abner T. "Sharp"

Dahl, Peter Andrew. "Battle at Beecher's Island." *Real West,* Jan. 1958, p. 6.

Mastin, Venita. "Sharp Grover: One Hundred Percent Hero or a Good Deal Less." *Old West,* Winter 1977, p. 18.

Oakes, George. "I Fought at Beecher's Island." *True West,* Oct. 1956, p. 18.

Walker, Wayne T. "Fighting Army Scouts of the Indian Wars." *Great West,* June 1972, p. 14. Rpt. *Authentic West,* Fall 1981, p. 16.

Guerrier, Edmund

Bird, Roy. "Edmund Guerrier, Half-Breed Army Scout." *Real West,* Dec. 1982, p. 34. Rpt. *Real West,* Yearbook, Fall 1983, p. 22.

Gunness, Belle

Ketchum, E.D. "The Gunness Monster." *Westerner,* Jan.-Feb. 1975, p. 26.

Gunnison, John W.

Dixon, Madoline C. "The Gunnison Massacre." *True West,* July 1985, p. 34.

Groesbeck, Kathryn D. "The Gunnison Massacre." *Frontier Times,* Winter 1961, p. 21.

Pendlove [sic, Spendlove], Earl S. "Massacre at Sevier Lake." *Real West,* March 1962, p. 26.

Spendlove, Earl S. "Moshoquop's Terrible Revenge." *The West,* April 1967, p. 10.

Hackett, George M.
Boessenecker, John. "George Hackett: Terror to Road Agents." *Old West,* Fall 1987, p. 14.

Hadji Ali "Hi Jolly" (see Ali, Hadji)

Hailey, John
Koller, Joe. "John Hailey: Stagecoach King of Idaho." *Golden West,* March 1965, p. 8.

Haines, Wiley Green
Haines, Joe D., Jr. "A Sensational Hold-Up." *True West,* Jan. 1984, p. 44.

_____. "Wiley Haines Was a Courageous Frontier Lawman." *NOLA Quarterly,* Vol. VIII, No. 1, Summer 1983, p. 1.

Shirley, Glenn. "His Guns Tamed the Osage Nation." *Westerner,* Sept. 1970, p. 22.

_____. "The Murdering Martins." *True Western Adventures,* Aug. 1960, p. 18.

Haldeman Brothers (Thomas and William)
Haynes, George. "Four Lives for Twenty Dollars." *Real West,* May 1959, p. 8.

Hale, William "Bill"
Gray, Morton. "The Cowboy Who Would Be King." *Real West,* May 1959, p. 32.

Holding, Vera. "King of the Killers." *True Frontier,* April 1973, p. 23.

Hall, Calvin
Robertson, Dorothy. "'Or Junipers Will Bear Strange Fruit.'" *True Frontier,* Oct. 1976, p. 36.

Hall, Dick Wick

Bloom, Sam. "Who Was Dick Wick Hall?" *Real West*, Nov. 1972, p. 42.

Kildare, Maurice. "Spinning Fancy Yarns Was a Fine Art." *Frontier West*, Dec. 1974, p. 36.

Hall, Lee (Jesse Leigh Hall)

DeMattos, Jack. "Lee Hall" ("Gunfighters of the Real West" column). *Real West*, Aug. 1984, p. 38. Rpt. *Real West*, Yearbook 1986, p. 63.

Young, Bob. "He Whipped Rowdy Denison Into Shape." *NOLA Quarterly*, Vol. XII, No. 2, Fall 1987, p. 13.

Halsell Brothers (H.H. and Oscar)

Halsell, H.H. "Cowboys and Cattleland." *Old West*, Fall 1971, p. 28.

Halsell, Oscar D. "O.D."

Roberts, Gary L. "Hamilton Rayner and the Shoot-Out at Pat Hanly's Saloon." *Real West*, Oct. 1985, p. 19.

Ham, Caiaphas Kennard

Yarbrough, C.L. "In Search of Los Almagres." *Vanishing Texas*, May 1981, p. 12.

Hamblin, Jacob

Armstrong, Nancy M. "Jacob Hamblin, Peacemaker to the Indians." *Real West*, May 1979, p. 50.

Clanton, Chet. "Jacob Hamblin: The Mormon Scout." *Great West*, Dec. 1969, p. 46.

Kildare, Maurice. "Jacob Hamblin: Cowardly Saint in Buckskin." *True Frontier*, March 1969, p. 28. Rpt. *True Frontier*, Aug. 1976, p. 42.

Koller, Joe. "Jacob Hamblin, Saint In Buckskins." *Golden West*, Jan. 1966, p. 10.

Olson, Roy J. "The Peacemaker." *Frontier Times*, Fall 1960, p. 22.

Spendlove, Earl. "Jacob and the Mormon Murder." *Real West*, March 1965, p. 32.

_____. "Let Me Die in Peace." *The West*, May 1971, p. 10.

Hamilton, Louis McLane

Irons, Angie. "Capt. Louis Hamilton: The Gentleman Officer." *Old West*, Spring 1988, p. 30.

Hand, Dora (Fannie Keenan)

Ferguson, John F. "Truth About Dora Hand." *The West*, Aug. 1965, p. 18. Rpt. *The West*, Sept. 1974, p. 12.

Hendricks, John S. Letter. *Real West,* Jan. 1962, p. 76.

Mays, Carelton. "Mystery of Dora Hand." *Real West,* May 1959, p. 14.

Moffat, Charles. "The Strange Life of Dora Hand." *Western Tales,* June 1960, p. 30.

Hanks Gang

Gettman, Lawrence. "The Leader of the Hanks Bunch Was the Town's Most Liberated Redhead." *Frontier West,* Oct. 1975, p. 26.

Hanks, Orlando Camilla (Camillo) "Deaf Charlie"

Kildare, Maurice. "Deaf Charley Hanks." *Real West,* Dec. 1973, p. 30.

Kindred, Wayne. "The Ice Wagon Affair." *True West,* Feb. 1987, p. 20.

Parsons, Chuck. "Deaf Charley and the Taylor-Sutton Feud" ("Answer Man" column). *True West,* June 1989, p. 12.

Stell, Col. Thomas M. "The Killing of Camilla Hanks." *Frontier Times,* March 1979, p. 9.

Hannan, James "Jim"

Kildare, Maurice. "My Name Is James Hannan." *The West,* Oct. 1974, p. 22.

Ha-Nu-Cah (Captain Jim)

Cerveri, Doris. "Paiute Leaders." *Real West,* Special Issue, Spring 1972, p. 14.

Hardin, Joe

Shoemaker, Arthur. "Mysterious Joe Hardin." *True West,* Feb. 1988, p. 56.

Hardin, John Wesley

Archer, Jules. "The Forty Notches of John Wesley Hardin." *Western Action,* Sept. 1960, p. 20.

Ballenger, Dean W. "The Violent Legend of John Wesley Hardin." *Frontier West,* Aug. 1971, p. 20.

Bourne, McNeal. "Keeping Score on John Wesley Hardin." *NOLA Quarterly,* Vol. X, No. 4, Spring 1986, p. 17.

Conant, Lora M. "Hang Them High." *Great West,* Feb. 1969, p. 12.

DeMattos, Jack. "John Wesley Hardin" ("Gunfighters of the Real West" column). *Real West,* April 1984, p. 44. Rpt. *Real West,* Annual, Spring 1985, p. 46.

Dixon, David. "Four Sixes to Beat." *True Western Adventures,* June 1960, p. 34.

Ellison, Douglas W. "Rivals in Texas: Hardin and Longley." *NOLA Quarterly,* Vol. XII, No. 4, Spring 1988, p. 10.

"Gallery of Gunmen: No. 1, John Wesley Hardin." *True Western Adventures*, Feb. 1960, p. 62.

Gluck, Harold. "Some Shooting!" *True West*, Aug. 1957, p. 13.

Lane, John M. "I Saw Wes Hardin Back Down." *Real West*, July 1963, p. 20.

Lawson, Norris. Letter, "John Wesley Hardin's Daughter." *Frontier Times*, Feb. 1985, p. 5.

Lehman, M.P. "Loose Guns and Notched Handles." *The West*, March 1966, p. 26. Rpt. *Western Frontier*, Sept. 1975, p. 16; and *Western Frontier*, July 1983, p. 16.

Metz, Leon C. "Last Days of John Wesley Hardin." *The West*, Sept. 1967, p. 10. Rpt. *Golden West*, March 1972, p. 18; *Western Frontier*, Special Issue, Fall 1974, p. 8; and *Western Frontier*, Jan. 1983, p. 8.

Nordyke, Lewis. "Killer Champ." *Frontier Times*, Spring 1958, p. 4.

Parsons, Chuck. "Answer Man" column. *True West*, Dec. 1983, p. 36.

————. "Destroying the Hardin Gang." *NOLA Quarterly*, Vol. V, No. 4, April 1980, p. 1.

————. "John Wesley Hardin and the Texas Rangers." *NOLA Quarterly*, Vol. II, No. 1, Spring 1975, p. 9.

————. "John Wesley Hardin as Author." *NOLA Quarterly*, Vol. V, No. 2, January 1980, p. 6.

————. "A Telegram for Mr. Hardin, August 19, 1895." *Real West*, Nov. 1977, p. 30.

————. "A Texas Gunfighter and the Kansas Murder Family." *Real West*, July 1980, p. 32. Rpt. *Real West*, Annual 1981, p. 14.

————. "Who Was the Fastest Gunman, James B. 'Wild Bill' Hickok or John W. 'Little Arkansas' Hardin?" *NOLA Quarterly*, Vol. I, No. 3, 1975, p. 8.

Repp, Ed Earl. "John Wesley Hardin: Rebel With a Six-Gun." *True Frontier*, July 1969, p. 22. Rpt. *True Frontier*, Special Issue No. 5, 1973, p. 6; and *True Frontier*, June 1976, p. 57.

Rothe, Aline. "Where Wes Hardin Started Running." *Frontier Times*, July 1977, p. 36.

Schuessler, Raymond. "Child Prodigy With a Six-Gun." *Pioneer West*, May 1969, p. 18.

"Shootout at Abilene." *Man's Western*, Jan 1960, p. 43.

Smith, Martin. "The Arrest of John Wesley Hardin." *Westerner*, Jan. 1971, p. 11.

Whittington, Michael. "Six Telegrams That Tell a Story: The Arrest of John Wesley Hardin." *NOLA Quarterly*, Vol. XI, No. 2, Fall 1986, p. 8.

Wiltsey, Norman B. "Forty Times a Killer." *Frontier Times*, Jan. 1964, p. 6.

_____. "Gunfighter." Part I, *Real West,* Oct. 1968, p. 34; Part II, *Real West,* Nov. 1968, p. 37.

Wright, A.J. "A Gunfighter's Southern Vacation." *NOLA Quarterly,* Vol. VII, No. 3, Autumn 1982, p. 12.

_____. "John Wesley Hardin's Missing Years." *Old West,* Fall 1981, p. 6.

Wukovits, John F. "Gunfighters and Lawmen" column. *Wild West,* June 1990, p. 12.

Hardwick, Thomas W.
Kildare, Maurice. "Thomas W. Hardwick: Green River Renegade." *Real West,* Oct. 1970, p. 13.

Hargins, Bertha
Williston, Avery. "It Took a Woman to Tame the Toughest Town in Wyoming." *Frontier West,* April 1972, p. 44.

Harkey, Dee
Lofton, Monk. "Mean As Hell." *True West,* April 1959, p. 20

Harney, William Shelby
Coyer, Richard J. "We'll Never Forgive Old Harney." *True West,* July 1982, p. 22.

Kutac, C. "The Sioux Called Him 'The Wasp.'" *Real West,* March 1981, p. 30. Rpt. *Real West,* Annual, Spring 1982, p. 57.

Harold, Jim (Jim Taylor, Jim Morgan)
Rasch, Philip J. "Death of a Bank Robber." *NOLA Quarterly,* Vol. VII, No. 2, Summer 1983, p. 10.

Harony, Mary Catherine "Big Nose Kate" (see Cummings, Mary K.)

Harowick, Tom
Howell, Deal. "The Sweet Grass Hills Massacre." *The West,* Feb. 1965, p. 20.

Harpe Brothers
Wert, Jeffry D. "Cutthroats of Ohio's Cave-in-Rock." *Wild West,* June 1989, p. 19.

Wiltsey, Norman B. "The Bloody Brothers Harpe." *Real West,* Aug. 1973, p. 55.

Harrell, Milvern
Howell, Montie. "The Woods Clan and the Dawson Massacre." *True West,* June 1988, p. 52.

Harrington, Frank
Qualey, Jake. "Frank Harrington's Bloody Revenge." *Real West,* May 1960, p. 24.

Harris, Frank "Shorty"
Buist, Lois W. "Personality" column. *Wild West,* Aug. 1990, p. 10.

Murray, Tom G. "Shorty Harris and the Bullfrog." *Old West,* Fall 1968, p. 30.

Robbins, Jhan and June. "America's Lowest Man." *True Western Adventures,* Feb. 1960, p. 22.

St. George, Tim. "Death Valley's Amazing Shorty Harris." *Real West,* Sept. 1961, p. 16.

Taylor, Paul. "The Man Who Walked to Gold." *Old West,* Fall 1989, p. 60.

Young, Bob and Jan. "The Man Who Was Buried Standing Up." *Old West,* Spring 1965, p. 32.

Harris, Sam
Ballenger, Dean W. "Sam Harris' Wild Journey Into Eternity." *Westerner,* Jan.-Feb. 1973, p. 42.

Preece, Harold. "Big Sam Harris." *Frontier West,* Aug. 1971, p. 16.

Harris, William H.
DeMattos, Jack. "Whatever Became of the Dodge City Peace Commission?" *Real West,* Jan. 1977, p. 38. Rpt. *Real West,* Yearbook, Summer 1978, p. 50.

Harrison, Charley
Brown, Alma Margaret. "Hand-Picked Jury in Hell." *True West,* Feb. 1968, p. 30.

Harshaw, David Tecumseh "Dave"
Miller, Halsey. "Silver From the Patagonias: The Harshaw Mines." *Old West,* Winter 1990, p. 37.

Hart, C.L. "Loss"
Mooney, Charles W. "The Man Who Killed Bill Dalton." *The West,* Feb. 1971, p. 38. Rpt. *Golden West,* Jan. 1974, p. 14; and *Western Frontier,* April 1983, p. 2.

Hart, Pearl

Auer, Louise. "Arizona's Lady Bandit." *Golden West,* March 1966, p. 14. Rpt. *Western Frontier,* May 1986, p. 32.

Breihan, Carl W. "Outlaw Lady: Pearl Hart." *Real West,* June 1970, p. 40. Rpt. *Real West,* Annual, Fall 1974, p. 74.

Brent, William and Milarde. "The Hell Hole." Part I, *Pioneer West,* July 1969, p. 18; Part II, *Pioneer West,* Sept. 1969, p. 28.

Grant, Maxwell. "Death Wore a Red Petticoat." *Westerner,* Jan.-Feb. 1972, p. 38.

Holding, Vera. "Pearl Hart: Last Lady Road Agent." *True Frontier,* Jan. 1970, p. 22. Rpt. *True Frontier,* April 1976, p. 22.

Kelley, Thomas P. "Unrequited Love Was the Secret Force That Drove the West's Lone Woman Bandit." *Frontier West,* April 1975, p. 34.

Kildare, Maurice. "Pearl Hart: Bandit Queen." *Real West,* Jan. 1967, p. 13.

Lake, Ivan Clyde. "Last Chance for the Widow Taylor's Pearl." *Golden West,* Nov. 1967, p. 14. Rpt. *Golden West,* Sept. 1972, p. 20; and *Western Frontier,* Special Issue, Fall 1974, p. 20.

Macklin, William F. "Pearl Hart: Scandal of the Southwest." *Real West,* Feb. 1985, p. 38. Rpt. *Real West,* Yearbook, Fall 1985, p. 44.

Mason, Frank. "Last Female Road Agent." *Real West,* Sept. 1960, p. 11.

"Pearl Hart." *Gunslingers of the West,* Winter 1966, p. 62.

Repp, Ed Earl. "Gunhawk in Skirts." *Pioneer West,* Jan. 1971, p. 42. Rpt. *Pioneer West,* Sept. 1975, p. 18.

Robbins, Lance. "Pearl Hart." *Real West,* Dec. 1970, p. 74.

Schreier, Konrad F., Jr. "Pearl Hart: More Sad Case Than Hard Case." *True West,* April 1983, p. 52.

Von Kreisler, Max. "Pearl Hart: Arizona's Girl Bandit." *Great West,* April 1973, p. 36.

Harvey, Alexander

Henry, R.C. "Butcher of the Piegans." *Western Round-Up,* Aug. 1970, p. 22. Rpt. *Oldtimers Wild West,* April 1976, p. 42.

Harvey, Ben

Phelps, Gary. "The Incredible Saga of Ben Harvey's All-Girl Desperado Gang." *Frontier West,* June 1975, p. 36.

Harvey, Fred

Howes, Nick. "Meals by Fred Harvey." *True Frontier,* Aug. 1975, p. 34.

Lambert, Fred. "The Harvey Houses." *Old West,* Summer 1966, p. 20.

Harvey, John "Captain Jack"
Rosa, Joseph G. "Captain Jack Harvey: The Story of An Unsung Hero." *Real West,*
    Aug. 1982, p. 18.

Harvey, William (Nicholas C. Creede)
Bayworth, Jerome. "Creede, Sin City of Colorado." *The West,* Sept. 1965, p. 40.

Hascal, Joel
Lupton, Glen. "The Merciless Justice Who Ruled the Frontier." *Frontier West,*
    June 1974, p. 32.

Haslam, Bob "Pony Bob"
Helfer, Harold. "Death Rides the Pony Express." *Western True Story,* Oct. 1971,
    p. 23.
Howes, Nick. "Haslam of the Pony Express." *Real West,* Sept. 1975, p. 12.
Sufrin, Mark. "The Pony Express Rider Who Saved the Nation." *Frontier West,*
    April 1972, p. 12.

Hastings, Lansford Warren
Grubb, Bob. "Death on the Devil's Trail." *True Frontier,* Jan. 1978, p. 12.
Simonds, A.J. "The Man Who Would Be President." *Real West,* Sept. 1970, p. 28.

Hathaway, John
Bailey, Tom. "Vengeance on the Oregon Trail." *True Western Adventures,* April
    1959, p. 42.

Hathaway, Seth
Hathaway, Seth. "The Adventures of a Buffalo Hunter." Rpt. *True West,* Feb.
    1969, p. 26.

Hauschel, Jake "Dutch"
Ballenger, Dean W. "Jake Hauschel's Gold Bars Were Buried in Blood."
    Westerner, May-June 1974, p. 36.

Haworth, James Mahlon
Irons, Angie. "Simpoquodle: The Fighting Quaker." *True West,* Aug. 1988, p. 40.

Hays, John C. "Jack"
Arnold, Jess. "Captain Jack." *True West,* Jan. 1955, p. 14.
Blount, Ben M. Letter, "Jack Hays." *True West,* Oct. 1979, p. 5.

Comtois, Pierre. "Gunfighters and Lawmen" column. *Wild West,* Feb. 1990, p. 8.

Davis, Russell. "He Founded the Texas Rangers." *Western True Story,* Oct. 1971, p. 30. Rpt. *America's Frontier West,* Issue No. 1, n.d., p. 20.

Hunter, J. Marvin, ed. "The Intrepid Texas Ranger." Rpt. *Old West,* Summer 1965, p. 68.

Nevin, David. "Rangers Who Wouldn't Die." *True Western Adventures,* Aug. 1960, p. 8.

"Plaque, Program in Memory of John C. Hays." *NOLA Quarterly,* Vol. VIII, No. 3, Winter 1983-84, p. 20.

Shulsinger, Stephanie C. "Colonel Jack Hays in California." *Real West,* Feb. 1973, p. 26.

————. "Colonel Jack Hays of the Texas Rangers." *Real West,* Dec. 1972, p. 24.

Head, Mark
Carson, Phil. "Personality" column. *Wild West,* Dec. 1989, p. 10.

Hearne, Samuel
Chapin, Earl V. "Samuel Hearne and His Journey to Coppermine." *Real West,* Sept. 1973, p. 28.

Heath, John (also spelled "Heith")
Carson, Xanthus. "The Tombstone Lynching of John Heith." *Real Frontier,* June 1970, p. 14.

Huber, Mrs. William C. Letter. *Real Frontier,* Dec. 1970, p. 4.

Mathers, Carolyn. "Hangman's Justice for a Bandit Judas." *True Frontier,* March 1968, p. 30. Rpt. *True Frontier,* Jan. 1974, p. 36; and *True Frontier,* Special Issue No. 17, Winter 1976, p. 10.

Ormes, Carl. "Blood at Bisbee." *Real West,* May 1959, p. 23.

Roensch, Dell. "Bisbee's Bath of Blood." *True Western Adventures,* Dec. 1959, p. 38.

Hedden, Cyrus
Collins, Orpha. "Ambush on the Coquille." *True West,* Aug. 1963, p. 44.

Wylie, Howard. "An Incredible Journey to Save a Friend." *Golden West,* Aug. 1974, p. 34. Rpt. *Western Frontier,* March 1977, p. 34.

Hedden, John
Collins, Ellen. "John Hedden of Scottsburg." *True West,* June 1963, p. 41.

Fitzgerald, Arlene. "Siege at Battle Rock." *The West,* May 1973, p. 32. Rpt. *Western Frontier,* May 1976, p. 18.

Meier, Gary. "Fifteen Days on Battle Rock." *True West,* April 1988, p. 14.

Hedgepeth, Marion

Cody, Lance. "The Deadly Dude." *Western Tales,* April 1960, p. 16.

Ditzel, Paul. "Have Derby: Will Kill!" *True Western Adventures,* June 1959, p. 8.

Fox, Charles. "The Outlaw in My Family." *NOLA Quarterly,* Vol. XII, No. 3, Winter 1988, p. 8.

Parsons, Chuck. "Little Known Badman" ("Answer Man" column). *True West,* Nov. 1990, p. 13.

Thomas, William. "Handsome Marion Hedgepeth, Montana Bank Robber." *Real West,* July 1966, p. 29.

Von Kreisler, Max. "The Killer in the Derby Hat." *Oldtimers Wild West,* Dec. 1978, p. 7.

Heinze, F. Augustus

Clark, Helen. "The Copper Kings." *Pioneer West,* Sept. 1969, p. 24. Rpt. *Pioneer West,* Aug. 1972, p. 36.

Harrison, John H. "A Man to Rule the Mines." *Westerner,* March 1971, p. 40.

Helm, Boone

Barker, Bill. "Boone Helm, Man Beast of the Frontier." *Real West,* Dec. 1971, p. 32. Rpt. *Real West,* Annual 1972, p. 38.

Freeman, Frank M. "Many's the Poor Devil I've Killed." *The West,* July 1969, p. 22.

LaTelle, G.H. "Boone Helm: Bloody Cannibal of the West." *Real West,* July 1965, p. 53.

Rickards, Colin. "Boone Helm: Man Eater." *True West,* April 1973, p. 6.

Weatherford, Anne. "Boone Helm: Murderer, Thief, Cannibal." *Great West,* Dec. 1969, p. 12. Rpt. *Great West,* Dec. 1970, p. 12.

Wiltsey, Norman B. "The Beast That Looked Like a Man." *True West,* Dec. 1958, p. 10.

Helmer, Bounce

Nelson, Andre. "The Last Sheepman-Cattleman War." *True West,* May 1988, p. 14.

Hennessey, Patrick "Pat"

Andre, Barbara E. "Horror On a Sunny Afternoon." *The West,* Jan. 1970, p. 38.

Kildare, Maurice. "Burned On a Wagon Wheel." *Real West,* May 1970, p. 38.

Turpin, Robert F. "The Hennessey Massacre." *Great West,* Dec. 1970, p. 10.

_____. "Who Were the Last Men Hennessey Saw?" *True West,* June 1967, p. 35.

Henry, Alexander

Chapin, Earl V. "The Pembina River Post: Diary of a Fur Trader." *Western Frontier,* Annual, Spring 1981, p. 3.

Hickman, William Adams "Wild Bill"

Carson, John. "'Use Him Up, Bill.'" *True West,* June 1964, p. 16.

Parsons, Chuck. "Ten Wives and Forty Children" ("Answer Man" column). *True West,* April 1990, p. 12.

Hickok, James Butler "Wild Bill"

Bayston, Phillip E. "They Called Him Wild Bill." *Great West,* Feb. 1969, p. 44.

Bird, Roy. "The Custer-Hickok Shootout in Hays City." *Real West,* May 1979, p. 28.

Boucher, Leonard Harold. "How Wild Bill Hickok Lost His Head." *True West,* June 1959, p. 37.

Bradley, Tom. "Dead Man's Hand." *Man's Western,* Aug.-Sept. 1959, p. 24.

Breihan, Carl W. "Blood On the Queen of Hearts." *Golden West,* May 1967, p. 16. Rpt. *The West,* Dec. 1971, p. 14.

_____. "The Hickok-McCanles Affair." *Real West,* Sept. 1967, p. 10.

Clark, J.B. "The Hickok-Tutt Duel." *Frontier Times,* Spring 1962, p. 45.

DeMattos, Jack. "Wild Bill Hickok" ("Gunfighters of the Real West" column). *Real West,* June 1980, p. 30.

Fielder, Mildred. "Wild Bill's Guns in Deadwood." *Old West,* Fall 1970, p. 14.

Frazier, Thomas A. "Wild Bill Hickok, the Man and the Legend." Part I, *Real West,* Jan. 1969, p. 26; Part II, *Real West,* Feb. 1969, p. 28. Rpt. as one-part article, *Real West,* Special Issue, Fall 1973, p. 42.

Hart, George. "Hays City Under the Guardian Care of Wild Bill." Part I, *Real West,* April 1971, p. 26; Part II, *Real West,* May 1971, p. 46.

_____. Letter, "Hickok: Hero or Heel?" *True West,* June 1956, p. 26.

_____. "The Mystery of Wild Bill Hickok's Remains." *Real West,* Oct. 1970, p. 32.

Hermon, Gregory. "Wild Bill's Sweetheart: The Life of Mary Jane Owen." *Real West,* Feb. 1987, p. 21.

Hockley, G.W. "Last Days of a Plainsman." *True West,* Dec. 1965, p. 22.

Jameson, Henry B. "Lay Off Abilene." *True West,* Sept. 1982, p. 16.

Jonson, Charles J. "The Strange Marriage of Wild Bill Hickok." *The West,* March 1964, p. 21. Rpt. *The West,* Aug. 1974, p. 14.

_____. "When Wild Bill Hickok Wouldn't Fight." *The West,* Dec. 1964, p. 18. Rpt. *Western Frontier,* April 1983, p. 20.

"Law Man or Bad Man: Wild Bill Hickok." *Gunslingers of the West,* Winter 1966, p. 2.

Lipton, Dean. "Wild Bill's Wild West." *Great West,* Dec. 1970, p. 6.

Mays, Carelton. "Wild Bill Was No Hero." *Real West,* March 1962, p. 8.

McCreight, M.I. Letter, "Hickok: Hero or Heel?" *True West,* June 1956, p. 27.

Naylor, Lee. "The Hated Nickname That Led to Wild Bill Hickok's Murder." *Frontier West,* Aug. 1973, p. 38.

Nolan, Paul T. "Jack Crawford's Account of Wild Bill." *Real West,* Sept. 1971, p. 27.

O'Neal, Bill. "'Duck Bill' Hickok vs The McCanles Gang" ("Great Western Gunfights" column). *True West,* April 1991, p. 56.

_____. "Wild Bill vs Phil Coe" ("Great Western Gunfights" column). *True West,* March 1988, p. 59.

Parsons, Chuck. "It's Wild Bill!" *True West,* July 1989, p. 42.

_____. "Who Was the Faster Gunman, James B. 'Wild Bill' Hickok or Wesley 'Little Arkansas' Hardin?" *NOLA Quarterly,* Vol. I, No. 3, 1975, p. 8.

_____. "'Wild Bill' Hickok Killed Two Men in Abilene." *NOLA Quarterly,* Vol. I, No. 1, 1974, p. 9.

Pryse, Dorothy. "Bill Hickok's Friends." *True West,* April 1978, p. 14.

Repp, Ed Earl. "Home Made Hero." *True Frontier,* Dec. 1974, p. 19.

_____. "Massacre at Rock Creek." *The West,* April 1970, p. 38.

Riske, Milt. "Wild Bill's Women." *Real West,* March 1980, p. 22.

Rosa, Joseph G. "The Girl and the Gunfighter: A Newly Discovered Photograph of Wild Bill Hickok." *Real West,* Dec. 1984, p. 18.

_____. "Wild Bill and the Timber Thieves." *Real West,* April 1982, p. 12. Rpt. *Real West,* Special Issue, Spring 1983, p. 54.

_____. Letter, "Hickok: Hero or Heel?" *True West,* June 1956, p. 26.

Rybolt, Robert. "Wild Bill Murder Plot." *True West,* July 1985, p. 42.

Sandell, Jay. "The Tragic Story of Wild Bill Hickok." *Real West,* Aug. 1959, p. 30. Rpt. *Real West,* Annual, Summer 1966, p. 34.

_____. "Wild Bill Hickok." *Real West*, Americana Series, Fall 1965, p. 10.

Secrest, William B. "Bill Hickok's Girl On the Flying Trapeze." *Old West*, Winter 1967, p. 26.

_____. "Wild Bill Hickok: On Shooting." *True Frontier*, March 1971, p. 32. Rpt. *True Frontier*, Special Issue No. 11, Winter 1974-75, p. 26.

_____. "Wild Bill's Wild Women." *True Frontier*, May 1969, p. 8.

Sooner, Norman. "Hickok: Longhaired Rebel or National Hero?" *Westerner*, Aug. 1971, p. 14.

Sparks, Elmer E. Letter, "Hickok: Hero or Heel?" *True West*, June 1956, p. 28.

Stevens, Ray W., Jr. "Hickok the Hero." *True West*, Dec. 1955, p. 12. Rpt. *Badman*, Annual 1971, p. 30.

Thorp, Raymond W. "Wild Bill's Famous Bullet." *Real West*, May 1961, p. 18.

"Truly Western Hall of Fame." *True Western Adventures*, June 1960, p. 72.

Uhlarik, Carl. Letter. *Real West*, April 1969, p. 75.

"Wild Bill's Rifle." *True West*, Winter 1953, p. 48.

Wilson, Robert L. "Slaughter at Rock Creek Station." *Westerner*, May-June 1969, p. 48.

Hicks Brothers (Milton and Will)

Rasch, Philip J. "The Unfinished Story of the Hicks Brothers." *NOLA Quarterly*, Vol. X, No. 1, Summer 1985, p. 2.

Hicks, John

Hicks, Bebe. "They Buried Uncle John in Boothill." *America's Frontier West*, Issue No. 1, n.d., p. 8. Rpt. *Western True Story*, Oct. 1971, p. 16.

Higgins, John Calhoun Pinckney "Pink"

Bell, Morris. Letter. *True West*, Dec. 1991, p. 7.

Breihan, Carl W. "The Horrell-Higgins Feud." *Real West*, Oct. 1970, p. 40.

_____. "The Lampasas County War." *Oldtimers Wild West*, Aug. 1977, p. 7.

DeArment, R.K. "The Protection Man." *Old West*, Spring 1991, p. 20.

Dodge, Matt. "Shootout in Standifer Thicket." *Oldtimers Wild West*, Dec. 1978, p. 20.

Northington, M.G. "I Saw Them Stack Their Guns." *Frontier Times*, Spring 1962, p. 18.

O'Neal, Bill. "The Horrell Brothers vs Pink Higgins" ("Great Western Gunfights" column). *True West*, Jan. 1991, p. 58.

Sandell, Jay. "I'll Stop This Damned Feud!" *Real West*, May 1962, p. 40.

Higley, Brewster

Friedman, Ralph. "Home On The Range." *Frontier Times,* March 1963, p. 28.

Sheller, Roscoe. "The Doctor's Home On The Range." *The West,* Nov. 1967, p. 14. Rpt. *Golden West,* March 1972, p. 22.

Thede, Marion, and Harold Preece. "The Story Behind the Song, Home On the Range." *Real West,* Dec. 1973, p. 18.

Hildebrand, Sam

Breihan, Carl W. "Death of Sam Hildebrand." *Real West,* April 1980, p. 40. Rpt. *Real West,* Special Issue, 1981, p. 60.

Hill, James Jerome "Jim"

Bangert, E. "Benefactor or Tyrant?" *Frontier Times,* Jan. 1966, p. 18.

Hite, Cass

Dana, Julian. "One Came Back." *True West,* Oct. 1962, p. 26.

Hobbs, Fern

Auer, L.C. "The Skirt Who Hog Tied a Town." *Western Frontier,* Special Issue, Dec. 1974, p. 5.

Freeman, Olga. "Clean-up at Copperfield, Oregon." *Real West,* Nov. 1969, p. 19.

Hodges, Ben

Chatfield, Harry E., and Carolyn Day. "Ben Hodges: Likeable Old Cuss of Dodge City." *Real West,* March 1974, p. 24.

Waddell, Cliff. "The Incredible One-Man Range War of Ben Hodges." *Frontier West,* Dec. 1974, p. 26.

Hodgkins, William L.

Compton, Ed. "The Tenderfoot Dude Who Out-Fought Colorado's Worst Badmen." *Frontier West,* Dec. 1974, p. 40.

Hoerster, Daniel

Johnson, Dave. "Daniel Hoerster and the Mason County War." *NOLA Quarterly,* Vol. IX, No. 3, Winter 1985, p. 15.

Hogan, Dan

Jones, Calico. "Grab Your Guns, Boys." *Real West,* Jan, 1968, p. 30.

Hogan, Frank
Meier, Gary. "Frank Hogan: Oregon Thief Taker." *True West,* June 1987, p. 12.

Holdman, Joseph "Joe"
Shannon, Ted. "Saga of the Amazing Professor Buckshot." *The West,* May 1964, p. 30.

Hole-in-the-Day
Czech, Kenneth P. "Warriors and Chiefs" column. *Wild West,* Feb. 1991, p. 10.

Holladay, Ben
Cheney, Louise. "Ben Holladay's Wild Ride." *Real West,* Sept. 1969, p. 42.

Hartley, William B. "The Fabulous Pony Express." *True Western Adventures,* June 1960, p. 12.

Lucia, Ellis. "Fastest Stage Run in History." *Frontier Times,* Fall 1961, p. 12.

———. "King of Wheels." *True Western Adventures,* April 1960, p. 25.

Pinot, B. Hale. "Ben Holladay's Overland Stage." *Westerner,* May-June 1969, p. 32.

Holliday, Cyrus K.
Berson, Jeffrey. "The Dream That Spanned the Prairies." *The West,* March 1964, p. 30. Rpt. *Western Frontier,* Special Issue, Summer 1974, p 6; and *Western Frontier,* Special Issue, Oct. 1983, p. 48.

Bowman, George. "Cyrus Holliday's Hell on Wheels." *Real West,* May 1965, p. 30.

Holliday, John Henry "Doc"
Breihan, Carl W. "Desperate Men, Desperate Guns." *Real West,* Annual, Winter 1977-78, p. 16.

Carson, John. "Doc Holliday" ("Backgrounds of Famous Western Badmen" column). *True West,* June 1962, p. 25.

DeMattos, Jack. "Doc Holliday." *Real West,* Special Issue, Spring 1985, p. 30.

———. "Doc Holliday" ("Gunfighters of the Real West" column). *Real West,* Jan. 1982, p. 36.

"'Doc' Holliday: He Pulled a Deadly Six-Gun After He Gave Up On Teeth." *Gunslingers of the West,* Winter 1966, p. 28.

Kantor, Seth. "Time: Oct. 26, 1881—Place: OK Corral." *Western Action,* Dec. 1960, p. 30.

Kirkpatrick, J.R. "Doc Holliday's Missing Grave." *True West,* Oct. 1990, p. 46.

Lazaru, Leon. "Deadliest Dentist of the West." *Man's Western,* Jan. 1960, p. 10.

Malocsay, Zoltan. "OK Corral: 100 Years of Lies." *Westerner,* July-Aug. 1973, p. 34.

Mays, Carelton. "What Really Happened at the OK Corral?" *Real West,* Jan. 1958, p. 14.

Montgomery, Wayne. "The Deadly Doctor Holliday." *Westerner,* April 1973, p. 14.

_____ "Gambling Gunslinger." *Great West,* July 1968, p. 27.

_____. "A Little Ride With Doc." *Real Frontier,* April 1971, p. 41. Rpt. *True Frontier,* Special Issue No. 13, 1975, p. 12.

_____. "Tom 'Pole Cat' Adams Recalls Doc Holliday." *NOLA Quarterly,* Vol. II, No. 2, Summer 1975, p. 14.

Myers, John Myers. "The West's Greatest Gunman." *True West,* Feb. 1960, p. 6.

Palmquist, Robert F. "Good-Bye Old Friend." *Real West,* May 1979, p. 24.

Quale, J.L. "The Strange Love Affair of Big Nose Kate and Doc Holliday." *Real West,* Sept. 1964, p. 36.

Qualey, J.S. "How Doc Holliday Died." *Real West,* Feb. 1959, p. 11. Rpt. *Real West,* Annual, Summer 1966, p. 76.

Ripple, Sam. "Doc Holliday's Girl." *Westerner,* Nov.-Dec. 1971, p. 48.

Sherman, Jory. "Death Dealing Dentist." *Big West,* Oct. 1967, p. 38.

Hollister, Cassius M. "Cash"

Walker, Wayne T. "Cash Hollister." *Real West,* Annual, Spring 1983, p. 44.

_____. "Cash Hollister: Border Lawman." *Real West,* March 1982, p. 14.

_____. "Cash Hollister, Gunfighter-Lawman." *Westerner,* June 1971, p. 25.

_____. "Cash Hollister, Kansas Lawman." *Oldtimers Wild West,* Feb. 1978, p. 24.

Hollow Horn Bear

Kay, Jay F. "Redskins in the White House." *Golden West,* March 1965, p. 18. Rpt. *Golden West,* June 1973, p. 28; and *Western Frontier,* Nov. 1975, p. 42.

Hollow Horn Dog

Carmody, Lee. "The Whiskey Vengeance of the Outraged Sioux." *Frontier West,* June 1975, p. 18.

Holman, Jake

Majors, John A. "Weird Killings in Blood Valley." *Real West,* Jan. 1963, p. 8.

Holszay, Reimond (Reymond) "Black Bart"
Bartholomew, Ed. "'Black Bart' Holszay." *NOLA Quarterly,* Vol. IV, No. 4, June
   1979, p. 17.

Holt, Adoniram Judson
Nolen, Oran Warder. "He Was a Missionary to the Wild Indians." *The West,* July
   1969, p. 28.

Hoover, George M.
Ernst, Robert R. "Dodge City Sued." *True West,* Nov. 1986, p. 32.

Horn, Sarah
Cheney, Louise. "Comanche Captive Sarah Horn." *The West,* Dec. 1966, p. 14.

Horn, Tom
Best, J.C. "More on Tom Horn." *Real West,* Aug. 1983, p. 12. Rpt. *Real West,*
   Yearbook, Fall 1984, p. 40.

Breihan, Carl W. "Desperate Men, Desperate Guns." *Real West,* Annual, Winter
   1977-78, p. 16.

Brown, Mildred. "Lawman Joe LeFors Sends Tom Horn to Gallows." *NOLA
   Quarterly,* Vol. VIII, No. 3, Winter 1983-84, p. 6.

Browning, Dwain. "Tom Horn." *Great West,* Oct. 1968, p. 18.

Carson, John. "Tom Horn: Was a Hero or a Villain Hanged?" *True West,* Dec.
   1960, p. 26.

Cortesi, Lawrence. "The Pinkerton Agent Who Became a Killing Renegade."
   Frontier West, Aug. 1973, p. 34.

DeMattos, Jack. "Tom Horn" ("Gunfighters of the Real West" column). *Real
   West,* Dec. 1980, p. 14.

Donoho, Ron. "He Hanged Tom Horn." *The West,* Sept. 1971, p. 28.

Gaddis, Bob. "The Sheriff They Hanged in Error." *True Frontier,* Oct. 1967, p.
   14.

Hart, Ernest H. "The Legend of Tom Horn: Was He a Vicious Killer or a Fine
   Lawman?" *Real West,* Sept. 1972, p. 14.

Jones, Calico. "The Hired Killer." *Wild West,* June 1969, p. 36.

Koller, Joe. "Tom Horn: Man of Mystery." *Real West,* March 1971, p. 38.

Krakel, Dean. "Was Tom Horn Two Men?" *True West,* Feb. 1970, p. 12.

Nickell, Phillip G. "The Family Tom Horn Destroyed." *Real West,* Dec. 1986, p.
   23.

_____. "Tom Horn in Arizona, or Who Killed Old Man Blevins?" *NOLA Quarterly,* Vol. XIV, Nos. 3 and 4 (combined issue), 1990, p. 15.

O'Neal, Bill. "Stock Detective Tom Horn vs Rustlers" ("Great Western Gunfights" column). *True West,* July 1991, p. 58.

Paine, Lauran. "The Passing of Tom Horn." *True West,* June 1957, p. 22. Rpt. *True West,* Annual, 1978, p. 24.

Repp, Ed Earl. "The Mystery of Tom Horn." *The West,* Nov. 1968, p. 30. Rpt. *Western Frontier,* Special Issue, Fall 1974, p. 5; and *Western Frontier,* Jan. 1983, p. 6.

Riske, Milt. "Guns and Gloves." *Oldtimers Wild West,* Aug. 1979, p. 6.

Scott, Jay. "Tom Horn: Hired Gun." *True Western Adventures,* April 1960, p. 12.

Whitehead, Eva Horn. Letter, "Tom Horn: A Relative's Viewpoint." *True West,* Dec. 1960, p. 4.

Williams, Gary. "Tom Horn: Killer or Martyr?" *The West,* March 1965, p. 30. Rpt. *Western Frontier,* Fall 1981, p. 30.

Horony, Mary (see Cummings, Mary K.)

Horner, W.H.
Stephenson, Peggy. "Those Busy Bogus Bond Boys." *True West,* May 1988, p. 40.

Horrel Brothers (Samuel, Thomas, Martin, Benjamin, Merritt)
Breihan, Carl W. "The Horrell-Higgins Feud." *Real West,* Oct. 1970, p. 40.

_____. "The Lampasas County War." *Oldtimers Wild West,* Aug. 1977, p. 7.

Cline, Donald. "The Horrell War." *The West,* Dec. 1966, p. 30. Rpt. *Golden West,* July 1973, p. 14; and *Western Frontier,* March 1976, p. 40.

Northington, M.G. "I Saw Them Stack Their Guns." *Frontier Times,* Spring 1962, p. 18.

O'Neal, Bill. "The Horrell Brothers of Lampasas." *Frontier Times,* May 1980, p. 6.

_____. "The Horrell Brothers vs Pink Higgins" ("Great Western Gunfights" column). *True West,* Jan. 1991, p. 58.

_____. "The Horrell Brothers vs the Texas State Police" ("Great Western Gunfights" column). *True West,* Dec. 1990, p. 57.

Sandell, Jay. "I'll Stop This Damned Feud." *Real West,* May 1962, p. 40.

Horse Back
Andre, Jim. "The Last War Chief of the Comanches." *Westerner,* April 1971, p. 10.

Ho-Tah-Moie (Ho-To-Moie; John Stink)

Bright, Davilla. "The Indian Who Came Back From the Dead." *True Frontier,*
Special Issue No. 2, 1972, p. 31.

Myers, Olevia E. "Ho-Tah-Moie: Roaring Thunder." *The West,* Dec. 1973, p. 10.
Rpt. *Western Frontier,* Special Issue, March 1975, p. 10.

Houck, James D. "Jim"

Kildare, Maurice. "Take a Walk to Doom." *Real West,* April 1970, p. 38.

Houston, Margaret Lea

Preece, Harold. "Raven's Mate: Margaret Lea Houston." *Real West,* April 1971,
p. 22.

Houston, Samuel "Sam"

Bean, Tom. "Sam Houston's Last Great Dream." *Real West,* June 1985, p. 36. Rpt.
Real West, Special Issue, Spring 1986, p. 42.

Brady, Cyrus Townsend. "Sam Houston and His Battles." *Golden West,* July
1965, p. 27. Rpt. *Western Frontier,* Nov. 1980, p. 23.

Brown, Epp. "Santa Anna and Sam Houston." *True West,* May 1987, p. 60.

Hoskinson, Jo H. "When Angelina Gave the Alarm." *The West,* April 1969, p. 16.

Hynds, Alexander. "General Sam Houston: A Great Man." *Golden West,* Nov.
1968, p. 10.

Houston, Sequoyah

Etter, Jim. "The Day Sequoyah Houston Fell to Cherokee Bill." *Frontier Times,*
Nov. 1972, p. 22.

Houston, Temple

Cheney, Louise. "Temple Houston: Frontier Lawyer." *Golden West,* Nov. 1965,
p. 26. Rpt. *Golden West,* Jan. 1972, p. 44.

Farmer, Melvin L. Letter, "Killing of the Jennings Brothers." *True West,* Aug.
1964, p. 4.

Powers, Mark. "Temple Houston: Defender of the Underdog." *Wild West,* July
1972, p. 24.

Robbins, Peggy. "Personality" column. *Wild West,* June 1990, p. 8.

Sandell, Jay. "Temple Houston" ("Famous Lawmen of the West" column). *Real
West,* Americana Series, Fall 1965, p. 34.

_____. "Two-Gun Lawyer." *Real West,* March 1960, p. 28.

Shirley, Glenn. "Temple Houston in Mobeetie and Tascosa." *Frontier Times,* Sept. 1980, p. 8.

_____. "Temple Houston: Lawyer With a Gun." *Western Tales,* April 1960, p. 12.

_____. "Temple Houston: The Man With the Silver Tongue." *Real West,* Sept. 1970, p. 14.

Speer, Bonnie. "Under the Wings of the Raven." *Frontier Times,* Sept. 1970, p. 34.

Tolbert, Frank X. "Sam's Youngest Boy." *True West,* Aug. 1963, p. 12.

Houston, William H. "Bill"
Bundy, Rex. "Bill Houston, Fearless Montana Sheriff." *Real West,* Jan. 1972, p. 38. Rpt. *Real West,* Special Issue, Fall 1973, p. 50.

Howard, Charles "Charley"
Hyatt, Frieda and Samuel. "Salt War of Texas." *True West,* Oct. 1956, p. 20.

Jones, George. "Great Salt War." *Real West,* March 1960, p. 12.

Lipton, Dean. "Shoot-Out at San Elizario." *Great West,* Dec. 1969, p. 16.

Preece, Harold. "Texas' Craziest War." *The West,* Sept. 1964, p. 36. Rpt. *The West,* June 1974, p. 20.

Howard, James "Tex"
Carson, Xanthus. "The Bisbee Massacre." *Westerner,* Nov. 1970, p. 48.

Ormes, Carl. "Blood at Bisbee." *Real West,* May 1959, p. 23.

Roensch, Dell. "Bisbee's Bath of Blood." *True Western Adventures,* Dec. 1959, p. 38.

Howard, Oliver Otis
Auer, L. "The Coming of the Christian General." *Wild West,* March 1970, p. 14.

Downs, Michael S. "A Foolhardy and Uncalled for Experiment." *True West,* Sept. 1989, p. 36.

Pinkerton, Robert E. "The Indian Who Beat the U.S. Army." *True Western Adventures,* June 1960, p. 38.

Wiltsey, Norman B. "Hawks of the Desert." *True West,* Dec. 1955, p. 19.

Howard, William James
Traywick, Ben T. "The Last California Ranger." *The West,* March 1974, p. 25.

Howie, Neil
"Bullets and Flour." *Western Frontier,* Nov. 1976, p. 10.

Hartwick, James C. "Neil Howie: Better Than His Times." *True West,* Nov. 1981, p. 44.

Hoy, George R.
Johnson, Dave. "George R. Hoy: Obscure Victim." *NOLA Quarterly,* Vol. XIV, No. 1, 1990, p. 8.

Hoy, Valentine
Norwood, John. "Brown's Hole: Historic Border Hideout." *Frontier Times,* Feb. 1985, p. 43.

Hoyt, Edward Jonathan "Buckskin Joe"
Shirley, Glenn. "White Man-Devil." *True West,* Dec. 1963, p. 28.

Hoyt, Henry F.
Rickards, Colin. "Bones of the Northfield Robbers." *Real West,* Jan. 1979, p. 28.

Hoyt, Henry F. "A Frontier Doctor." Rpt. Part I, *Old West,* Fall 1980, p. 49; Part II, *Old West,* Winter 1980, p. 49; Part III, *Old West,* Spring 1981, p. 53.

Hubbard, Cal
Bailey, Tom. "Devil in the Driver's Seat." *True Western Adventures,* June 1961, p. 28.

Hudson, William Wesley "Wes"
Rose, Sammie, and Pat Wood. "Little Wes Hudson." *True West,* May 1991, p. 27.

Huelsdonk, John
Betts, William J. "Iron Man of the Hoh." *Real West,* Annual, Summer 1970, p. 10.

Hueston, Thomas "Tom"
"Bloody Ingalls Under Siege." *Western Frontier,* July 1976, p. 6.

Hughes, John R.
Breihan, Carl W. "Captain John R. Hughes: Texas Ranger." *The West,* Aug. 1967, p. 34. Rpt. *The West,* Aug. 1972, p. 26; and *Western Frontier,* April 1983, p. 6.

_____. "Ranger John Hughes." *Real West,* Sept. 1975, p. 22. Rpt. *Real West,* Yearbook, Summer 1978, p. 20.

Ferguson, Henry N. "Zane Grey's Original 'Lone Star Ranger.'" *Old West,* Spring 1978, p. 10.

Hancock, William CX. "Ranger's Ranger." *True West,* April 1961, p. 23.

Jurgens, Enos. "The Most Wanted Corpse in Texas." *America's Frontier West,* Issue No. 1, n.d., p. 36. Rpt. *Western True Story,* Oct. 1971, p. 38.

Michaels, Kevin. "Tracker." *Authentic West,* Summer 1981, p. 22.

Qualey, Jake. "Test of a Texas Ranger." *Real West,* Jan. 1961, p. 12.

"True Western Hall of Fame" column. *True Western Adventures,* Aug. 1961, p. 60.

Hulse, Alfred "Al"
Edwards, Harold L. "California's Ruthless Outlaw." *Old West,* Summer 1985, p. 52.

_____. "Who Killed William Tibbet?" *Real West,* June 1987, p. 23.

Secrest, William B. "The Return of Jim McKinney." *True West,* Feb. 1963, p. 14.

Hume, James B. "Jim"
Chandler, Robert J. "Wells Fargo: 'We Never Forget.'" Part I, *NOLA Quarterly,* Vol. XI, No. 3, Winter 1987, p. 6; Part II, *NOLA Quarterly,* Vol. XI, No. 4, Spring 1988, p. 7.

Cheney, Louise. "The Royal Embezzler." *Western Frontier,* Special Issue, Fall 1974, p. 30.

Coe, Clint. "The Vengeance of Wells Fargo." *True Western Adventures,* Aug. 1961, p. 26.

Dillon, Richard. "The Hangtown Apprenticeship of a Wells Fargo Detective." *NOLA Quarterly,* Vol. IV, No. 2, Autumn 1978, p. 1.

_____. "Wells Fargo's Jekyll and Hyde." *The American West,* Vol. VIII, No. 2, March 1971, p. 28.

Gault, Owen. "Gun for a Lawman." *Old West,* Oct. 1968, p. 42.

"The Raiders of Bullion Bend." *Authentic West,* Summer 1981, p. 34.

"When Wells Fargo Policed the West." *Authentic West,* Summer 1981, p. 14.

Hunt, Thomas "Tom"
Winfield, Craig. "I Did Time for Jesse James." *Westerner,* May-June 1972, p. 30.

Hunt, Wilson Price
Jerrells, Michael W. "Perilous Journey." *Wild West,* April 1989, p. 18.

Hunt, Richard (Zweig, Zwing)

Bailey, Tom. "Arizona's Buried Treasure Mystery." *True Western Adventures,* Summer 1958, p. 8.

Boyer, Glenn G. "Murder at Millville." *Real West,* April 1983, p. 10.

Chatfield, Harry, E. and Carolyn Day. "Skeleton Canyon's Lost Treasure." *Real West,* Nov. 1977, p. 40.

Kildare, Maurice. "The Desperado Kids." *Real West,* Dec. 1968, p. 11.

O'Neal, Bill. "Deputy Sheriff Billy Breakenridge vs Zweig Hunt and Billy Grounds" ("Great Western Gunfights" column). *True West,* July 1991, p. 59.

Rasch, Philip J. "The Brief Careers of Billy Grounds and Zwing Hunt." *Real West,* Feb. 1985, p. 12. Rpt. *Real West,* Yearbook, Winter 1986, p. 57.

Hunting Horse

Ryan, M.E. "Indian Scout for Custer." *True West,* Feb. 1956, p. 16.

Hurst, John

Hurst, John. "I Was at Beecher's Island." *The West,* June 1965, p. 40.

Huston, "Ma" (and sons, Barney and Jeff)

Ballenger, Dean W. "Ma Huston and Her Raiders." *Westerner,* May-June 1973, p. 32.

Hyatt, W.L.

Wallis, George A. "Cattle Kings." Part I, *True West,* April 1964, p. 8.

Ide, William B.

Martin, Cy and Jeannie. "William B. Ide: President for Twenty-six Days." *Real West,* Feb. 1973, p. 10.

Ieuch, "Dutch Henry" (also spelled "Euach")

Coburn, Walt. "The Night Dutch Henry Played Santa Claus." *True West,* Oct. 1969, p. 12.

Walker, Wayne T. "Born and Ieuch: The Two Dutch Henrys." *Real West,* Oct. 1983, p. 46. Rpt. *Real West,* Special Issue, Spring 1984, p. 8.

Ikard, Bose

Chatfield, Harry E. "Bose Ikard, Top Hand." Part I, *Real West,* Dec, 1968, p. 32; Part II, *Real West,* Jan. 1969, p. 23.

Iliff, John Wesley

Koller, Joe. "John W. Iliff: Cowcountry Mogul." *Golden West,* Sept. 1969, p. 22.

Indian Em'ly (Emily)

Atkinson, Fred T. "The Legend of Indian Emily." *Big West,* Oct. 1968, p. 20.

Booker, Pauline. "Indian Emily" ("Nuggets" column). *Frontier Times,* Spring 1958, p. 27.

Cerveri, Doris. "Romance of Indian Emily." *Real West,* Sept. 1969, p. 44.

Cheney, Louise. "Why Indian Em'ly Saved Fort Davis." *The West,* March 1967, p. 42. Rpt. *Golden West,* Jan. 1973, p. 28; and *Western Frontier,* Feb. 1985, p. 3.

"Grave of Heroine." *Real West,* July 1963, p. 62.

Rothe, Aline. "The Heroism of Indian Emily." *Real West,* March 1978, p. 19.

Indian Peggy

Repp, Ed Earl. "Indian Peggy." *True Frontier,* July 1971, p. 28. Rpt. *True Frontier,* Special Issue No. 7, Fall 1973, p. 28.

Inkpaduta

Van Nuys, Maxwell. "Inkpaduta: The Scarlet Point." Part I, *The West,* May 1967, p. 18; Part II, *The West,* June 1967, p. 16.

Iron Jacket

Cheney, Louise. "Chief Iron Jacket." *Real West,* Jan. 1971, p. 33. Rpt. *Real West,* Special Issue, Spring 1972, p. 11.

McKechnie, Logan. "The Indian Who Wouldn't Die." *True Frontier,* Oct. 1972, p. 20.

Iron Shirt

Coleman, Neil. "When 'Iron Shirt' Clashed With 'Old Rip.'" *Pioneer West,* Sept. 1967, p. 42.

Freeman, Frank H. "Spanish Bones and Comanche Armor." *Pioneer West,* March 1976, p. 28.

Irvin, Jim Tom
Parsons, Chuck. "Tragic End to a McNelly Ranger." *Real West,* March 1979, p. 38.

Irwin, Bernard J.D.
Chase, Bob. "Better Late Than Never." *Real West,* April 1984, p. 28.

Eherts, Walter. "The Fighting Doctor of Apache Pass." *Real West,* April 1987, p. 40.

Kelsh, James M. "Personality" column. *Wild West,* Oct. 1988, p. 10.

Irwin, Calvin "Cal"
McBee, Fred. "The Gunslinger." *Great West,* Oct. 1972, p. 8.

Isa-Tai
Phillips, Gary. "The Judas Medicine Man Who Destroyed His Own Braves." *Frontier West,* June 1974, p. 10.

I-See-O (Tahbone-Mah)
Walker, Wayne T. "I-See-O: Kiowa Scout and Peacemaker." *Great West,* Dec. 1974, p. 14.

Ishi
Hall, Ann. "Ishi, Last of the Stone Age Men." *Western Round-Up,* May 1970, p. 12. Rpt. *Wild West,* May 1972, p. 12; and *Oldtimers Wild West,* Dec. 1973, p. 44.

Scullin, George. "Ishi: Last Man in His World." *True Western Adventures,* June 1961, p. 42.

Shaw, Ruth Mepham. "Ishi: A Most Remarkable Indian." *True West,* June 1972, p. 15.

Jack, Ellen E. (Captain Jack)
Dickerson, B. "The Lady Captain Jack." *Westerner,* Summer 1975, p. 34.

Jackson, Frank
Beverly, Bob. "Sam's Cohort: Frank Jackson." *Frontier Times,* Sept. 1978, p. 15.
Parsons, Chuck. "Unknown Fate" ("Answer Man" column). *True West,* May 1991, p. 12.

Jackson, Fred
Secrest, William B. "The Gunfight at Stone Corral." *True Frontier,* June 1973, p. 26.

Jackson, Helen Hunt
Cheney, Louise. "Helen Hunt Jackson, Great Friend of the Indians." *Golden West,* Aug. 1974, p. 32.

Jackson, T.V.
Neville, Fonville. "The Hound Who Ran Down Burrows [sic]." *Western Frontier,* Special Issue, Summer 1974, p. 10.

Jackson, William C. "Teton" (Harvey Gleason)
Canton, Chet. "Three Hundred Outlaws." *Great West,* Sept. 1967, p. 26.
Parsons, Chuck. "Answer Man" column. *True West,* Jan. 1983, p. 18.

James Brothers (Frank and Jesse)
Breihan, Carl W. "The Day the James' Home Was Bombed." *Real West,* Jan. 1980, p. 38. Rpt. *Real West,* Yearbook 1980, p. 48.
_____. "Did the James Boys Take Part in the Muscle Shoals Robbery?" *Real West,* March 1972, p. 40.
_____. "The Glendale Train Robbery." *Real West,* May 1972, p. 29.
_____. "Holdup of the Omnibus at North Lexington." *Real West,* March 1979, p. 32.
_____. "The James Boys at Bardstown." *Real West,* June 1975, p. 28.
_____. "The James Gang and the Huntington Bank Robbery." *Real West,* June 1973, p. 38.

_____. "The Jameses in California." *Real West,* Feb. 1975, p. 36.

_____. "The Night They Bombed 'Castle James.'" *Oldtimers Wild West,* April 1980, p. 22.

_____. "The Northfield Raid." *The West,* Nov. 1966, p. 10. Rpt. *Western Frontier,* Sept. 1980, p. 34.

_____. "Who Robbed the Store at Westport, Mo.?" *Real West,* July 1975, p. 44.

DeMattos, Jack. "Frank and Jesse James." Part I ("Gunfighters of the Real West" column), *Real West,* Oct. 1984, p. 32; Part II ("Gunfighters of the Real West" column), *Real West,* Dec. 1984, p. 38. Rpt. as one-part article, *Real West,* Yearbook, Fall 1985, p. 28.

Dullenty, Jim. "Bombing of the Jesse James Home." *True West,* Jan. 1983, p. 20.

Elliott, Susan. "Sixguns at Northfield." *Great West,* May 1968, p. 16.

Gaddis, Robert W. "They Headed North to Death." *True Frontier,* June 1967, p. 32.

Hart, George. "Identifying Frank and Jesse James: The Case of the Missing Finger." *NOLA Quarterly,* Vol. XI, No. 1, Summer 1986, p. 14.

Hoctor, Emmett C. "'Safe Retreat' Found." *NOLA Quarterly,* Vol. XV, No. 4, Oct.-Dec. 1991, p. 20.

Jameson, Henry B. "Lay Off Abilene." *True West,* Sept. 1982, p. 16.

Linn, William C. "The James-Younger Gang: Murderers." *NOLA Quarterly,* Vol. III, No. 4, Autumn 1978, p. 7.

MacLean, Angus. "The Ghosts of Frank and Jesse James." *Golden West,* Nov. 1965, p. 22. Rpt. *Western Frontier,* Jan. 1978, p. 16; and *Western Frontier,* May 1985, p. 26.

Mangum, William P. "Frank and Jesse James Raced Horses Between Their Holdups." *NOLA Quarterly,* Vol. XIII, No. 2, Fall 1989, p. 8.

Mangum, William Preston. "Near Disaster at Brandenburg." *NOLA Quarterly,* Vo. XII, No. 4, Spring 1988, p. 14.

McLeod, Norman. "The Northfield Raid and Whiskey." *NOLA Quarterly,* Vol. XIII, No. 3, Winter 1989, p. 25.

Parsons, Chuck. "In Pursuit of the Northfield Robbers." *NOLA Quarterly,* Vol. IV, No. 4, June 1979, p. 14.

Steele, Phillip. "James Brothers Death Hoax." *NOLA Quarterly,* Vol. VIII, No. 3, Winter 1983-84, p. 14.

Turner, Brian P. "The James-Younger Gang in Kentucky." *Real West,* Special Issue, Spring 1985, p. 8.

_____. "The James-Younger Gang: Some Profitable Times Spent in Kentucky." *Real West,* Dec. 1982, p. 40.

_____. "The James-Younger Robbery in Columbia." *True West,* Feb. 1982, p. 61.

Winfield, Craig. "The Blue Cut Train Robbery." *Pioneer West,* July 1977, p. 15.

Winters, Frank. "The Day the Gangs Were Born." *Golden West,* Sept. 1965, p. 42. Rpt. *Western Frontier,* May 1985, p. 10.

Wukovits, John F. "Raiders Repulsed by Fire." *Wild West,* Oct. 1988, p. 18.

James Family (Drury Woodson, Robert)

Brant, Marley. "Outlaws' Inlaws in California." *Frontier Times,* Feb. 1985, p. 18.

Croy, Homer. "I Knew Jesse James' Mother." *True West,* June 1959, p. 35.

James, Frank

Breihan, Carl. W. "Death of Frank James." *Real West,* March 1975, p. 38.

_____. "Frank James' Terrible Revenge." *Westerner,* Nov.-Dec. 1973, p. 34.

_____. "Frank James' Terrible Revenge." *NOLA Quarterly,* Vol. III, No. 2, Autumn 1977, p. 11.

Carson, John. "Frank James In Wyoming." *Real West,* March 1967, p. 50.

Johnson, Norman K. "General Joe Shelby and the Trial of Frank James." *Real West,* Oct. 1988, p. 14.

"Letter From Frank James." *Old West,* Spring 1982, p. 48.

Mangum, William P. "Frank James' Secret Travels Authenticated." *NOLA Quarterly,* Vol. IX, No. 4, Spring 1984, p. 18.

Montgomery, Wayne. "More Unpublished Writings of Frank James." *Westerner,* July-Aug. 1973, p. 38.

_____. "The Secret Diary of Frank James." *Westerner,* Jan.-Feb. 1973, p. 34.

_____. "Revealed: The Secret Writings of Frank James." *Westerner,* May-June 1973, p. 26.

Nieberding, Velma, and Harold Preece. "The West's Outlaws Found No Peace Even in Death." *Frontier West,* Dec. 1971, p. 42.

Rickell, Walter. "Found: The Revolver Frank James Used." *Westerner,* July-Aug. 1974, p. 41.

Wiltsey, Norman B. "Frank James: The Hard Road Back." *Real West,* Feb. 1974, p. 38.

James, Jesse

Bird, Roy. "Those Dirty Little Cowards." *Real West,* May 1988, p. 32.

Black, Hugh E. "Did Jesse James Play Poker in Brownville Saloon?" *WOLA Journal Quarterly,* Vol. I, No. 2, Fall-Winter 1991, p. 2.

Breihan, Carl W. "Bob Ford Did Kill Jesse James." *Real West,* May 1959, p. 28.

_____. "The Bombing of Castle James." *Real West,* Aug. 1969, p. 24.

_____. "The Day Jesse James Attempted Suicide." *NOLA Quarterly,* Vol. I, No. 4, Winter 1975-76, p. 11.

_____. "The Day Jesse James Tried to Surrender." *Real West,* May 1974, p. 43.

_____. "Jesse James and the Gallatin Bank Robbery." *Real West,* Oct. 1971, p. 33.

_____. "Jesse James and the Liberty Bank Robbery." *Real West,* Aug. 1972, p. 40.

_____. "Jesse James and the Winston Train Robbery." *Real West,* Oct. 1972, p. 53.

_____. "Jesse James' Attempted Suicide." *True West,* Nov. 1982, p. 21.

_____. "Jesse James in Mexico." *Real West,* Jan. 1968, p. 24.

_____. "Jesse James' First Train Robbery." *Real West,* June 1971, p. 30. Rpt. *Real West,* Annual, 1972, p. 43.

_____. "Jesse James' Last Train Robbery." *Real West,* March 1969, p. 40. Rpt. *Real West,* Annual, Summer 1970, p. 20.

_____. "Jesse James: The King of Bandits." Part I, *Oldtimers Wild West,* April 1978, p. 16; Part II, *Pioneer West,* May 1978, p. 12.

_____. "King of Bandits." *The West,* May 1967, p. 10. Rpt. *Golden West,* April 1972, p. 34; *Western Frontier,* July 1976, p. 34; and *Western Frontier,* Nov. 1982, p. 34.

_____. "The Truth About Jesse James' Death?" *Real West,* Dec. 1971, p. 21.

_____. "What Brought About Jesse James' Death?" *Frontier Times,* Jan. 1964, p. 31.

Burkholder, Edwin V. "Who Killed Jesse James?" *True Western Adventures,* April 1959, p. 20.

Burton, Jeff. "Attributed to the James Gang." *English Westerners Brand Book,* April 1964, p. 1.

Cheney, W.D. "Who Lies Buried in Jesse James' Grave?" *Real West,* Jan. 1967, p. 32.

Croy, Homer. "The Book, the Gun and Jesse James." *True Western Adventures,* Oct. 1959, p. 36.

_____. "My Good Neighbor Jesse James." *True Western Adventures,* Aug. 1961, p. 10.

DeGregorio, Armand. "The Death Hoax of Jesse James." *NOLA Quarterly,* Vol. X, No. 4, Spring 1986, p. 4.

Edmondson, Wilson. "Did Jesse James Attend His Own Funeral?" *True Frontier,*

March 1968, p. 8. Rpt. *True Frontier,* Oct. 1972,. p. 12; and *True Frontier,* Special Issue No. 17, Winter 1976, p. 40.

Frazier, Thomas A. "Jesse James: The Man and the Legend." Part I, *Real West,* May 1970, p. 16; Part II, *Real West,* June 1970, p. 44.

Gibson, Marijo. "Jesse and the Cloth." *The West,* June 1970, p. 20. Rpt. *Western Frontier,* Special Issue, Fall 1974, p. 40.

Graham, J.W. "I Photographed Jesse James' Body." *True West,* Oct. 1959, p. 9.

Hale, Donald R. "Resurrection of Jesse James." *NOLA Quarterly,* Vol. V, No. 3, April 1980, p. 1.

Hart, George. "Stanley Waterloo Meets the Fords." *NOLA Quarterly,* Vol. XIV, No. 1, 1990, p. 1.

Hines, James. "Jesse James Attempted Suicide." *Real West,* Jan. 1962, p. 52.

_____. "Scandal That Killed Jesse James." *Real West,* May 1965, p. 40.

Hoctor, Emmett C. Letter. *WOLA Journal Quarterly,* Vol. I, No. 2, Fall-Winter 1991, p. 2.

_____. "Safe Retreat Found." *NOLA Quarterly,* Vol. XV, No. 4, Oct.-Dec. 1991, p. 20.

James, J. Coleman. "His Legs Are Missing." *Great West,* Nov. 1967, p. 14.

James, Stella. "Some Notes on Jesse James." *True West,* Aug. 1962, p. 28.

"Jesse James" ("Gallery of Gunmen" column). *True Western Adventures,* No. 4, Aug. 1960, p. 56.

Knellton, Ives. "Get Away Ridge." *True Frontier,* Special Issue No. 1, 1971, p. 6.

Linn, William C., and Carl W. Breihan. "Two Views of Jesse James: Ruthless Killer and Tender Lover." *NOLA Quarterly,* Vol. IV, No. 3, March 1979, p. 6.

Mahon, Howard. "Bob Ford Did Not Kill Jesse James." *Real West,* Nov. 1958, p. 22.

Mays, Carelton. "Jesse James." *Real West,* Special Issue, Fall 1964, p. 22.

Montgomery, Wayne. "Was Jesse James Really Murdered?" *Big West,* Feb. 1968, p. 28.

Nieberding, Vera, and Harold Preece. "The West's Outlaws Found No Peace Even in Death." *Frontier West,* Dec. 1971, p. 42.

Patterson, Richard. "Jesse James' First Train Robbery." *Old West,* Summer 1991, p. 14.

Rasch, Philip J. "Jesse James in New Mexico Folklore." *New York Westerners' Brand Book* , Vol. IV, 1957, p. 62.

Reed, Linda. "The Pulp Heroics of a Bandit King." *NOLA Quarterly,* Vol. V, No. 4, April 1980, p. 9.

Spivey, Louie E. "James Home Restoration." *Frontier Times,* Feb. 1985, p. 62.

Steele, Phillip W. "The Bullet That Killed Jesse James." *True West,* Oct. 1987, p. 50.

_____. "Jesse James Slept Here." *True West,* June 1986, p. 40.

_____. "Jesse James' Tombstone." *True West,* Dec. 1988, p. 46.

Stewart, Judge R. Lee. "Jesse James: Backgrounds of Famous Western Badmen." *True West,* April 1961, p. 37.

Thede, Marion, and Harold Preece. "The Ballad of Jesse James: The Story Behind the Song." *Real West,* Sept. 1973, p. 8.

Walker, Wayne T. "How Many Bullets Did It Take to Kill Jesse James?" *Frontier West,* Jan. 1976, p. 41.

Walters, Raymond L. "Jesse James' Double." *True West,* July 1984, p. 17.

Winfield, Craig. "Jesse James and the Winston Train Robbery." *Oldtimers Wild West,* Aug. 1977, p. 14.

_____. "Jesse's Bloodiest Escape." *Westerner,* Nov.-Dec. 1974, p. 27.

Wybrow, Robert J. "From the Pen of a Noble Robber: Letters From Jesse Woodson James, 1847-1882." *English Westerners' Brand Book,* Vol. XXIV, No. 2, Summer 1987, p. 1.

_____. "The James Gang in Kentucky." *English Westerners' Brand Book,* Vol. XV, No. 12, Jan. 1973, p. 1.

_____. "Jesse's Juveniles." Part I, *English Westerners' Brand Book,* Vol. XI, No. 3, April 1969, p. 1; Part II, *English Westerners' Brand Book,* Vol. XII, No. 1, Oct. 1969, p. 1.

_____. "Ravenous Monsters of Society: The Early Exploits of the James Gang." *English Westerners' Brand Book,* Vol. XXVII, No. 2, Summer 1990, p. 1.

Yeatman, Ted P. "Jesse James in Tennessee." *True West,* July 1985, p. 10.

James, Jesse, Jr.

Patterson, Richard. "The Trial of Jesse James, Jr." *Old West,* Summer 1987, p. 12.

James, Susan (Susan Parmer)

Keyser, Mary. "Susan James: Outlaw's Pawn." *True West,* Sept. 1981, p. 74.

James-Younger Gang

Breihan, Carl W. "The Gads Hill Train Robbery." *Real West,* Sept. 1969, p. 10.

_____. "The James Gang and the Huntington Bank Robbery." *Real West,* June 1973, p. 38.

_____. "Jesse James: The Russellville Bank Robbery." *Real West,* Oct. 1969, p. 16.

_____. "Raid on Columbia." *Westerner,* Jan.-Feb. 1972, p. 26.

_____. "The Rocky Cut Train Hold Up." *Real West,* May 1969, p. 10.

Stiles, Bill. "The James Gang and the Bounty Hunters." *Real Frontier,* Aug. 1970, p. 16. Rpt. *True Frontier,* Special Issue No. 1, 1971, p. 24.

Winfield, Craig. "The Northfield Bank Job." *Westerner,* Jan.-Feb. 1972, p. 29.

_____. "Raid On the Missouri Pacific." *Westerner,* Sept.-Oct. 1973, p. 24.

Jancigaj, Matthias
Espy, Watt. "The Crime and Execution of Matthias Jancigaj." *NOLA Quarterly,* Vol. V, No. 1, Oct. 1979, p. 3.

Jeffers, Claude
Wallis, George A. "Cattle Kings." Part II, *True West,* June 1964, p. 6.

Jeffords, Thomas "Tom"
Breihan, Carl W. "Blood Brother to the Apache." *Westerner,* March-April 1970, p. 34.

_____. "Blood Brother of Cochise." *Real West,* July 1973, p. 8.

Downs, Michael S. "A Foolhardy and Uncalled for Experiment." *True West,* Sept. 1989, p. 36.

Noel, Reuben. "Tom Jeffords and Cochise." *Frontier Times,* March 1966, p. 26.

Jenkins, James Gilbert
Beatty, Monroe R. "The Gentle Killer." *The West,* June 1965, p. 21.

Majors, John. "West's Gentle Killer." *Real West,* Nov. 1961, p. 22.

Jennings, Alphonso Jackson "Al"
Briehan, Carl W. "Al Jennings: Why the Outlaw Ran for Governor." *Westerner,* Nov.-Dec. 1974, p. 37.

Echols, Lee E. "Old Al Jennings." *Frontier Times,* May 1978, p. 14.

Gilles, Albert S., Sr. "Bill Gilbert and Al Jennings." *Western Frontier,* Stagecoach Series, Fall 1974, p. 16.

Gilles, Albert S., Sr. "The Outlaw Who Ran for Governor." *True Frontier,* Oct. 1967, p. 36. Rpt. *True Frontier,* Special Issue No. 1, 1971, p. 8; and *True Frontier,* Special Issue No. 13, 1975, p. 4.

Kelly, Bill. "The Outlaw Who Ran for Governor." *Oldtimers Wild West,* June 1978, p. 10.

Largent, H.M. Letter. *True West,* April 1962, p. 57.

Majors, John. "Al Jennings: Comic Opera Bandit." *Real West,* Nov. 1962, p. 20.

Patterson, Richard "Pat." "The Trial of Al Jennings." *NOLA Quarterly,* Vol. XIII, No. 3, Winter 1989, p. 16.

Powers, Mark. "Al Jennings." *Great West,* June 1971, p. 14.

Sasser, Charles W. "Gunfighters and Lawmen" column. *Wild West,* Aug. 1989, p. 8.

Jennings Gang

Huston, Fred. "The Jennings Gang vs Progress." *Golden West,* June 1972, p. 24.

Parsons, Chuck. "Oklahoma Outlaws" ("Answer Man" column). *True West,* Oct. 1990, p. 13.

Jennings, John

Gilles, Albert S., Sr. "John Jennings' Diamond." *True West,* Feb. 1969, p. 20.

Jennison, Charles R.

Hale, Donald R. "Dr. Jennison of Kansas: Hero or Killer?" *Golden West,* Sept. 1968, p. 28. Rpt. *Golden West,* June 1972, p. 36.

John (Old Chief John)

Bauguess, John. "Chief John's Last Battle." *Real West,* Americana Series, Winter 1966, p. 26.

Johnny-Behind-the-Duece" (see O'Rourke, Michael)

Johns, Robert "Buck"

Kildare, Maurice. "Greatest Rustler of Them All." *True Frontier,* Sept. 1968, p. 8. Rpt. *True Frontier,* Special Issue No. 1, 1971, p. 12.

Johnson, Britt

Catlin, W.S. "The Texas Slave Followed the Comanches Straight to Hell." *Frontier West,* Aug. 1973, p. 42.

Johnson County Invaders

Boucher, Leonard H. "The Wyoming Invaders." *Great West,* Sept. 1969, p. 16.

Cortesi, Lawrence. "The Day the Vigilantes Invaded Wyoming." *Frontier West,* June 1972, p. 20.

"The Hired Killers." *Great West,* Sept. 1967, p. 4.

Newton, Allen. "Explosion on Powder River." *Westerner,* July-Aug. 1969, p. 16.

Williams, Gary. "Dunning's Strange Confession: Five Dollars a Day to Ride, Fifty Dollars to Kill." *The West,* July 1964, p. 14.

Johnson, Ed.

"Ed Johnson Kills 'Gunplay' Maxwell." *NOLA Quarterly*, Vol. VII, No. 1, Spring 1982, p. 6.

Johnson Family

Chrisman, Harry E. "The Johnson-Eldridge Feud." *Golden West*, June 1974, p. 18.

Johnson, George

Guttman, Jon. "Gunfighters and Lawmen" column. *Wild West*, Dec. 1991, p. 10.

Johnson, Henry

Clatworthy, Alan. "The Black Private Whose Battle Plan Smashed the Utes." *Frontier West*, Feb. 1972, p. 38.

Johnston, Albert Sydney

Fleek, Sherman F. "Advancing Column Defied." *Wild West*, Feb. 1989, p. 34.

Johnston, John "Liver Eating" (also spelled Johnson)

Bundy, Rex. "Liver Eatin' Johnson." *Wild West*, March 1971, p. 20. Rpt. *Oldtimers Wild West*, Aug. 1973, p. 30, and *Pioneer West*, Bicentennial Souvenir Edition, 1976, p. 19.

Carpenter, Will. "Liver-Eating Johnson." *Westerner*, Nov.-Dec. 1971, p. 36.

Freeman, Frank M. "The Man Who Ate Indian Livers." *True Frontier*, Nov. 1969, p. 24. Rpt. *True Frontier*, Special Issue No. 3, 1972, p. 22.

Guttman, Jon. "Gunfighters and Lawmen" column. *Wild West*, Aug. 1990, p. 12.

Kelly, Bill. "The Vengeance of Liver Eatin' Johnson." *Real West*, April 1981, p. 40. Rpt. *Real West*, Annual, Spring 1982, p. 46.

Owens, Harry J. "He Never Ate Crow." *Old West*, Spring 1983, p. 10.

Preston, N.E. "Mountain Men Called Him Liver-Eatin' Johnson, the Crow Killer." *Great West*, July 1969, p. 46.

Thorp, Raymond. "Revenge of Liver Eating Johnson." *The West*, Sept. 1964, p. 26. Rpt. *The West*, Annual 1971, p. 22.

Thorp, Raymond W. "Liver Eating Johnson's Last Trail." *True West*, Oct. 1965, p. 18.

Whithorn, Doris. "Liver Eating Johnson's Fearsome Name." *True West*, June 1966, p. 45.

Jolsanny
Olson, James R. "The Greatest Apache Warrior." *True Frontier,* May 1970, p. 20.

Jones, Bradford D.
Jones, Bradford D. "Diary and Account Book of a 49'er." Rpt. *Western True Story,* Oct. 1971, p. 24.

Jones, Charles Jesse "Buffalo Jones"
Chatfield, Harry E. "The Man Who Saved the Buffalo." *The West,* April 1967, p. 30. Rpt. *Golden West,* March 1974, p. 14; and *Western Frontier,* Annual No. 4, 1976, p. 6.

Helminiak, Raymond. "The About Face of a Buffalo Hunter." *Frontier Times,* Nov. 1971, p. 26.

Koller, Joe. "The Destiny of Buffalo Jones." *Golden West,* March 1971, p. 16.

Renstrom, Evelyn. Letter. *Old West,* Spring 1968, p. 59.

Jones, Clifford B.
Wallis, George A. "Cattle Kings." Part I, *True West,* April 1964, p. 8.

Jones, Ewell
Kildare, Maurice. "Blood on the Reins." *Westerner,* Sept.-Oct. 1974, p. 34.

Jones, Frank
Bailey, Tom, and Ralph J. Weaver. "The Nine Lives of Captain Frank Jones." *Frontier Times,* Spring 1960, p. 6. Rpt. *Old West,* Summer 1979, p. 6.

Jameson, W.C. "Incident at Pirate Island." *True West,* Nov. 1988, p. 42.

Majors, Frederick. "Bass Outlaw Was a Texas Riddle." *Golden West,* Aug. 1974, p. 19.

Rosson, Mary'n. "How Four Texas Rangers Declared War On the Frontier's One Hundred Worst Desperadoes." *Frontier West,* Dec. 1973, p. 8.

Jones, Gus T. "Buster"
Walker, Wayne T. "Gus Jones: From Texas Ranger to Special Agent-in-Charge." *Real West,* April 1982, p. 20. Rpt. *Real West,* Special Issue, Spring 1983, p. 25.

Jones, Horace Pope
Henderson, Sam. "Horace Pope Jones: Indian Scout." *Wild West,* Jan. 1972, p. 22.

Irons, Angie. "H.P. Jones, the Gentleman Scout." *Old West,* Spring 1990, p. 24.

Jones, John A.
Lofton, Monk. "Bleeding Hills." *Real West*, May 1961, p. 33.

Jones, John B.
Walker, Wayne T. "Major John B. Jones, Ranger Who Tamed West Texas." *Real West*, April 1981, p. 6. Rpt. *Real West*, Fall Yearbook 1982, p. 30.

Robinson, Charles M., III. "The Tough Little Ranger of Lost Valley." *True West*, July 1991, p. 18.

Jones, Joseph "Joe"
King, Dale. "They Died in the Crater of the Moon." *Real West*, April 1958, p. 42.

Jones, Sam
Hayes, Frederick. "Sherlock Holmes of the West." *Real West*, Jan. 1960, p. 20.

Tachman, Art. "The West's Greatest Detective." *The West*, Oct. 1965, p. 14.

Jones, William "Canada Bill"
Secrest, William B. "A Gamblin' Man." *Real West*, March 1979, p. 20.

Jones, William "Hell-Roarin' Bill"
Carpenter, Will. "Hell-Roarin' Bill." *True Frontier*, Special Issue No. 7, Fall 1973, p. 30.

Jones, Wilson N.
Charlet, Valerie. "Saga of a Territory Chief." *Great West*, Dec. 1972, p. 33.

Jordan, Thomas "Tom"
Staniford, Mike. "Tom Jordan, Cherokee Outlaw." *True West*, Nov. 1985, p. 20.

Joseph (Chief)
Allenbaugh, Carl. "The 1,500 Mile Retreat." *Westerner*, Jan.-Feb. 1970, p. 14.

Clark, Helen. "The Battle of the Big Hole." *Pioneer West*, March 1969, p. 36.

_____. "Red Napoleon of the West." *Big West*, Oct. 1967, p. 24.

_____. "The Tragedy of Chief Joseph." *Wild West*, Sept. 1970, p. 60. Rpt. *Oldtimers Wild West*, Oct. 1974, p. 56; and *Pioneer West*, March 1978, p. 26.

Dickson, Marie Maziarz. "A Girlhood Spent With Chief Joseph." *Old West*, Winter 1982, p. 18.

Dunn, J.P., Jr. "The Nez Percé Tragedy." Part I, *Real West*, May 1965, p. 28; Part II, *Real West*, July 1965, p. 29.

_____. "Treachery and Tragedy." *Real West*, Americana Series, Fall 1966, p. 26.

Forrest, Earle R. "Big Hole Battlefield." *Frontier Times*, Sept. 1965, p. 6.

Howard, Helen Addison. "Did Chief Joseph Slay Mrs. Manuel?" *Frontier Times*, Jan. 1972, p. 22.

_____. "A Divided Command Doomed the Nez Percé." *Frontier Times*, Sept. 1967, p. 10.

Lehman, Leola. "Chief Joseph, Nez Percé General." *True Frontier*, Nov. 1967, p. 16.

Mason, John. "How Great Was Chief Joseph?" *Real West*, Aug. 1959, p. 34.

Pinkerton, Robert E. "The Indian Who Beat the U.S. Army." *True Western Adventures*, June 1960, p. 38.

Ryker, Lois. "Fort Fizzle." *Real West*, Annual, Spring 1968, p. 54.

Scott, Mike. "The Indian Chief Who Outfought the U.S. Army's Top Generals." *Frontier West*, Aug. 1971, p. 10.

Shulsinger, Stephanie Cooper. "Chief Joseph, Indian Statesman." *Real West*, Dec. 1970, p. 10. Rpt. *Real West*, Special Issue, Spring 1972, p. 43.

Spendlove, Earl. "Battle at Big Hole Basin." *Great West*, Dec. 1973, p. 6. Rpt. *Authentic West*, Spring 1981, p. 6.

Stanley, Samuel. "Joseph's Nez Percé: The Last Retreat." *The West*, Jan. 1967, p. 38. Rpt. *The West*, Aug. 1973, p. 28; *Western Frontier*, Annual No. 4, 1976, p. 30.; and *Western Frontier*, May 1981, p. 37.

Taylor, Barry M. "Warriors and Chiefs" column. *Wild West*, Aug. 1988, p. 8.

"True Western Hall of Fame" column. *True Western Adventures*, June 1959, p. 55.

Weddle, Ferris. "Horse for a Nez Percé Warrior." *Real West*, Special Issue, Winter 1963, p. 56.

Werner, Fred H. "Big Hole: Nez Percé Badge of Courage." *Real West*, Jan. 1981, p. 36.

Wiltsey, Norman B. "Brave Warriors." *True West*, Winter, 1953, p. 8.

_____. "Hear Me, My Chiefs." *True West*, Oct. 1961, p. 18.

Wingo, Ella Mae. "Life and Death of a Chief." *Wild West*, Nov. 1971, p. 30. Rpt. *Pioneer West*, Jan. 1976, p. 20.

Wood, C.E.S. "The Surrender of Young Joseph." *The West*, July 1968, p. 26.

Yarbrough, Leroy. "The March of Chief Joseph." *Real West*, Oct. 1968, p. 23.

Journeycake Clan

Henderson, Sam. "The Sons of Charles Journeycake." *Real West*, Yearbook, Summer 1978, p. 60.

Joy, Kit

Caldwell, George A. "New Mexico's First Train Robbery." *NOLA Quarterly,* Vol. XIII, No. 3, Winter 1989, p. 14.

Holben, Richard E. "Kit Joy's Gang." *Frontier Times,* Sept. 1971, p. 20.

Juanita

Jordan, Phil. "Mysterious Juanita." *Westerner,* Sept.-Oct. 1974, p. 18.

Judah, Theodore

DeVries, Laura L. "The Invisible Man at Promontory, Utah." *True West,* Jan. 1991, p. 38.

Martin, Cy. "Theodore Judah: Engineering Genius of the Pacific Railway." *Real West,* Feb. 1970, p. 12.

Rosenhouse, Leo. "Race to a Rendezvous." *Real Frontier,* April 1971, p. 28. Rpt. *True Frontier,* Jan. 1978, p. 26.

Young, Bob. "Here Comes Crazy Judah." *The West,* Feb. 1965, p. 10. Rpt. *Western Frontier,* Special Issue, Oct. 1983, p. 6.

Judson, Edward Z.C. (Ned Buntline)

Fink, Clarence M. "Ned Buntline: The Discoverer of Buffalo Bill." *Real West,* Dec. 1971, p. 29.

Hart, George. "The Myth of the Buntline Special." *Real West,* June 1973, p. 50.

Hayes, Frederick. "Buntline Hated the West." *Real West,* March 1960, p. 36.

Henderson, Sam. "Love, War, Liquor and Rebellion." *Pioneer West,* April 1970, p. 38. Rpt. *Pioneer West,* June 1974, p. 8; *Oldtimers Wild West,* June 1976, p. 16, and *Western Frontier,* Annual, Winter 1977, p. 22.

Lowe, Tom. "The Man Who Made 'Buffalo Bill.'" *True Western Adventures,* April 1961, p. 24.

Martin, Cy. "Legend Maker of the West." *Real West,* Sept. 1973, p. 22.

Melton, Horace A. "King of the Dime Novel Writers." *The West,* Sept. 1965, p. 24. Rpt. *Golden West,* Nov. 1973, p. 16; and *Western Frontier,* Annual No. 1, 1975, p. 22.

Kalloch, Isaac M.
Henderson, Sam. "Bulletins and Bullets." *Golden West,* Oct. 1974, p. 12.

Kamiakin
Ballard, David M. "War of Extermination Backfired." *Wild West,* June 1989, p. 43.

Gulick, Bill. "Kamiakin: War Chief of the Yakimas." *True West,* May 1984, p. 12.

Red Hawk, Richard. "Neither Saint Nor Savage." *True West,* Jan. 1988, p. 30.

Kanim, Pat
Steele, Corbin. "Chief Pat Kanim's Mad Dream." *Real West,* Jan. 1963, p. 16.

Kaytennae
Norton, Hana Samek. "Katennae and the End of the Apache Wars." *True West,* June 1988, p. 14.

Kearny, Stephen W.
Bloom, Sam. "The General Was Wrong." *Great West,* Dec. 1972, p. 14.

Kells, Robert E., Jr. "Farthest Western Victory." *Wild West,* Aug. 1988, p. 18.

Kessinger, Dennis. "Kearny and Pico: The Battle of San Pasqual." *Old West,* Winter 1991, p. 20.

Krec, Ted. "The Restless Dead of San Pasqual." *True Western Adventures,* April 1961, p. 24.

Pearson, Robert E. "California's Great Lancers and Sabers War." *Pioneer West,* March 1968, p. 34.

Keeler, Fred
Ernst, Robert R. "Gunfire in Bartlesville." *NOLA Quarterly,* Vol. XV, No. 4, Oct-Dec. 1991, p. 26.

Keener, John
Boessenecker, John. "John Keener Cashes In." *Old West,* Winter 1991, p. 14.

Keil, Wilhelm

Fee, Art. "Dead Man's Wagon Train." *Pioneer West,* April 1971, p. 41. Rpt. *Oldtimers Wild West,* July 1974, p. 40; and *Pioneer West,* July 1976, p. 41.

_____. "The Remarkable Dr. Keil." *Golden West,* Nov. 1966, p. 28. Rpt. *The West,* July 1972, p. 28.

Gille, Marcia. "'King' Keil." *Old West,* Summer 1987, p. 18.

Ryland, Lee. "Wagon Train of the Dead." *Real West,* Jan. 1964, p. 24.

Talabere, Annie. "The Church That Died" ("Wild Old Days" column). *True West,* Oct. 1972, p. 38.

_____. "The Communistic Colony." *True Frontier,* Sept. 1973, p. 14.

_____. "The Unusual Dr. Keil." *Real West,* March 1977, p. 36.

Keil, William "Willie"

Herberg, Ruth. "The Whiskey Coffin." *Great West,* April 1971, p. 10.

Keller, James Madison "Jim"

Repp, Ed Earl. "Perils of a Frontier Scout." *The West,* Sept. 1973, p. 10.

Kelley, Edward O. (see O'Kelley, Edward)

Kellogg, Noah

Ryker, Lois. "The Jackass' Sixty-Million-Dollar Mine." *Real West,* May 1962, p. 14.

Kelly, Daniel "Dan"

Carson, Xanthus. "The Bisbee Massacre." *Westerner,* Nov. 1970, p. 48.

Ormes, Carl. "Blood at Bisbee." *Real West,* May 1959, p. 23.

Roensch, Dell. "Bisbee's Bath of Blood." *True Western Adventures,* Dec. 1959, p. 38.

Kelly, Edward M.

Rasch, Philip J. "Death in Las Vegas." *English Westerners Brand Book* No. 2, Jan. 1960, p. 10.

_____. "The Curious Case of Edward M. Kelly." *NOLA Quarterly,* Vol. XII, No. 2, Fall 1987, p. 8.

Kelly, Francis "Fanny"

Cheney, Louise. "White Captive of the Savage Sioux." *Oldtimers Wild West,* Jan. 1975, p. 20.

Kelly, Luther Sage "Yellowstone Kelly"

Breihan, Carl W. "Yellowstone Kelly." *Real West,* Sept. 1980, p. 32. Rpt. *Real West,* Yearbook 1981, p. 42.

Bundy, Rex. "Yellowstone Kelly, the Little Man With a Strong Heart." *Real West,* Aug. 1970, p. 33.

Gray, Fred Morton. "Yellowstone Kelly, Indian Fighter." *The West,* April 1965, p. 26. Rpt. *The West,* May 1972, p. 25; and *Western Frontier,* March 1976, p. 14.

_____. "Saga of Yellowstone Kelly." *Real West,* Jan. 1960, p. 37.

Martin, Manning. "Yellowstone Kelly." *Frontier Times,* Jan. 1974, p. 39.

Kelly, Scott

Lanza, Ruth Willet. "Scott Kelly: Man of Mystery." *True West,* Feb. 1989, p. 26.

Kelsey, Nancy

Ault, Phillip H. "Nancy Kelsey." *True West,* December 1989, p. 30.

Shaw, Ruth Mepham. "Nancy Kelsey, Barefoot on the Sierra Trail." *Real West,* May 1974, p. 32.

Kelsey, Sam

McNeil, Ray. "When the Killer Sat In the Judge's Seat." *Westerner,* May-June 1972, p. 16.

Kemp, David Lyle

O'Neal, Bill. "They Called Him Mister Kemp." *True West,* April 1991, p. 31.

Kennard, William "Willie"

Chamberlain, Kathleen P. "Colorado's Amazing Black Lawman." *NOLA Quarterly,* Vol. XIII, No. 2, Autumn 1989, p. 13.

McDermott, Burton. "The Incredible Saga of the Black Marshal Who Tamed Colorado." *Frontier West,* April 1974, p. 29.

Kennedy, Charles "Big Charley"

Ballenger, Dean W. "Strangler Kennedy and His Tavern of Death." *Westerner,* Sept.-Oct. 1972, p. 22.

Jones, Calico. "The Monster of Palo Flechado." *Real West,* May 1965, p. 13.

Kennedy, James "Jim"

Walker, Wayne T. "Jim Kennedy, Murderer." *Great West,* April 1970, p. 6.

Keogh, Myles W.

Dary, David A. "Comanche, a Century Later." *Frontier Times,* Sept. 1977, p. 18.

Ege, Robert J. "The Bravest Man the Sioux Ever Fought." *Real West,* Sept. 1967, p. 12.

Fee, Art. "Captain Keogh's Faithful Horse." *Golden West,* Sept. 1973, p. 12.

Redmond, Richard C. "He Rode Comanche" ("Nuggets" column). *Frontier Times,* Winter 1961, p. 33.

Thane, Eric. "Custer's Last Man." *True Frontier,* Sept. 1969, p. 22.

Keseberg, Lewis

Cerveri, Doris. "Keseberg: Cannibal of Donner Pass." *Real West,* Jan. 1967, p. 15.

Ketchel, Stanley

Mays, Carelton. "Six-Gun Killing of a World Champion." *Real West,* Aug. 1959, p. 20.

Ketchum, Ami

Carsten, Lyle. "The Nebraska Man Burner." *Pioneer West,* April 1972, p. 32.

Chrisman, Harry E. "When 'Slow Elk' Came High." *Old West,* Summer 1965, p. 46.

Preece, Harold. "Strange Truth About Print Olive." *Golden West,* June 1974, p. 38.

Swanson, Budington. "Death at Devil's Gap." *Great West,* Aug. 1973, p. 10. Rpt. *Great West,* Fall 1981, p. 10.

Ketchum, Sam

Burton, Jeff. "Suddenly in a Secluded and Rugged Place." *English Westerners Brand Book,* Vol. XIV, No. 3, April 1972, and No. 4, July 1972 (combined issue).

Cooke, Phil. Letter. *Frontier Times,* Fall 1962, p. 56.

Titsworth, B.D. "Hole-in-the-Wall Gang." Part I, *True West,* Dec. 1956, p. 10.; Part II, *True West,* Feb. 1957, p. 20. Rpt. as one-part article, *Badman,* Fall 1972, p. 4.

Ketchum, Tom "Black Jack"

Breihan, Carl W. "The Day They Hung Black Jack Ketchum." *Westerner,* Sept. 1970, p. 10.

————. "The Meteoric Rise—and Bloody Fall—of Black Jack Ketchum." *The West,* Oct. 1967, p. 34. Rpt. *The West,* Oct. 1972, p. 26.

Carson, Xanthus. "The Wild Escape of Texas' Train-Robbing Badman." *Frontier West,* June 1972, p. 42.

Cortesi, Lawrence. "The Black Jack Ketchum Gang." *Pioneer West,* Nov. 1978, p. 6.

_____. "Showdown at Emery Gap." *Frontier West,* June 1974, p. 14.

Hines, Jack. "Blackjack Ketchum, Texas Gunslinger." *Real West,* July 1961, p. 37.

Honig, Donald. "Moon-Mad Gunslinger." *Western Tales,* April 1960, p. 24.

Hovey, Walter C. "Black Jack Ketchum Tried to Give Me a Break." Ed. Doris Sturges. *True West,* April 1972, p. 6.

Reiss, Malcolm. "Blackjack Ketchum: The End of His Gang." *True Western Adventures,* June 1961, p. 20.

Repp, Ed Earl. "Brothers of El Diablo." *True Frontier,* March 1970, p. 22. Rpt. *True Frontier,* Special Issue No. 5, 1973, p. 26.

Robbins, William. "He Lost His Head Twice." *True Frontier,* June 1967, p. 30.

Romero, Trancito. "I Saw Black Jack Hanged." *True West,* Oct. 1958, p. 27.

Sturges, Richard W. "I Trailed Black Jack Ketchum." *True West,* Aug. 1963, p. 40.

Titsworth, B.D. "Hole-in-the-Wall Gang." Part I, *True West,* Dec. 1956, p. 4; Part II, *True West,* Feb. 1957, p. 20. Rpt. as one-part article, *Badman,* Fall 1972, p. 4.

Young, Bob. "Black Jack Ketchum Was a Ruthless Killer." *NOLA Quarterly,* Vol. VIII, No. 2, Fall 1983, p. 11.

Youngs, C. Daniel. "How Black Jack Lost His Head." *Real West,* Nov. 1958, p. 46.

Keyser, Peter

Catlin, W.S. "Texas Fences Made Bad Neighbors." *Frontier West,* June 1975, p. 30.

Kicking Bird

Gilstrap, Lou. "Peacemakers Walk a Dangerous Road." *Old West,* Fall 1973, p. 34.

Grove, Fred. "Kicking Bird: Kiowa Martyr." *The West,* Aug. 1967, p. 16. Rpt. *Western Frontier,* Jan. 1978, p. 28.

"Kid Curry" (see Logan, Harvey)

Kidder, Jefferson C. "Jeff"

DeArment, Robert K. "Jeff Kidder: Arizona Ranger." *NOLA Quarterly,* Vol. VII, No. 4, Winter 1972-73, p. 6.

Kildare, Maurice. "Arizona's Toughest Ranger." *Old West,* Summer 1967, p. 10.

O'Neal, Bill. "Jeff Kidder vs Mexican Policia." *True West,* Jan. 1989, p. 54.

Kidder, Lyman S.

Frost, Lawrence A. "Custer and the Kidder Massacre." *Westerner,* Sept. 1970, p. 26.

Gray, Monclair. "Mystery of the Eleventh Skeleton." *Real West,* Nov. 1962, p. 23.

Shockley, Philip M. "Triangle of Death." *Frontier Times,* May 1966, p. 10.

Sutton, E.S. Letter. *True West,* June 1968, p. 47.

Kilpatrick, Ben.

Carson, Xanthus. "Gunfight on the Sunset Limited." *Real Frontier,* Aug. 1971, p. 14. Rpt. *True Frontier,* Feb. 1975, p. 8.

Cortesi, Lawrence J. "Death on the Sunset Limited." *Oldtimers Wild West,* Feb. 1980, p. 10.

Gann, Walter W. "Ben Kilpatrick's Last Stand." *True West,* Aug. 1979, p. 14.

Mallory, Burr H. "The Jest That Backfired." *True West,* Aug. 1957, p. 22.

Parsons, Chuck. "Ben Kilpatrick's Family" ("Answer Man" column). *True West,* May 1987, p. 12.

Kind, Ezra

Carroll, John M. "Ezra Kind's Mysterious Message." *Real West,* Dec. 1971, p. 13.

King, Charles

Eherts, Walter. "Personality" column. *Wild West,* April 1991, p. 12.

King, Clarence

Hill, Leonard. "The Great Diamond Hoax." *True Frontier,* Special Issue No. 12, 1975, p. 38. Rpt. *True Frontier,* Special Issue No. 20, Winter 1977, p. 8.

Scullin, George. "They Salted the Desert With Diamonds." *True Western Adventures,* June 1960, p. 30.

Voynick, Steve. "Behind the Great Diamond Hoax." *True West,* January 1989, p. 18.

King, Ed
Kildare, Maurice. "The Gut Fighters Who Made 'Hell Town' the Bloodiest Place in Texas." *Frontier West,* Dec. 1972, p. 28.

Pickering, L.H. "Funeral in Tascosa." *Real West,* March 1978, p. 40.

King, James
Cheney, Louise. "James King of William." *Real West,* May 1975, p. 30.

King, Lizzie
Cheney, Louise. "Lizzie King of Bonanza City." *Real West,* Feb. 1970, p. 20.

King, Melvin A.
Dittmos, Henry. "The Bat and the Rose." *True Western Adventures,* Issue No. 1, 1957, p. 16.

Roberts, Gary L. "Corporal Melvin A. King: The Gunfighting Soldier of the Great American West." *Real West,* Sept. 1987, p. 4.

King, Richard
Dyer, Robert. "Richard King: A Man for Texas." *True West,* March 1988, p. 28.

Waltrip, Lela and Rufus. "Richard King's Handsome Pastures." *The West,* April 1968, p. 8. Rpt. *Western Frontier,* July 1980, p. 11.

King, Thomas Starr
Wingfield, William. "Thomas Starr King, the Preacher Who Saved California's Soul." *Real West,* Annual, Summer 1973, p. 20.

Kinkead, James H.
McDonald, Douglas B. "The First Far-Western Train Robbery." *The West,* April 1967, p. 8.

Kinman, Seth
Harrison, John H. "The Man With a Sunday Shot." *Real Frontier,* Nov. 1971, p. 14. Rpt. *True Frontier,* Oct. 1976, p. 6.

Hoopes, Chad L. "Kinman's Elk Horn Throne." *Big West,* April 1968, p. 34.

Miller, Don. "Seth Kinman, Presidents, and Grizzly Bears." *Real West,* June 1982, p. 26. Rpt. *Real West,* Special Issue, 1985, p. 14.

Kinney, Henry Lawrence
Woods, Dee. "King of the Wild Horse Desert." *The West,* March 1967, p. 28.

Kinney, John

DeMattos, Jack. "John Kinney: Gunfighter of the Real West." *Real West,* Feb. 1984, p. 20. Rpt. *Real West,* Yearbook, Winter 1986, p. 10.

Rasch, Philip J. "John Kinney, King of the Rustlers." *English Westerners' Brand Book,* Vol. IV, No. 1, Oct. 1961, p. 9.

Kinney, Nathaniel N.

Hartman, Viola R. "Terror in the Night: The Bald Knobbers." *Old West,* Fall 1983, p. 48.

Ingenthron, Elmo, and Mary Hartman. "Death of the Bald Knobbers." *Old West,* Fall 1988, p. 44.

Kino, Eusebio Francisco

Clark, Helen. "Black Robe of Pimeria Alta." *Wild West,* June 1970, p. 26.

Kirker, James "Jim"

Carson, Kit. "Capt. James Kirker, King of the Scalpers." *Real West,* Sept. 1968, p. 40.

Martin, Don. "Jim Kirker, King of the Scalpers." *The West,* Dec. 1964, p. 10. Rpt. *The West,* June 1974, p. 14.

Wilson, Steve. "Don Santiago Querque: Reckless Adventurer." *The West,* April 1969, p. 10.

Kirkpatrick, John M.

Beckham, Joe. "The Cannon on Battle Rock." *True Frontier,* May 1969, p. 20.

Betts, William J. "The Captain Called Them Friendly." *Real West,* March 1978, p. 20.

Fitzgerald, Arlene. "Siege at Battle Rock." *The West,* Sept. 1965, p. 34.

Meier, Gary. "Fifteen Days on Battle Rock." *True West,* April 1988, p. 14.

Traywick, Ben T. "Battle Rock." *Real West,* Dec. 1968, p. 37.

Kishkalwa

Minor, Nono. "Kish-Kal-Wa, Shawnee Chief." *Real West,* Jan. 1967, p. 49.

Kitchen, Pete

Kubista, Arizona Bob. "Sixty Miles to Hell." *The West,* Feb. 1966, p. 14. Rpt. *Western Frontier,* Winter 1978, p. 44.

Pinkerton, Robert E. "He Filled His Own Boot Hill." *True Western Adventure,* Issue No. 1, 1957, p. 34.

Preece, Harold. "Saga of the Amazing Pete Kitchen." *Real West,* May 1963, p. 24.

Thorp, Raymond W. "Pete Kitchen's Road of Dead Men." *True West,* Dec. 1964, p. 6.

"Kitty Tango" (Katherine Mendenez)

Henry, R.C. "The Shebang of Kitty Tango." *Oldtimers Wild West,* Aug. 1973, p. 20. Rpt. *Pioneer West,* March 1976, p. 24.

Klein, James "Jim"

Kelly, Bill. "End of the Line for Jim Klein." *Real West,* Jan. 1980, p. 22.

"Klondike Kate" (see Rockwell, Kathleen Eloisa)

Knight, Andrew J.

Osterhout, Richard C. "Another Sheriff of Deadwood." *NOLA Quarterly,* Vol. XV, No. 4, Oct.-Dec. 1991, p. 22.

Knowles, John Randolph

Majors, John A. "Weird Killings in Blood Valley." *Real West,* Jan. 1963, p. 8.

Knox, Charley

Brennan, George. "Charles Knox: The Man Who Breathed Life Back Into a Dead Town." *Frontier West,* Feb. 1972, p. 28.

Kohrs, Conrad

Holding, Vera. "Conrad Kohrs...Butcher in Old Montana." *True Frontier,* Feb. 1972, p. 33. Rpt. *True Frontier,* Special Issue No. 15, Summer 1976, p. 27.

Huston, Fred. "From Cabin Boy to Cattle King." *Frontier West,* Jan. 1976, p. 26.

Wright, Kathryn. "Conrad Kohrs' Race With the Innocents." *Old West,* Summer 1981, p. 8.

Kosterlitzky, Emilio (also spelled Kosterlitsky, Kosterlitzsky)

Bentz, Donald N. "The Dazzling Mexican Cossack." *The West,* Dec. 1966, p. 16. Rpt. *Western Frontier,* Summer, 1979, p. 6.

Chegwyn, Michael. "The West's Most Competent Mercenary: Emilio Kosterlitzsky." *Frontier Times,* Sept. 1970, p. 20.

Parsons, Chuck. "The Eagle of Sonora ("Answer Man" column). *True West,* Oct. 1989, p. 14.

Winfield, Craig. "Mexican Cossack." *Westerner,* Jan.-Feb. 1970, p. 36.

Kreeger, Lewis Michael "Lew"
DeArment, Robert K. "Kreeger's Toughest Arrest." *True West,* June 1986, p. 14.

Kuhl, Ben
Murbarger, Nell. "When Death Rode the Jarbidge Stage." *True West,* Oct. 1956, p. 16.

Web, Edgar. "The Day the Jarbridge [sic] Stage Was Late." *Westerner,* Jan.-Feb. 1975, p. 16.

LaFitte, Jean
Rieseberg, Harry. "LaFitte's Pirate Gold." *Real West,* Sept. 1961, p. 26.

_____. "Lafitte's Sunken Pirate Treasure." *Real West,* Special Issue, Summer 1964, p. 8.

_____. "New Search for LaFitte's Treasure." *Real West,* Nov. 1966, p. 16.

Laframboise, Jean Baptiste
Kildare, Maurice. "Jean Baptiste Laframboise: Oregon's Toughest Fur Trapper." *Real West,* Feb. 1972, p. 29.

Lamb, Charity
Ryland, Lee. "Charity Lamb: Murder On a Summer Night." *Real Frontier,* June 1970, p. 32. Rpt. *True Frontier,* June 1973, p. 42.

Lamb, Graham
Berk, Lee. "A Tough Nevada Lawman." *True West,* Jan. 1983, p. 22.

Lambert, Fred
Conant, Lora M. "Little Giant of the Cimarron." *Great West,* Feb. 1971, p. 18.

Harris, Fredie Steve. "Fred Lambert and the Whistling Billy." *The West,* Feb. 1969, p. 29.

Hornung, Chuck. "Fred Lambert: New Mexico Lawman." *The West,* Jan. 1970, p. 22.

_____. "The Motor Pony." *The West,* Aug. 1970, p. 28.

_____. "The Roan Horse Case." *Real West,* June 1980, p. 7.

White, Jerry. "Good Men and Bad." *Frontier Times,* May 1961, p. 38.

Lammy, John

Underwood, Larry. "Who Killed Sheriff John Lammy?" *NOLA Quarterly,* Vol. VIII, No. 3, Winter 1983-84, p. 10.

Lamont, Ada

Robbins, Lance. "Ada Lamont." *Real West,* Jan. 1971, p. 62.

Landusky, Pike

Gibson, Jay. "The Killing of Pike Landusky." *NOLA Quarterly,* Vol. X, No. 2, Fall 1985, p. 15.

Greenfield, Charles D. "Pike Landusky, The Violent Peace Officer." *The West,* Oct. 1967, p. 37.

Hamilton, Wade. "The Shooting of Pike Landusky." *True West,* Dec. 1959, p. 37.

Meredith, Henry. "The Man Who Ripped His Jaw Off." *Great West,* Nov. 1967, p. 28.

Turner, Len. "Incident on the Musselshell." *Frontier Times,* Summer 1959, p. 15.

Lane, George "Clubfoot"

Laughlin, E. "The Strange Story of 'Club Foot' George." *The West,* Sept. 1964, p. 30. Rpt. *Golden West,* June 1974, p. 28; *Western Frontier,* Annual, 1977, p. 42; and *Western Frontier,* May 1986, p. 42.

Lane, James "Jim"

Mosny, Roy. "The Bloody Border War." *Great West,* April 1967, p. 4.

Shulsinger, Stephanie Cooper. "Jim Lane: Firebrand From Kansas." *Real West,* Sept. 1971, p. 8.

Lane, Joseph "Joe"

Ankeny, Levi. "Treaty on the Rock." *True West,* Oct. 1962, p. 44.

Beckham, Joe. "Oregon's Joe Lane." *Pioneer West,* Oct. 1971, p. 34. Rpt. *Pioneer West,* March 1974, p. 26.

Lant, Dave

Burton, Doris Karren. "A Clue to the Fate of Outlaw David Lant." *The Outlaw Trail Journal,* Vol. I, No. 1, Summer 1991, p. 31.

Conway, Cliff. "Oldtimer Remembers Cassidy, Tracy, Lant, Warner." Interview of J.M. Blankenship. *NOLA Quarterly,* Vol. III, No. 1, Summer 1977, p. 9.

Ellison, Douglas W. "Tracy and Lant Escape From Aspen Jail." *The WOLA Journal,* Vol. I, No. 1, Spring-Summer 1991, p. 17.

LaRamee, Jacques
Vivdor, Paul J. "Who Was Jacques LaRamee?" *The West,* Jan. 1966, p. 17.

Larn, John
Gard, Wayne. "Night Justice on Clear Fork." *Western Frontier,* Special Issue, Fall 1974, p. 22.

Metz, Leon C. "The Rise and Fall of John Larn." *Real West,* Jan. 1967, p. 25.

Robinson, Charles M., III. "John Larn." *True West,* Oct. 1989, p. 21.

Sonnichsen, C.L. "Justice After Dark." *True West,* Feb. 1966, p. 18.

Lash, Tom
Carl, Levi. "Terror Rides the Chisholm Trail." *Man's Western,* Jan. 1960, p. 32.

Lassen, Peter
Bangert, Ethel. "Peter Lassen: The Great Chief." *True Frontier,* April 1973, p. 36.

Cerveri, Doris. "The Curse at Black Rock." *True Frontier,* June 1973, p. 20.

Murbarger, Nell. "Pete Lassen: The Venerable Voyager." *Frontier Times,* March 1963, p. 14.

Repp, Ed Earl. "Who Killed Peter Lassen?" *The West,* Sept. 1971, p. 18. Rpt. *Western Frontier,* Nov. 1978, p. 18.

Rosenhouse, Leo. "The Lost 'Lassen' Treasure." *Pioneer West,* Jan. 1970, p. 20.

Ross, Leonard. "Peter Lassen's Lost Gold." *True Frontier,* May 1969, p. 16. Rpt. *True Frontier,* Special Issue No. 12, 1975, p. 14.

Lathrop, Mary
Peabody, Olive B. "Portia of the West." *The West,* Sept. 1973, p. 24. Rpt. *Western Frontier,* Special Issue, Dec. 1974, p. 18.

Laverdure, Pierre
Bundy, Rex. "Pierre Laverdure, Metís Wanderer of the Far West." *Real West,* Yearbook, Spring 1974, p. 68.

La Verendrye, Pierre
Chapin, Earl V. "The Man Who Discovered a Mystery." *The West,* June 1974, p. 38.

Lawrence, John

Martin, Bernice. "A Pair of Kings." *Frontier Times,* Sept. 1963, p. 30.

Lawyer

Drury, Clifford M. "I, The Lawyer: Head Chief of the Nez Percé." *New York Westerners Brand Book,* Vol. VII, No. 1, May 1960, p. 1.

Lay, Elzy (Elza, alias William H. McGinnis)

Boren, Kerry Ross. "Elza Lay: Butch Cassidy's Mystery Partner." *Westerner,* Winter 1976, p. 22.

Burton, Jeff. "Suddenly in a Secluded and Rugged Place." Part I, *English Westerners' Brand Book,* Vol. XIV, No. 3, April 1972, p. 1; Part II, *English Westerners' Brand Book,* Vol. XIV, No. 4, July 1972, p. 1.

Carson, John. "They Called Him 'Elza.'" *True West,* Feb. 1973, p. 20.

Cole, William D. "Elza Lay: Intellectual Gunman." *True Western Adventures,* Dec. 1959, p. 12.

Parsons, Chuck. "Outlaw Elza Lay" ("Answer Man" column). *True West,* Sept. 1988, p. 12.

Titsworth, B.D. "Hole-in-the-Wall Gang." Part I, *True West,* Dec. 1956, p. 4; Part II, *True West,* Feb. 1957, p. 20. Rpt. as one part article, *Badman,* Fall 1972, p. 4.

Lazier, Jules

Nelson, Andre. "The Last Sheepman-Cattleman War." *True West,* May 1988, p. 14.

Lease, Mary Elizabeth Clyens

Souder, Eunice. "Kansas' Yellen Ellen." *Pioneer West,* Aug. 1972, p. 24.

Leatherwood, Robert N. "Bob"

Roensch, Dell. "Outlaws of the Desert Hole." *True Western Adventures,* Feb. 1960, p. 8.

Leaton, Benjamin "Ben"

Myers, Lee. "El Fortin." *Frontier Times,* Jan. 1966, p. 20.

Leavenworth, Henry

Lee, James C. "Fort Leavenworth: The Gateway to the West." *Pioneer West,* March 1977, p. 6.

Leonard, Leslie. "Bungled River Attack." *Wild West,* Oct. 1988, p. 34.

Ledbetter, James Franklin "Bud"

Henderson, Sam. "Bud Ledbetter's Last Showdown." *The West*, Nov. 1969, p. 30. Rpt. *Western Frontier,* May 1981, p. 30.

Turpin, Robert F. "Sand Hills Marshal." *Great West,* April 1970, p. 16.

Shirley, Glenn. "James Ledbetter: Hero of a Hundred Battles and Nary a Scratch." *Real West,* Jan. 1973, p. 24.

Ledford, John H. "Jack"

Breihan, Carl W. "Jack Ledford: Murdered in Wichita." *Real West,* Feb. 1972, p. 38.

McKay, Charles. "Killing of Jack Ledford." *Real West,* Nov. 1960, p. 42.

Lee Brothers ("Pink," "Jim," and "Tom")

Turpin, Robert F. "Wanted Dead or Alive: The Lee Brothers." *Great West,* Feb. 1970, p. 12.

Lee, Emma Bachellor (wife of John D. Lee)

Sellers, G. "The Courage of Emma Lee." *The West,* Sept. 1973, p. 20.

Lee, Jason

Lavender, David. "Sky of Brass, Earth of Iron." *Old West,* Fall 1966, p. 2.

Lee, Jesse Matlock

Nelson, Vance. "A Founder of Fort Robinson." *True West,* July 1984, p. 49.

Lee, John D.

Altman, Larry. "Mountain Meadows Massacre." *Real West,* Nov. 1958, p. 26.

Harrison, John H. "The Day the Mormons Found the End of the Blood Trail." *Frontier West,* April 1975, p. 10.

Kildare, Maurice. "Last of the Lees." *Real West,* July 1966, p. 20.

Kutac, C. "John D. Lee's Lost Mine." *Real West,* March 1977, p. 29.

McLane, Bruce. "What Happened at Mountain Meadows?" *True Western Adventures,* Oct. 1966, p. 20.

Sasser, Charles W. "Massacre at Mountain Meadows." *Old West,* Fall 1989, p. 14.

Swanson, Budington. "Murders in the Meadows." *Pioneer West,* Sept. 1979, p. 26.

Walker, Dale L. "Death of the Fancher Train." *Real West,* Jan. 1980, p. 18.

Lee, Oliver

Carson, Xanthus. "This Was Rangeland Justice: The Fantastic Courtroom Saga of the Lion of the West." *Frontier West,* Oct. 1972, p. 38.

Lofton, Monk. "Who Killed Judge Fountain?" *True West,* April 1963, p. 40.

Molthan, Ruth. "Battle at the Wildy Well." *Real Frontier,* Aug. 1970, p. 24. Rpt. *True Frontier,* Oct. 1974, p. 26; and *True Frontier,* Special Issue No. 7, Winter 1976, p. 26.

O'Neal, Bill. "Pat Garrett's Posse vs Oliver Lee and James Gililland." *True West,* Nov. 1991, p. 60.

Williams, Gary. "Mystery in the White Sands." *The West,* April 1965, p. 20.

Lee, Robert "Bob"

Jones, Nick. "The Lee-Peacock Feud." *Real West,* Jan. 1979, p. 12. Rpt. *Real West,* Annual, Winter 1980, p. 20.

Lee, Robert E.

Kyllo, Joan. "Robert E. Lee on the Texas Frontier." *The West,* Sept. 1974, p. 38.

Robinson, Charles M., III. "Outlaws, Indians, and Robert E. Lee." *True West,* March 1990, p. 14.

LeFors, Joseph S. "Joe"

Brown, Mildred. "Lawman Joe LeFors." *NOLA Quarterly,* Vol. VIII, No. 3, Winter, 1983-84, p. 6.

Kelly, Bill. "In Pursuit of Jim Tosah." *Real West,* Nov. 1977, p. 22.

Saban, Vera D. "Joe LeFors: Lawman on the Run." *Frontier Times,* Oct. 1984, p. 42.

Left Hand ("Nawat," "Ni Wot," "Nawathit")

"The Losing of a Nation." *Western Frontier,* Annual No. 4, 1976, p. 22.

"The Saga of Chief 'Nawat' Whose Best Friend Cut the Chisholm Trail." *Pioneer West,* Bicentennial Souvenir Edition, 1976, p. 14.

Brown, Saletha A. "Left-Hand Pledged to Peace." *The West,* March 1969, p. 34.

Lehman, Sam

Ballenger, Dean. "Get Marshal Sam Lehman." *Westerner,* Nov.-Dec. 1973, p. 44.

Lehmann, Herman

Lehmann, Herman. "Nine Years Among the Indians, 1870-1879." Part I, *Frontier Times,* March 1963, p. 6; Part II *Frontier Times,* May 1963, p. 8.

Leonard, Ira E.

Rasch, Philip J. "The Would-Be Judge: Ira E. Leonard." *Denver Westerners' Brand Book* , Vol. XX, 1965, p. 219.

Leonis, Miguel

Cole, Martin. "The Giant Basque of Calabasas." *Oldtimers Wild West,* Jan. 1975, p. 12.

Norrish, Rosie M. "The King of the Calabasas: Miguel Leonis." *Great West,* May 1969, p. 36.

Yancey, Fred. "King of Calabasas." *The West,* Feb. 1965, p. 24.

LeRoy, Billy

Cline, Don. "Billy LeRoy: The Original Billy the Kid." *Frontier Times,* Feb. 1985, p. 25.

Rasch, Philip J. "Billy LeRoy: Incompetent Highwayman." *Real West,* March 1988, p. 6.

Reilly, Jim. "They Died on Lonesome Road." *Real West,* July 1962, p. 9.

Leschi

Holden, Larry. "Leschi: Did They Hang an Innocent Man?" *True Frontier,* Dec. 1972, p. 16. Rpt. *True Frontier,* Special Issue No. 17, Winter 1976, p. 18.

"Warcry at Puget Sound." *Great West,* Aug. 1971, p. 20.

Leslie, Frank "Buckskin Frank"

Breihan, Carl W. "Blond Adonis of Tombstone." *Real West,* May 1962, p. 26.

_____. "Buckskin Frank Leslie." *Real West,* Aug. 1968, p. 12.

Brent, William and Milarde. "The Hinged-Frame Killer." *Pioneer West,* May 1969, p. 12.

DeMattos, Jack. "Buckskin Frank Leslie" ("Gunfighters of the Real West" column). *Real West,* Sept. 1981, p. 36.

Guttman, Jon. "Gunfighters and Lawman" column. *Wild West,* Dec. 1989, p. 12.

Lake, Ivan Clyde. "The Lady Killer." *The West,* June 1967, p. 14. Rpt. *The West,* Sept. 1973, p. 38; and *Western Frontier,* Annual, Summer 1978, p. 34.

O'Neal, Bill. "Buckskin Frank Leslie vs Billy the Kid Claiborne" ("Great Western Gunfights" column). *True West,* March 1991, p. 60.

Scott, Jay. "Buckskin Frank: Tombstone Ladykiller." *True Western Adventures,* April 1961, p. 18.

Wolfe, George D. "Buckskin Frank Leslie." *Frontier Times,* Spring 1961, p. 14. Rpt. *Old West,* Spring 1979, p. 14.

Youngs, C. Daniel. "Loves of Buckskin Leslie." *Real West,* May 1959, p. 10.

Lesueur, Frank
Rasch, Philip J. "Death Comes to Saint Johns." *NOLA Quarterly,* Vol. VII, No. 3, Autumn 1982, p. 1.

Levi, Jim
Sheldon, Edmond. "Gunfighters and Lawmen" column. *Wild West,* Dec. 1990, p. 10.

Lewis, Alexander
Walker, Wayne T. "The Man Judge Parker Couldn't Hang." *Western Frontier,* Nov. 1982, p. 2.

Lewis and Clark Expedition Members
Timmen, Fritz. "The Men of Lewis and Clark." *Real West,* Jan. 1968, p. 12.

Lewis, David "Cougar Dave"
Preece, Harold. "The Forgotten Fracas." *Real West,* Americana Series, Fall 1966, p. 30.

Lewis, Elmer "Kid"
Burton, Jeff. "The Mysterious Kid." *English Westerners Tally Sheet,* Vol. XX, No. 4, July 1974, p. 4.
Kelly, Bill. "The Odyssey of Kid Lewis." *Real West,* March 1977, p. 24. Rpt. *Real West,* Annual, Winter 1977-78, p. 34.
McBee, Fred. "The Newspapers Called Him the Mysterious Kid." *Great West,* June 1971, p. 28.
Rasch, Philip. "Three More Named 'Kid' Lewis." *Real West,* Annual, Spring 1982, p. 6.
Wilson, Steve. "How a Lynching Helped Open a Territory." *True Frontier,* Oct. 1967, p. 24.

Lewis, Joe
Larson, Jack. "The Devil Half Breed and the Columbia River Massacre." *Frontier West,* June 1975, p. 40.

Lewis, Meriwether
Henry, R.C. "Kin to the Grizzly." *The West,* July 1969, p. 26.

Hurdy, John Major. "The Impossible Mission of Lewis and Clark." *Pioneer West,* April 1971, p. 22.

Spivey, Louie E. "The Broken Dreams and Puzzling Death of Meriwether Lewis." *Old West,* Winter 1985, p. 36.

White, Marian B. "A Great Explorer's Final Hours." *Frontier Times,* May 1980, p. 8.

Lewis, Robert Ernest

Ernst, Robert R. "Gunfire in Bartlesville." *NOLA Quarterly,* Vol. XV, No. 4, Oct.-Dec. 1991, p. 26.

Lewis, Silan (also "Silon")

Robinson, Max. "Silon Lewis: Choctaw Code Martyr." *The West,* Oct. 1974, p. 14.

Scott, Jay. "End of a Tribal Law." *True Western Adventures,* Aug. 1961, p. 28.

Shirley, Glenn. "The Honorable Death of Silan Lewis." *True West,* June 1991, p. 27.

_____. "Witness to Choctaw Punishment." *Westerner,* Nov.-Dec. 1973, p. 14.

Liddil, Richard "Dick" (also spelled "Liddill")

Parsons, Chuck. "James Gang Traitor" ("Answer Man" column). *True West,* July 1984, p. 31.

Stiles, Bill. "King of the Buscaderos." *The West,* April 1969, p. 20.

Light, Zach

Rasch, Philip J. "Zach Light, New Mexico Badman." *NOLA Quarterly,* Vol. IV, No. 4, June 1979, p. 1.

Light Horse Indian Lawmen

Walker, Wayne T. "The Light Horse Indian Lawmen." *Great West,* Aug. 1973, p. 6. Rpt. *Great West,* Fall 1981, p. 6.

Lijon, Paul J.

Lyon, Paul J., with Dell Roensch. "Geronimo's Last Raid." *True Western Adventures,* Summer 1958, p. 45.

Lillie, Gordon "Pawnee Bill"

Beardsley, J.L. "Pawnee Bill: Oklahoma Giant." *The West,* March 1973, p. 20.

Long, Paul F. "Pawnee Bill Lillie: The Other Bill." *Real West,* Aug. 1984, p. 26. Rpt. *Real West,* Annual, Spring 1985, p. 58.

Savage, G.L. "Pawnee Bill: Little Giant of Oklahoma." *Old West,* Fall 1966, p. 54.

Lilly, Ben
Dobie, J. Frank. "The Man Who Thought Like a Panther." *True West,* Dec. 1963, p. 35.

Lilly, Ben. "Ben Lilly and the Creation Bear." *Westerner,* Jan.-Feb. 1973, p. 18.

Woolsey, Norman G. "Ben Lilly's Longest Grizzly Chase." *True West,* April 1958, p. 18.

Lin, Gin
Meier, Gary. "Gin Lin: Chinese Gold King." *True West,* Feb. 1991, p. 30.

Lincoln County Gang
Deac, Wilfred P. "War Without Heroes." *Wild West,* April 1991, p. 18.

Martin, Cy. "The Lincoln County War." *Real West,* Yearbook, Summer 1978, p. 12.

Rasch, Philip J. "Chaos in Lincoln County." *Denver Westerners Brand Book,* Vol. XVIII, 1963, p. 150.

_____. "Five Days of Battle." *Denver Westerners' Brand Book,* Vol. XI, 1956, p. 295.

_____. "Gunfire in Lincoln County." *English Westerners Brand Book,* Vol IX, No. 3, April 1967, p. 6.

Little Big Man
Swanson, Budington. "How Little Big Man Tried to Save the Black Hills." *Western Frontier,* Special Issue, March 1975, p. 34.

Little Crow
Arthur, Jim. "The Sioux Chief Whose Rage Turned the Prairie Red With Blood." *Frontier West,* Oct. 1973, p. 8.

Boswell, Charles. "The Last Flight of Little Crow the Fifth." *True Western Adventures,* Aug. 1959, p. 36.

Deac, Wilfred P. "The Indians Are Raising Hell." *True West,* Sept. 1988, p. 38.

Lipton, Dean. "Tell 'em to Eat Grass." *Great West,* Feb. 1968, p. 8.

Lowenkopf, Shelly. "The West's Bloodiest Massacre." *Man's Western,* Jan. 1960, p. 22. Rpt. *Pioneer West,* Nov. 1967, p. 16.

Mays, Carelton. "Blood Bath at Red River." *Real West,* Americana Series, Fall 1966, p. 18.

Quale, Charles. "Bloody Revenge of Little Crow." *Real West,* Nov. 1961, p. 28. Rpt. *Real West,* Americana Series, Winter 1964, p. 22.

Little Dog
Greenfield, Charles D. "Little Dog Became the Best Friend the Montana Whites Ever Had." *Frontier West,* Feb. 1973, p. 20.

Littlefield, George W.
Wallis, George A. "Cattle Kings." Part I, *True West,* April 1964, p. 8.

Little Wolf
Bailey, Tom. "The White Invaders." *True West,* Aug. 1963, p. 14.

Bird, Roy. "The Last Indian Raid in Kansas." *Real West,* Sept. 1980, p. 26. Rpt. *Real West,* Annual, 1981, p. 38.

Guttman, John. "Warriors and Chiefs" column. *Wild West,* Oct. 1989, p. 10.

Kiewit, Fred. "Outrage at Oberlin." *Frontier Times,* Sept. 1965, p. 18.

Long, James. "Death Trail of the Cheyenne." *Real West,* Sept. 1964, p. 20.

Lowenkopf, Shelly. "Little Wolf's Invincible Yellow Paint." *Wild West,* Dec. 1969, p. 4.

Millard, Joseph. "The Reluctant Warriors." *True Western Adventures,* Feb. 1959, p. 40.

Smith, Ann M. "Let My People Go." *Western Round-up,* May 1970, p. 40. Rpt. *Pioneer West,* Nov. 1973, p. 52; and *Oldtimers Wild West,* Dec. 1976, p. 16.

————. "The Cheyenne Shadows." *Pioneer West,* June 1972, p. 48.

Stanley, Samuel. "Breakout at Fort Robinson: The Cheyennes Vowed No Stockade Would Hold Them." *Frontier West,* April 1975, p. 36.

————. "Their Hearts Yearned for Home." *The West,* Aug. 1968, p. 36. Rpt. *Golden West,* April 1972, p. 8; and *Western Frontier,* Special Issue, March 1975, p. 28.

Turpin, Robert F. "Little Wolf's Fight." *Great West,* Aug. 1970, p. 10.

Livingston, Gus
Rube, Bernts. "A Yuma Tragedy." *NOLA Quarterly,* Vol. V, No. 1, October 1979, p. 16.

Llewellyn, William Henry Harrison
Carson, John. "Iron Man Llewellyn." *Frontier Times,* Jan. 1972, p. 20.

Lloyd, Ira
Bird, Roy. "Ira Lloyd, Gun-toting Lawyer in a Lawless Cowtown." *Real West,* April 1981, p. 24. Rpt. *Real West,* Annual, Spring 1982, p. 31.

Lloyd, Richard "Dick"
Rasch, Philip J. "Adios, Dick Lloyd." *NOLA Quarterly,* Vol. VIII, No. 1, Summer 1983, p. 7.

Loco, Pedro
Dobie, J. Frank. "Pedro Loco." *True West,* Winter 1953, p. 18.

Logan Brothers
Dullenty, Jim, and Ben Garthofner with Robert C. Lucke. "New Gold Rush in the Little Rockies." *True West,* March 1984, p. 46.

Dullenty, Jim. "George Currie and the Curry Brothers." *NOLA Quarterly,* Vol. II, No. 3, Fall 1976, p. 11.

Greenfield, Charles. "How the Logan Boys Got That Way." *Golden West,* Sept. 1969, p. 16. Rpt. *Golden West,* April 1973, p. 16; and *Western Frontier,* Nov. 1982, p. 16.

Johnson, Dorothy M. "The Brothers Left a Crimson Trail." *True Western Adventures,* Aug. 1959, p. 24.

Mac, 'Tana. "The Long Long Trail." *Frontier Times,* Spring 1961, p. 23.

Logan, Harvey "Kid Curry"
Boren, Kerry Ross. "The Mysterious Pinkerton." *True West,* Aug. 1977, p. 28.

Borger, Ed. "The Sundance Kid's Attack at Wilcox." *Westerner,* Nov.-Dec. 1973, p. 28.

DeMattos, Jack. "Harvey Logan" ("Gunfighters of the Real West" column). *Real West,* Oct. 1983, p. 24.

Graham, Nortron. "Dynamite Kid." *Real West,* Aug. 1958, p. 38.

"Harvey Logan, Alias Kid Curry." *Great West,* Oct. 1972, p. 30.

Humbolt, Fred. "Harvey Logan: Tiger of the Wild Bunch." *Westerner,* Nov.-Dec. 1973, p. 39.

Kerry, Dane. "Kid Curry: Sheriff Buster of the Wild Bunch." *Western Action,* Dec. 1960, p. 26.

Kindred, Wayne E. "Harvey Logan's Escape." *True West,* May 1986, p. 20.

_____. "Knoxville's Favorite Outlaw." *NOLA Quarterly,* Vol. X, No. 2, Fall 1985, p. 6.

Kirk, C.N. "Kid Curry's Wild Bunch." *True West,* Feb. 1956, p. 8.

Lamb, F. Bruce. "How My Family Met Outlaw Kid Curry." *WOLA Journal Quarterly,* Vol. I, No. 2, Fall-Winter 1991, p. 6.

North, Dick. "When the Tiger of the Wild Bunch Broke Out of the Knoxville Jail." *Frontier Times,* Sept. 1975, p. 16.

Osgood, Stacy W. "Gun and Gunman." *Chicago Westerners Brand Book,* Vol. XVIII, No. 1, March 1961, p. 1.

_____. "Wildest of the Wild Bunch." *Chicago Westerners Brand Book,* Vol. XVII, No. 5, July 1960, p. 1.

Owens, Harry J. "The Thrilling Capture of the Sundance Kid and Kid Curry." *NOLA Quarterly,* Vol. X, No. 4, Spring 1986, p. 9.

Rasch, Philip J. "He Saw Kid Curry Rob Great Northern Train." *NOLA Quarterly,* Vol. IX, No. 3, Winter 1985, p. 8.

Williams, Gary. "New Facts About Kid Curry, Last of the Wild Bunch." *The West,* March 1964, p. 6. Rpt. *The West,* Annual 1971, p. 12.

Logan, Lonny ("Lonny Curry")

Bell, Mike. "The Killing of Lonny Logan." *English Westerners Tally Sheet,* Vol. XXXVI, No. 2, Spring 1990, p. 1.

Logan, Thomas W.

Boor, Jackie. "The Killing of Sheriff Logan." *True West,* April 1987, p. 14.

London, Jack.

Browning, Dwain. "The Stormy Life of Jack London." *Golden West,* Oct. 1974, p. 30.

Lone Wolf

Jones, Calico. "Lone Wolf: Death Defying Kiowa Chief." *Real West,* Aug. 1971, p. 6.

Kildare, Maurice. "Lone Wolf, Death Defiant Kiowa Chief." *Real West,* Special Issue, Spring 1972, p. 57.

Lehman, Leola. "Lone Wolf's Vengeance." *Real West,* Americana Series, Fall 1966, p. 38.

Robinson, Charles M., III. "The Tough Little Ranger of Lost Valley." *True West,* July 1991, p. 18.

Long, Jane

Cheney, Louise. "Jane Long, Mother of Texas." *The West,* Feb. 1966, p. 20. Rpt. *The West,* July 1973, p. 38; and *Western Frontier,* Annual No. 4, 1976, p. 2.

Marks, Paula Mitchell. "Jane Long's Long Vigil." *Old West,* Winter 1984, p. 28.

Long, Steve "Big Steve"

Griswold, John. "The Outlaw Who Wore a Sheriff's Star." *Frontier West,* Feb. 1972, p. 24.

Longabaugh, Harry "Sundance Kid"

Boren, Kerry Ross. "How They Killed the Sundance Kid." *Real West,* Nov. 1979, p. 14.

Borger, Ed. "The Sundance Kid's Attack at Wilcox." *Westerner,* Nov.-Dec. 1973, p. 28.

Ernst, Donna. "Longabaugh Family Breaks Long Silence." *NOLA Quarterly,* Vol. XIII, No. 2, Fall 1989, p. 9.

Kirby, Edward M. "Butch Cassidy and the Sundance Kid: An Historical Essay." *The Outlaw Trail Journal,* Vol. I, No. 1, Summer 1991, p. 23.

_____. "Butch, Etta and Sundance in the Big Apple." *Real West,* Jan. 1978, p. 46.

_____. "Butch, Sundance and Etta Place Frolicked in 'Fun City.'" *NOLA Quarterly,* Vol. I, No. 4, 1975, p. 5.

_____. "The Sundance Kid and the Belle Fourche Bank Robbery." *True West,* Jan. 1983, p. 10.

_____. "The Sundance Kid and the Belle Fourche Robbery." *NOLA Quarterly,* Vol. VII, No. 2, Summer 1982, p. 5.

Meadows, Anne, and Daniel Buck. "Running Down a Legend." *Americas,* Vol. XLII, No. 6, 1990-1991, p. 21.

Owens, Harry J. "The Thrilling Capture of the Sundance Kid and Kid Curry." *NOLA Quarterly,* Vol. X, No. 4, Spring 1986, p. 9.

Parsons, Chuck. "A Tough One to Track" ("Answer Man" column). *True West,* April 1991, p. 12.

Robinson, Howard. "The Day the American West Died." *America's Frontier West,* Issue No. 1, n.d., p. 30.

Longley, James Stockton "Jim"

Spiller, Wayne. "His Brother's Long Shadow." *True West,* Feb. 1972, p. 6.

Longley, William Preston "Wild Bill"

Briehan, Carl. W. "Wild Bill Longley: He Didn't Believe in Surrender." Part I, *Real West,* March 1970, p. 46; Part II *Real West,* April 1970, p. 56.

DeMattos, Jack. "Bill Longley" ("Gunfighters of the Real West" column). *Real West*, Feb. 1983, p. 32.

Ellison, Douglas W. "Rivals in Texas: Hardin and Longley." *NOLA Quarterly*, Vol. XII, No. 4, Spring 1986, p. 10.

Forbes, Stanley G. "Fast Gun From Texas." *Golden West*, Sept. 1965, p. 37. Rpt. *Western Frontier*, Special Issue, Fall 1974, p. 37; and *Western Frontier*, Jan. 1983, p. 5.

Hagen, Everett. "I Saw Wild Bill Longley Hang." *Real West*, May 1959, p. 20.

Longley, Dewey Byron. "My Uncle, Bill Longley." *True Western Adventures*, June 1959, p. 18.

O'Neal, Bill. "Wild Bill Longley vs Bill Scrier" ("Great Western Gunfights" column). *True West*, April 1989, p. 56.

Parsons, Chuck. "Outlaw Genealogy" ("Answer Man" column). *True West*, Nov. 1989, p. 12.

Rhodes, L. Patschke. "Wild Bill Longley." *True West*, Jan. 1955, p. 24. Rpt. *Old West*, Winter 1965, p. 44; and *Badman*, Summer 1971, p. 12.

Robbins, Lance. "Young Rebel." *Real West*, Annual, Spring 1968, p. 78.

Schuessler, Raymond. "Bill Longley: Thirty Notch Gunman." *Real West*, Feb. 1969, p. 17.

Stanley, Sam. "Wild Bill Longley." *Pioneer West*, Nov. 1978, p. 26.

"Wild Bill Longley" ("Gallery of Gunmen" column). *True Western Adventures*, No. 3, June 1960, p. 64.

Longstreet, Andrew Jackson "Jack"

Lewis, Georgia. "Jack Longstreet." *Real Frontier*, June 1970, p. 28. Rpt. *True Frontier*, Special Issue No. 3, 1972, p. 38.

Longwell, James

Rosson, Mary'n. "James Longwell: Deputy-Scout-Western Banker." *Frontier West*, Dec. 1972, p. 18.

Looking Glass

Howard, Helen Addison. "A Divided Command Doomed the Nez Percé." *Frontier Times*, Sept. 1967, p. 10.

McKinnon, L.C. "A Courageous Try for Freedom." *Real West*, June 1983, p. 10. Rpt. *Real West*, Annual, Spring 1984, p. 50.

Lopez, Rafael

Wolfe, George D. "Utah's Greatest Manhunt." *Frontier Times*, Fall 1962, p. 32.

"Lottie Deno" (see Thurmond, Charlotte)

Love, Harry
Ryall, William. "Captain Love's Bounty." *True Western Adventures,* Feb. 1960, p. 28.

Secrest, William B. "Hell for Leather Rangers." *True West,* April 1968, p. 20.

_____. "Who Died at Cantua Creek?" *Real West,* April 1984, p. 36. Rpt. *Real West,* Special Issue, Spring 1985, p. 20.

Love, H.M.
Titsworth, B.D. "Hole-in-the-Wall Gang." *True West,* Dec. 1956, p. 10. Rpt. *Badman,* Fall 1972, p. 4.

Loving, Frank "Cockeyed Frank"
DeArment, R.K. "The Gunfights of Cockeyed Frank." *True West,* Sept. 1989, p. 22.

O'Neal, Bill. "Cockeyed Frank Loving vs Levi Richardson" ("Great Western Gunfights" column). *True West,* June 1991, p. 62.

Wadly, Jerome. "The Gunfighter's Ladies." *Westerner,* July-Aug. 1973, p. 48.

Loving, Oliver
Garner, E.L. "Bill Williams' Getaway." *Frontier Times,* March 1968, p. 21.

Koller, Joe. "Oliver Loving's Last Stand." *Golden West,* May 1966, p. 16. Rpt. *Western Frontier,* Sept. 1980, p. 16.

Peterson, Marc. "The Death of Joe [sic] Loving." *True West,* April 1957, p. 9.

Preece, Harold. "Oliver Loving, Texas Trail Driver." *Real West,* July 1964, p. 32.

Loveland, William Austin Hamilton
Jessen, Kenneth. "W.A.H. Loveland, Railroad Builder." *Old West,* Fall 1982, p. 30.

Lowe, Joe "Rowdy Joe"
Koop, W.E. "Rowdy Joe Low and His Bloody Delano." *The West,* June 1965, p. 22. Rpt. *The West,* Jan. 1972, p. 34.

O'Neal, Bill. "Rowdy Joe Lowe vs Red Beard" ("Great Western Gunfights" column). *True West,* Aug. 1989, p. 61.

Phillips, Bill. "Wild and Wooly Wichita." *True Frontier,* Oct. 1977, p. 6.

Walker, Wayne T. "Killer in a Top Hat." *Great West,* Oct. 1972, p. 20. Rpt. *Real West,* May 1979, p. 32.

Lucas, Orrington "Red"
Wallace, John. "The Story of a U.S. Marshal: Red Lucas." *Frontier Times,* July 1974, p. 6.

Lull, Louis J.
Zink, Wilbur A. "Gun Battle at Roscoe." *Frontier Times,* March 1969, p. 6.

McAlister, J.E.
O'Neal, Bill. "The LS Ranch in Texas: Cattle Kingdom of the Caprock County." *Real West,* April 1983, p. 14.

McCabe, Francis
Vanderwerth, W.C. "Which Way Did They Go?" *Real West,* Yearbook, Summer, 1978, p. 52.

McCall, John "Jack"
Harrison, Fred. "The Trial of Jack McCall." *Real West,* Nov. 1966, p. 20.

Hart, George. "Jack McCall: Frontier Enigma." *Real West,* Nov. 1972, p. 18. Rpt. *Real West,* Yearbook, Spring 1974, p. 51.

Rosa, Joseph G. "Draw It Tighter, Marshal." *Old West,* Summer 1971, p. 6.

McCanles, David Colbert "Dave"
Breihan, Carl W. "The Hickok-McCanles Affair." *Real West,* Sept. 1967, p. 10.

"Hickok: Hero or Heel?" *Badman,* Annual 1971, p. 32.

O'Neal, Bill. "'Duck Bill' Hickok vs The McCanles Gang." *True West,* April 1991, p. 56.

Repp, Ed Earl. "Home Made Hero." *True Frontier,* Dec. 1974, p. 19.

Wilson, Robert L. "Slaughter at Rock Creek Station." *Westerner,* May-June 1969, p. 48.

McCarty Boys (Tom, Bill, and Fred)
Fishell, Dave. "The McCarty Gang and the Delta Holdup." *Old West,* Spring 1985, p. 10.

Henderson, Grace G. "The McCarty Gang in Oregon." *Old West,* Summer 1977, p. 39.

Kirkpatrick, J.R. "Butch Cassidy and the McCarty Gang." *Westerner,* Feb. 1971, p. 44.

"The McCarty Gang." *Great West,* Dec. 1969, p. 6.

Skovlin, John. "The McCarty Gang." *NOLA Quarterly,* Vol. V, No. 3, April 1980, p. 16.

Stewart, Patricia. "They Knew the McCartys." *The West,* Dec. 1970, p. 24.

McCarty, Joe
Rasch, Philip J. "The Bonney Brothers." *Frontier Times,* Jan. 1965, p. 43.

McCarty, Patrick Henry "Billy the Kid" (Kid Antrim, Billy Bonney)
Adams, Jeff. "Hellacious Young Hellion." *Old West,* Spring 1965, p. 38. Rpt. *Badman,* Summer 1971, p. 21.

Barker, Allen. "I Refound Stinking Springs." *True West,* Feb. 1989, p. 14.

"Billy the Kid" ("Gallery of Gunmen" column). *True Western Adventures,* No. 2, June 1960, p. 49.

Blazer, Paul. "Billy the Kid: The Coward at Blazer's Mill." *Westerner,* Sept.-Oct. 1974, p. 12.

Breihan, Carl W. "Billy the Kid's Date With Destiny." Part I, *Pioneer West,* May 1977, p. 6; Part II, *Pioneer West,* July 1977, p. 6.

———. "The Day Billy the Kid Was Killed." *Real West,* Dec. 1974, p. 38.

Callon, Milton W. "Billy the Kid's Last Christmas." *Frontier Times,* Jan. 1968, p. 34.

Carson, Kit. "Billy the Kid's Restless Bones." *Real West,* March 1962, p. 14.

———. "The Day Billy the Kid Died." *Real West,* March 1964, p. 15.

Carson, William J. "What Was Billy the Kid's Real Name?" *Real West,* May 1969, p. 46.

Carson, Xanthus. "The Riddle of Billy the Kid: Living Phantom or Walking Dead Man?" *Frontier West,* Oct. 1975, p. 40.

———. "They All Loved Billy the Kid." *True Frontier,* July 1970, p. 30. Rpt. *True Frontier,* Special Issue No. 9, 1974, p. 28.

Cline, Don. "Battle Over Billy the Kid's Horse." *NOLA Quarterly,* Vol. XII, No. 3, Winter, 1988, p. 12.

———. "Billy the Kid and Escape From Jail in Albuquerque." *NOLA Quarterly,* Vol. X, No. 2, Fall 1985, p. 9.

————. "Billy the Kid Photos: The Faces, the Places, the Facts." *Old West,* Spring 1986, p. 46.

————. "The Mystery of Billy the Kid's Home." *NOLA Quarterly,* Vol. XIII, No. 2, Fall 1988, p. 16.

————. "The Secret Life of Billy the Kid." *True West,* April 1984, p. 12.

Cronyn, George. "Who Really Shot Billy the Kid?" *Real West,* Sept. 1966, p. 42.

Deac, Wilfred P. "War Without Heroes." *Wild West,* April 1991, p. 18.

DeMattos, Jack. "Henry McCarty" ("Gunfighters of the Real West" column). *Real West,* Aug. 1983, p. 40.

————. "The Kid." *Real West,* Special Issue, Spring 1984, p. 42.

————. "The Search for Billy the Kid's Roots Is Over." *Real West,* Jan. 1980, p. 26.

————. "The Search for Billy the Kid's Roots." *Real West,* Nov. 1978, p. 12.

Dyer, Robert. "Billy the Kid: The Photos Face Forensics." *True West,* March 1990, p. 26.

Erwin, Allen A. Letter. *True West,* Aug. 1957, p. 44.

Gregg, Andy. "Who Was the Real Billy the Kid?" *Real West,* Nov. 1963, p. 35.

Guinon, J.P. "The Last Days of Billy the Kid." *Real West,* Special Issue, Fall 1964, p. 40.

Harshbarger, I. Letter. *True West,* Aug. 1957, p. 46.

Holder, Gene. Letter. *True West,* Aug. 1957, p. 43.

Kemp, Ben W. "Ride for Mexico, Billy." *Frontier Times,* March 1980, p. 6.

Kruse, Mel C. Letter. *True West,* Aug. 1957, p. 44.

Martinez, Roberto. Letter. *True West,* Aug. 1957, p. 3.

Mays, Carelton. "Angel From Hell." *Real West,* Jan. 1961, p. 8. Rpt. *Real West,* Annual, Spring 1968, p. 34.

McCarty, Lea F. "Billy the Kid's Funeral." *True West,* Dec. 1960, p. 6.

————. Letter. *True West,* Aug. 1957, p. 48.

McCright, Grady E. "Who Sleeps in Billy the Kid's Tomb?" *True Frontier,* April 1978, p. 12.

Metz, Leon. "My Search for Pat Garrett and Billy the Kid." *True West,* Aug. 1983, p. 35.

Overly, William. W. Letter. *True West,* Aug. 1957, p. 48.

Poe, John W. Rpt. "Death of Billy the Kid." *True West,* June 1962, p. 6.

Rasch, P.J. Letter. *True West,* Aug. 1957, p. 45.

Rasch, Philip J. "A Billy the Kid Incident." *NOLA Quarterly,* Vol. IV, No. 1, Fall 1978, p. 6.

_____. "Clues to the Puzzle of Billy the Kid." *English Westerners' Brand Book,* Vol. IV, Dec. 1957-Jan. 1958, p. 1.

_____. "Did Billy the Kid Kill Broncho Jake?" *NOLA Quarterly,* Vol. III, No. 2, Autumn 1977, p. 12.

_____. "The Governor Meets the Kid." *English Westerners' Brand Book,* Vol. VIII, April 1966, p. 5.

_____. "A Second Look at the Blazer's Mill Affair." *Frontier Times,* Jan. 1969, p. 30.

_____. "Sidelights on Billy the Kid." *NOLA Quarterly,* Vol. VIII, No. 2, Fall 1983, p. 2.

_____. "The Trials of Billy the Kid." *Real West,* Nov. 1987, p. 32.

Rickards, Colin. "Pat Garrett Tells 'How I Killed Billy the Kid.'" *Real West,* Special Issue, Fall 1973, p. 30.

Ripple, Sam. "Billy's Murderous Deed." *Westerner,* Nov.-Dec. 1973, p. 37.

Roberts, J.B. Letter. *Real West,* April 1980, p. 6.

Sanchez, Lynda A. "They Loved Billy the Kid: To Them He Was 'Billito.'" *True West,* Jan. 1984, p. 12.

Siringo, Charles A. "The Capture of Billy the Kid." *Big West,* Dec. 1969, p. 12.

Sooner, Paul. "The Kid." *Westerner,* Nov.-Dec. 1971, p. 16.

Steinke, Rick. Letter. *True West,* Aug. 1957, p. 46.

Stillman, W.K., and Cy Martin. "Was Billy the Kid a Psychopathic Killer?" *Golden West,* Sept. 1965, p. 30. Rpt. *Western Frontier,* Jan. 1978, p. 12; and *Western Frontier,* Nov. 1982, p. 28.

Turner, Russell M. Letter. *True West,* Aug. 1957, p. 47.

Weisner, Herman B. "Outlaw Rock." *True West,* March 1982, p. 48.

_____. "Pistol or Shotgun: Which Killed Billy?" *Old West,* Summer 1981, p. 12.

"A Western Desperado." Rpt. *NOLA Quarterly,* Vol. XV, No. 1, 1991, p. 29.

Westwood, Dick. "Secret Meetings with Billy the Kid." *NOLA Quarterly,* Vol. XI, No. 4, Spring 1987, p. 12.

Wiltsey, Norman B. "Billy the Kid." *True Western Adventures,* Feb. 1959, p. 14.

_____. "Billy the Kid: Ruffian or Robin Hood?" Part I, *Real West,* Oct. 1970, p. 35; Part II, *Real West,* Nov. 1970, p. 46.

_____. "Killer Kid." *True West,* April 1957, p. 4.

Wright, Thomas W. Letter. *True West,* Aug. 1957, p. 48.

McCarty, Thomas "Tom"

Boren, Kerry Ross. "The Mysterious Pinkerton." *True West,* Aug. 1977, p. 28.

"The McCarty Gang." *Great West,* Dec. 1969, p. 6.

McCloud, James "Jim"
Carlson, Chip. "An Outlaw on Outlaw Horses." *True West,* July 1991, p. 23.

McCloud, Sadie
Pennard, Lee. "The Bloody Vengeance Trail of Sadie McCloud." *Frontier West,* June 1973, p. 36.

McCluskey, Mike (also McCluskie, McCloskie; Arthur Delaney)
Allegro. "The West's Bloodiest Duel." Ed. Colin Rickards. Rpt. *Old West,* Summer 1965, p. 25.

Arango, Douglas. "The Deepest Pit of Hell." *Great West,* June 1967, p. 22.

Campagnon, Frank D. "Mike's Mad Shadow." *True Western Adventures,* Issue No. 1, 1957, p. 23.

Coulter, Eugene. "The Bloody Newton Shoot-Out." *Frontier West,* April 1971, p. 24.

Crane, Ray. "Shoot-Out at Newton." *Great West,* Oct. 1968, p. 4.

Holding, Vera. "Bloodiest Night in Kansas History." *True Frontier,* March 1970, p. 30.

O'Neal, Bill. "McCluskie vs Anderson" ("Great Western Gunfights" column). *True West,* Feb. 1988, p. 41.

_____. "The Newton General Massacre" ("Great Western Gunfights" column). *True West,* Jan. 1988, p. 47.

Richmond, Robert W. "Killing of Mike McCluskie." *The West,* May 1965, p. 38.

Wiltsey, Norman B. "Thundering Guns at Tuttle's Dancehall." *Golden West,* Nov. 1966, p. 8.

McComas, Charlie
Wellman, Paul I. "The White Apache." *True Western Adventures,* April 1959, p. 12.

McCormick, "Frenchy" and "Mickey"
Bean , Tom. "Frenchy." *True West,* May 1990, p. 61.

Daniel, Beverly. "Frenchy McCormick: The Sweetheart of Tascosa's Saloon." *Westerner,* Jan.-Feb. 1974, p. 12.

_____. "They Died Together, Frenchy McCormick and Old Tascosa." *Real West,* Aug. 1973, p. 66.

Wallace, George A. "Cattle Kings." *True West,* Feb. 1964, p. 70.

McCoy Gang (Dick, Joe, and Streeter)
Miller, Victor W. "The McCoy Gang." *Old West,* Summer 1970, p. 22.

McCoy, Joseph G. "Joe"
Cheney, Louise. "Abilene's Stampede of Death." *Real West,* Sept. 1962, p. 18.
Holman, John. "Fantastic Dream of Joe McCoy." *Real West,* Jan. 1961, p. 20.
Koller, Joe. "McCoy's River of Cattle." *Golden West,* May 1971, p. 20.
Richmond, Robert W. "Joe McCoy Scouts Texas." *True West,* Feb. 1973, p. 32.

McCulloch, Ben
Brown, John Henry. "Gen. Ben McCulloch: His Indian Fighting Days." *Frontier Times,* Nov. 1978, p. 22.

McCurdy, Elmer
Kelly, Bill. "The Triumphal Return of Elmer McCurdy." *Real West,* July 1977, p. 8. Rpt. *Real West,* Yearbook, Summer 1978, p. 32.

McCurtain, Jackson E.
Smith, Jay McDougal. "Grand Lady of the Choctaws." *Real West,* Feb. 1987, p. 32.

McDaniels, Charley
Stone, Fred A. "Flowers for Charley McDaniels." *True West,* Winter 1953, p. 13.

McDonald, John
Southworth, John. "An Unlikely Pair of Outlaws" ("Wild Old Days" column). *True West,* Feb. 1991, p. 60.

McDonald, William "Bill"
Andre, Jim. "The Fastest Tongue in Texas." *Westerner,* May-June 1969, p. 19.
DeMattos, Jack. "Bill McDonald, Bull-headed Ranger." *Real West,* Annual, Spring 1984, p. 44.
_____. "Bill McDonald" ("Gunfighters of the Real West" column). *Real West,* June 1983, p. 22.
Paine, Albert Bigelow. "Buzzard's Water Hole Gang." Rpt. *Frontier Times,* March 1980, p. 12.
Repp, Ed Earl. "The King of the Outlaw Busters." *The West,* Feb. 1969, p. 10. Rpt. *The West,* Dec. 1972, p. 16; *Western Frontier,* July 1977, p. 24; and *Western Frontier,* April 1983, p. 16.

St. John, Robert. "The Charmed Life of Ranger McDonald." *Real West,* July 1966, p. 38.

McElroy, John T.
Wallis, George A. "Cattle Kings." Part I, *True West,* April 1964, p. 8.

McFarlane, Robert L.
Edwards, Harold L. "No Monument for Robert McFarlane." *Old West,* Winter 1989, p. 28.

McGillycuddy, Valentine T.
Kutac, C. "Valentine McGillycuddy Who Understood Hurt." *Frontier Times,* Jan. 1980, p. 18.

Miller, Don. "Pine Ridge Standoff." *Real West,* July 1981, p. 10. Rpt. *Real West,* Annual, Spring 1982, p. 34.

McGinty, William M. "Billy"
Walker, Wayne T. "Billy McGinty: Just a Plain Old Bronc Rider." *Golden West,* Aug. 1972, p. 40.

McGirl, Thomas
Bundy, Rex. "No Girl Was McGirl." *Real West,* Dec. 1974, p. 14.

McGowan, Edward "Ed"
Traywick, Ben T. "Big Ed McGowan's Many Feuds." *The West,* March 1974, p. 29.

McGrew, Alexander O.
Robbins, Lance. "Wheelborrow [sic] McGrew." *Real Frontier,* Nov. 1971, p. 31. Rpt. *True Frontier,* Special Issue No. 11, Winter 1974-75, p. 7.

McIntire, James "Jim"
Kildare, Maurice. "American Valley Went Up in Smoke." *Frontier Times,* Nov. 1975, p. 8.

DeArment, R.K. "The Great Outlaw Confederacy." *True West,* Sept. 1990, p. 14.

McJunkin, George
Germond, Mary F. "The Black Cowboy Who Made the Folsom Discoveries." *True Frontier,* April 1972, p. 12.

Mackay, John W.
Pearson, Robert E. "The Bonanza Giant of 1873." *Big West,* Dec. 1967, p. 22.

Wingfield, William. "The Prince of Miners." *Real West,* May 1977, p. 14. Rpt. *Real West,* Annual, Winter 1977-78, p. 55.

McKee, Anthony
Read, Steve. "Raiders of the Blue Hills." *True West,* Jan. 1990, p. 16.

MacKenzie, Murdo
Wallis, George A. "Cattle Kings." Part II, *True West,* June 1964, p. 6.

Mackenzie, Ranald S.
Allenbaugh, Carl. "When Bad-Hand Rode to Oblivion." *Westerner,* March-April 1969, p. 28. Rpt. *Old Trails,* Winter 1977, p. 30.

Bloom, Sam. "Ambush! The Day the Fourth Cavalry Walked Into Hell." *Frontier West,* June 1974, p. 40.

Breihan, Carl W. "Mackenzie's Raiders." *Pioneer West,* March 1977, p. 19.

_____ "The Abbreviated Career of a Brilliant Soldier." *Golden West,* Nov. 1968, p. 18. Rpt. *Golden West,* Oct. 1973, p. 14.

Collett, James. "Mackenzie's Secret Raid." *Old West,* Spring 1984, p. 54.

Jones, Orlan and Wini. "Palo Duro, Canyon of the Dead." *Real West,* May 1964, p. 34.

Judge, Bill. "Battle of the Mighty Three." *True West,* June 1963, p. 26.

Knox, William. "The Last Campaign." *The West,* March 1966, p. 16.

Mclaine, Bruce. "Damn the Orders! Go Get 'Em." *True Western Adventures,* Aug. 1959, p. 28.

Richardson, Gladwell. "McKensie [sic]." *Westerner,* March-April 1972, p. 27.

Robinson, Charles M., III. "Mackenzie's Madness." *Old West,* Spring 1989, p. 14.

Skaggs, J. M. "The Insanity and Death of General Ranald S. Mackenzie." *True West,* Oct. 1971, p. 24.

Truby, J. David. "The American West's Best Indian Fighter." *Real West,* May 1978, p. 22.

Winski, Norman. "'Bad Hand' Mackenzie (Custer's Avenger)." *Pioneer West,* July 1967, p. 28.

_____. "The Human Fighting Machine." *Big West,* Oct. 1968, p. 32.

Wolfe, George D. "The Indians Named Him Bad Hand." *True West,* Dec. 1961, p. 16.

McKimie, Robert "Little Reddy"
Parsons, Chuck. "Little Reddy" ("Answer Man" column). *True West,* Feb. 1991, p. 12.

McKinney, Charles B.
Stephens, Robert W. "Ambush in the Chaparral." *Frontier Times,* May 1967, p. 30.

McKinney, James "Jim"
DeMattos, Jack. "Jim McKinney" ("Gunfighters of the Real West" column). *Real West,* July 1979, p. 16.

Edwards, Harold L. "Affairs of Gunman Jim McKinney." *NOLA Quarterly,* Vol. XI, No. 4, Spring 1987, p. 5.

_____. "California's Ruthless Outlaw." *Old West,* Summer 1985, p. 52.

_____. "Who Killed William Tibbet?" *Real West,* June 1987, p. 23.

Martin, Larry J. "Bad Boy Jim McKinney Becomes a Killer." *NOLA Quarterly,* Vol. VIII, No. 1, Summer 1983, p. 15.

Parsons, Chuck. "West Coast Badman" ("Answer Man" column). *True West,* June 1987, p. 10.

Secrest, William B. "McKinney's Way." *True Frontier,* Feb. 1972, p. 8. Rpt. *True Frontier,* Oct. 1976, p. 24.

Thorp, Raymond W., and William B. Secrest. "The Return of Jim McKinney." *True West,* Feb. 1963, p. 14.

McLaughlin, James "White Hair"
Clayton, Juliana. "The Private War of White Hair McLaughlin." *True West,* Nov. 1989, p. 52.

McLaury Brothers (also spelled McLowery)
Deac, Wilfred P. "Two Minutes in Tombstone." *Wild West,* Aug. 1991, p. 42.

Kantor, Seth. "Time: Oct. 26, 1881—Place: OK Corral." *Western Action,* Dec. 1960, p. 30.

Malocsay, Zoltan. "OK Corral: One Hundred Years of Lies." *Westerner,* July-Aug. 1973, p. 34.

Mays, Carelton. "What Really Happened at the OK Corral?" *Real West,* Jan 1958, p. 14.

Potter, Pam. "Murdered on the Streets of Tombstone." *NOLA Quarterly,* Vol. V, No. 1, Oct. 1979, p. 9.

Roberts, Gary L. "The Fight That Never Dies." *Frontier Times,* Nov. 1965, p. 6.

_____. "The Fremont Street Fiasco." *True West,* July 1988, p. 14.

McLoughlin, John

Darwin, Wayne. "The White Eagle Comes to Grief." *Golden West,* May 1971, p. 36.

Hall, Patrick A. "The Star of Oregon." *Golden West,* July 1968, p. 14. Rpt. *The West,* Oct. 1973, p. 26.

McMains, Oscar P.

Holben, Richard. "The Incredible Cimarron War of the Vigilante Minister." *Frontier West,* April 1973, p. 38.

McMasters, Thomas "Tom"

Bailey, Tom. "Satan's Brand." *True Western Adventures,* Oct. 1960, p. 30.

McMillen, Frank

Winfield, Craig. "Jesse James and the Winston Train Robbery." *Oldtimers Wild West,* Aug. 1977, p. 14.

McNelly, Lee H.

Bolon, R. "McNelly's Raiding Rangers." *Big West,* Oct. 1967, p. 42.

Boswell, Charles. "Ranger McNelly's Desperate Bargain." *True Western Adventures,* June 1961, p. 16.

Harrison, John H. "The Day McNelly's Thirty-One Texas Rangers Declared War On Mexico." *Frontier West,* June 1975, p. 6.

Kildare, Maurice. "McNelly's Texas Blood Bath." *Westerner,* Nov. 1970, p. 38.

McDaniel, Ruel. "Captain McNelly versus Five Thousand Outlaws." *Real West,* March 1961, p. 16.

Webb, Walter Prescott. "McNelly's Rangers." *True West,* Feb. 1962, p. 6. Rpt. *True West,* Aug. 1983, p. 68.

_____. "The Bandits of Las Cuevas." *True West,* Oct. 1962, p. 8.

McSween-Tunstal Faction

Mays, Carelton,. "The Cattle Baron Who Wouldn't Fight." *Real West,* Aug. 1958, p. 6.

Pryor, Rafaelita. "Siege of the McSween House." *Frontier Times,* May 1969, p. 24.

Rasch, Philip J. "How the Lincoln County War Started." *True West,* April 1962, p. 30.

McSween, Susan "Sue"

Best, J.C. "I Beg You, Colonel Dudley." *Real West,* Aug. 1988, p. 40.

Cline, Don. "Sue McSween and Colonel Dudley." *NOLA Quarterly,* Vol. XV, No. 1, 1991, p. 17.

Henn, Nora. "Was a Piano in the McSween House During the Five-day Battle?" *Real West,* Feb. 1984, p. 26. Rpt. *Real West,* Annual, Spring 1985, p. 30.

"Madame Moustache" (Elenore Dumont)

Bell, Maureen. "Madame Moustache: Notorious Gambler." *True West,* July 1991, p. 50.

Cheney, Louise. "The Petticoat Gambler Made Faro a Lethal Game." *Frontier West,* Oct. 1973, p. 34.

Coriell, Marian M. "Madame Moustache: The Perfumed Dove Who Mined the Miners." *Great West,* Sept. 1969, p. 30.

Harrison, John H. "Madame Moustache." *Real West,* Dec. 1982, p. 32. Rpt. *Real West,* Special Issue, Spring, 1985, p. 64.

Sandell, Jay. "Madame Moustache, the Angel of Sin." *Real West,* April 1958, p. 28. Rpt. *Real West,* Annual, Summer 1966, p. 50.

Young, Bob and Jan. "Madame Moustache." *True West,* June 1956, p. 12.

Madame Vestal (Belle Siddons)

Auer, Louise. "Deadwood's Gambling Lady." *Real West,* Oct. 1972, p. 48. Rpt. *Real West,* Annual, Summer 1973, p. 52.

Madsen, Chris

Sufrin, Mark. "Desperate Manhunt in the Oklahoma Territory." *Frontier West,* June 1971, p. 10.

Barbieri, M.I. "Chris Madsen." *Real West,* Americana Series, Fall 1965, p. 43.

Breihan, Carl. W. "Chris Madsen: The Fighting Dane." Part I, *Real West,* Dec. 1970, p. 24; Part II, *Real West,* Jan. 1971, p. 38. Rpt. as one-part article, *Real West,* Special Issue, Fall 1973, p. 24.

Burkholder, Edwin V. "The Last of the Fighting Marshals." *True Western Adventures,* Feb. 1959, p. 24.

Darlington John C. "Chris Madsen versus a Hundred Outlaws." *The West,* June 1965, p. 36. Rpt. *Western Frontier,* July 1983, p. 24.

Murach, I.B. "Cotton Pickin' Marshal." *Real Frontier,* Oct. 1970, p. 6. Rpt. *True Frontier,* Special Issue No. 11, Winter 1974-75, p. 12.

_____. "The Fighting Cotton Picker." *Golden West,* Jan. 1967, p. 40. Rpt.

Golden West, Sept. 1972, p. 37; *Western Frontier,* Annual, 1976, p. 23; and *Western Frontier,* Nov. 1986, p. 41.

Parsons, Chuck. "The Three Guardsmen" ("Answer Man" column). *True West,* March 1990, p. 12.

"Truly Western Hall of Fame" column. *True Western Adventures,* Aug. 1960, p. 74.

Magana, Juan

Edwards, Harold L. "Quick Justice for Juan Magana." *NOLA Quarterly,* Vol. XIV, No. 2, Summer 1990, p. 7.

Magoffin, James Wiley

Cortesi, Lawrence. "The Fantastic Spy Who Smashed the Mexicans." *Frontier West,* Dec. 1972, p. 22.

Eherts, Walter. "Secret Agent in the Southwest." *Real West,* Special Issue, Spring 1983, p. 22.

Walker, Wayne T. "Special Agent to the President." *Oldtimers Wild West,* Oct. 1977, p. 14.

Magoffin, Susan

Cheney, Louise. "Adventures of a Charming Lady." *The West,* April 1967, p. 14.

Russell, Sharman Apt. "'Lo, We Are Camping Again!'" *True West,* May 1989, p. 42.

Magruder, Lloyd

Agnew, Henry T. "Beachy's Murderous Dream." *Real West,* Jan. 1965, p. 38.

Cheney, Louise. "Hill Beachy's Nightmare." *Golden West,* May 1967, p. 36.

Ford, H.D. "Nightmare in the Bitterroots." *Frontier Times,* Spring 1960, p. 14.

Hansen, John. "They Murdered Magruder." *Great West,* Oct. 1973, p. 14.

Morgan, Thomas. Letter. *True West,* Feb. 1963, p. 4.

Pratt, Grace Roffey. "Hill Beachy's Prophetic Dream." *True West,* Dec. 1962, p. 24.

Stanley, Samuel. "Hill Beachy's Journey for Justice." *Real West,* April 1981, p. 28.

Weddle, Ferris M. "Murder in the Bitterroots." *Old West,* Winter 1964, p. 21. Rpt. *Badman,* Summer 1971, p. 57.

_____. "How Bitter Were the Roots." *Real West,* May 1959, p. 41.

Majors, Alexander

Shead, Ted. "They Rode the Wild and Vacant Land." *Real West,* Jan. 1972, p. 30.

Majors, John

Hartley, William B. "The Fabulous Pony Express." *True Western Adventures,* June 1960, p. 12.

Mays, Carelton. "Tragedy of the Pony Express." *Real West,* Nov. 1960, p. 8. Rpt. *Real West,* Annual, Spring 1968, p. 18.

Malcolm, John G.

Squires, Harry A. "It Was Great While It Lasted." *Golden West,* Nov. 1973, p. 13.

Maledon, George

Belton, George. "He Hanged Them With Silk." *Real West,* May 1960, p. 27.

Breihan, Carl W. "George Maledon, Hangman From Hell." *Real West,* May 1968, p. 10. Rpt. *Real West,* Annual, Summer 1970, p. 22.

_____. "Hangman From Hell." *Real West,* Sept. 1978, p. 40. Rpt. *Real West,* Annual, Winter 1980, p. 14.

French, Charles A. "Judge Parker's Hangman: The Noose Was His Only Friend." *Westerner,* Jan. 1971, p. 42.

Goolsby, Bruce. "The Hangman." *Frontier Times,* March 1963, p. 47.

Henshaw, Clay. "George Maledon: The Hanging Judge's Hangman." *Western Tales,* June 1960, p. 34.

Kildare, Maurice. "The Hangman's Daughter." *True Frontier,* Nov. 1973, p. 24.

Naylor, Lee. "Somebody Had to Do the Hanging Judge's Dirty Work." *Frontier West,* Dec. 1973, p. 22.

Repp, Ed Earl. "King of the Frontier Hangmen." *True Frontier,* Jan. 1970, p. 18. Rpt. *True Frontier,* Dec. 1972, p. 24.

Wilson, William R. "Justice on the Sooner Border." *Golden West,* June 1972, p. 38.

Malone, Washington "Wash"

Long, Gordon. "The Most Bizarre Cattle Drive of Them All." *The West,* Feb. 1965, p. 38.

Maman-Ti

Lamb, Lucylle M. "The Cry of the Owl." *Real Frontier,* June 1971, p. 34.

Maney, Michael Erskin

Edwards, Harold L. "The Short and Violent Life of Juan Patron." *True West,*
March 1991, p. 28.

Mangas Coloradas

Cortesi, Lawrence. "The Apache Conference That Set the Southwest Aflame."
Frontier West, April 1975, p. 14.

Hansard, Thom. "Apache Vengeance." *True West,* Winter, 1953, p. 25.

Majors, John. "Apache Vengeance: The Crime Against Mangas Coloradas." *Real
West,* Jan. 1962, p. 42. Rpt. *Real West,* Special Issue, Winter 1963, p. 43.

Myers, Lee. "Mangus Colorado's [sic] Favorite Ambush Site." *Old West,* Winter
1968, p. 24.

_____. "Retribution at Fort McLane." *True West,* Dec. 1969, p. 30.

Wiltsey, Norman B. "The Ordeal of Mangas Coloradas." *The West,* Jan. 1967, p.
26. Rpt. *The West,* Oct. 1971, p. 34.

Yarbrough, Leroy. "Mangus Colorado [sic]: Giant of the Desert." *Real West,* May
1971, p. 8. Rpt. *Real West,* Special Issue, Spring 1972, p. 19.

_____. "The Apache and the Sioux." *Real West,* Special Issue, Winter 1970,
p. 26.

Manley, W. Lee (William Lewis)

Cheney, Louise. "Manley's Return to Death Valley." *Real West,* Feb. 1971, p. 30.

Copeland, John A. "The Death Thirst." *True Western Adventures,* Feb. 1961, p.
26.

Mann, Harvey

Bird, Roy. "The Ambiguous Dr. Mann: Seventh Cavalry Surgeon." *Real West,*
Special Issue, Spring 1983, p. 65.

Manning, Anselm R.

Parsons, Chuck. "Hero of the Northfield Raid" ("Answer Man" column). *True
West,* Nov. 1990, p. 12.

Manning Brothers (James "Jim," George "Doc," and Frank)

Barstow, Bob. "The Patch-Pocket Marshal Took to Drink." *America's Frontier
West,* Issue No. 1, n.d., p. 42.

Bristow, Bob. "Patch Pocket Gunman." *True Western Adventures,* April 1959, p.
8.

Dial, Scott. "Dallas Stoudenmire and the El Paso Saloon War." *Westerner,* Spring
1975, p. 26.

Metz, Leon C. "The Death of Dallas Stoudenmire." *Real West,* Feb. 1973, p. 38.

Nolen, Oran Warder. "Gunfire in El Paso." *True Frontier,* Jan. 1969, p. 42.

Wolfgang, Otto. "Hell Town of Texas." *Pioneer West,* Jan. 1976, p. 50.

Manning, Charley
Stoner, Mary E. "My Father Was a Train Robber." *True West,* Aug. 1983, p. 14.

Manuel, Moses
Cheney, Louise. "The Fabulous Homestake Mine." *Real West,* Sept. 1970, p. 54.

Manuelito
Traywick, Ben. T. "Fiery War Chief of the Navajos." *The West,* April 1970, p. 26. Rpt. *Western Frontier,* April 1982, p. 5.

Maples, Daniel "Dan"
McKibben, Mike. "Siege at Rabbit Trap." *True Western Adventures,* Spring 1958, p. 16.

Marcy, R.B.
Jameson, J. Harold. "Ordeal in the Snow." *Frontier Times,* May 1963, p. 18.

Marcy, R.B. "Captain Marcy's Impossible Mission." *The West,* Jan. 1968, p. 20.

Markham Brothers (Sam and Abe)
Hallitson, John G. "The Markham's Traveling Sin Towns." *Frontier West,* June 1971, p. 24.

Marlow Brothers (Boone, "Alf," "Epp," George, and Charlie)
Hartley, William B. "The Men Who Wouldn't Be Lynched." *True Western Adventures,* Aug. 1959, p. 8.

Johnson, Edward W. "Deputy Marshal Johnson Breaks a Long Silence." *True West,* Feb. 1980, p. 6.

Parsons, Chuck. "Answer Man" column. *Frontier Times,* June 1985, p. 19.

Patten, Josephine. "He Killed a Heap of Men." *Old West,* Winter 1966, p. 27.

Stanley, Samuel. "A Desperate Escape." *Real West,* Dec. 1986, p. 16.

Taylor, Nat M. "Story of the Marlow Boys." *True West,* Feb. 1962, p. 32.

Marquis de Mores
Boswell, Charles. "His Lordship of the Badlands." *True Western Adventures,* April 1960, p. 14.

Clough, Bob. "The Napoleon of the Dakota Badlands." *Real West*, Yearbook, Fall 1979, p. 43.

Marsh, Grant

Wiltsey, Norman B. "The Epic Voyage of the Far West." *Real West*, July 1968, p. 15.

Brooks, Ken. "Custer's Navy: The Tragic Journey of the Sternwheeler *Far West.*" *True West*, October 1986, p. 14.

Marsh, John "Doc"

"Doc John Marsh." *Great West*, Summer 1981, p. 26.

Marshall, James W.

Marshall, James W. "James Marshall's Own Account of His Discovery of Gold at Sutter's Mill." *The West*, April 1966, p. 10. Rpt. *Golden West*, Jan. 1972, p. 24; and *Western Frontier*, Feb. 1984, p. 14.

Nadeau, Remi. "John [sic] Marshall's Boom Town." *True West*, April 1964, p. 36.

O'Brien, Robert. "James Marshall and the Curse of Gold." *True Western Adventures*, Feb. 1960, p. 12.

Rosenhouse, Leo. "El Dorado at the Sawmill." *Pioneer West*, April 1970, p. 16. Rpt. *Pioneer West*, Aug. 1972, p. 40; and *Pioneer West*, June 1974, p. 28.

Marshal, John E. "Curly"

Koop, W.E. "A Rope for One-Armed Charlie." *True West*, Feb. 1967, p. 22.

Walker, Wayne T. "The Curly Marshal Gang." *Real West*, Sept. 1979, p. 18.

Wilson, Roger. "The Curly Marshal Gang." *Great West*, Sept. 1974, p. 30. Rpt. *Authentic West*, Summer 1981, p. 30.

Martin Brothers (Sam and Will)

Haines, Joe D., Jr. "Wiley Haines Was Tough on Horse Thieves." *NOLA Quarterly*, Vol. VIII, No. 1, Summer 1983, p. 4.

Shirley, Glenn. "The Murdering Martins." *True Western Adventures*, Aug. 1960, p. 18.

Martin, John A.

Ross, Raymond J. "John A. Martin: Custer's Last Courier." *The West*, April 1967, p. 24.

Martin, William A. "Hurricane Bill"

DeArment, R.K. "Hurricane Bill Martin: Horsethief." *True West,* June 1991, p. 38.

Martinez, Antonio Jose

Duncan, Gra'Delle. "New Mexico's Game of Death." *Golden West,* May 1966, p. 28. Rpt. *Golden West,* July 1974, p. 10.

Odendahl, Eric M. "Saint or Devil." *True West,* April 1967, p. 34.

Mason, Barney

Edwards, Harold L. "Barney Mason: In the Shadow of Pat Garrett and Billy the Kid." *Old West,* Summer 1990, p. 14.

Parsons, Chuck. "Pat Garrett's Deputy" ("Answer Man" column). *True West,* Aug. 1990, p. 13.

Massai

Begay, Alberta. "Massai: Broncho Apache." *True West,* Aug. 1959, p. 6.

Hayes, Mike. "Massai: Legendary Apache Outlaw." *Real West,* Aug. 1988, p. 4.

Lutske, Harvey. "The Apache the Army Never Defeated." *Pioneer West,* Jan. 1968, p. 28. Rpt. *Wild West,* Oct. 1969, p. 16.

Massie, William Rodney

Thorp, Raymond W. "Wild Bill's Famous Bullet." *Real West,* May 1961, p. 18.

Masterson, Bertholomiew "Bat" (also spelled "Bartholomew")

Breihan, Carl W. "Bat Masterson, Law Man." Part I, *Real West,* Nov. 1969, p. 44; Part II, *Real West,* Dec. 1969, p. 17. Rpt. as one-part article, *Real West,* Special Issue, Fall 1973, p. 8.

————. "They Called Him Bat." *Oldtimers Wild West,* Oct. 1978, p. 17.

Burkholder, Edwin V. "Bat Masterson." *Real West,* Americana Series, Fall 1965, p. 13.

————. "Bat Masterson: Gunslinging Dude from Dodge." *Western Action,* Sept. 1960, p. 28.

————. "I Knew the Real Bat Masterson." *Real West,* May 1960, p. 12. Rpt. *Real West,* Annual, Summer 1966, p. 6.

Chatfield, Harry. "Bat Masterson's Railroad War." *Real West,* March 1965, p. 20.

DeArment, Robert K. "Bat Masterson's Rescue of Bully Bill." *True West,* Oct. 1979, p. 10.

DeMattos, Jack. "Bat Masterson" ("Gunfighters of the Real West" column). *Real*

West, Feb. 1985, p. 32. Rpt. *Real West,* Special Issue, Spring 1986, p. 56.

————. "Bat Masterson Was Colorful Lawman and Sport." *NOLA Quarterly,* Vol. II, No. 4, Winter 1976, p. 4.

————. "The President and the Gunfighter." *True West,* Feb. 1976, p. 18.

————. "Those Guns of Bat Masterson." *Frontier Times,* March 1977, p. 10.

Dittmos, Henry. "The Bat and the Rose." *True Western Adventures,* Issue No. 1, 1957, p. 16.

Earp, Wyatt. "Wyatt Earp's Tribute to Bat Masterson, the Hero of 'Dobe Walls." Part I, *Real West,* Sept. 1978, p. 8; Part II, *Real West,* Nov. 1978, p. 36. Rpt. as one-part article, *Real West,* Yearbook, Fall 1979, p. 16.

Harmon, John. "A Rose to Death." *Real West,* Aug. 1958, p. 28.

Hinkle, Milt. "The Earp and Masterson I Knew." *True West,* Dec. 1961, p. 24.

Malocsay, Zoltan. "Bat!" *Westerner,* Nov.-Dec. 1972, p. 13.

————. "Defiance in the Street." *Westerner,* Sept.-Oct. 1972, p. 28.

Penn, Chris. "A Note on Bartholomew Masterson." *English Westerners Brand Book,* Vol. IX, No. 3, April 1967, p. 11.

Wiltsey, Norman B. "A Man Called Bat." *True West,* Dec. 1956, p. 16. Rpt. *Real West,* Nov. 1973, p. 24.

Masterson Brothers

Mays, Carelton. "Those Amazing Mastersons." Part I, *Real West,* Jan. 1964, p. 10; Part II, *Real West,* March 1964, p. 26.

Masterson, Edward J. "Ed"

Ernst, Robert R. "Dodge City Sued." *True West,* Nov. 1986, p. 32.

Huston, Fred. "Ed Masterson: He Was More Than Just Bat's Brother." *Golden West,* Jan. 1974, p. 34.

O'Neal, Bill. "Marshal Ed Masterson vs Texas Cowboys" ("Great Western Gunfights" column). *True West,* Aug. 1988, p. 61.

Penn, Chris. "Edward J. Masterson: Marshal of Dodge City." Part I, *English Westerners' Brand Book,* Vol. VII, No. 4, July 1965, p. 6; Part II, *English Westerners' Brand Book,* Vol. VIII, No. 1, Oct. 1965, p. 1.

Roberts, Gary L. "The Brother of Bat Masterson." *Frontier Times,* June-July 1963, p. 23.

Masterson, James "Jim"

Peters, James Steven. "Masterson's Militia." *Old West,* Fall 1983, p. 54.

Walker, Wayne T. "Jim Masterson: Quiet Marshal." *Real West,* July 1976, p. 28. Rpt. *Real West,* Yearbook, Summer 1978, p. 40.

_____. "Jim Masterson: The Loner." *Great West,* Aug. 1971, p. 10.

Mather, Dave "Mysterious Dave"

Dahl, Peter Andrew. "Mysterious Dave and the Gold Brick Swindle." *Real West,* July 1960, p. 12.

DeMattos, Jack. "Here's to Mysterious Dave Mather." *NOLA Quarterly,* Vol. I, No. 4, Winter 1975-76, p. 15.

_____. "Mysterious Dave Mather" ("Gunfighters of the Real West" column). *Real West,* March 1978, p. 26.

Jones, Calico. "Mysterious Dave Mather." *Real West,* April 1974, p. 39.

Moyer, S.R. "Dave Mather: The West's Greatest Puzzle." *The West,* Dec. 1965, p. 10. Rpt. *Western Frontier,* May 1981, p. 14.

Robbins, Lance. "Mysterious Was the Word for Dave." *Real West,* Americana Series, Fall 1965, p. 74.

Walker, Wayne T. "Mysterious Dave Mather." *True Frontier,* Dec. 1971, p. 27.

Mathewson, William "Buffalo Bill"

Henderson, Sam. "Those Other Buffalo Bills." *Real West,* June 1975, p. 14.

Walker, Wayne T. "The First 'Buffalo Bill.'" *Frontier Times,* May 1980, p. 26.

_____. "The Life of William Mathewson." *The West,* Jan. 1969, p. 12.

Wilson, Roger. "William Mathewson: The First 'Buffalo Bill.'" *Great West,* Feb. 1973, p. 12.

Matney, Samuel K. "Tule Dad"

Robertson, Dorothy. "Tuledad: Rampaging Senior Citizen." *True Frontier,* July 1971, p. 33. Rpt. *True Frontier,* Special Issue No. 11, Winter 1974-75, p. 36.

Maus, Marion P.

Murphy, Edward F. "The Valiant Marion P. Maus." *True West,* Sept. 1982, p. 46.

Maverick, Samuel Augustus

Beaty, Opal Waymire. "Maverick: Man and Legend." *The West,* July 1967, p. 38. Rpt. *The West,* Feb. 1973, p. 38, and *Western Frontier,* Nov. 1979, p. 28.

Smith, Helena Huntington. "Long Ropes and Branding Irons." *True West,* Feb. 1967, p. 20.

Maximilian I

Carson, Kit. "Maximilian's Buried Millions." *Real West,* Summer 1964, p. 44.

_____. "Mystery of Maximilian's Gold." *Real West,* Jan. 1962, p. 22.

Maxwell, C.L. "Gunplay" (Richard Seaman)
"Ed Johnson Kills 'Gunplay' Maxwell." *NOLA Quarterly,* Vol. VII, No. 1, Spring 1981, p. 6.

Johnson, Richard. "The Outlaw and the Jewel Thief." *NOLA Quarterly,* Vol. III, No. 3, Winter 1978, p. 1.

Kelly, Bill. "The Great Gunplay." *Real West,* May 1976, p. 20.

Zehnder, Chuck. "Gunfighters and Lawmen" column. *Wild West,* June 1991, p. 8.

Maxwell, Lucien Bonaparte
Ansell, Charles F. "Massacre at Manco Burro Pass." *True West,* Dec. 1985, p. 30.

Chapman, Hank and Toni. "Midas of New Mexico." *The American West,* Vol. VIII, No. 1, Jan. 1971, p. 4.

Holben, Richard E. "Emperor of the Santa Fe Trail." *Wild West,* March 1971, p. 50. Rpt. *Oldtimers Wild West,* Aug. 1973, p. 40; and *Pioneer West,* Bicentennial Souvenir Edition, 1976, p. 34.

Koller, Joe. "The Duke of Maxwell's Grant." *Golden West,* May 1970, p. 20.

Tidwell, Dewey. "Lucien Maxwell's Vast Land Grant." *Real West,* Oct. 1983, p 44. Rpt. *Real West,* Special Issue, Spring 1984, p. 67.

Wolfe, George D. "Maxwell Empire." *True West,* June 1962, p. 26.

Maxwell, Ralph "King Max"
Young, John Richard. "Maxwell: Boss of No Man's Land." *True Western Adventures,* Summer 1958, p. 40.

May, Boone
Hansen, John. "Boone May: Shotgun Messenger." *Great West,* Dec. 1974, p. 18.

Mayer, Frank
Cary, Lucian. "Buffalo Killer." *True Western Adventures,* Oct. 1958, p. 12.

_____. "Last of the Buffalo Hunters." *True Western Adventures,* Dec. 1959, p. 34.

Wiltsey, Norman B. "Frank Mayer, Scientific Buffalo Hunter." *Real West,* March 1974, p. 48.

_____. "Last of the Hide Hunters." *True West,* Oct. 1957, p. 12.

Meadors, Albert
Stoner, Mary E. "My Father Was a Train Robber." *True West,* Aug. 1983, p. 14.

Meagher, John

Henderson, Sam. "Brothers of Fortune." *Golden West,* July 1965, p. 18.

Meagher, Michael "Mike"

"A .44 Slug Through the Lungs." *Big West,* Dec. 1969, p. 26.

DeMattos, Jack. "Mike Meagher" ("Gunfighters of the Real West" column). *Real West,* Jan. 1979, p. 32.

Henderson, Sam. "Brothers of Fortune." *Golden West,* July 1965, p. 18.

"The Quiet Marshal." *Great West,* Dec. 1968, p. 4. Rpt. *Great West,* Feb. 1971, p. 30.

Snell, Joseph W. "The Murder of Mike Meagher." *The West,* Jan. 1965, p. 20. Rpt. *The West,* July 1972, p. 38.

Walker, Wayne T. "Mike Meagher: The Man Who Tamed Wichita." *Oldtimers Wild West,* Feb. 1980, p. 6.

Meagher, Thomas Francis

Henry, R.C. "What Happened to the Great Dreamer?" *Golden West,* March 1971, p. 34. Rpt. *Western Frontier,* July 1980, p. 38.

MacLaine, Robert B. "The Hectic Life of Thomas Meagher." *Real West,* Jan. 1968, p. 40.

————. "Thomas Meagher, Soldier of Fortune." *Real West,* Nov. 1967, p. 12.

Moffat, George A. "Mystery of the Disappearing Governor." *The West,* Aug. 1965, p. 8.

Mears, Otto

Martin, Bernice. "A Pair of Kings." *Frontier Times,* Sept. 1963, p. 30.

Sooner, Paul. "Otto Meers [sic]: The Mountain Slayer." *Westerner,* Sept.-Oct. 1974, p. 40.

Stone, Kit. "He Put Wheels on Mountains." *Real Frontier,* Dec. 1970, p. 39. Rpt. *True Frontier,* Feb. 1973, p. 27; *True Frontier,* June 1973, p. 36.

Walker, Wayne T. "Otto Mears: From an Orphan to a Railroad Tycoon." *Golden West,* Nov. 1972, p. 38. Rpt. *Western Frontier,* Special Issue, Summer 1974, p. 42; and *Western Frontier,* Summer 1978, p. 20.

Meek, Joseph "Joe"

Beckham, Joe. "Buckskin Envoy to Washington." *Golden West,* March 1970, p. 22. Rpt. *The West,* Aug. 1973, p. 16; and *Western Frontier,* Annual No. 3, 1976, p. 16.

————. "Men With the Strength of Mountains." *True Frontier,* July 1970, p. 14.

Freeman, Olga. "Joe Meek: Mountain Man and Envoy Extraordinary." *Real West,*
    Yearbook, Fall 1979, p. 46.
Judge, Bill. "Half-Horse, Half-Alligator." *Frontier Times,* Spring 1961, p. 10.
Wiltsey, Norman B. "Blood Oath." *Westerner,* Dec. 1970, p. 46.
————. "I Will Have Blood for Blood." *Real West,* Oct. 1974, p. 36.
————. "The Vengeance of Joe Meek." *True West,* Aug. 1955, p. 20.

Meek, Stephen Hall "Steve"
Hicks, Flora Weed. "They Wanted to Hang Steve Meek." *The West,* July 1969,
    p. 10.

Meeker, Ezra
Auer, L.C. "Saga of the Oregon Trail." *The West,* Sept. 1966, p. 16. Rpt. *True
    West,* May 1973, p. 26; *Western Frontier,* March 1976, p. 24; and *Western
    Frontier,* Aug. 1985, p. 2.
Bolon, R. "The Pen, the Sword and Scalp." *Big West,* Aug. 1967, p . 40.
————. "The Utopia That Turned Into Hell." *Wild West,* Sept. 1971, p. 52.
Clifford, Howard. "Ezra Meeker's Peculiar Search for Gold." *Westerner,*
    Jan.-Feb. 1975, p. 42.
Main, Mildred Miles. "A Trail Blazer and a Sculptress." *True West,* June 1975,
    p. 14.
Mathisen, Jean A. "A Pioneer's Dream." *True West,* June 1990, p. 48.
Meeker, Ezra. "The Oregon Trail." *True West,* April 1963, p. 8.

Meeker, Josephine "Josie"
Harrison, Fred. "A White Squaw for the Chief." *Real Frontier,* Aug. 1970, p. 12.
Payne, John L. "Sex Horror of Josephine Meeker." *Real West,* Feb. 1959, p. 8.

Meeker, Nathan
Bloom, Sam. "Crossing the Milk Creek Line." *Real West,* July 1979, p. 32.
Cortesi, Lawrence J. "The White River Tragedy." *Oldtimers Wild West,* Dec.
    1978, p. 17.
Harrison, Fred. "A White Squaw for the Chief." *True Frontier,* Special Issue No.
    14, 1975, p. 10.
Hines, Lawrence. "The Utes Wanted No Part of the White Man's Ways." *Frontier
    West,* Dec. 1972, p. 32.
Malsbary, George. "Massacre at the Agency." *Pioneer West,* Dec. 1971, p. 12.
Mays, Carelton. "Blood at White River." *Real West,* Americana Series, Winter
    1964, p. 46.

_____. "Why Blood Flowed at White River." *Real West,* Nov. 1962, p. 8.

Tibbets, Robin. "The White River Massacre." *True West,* June 1961, p. 30.

Meeks, Henry "Bub"

Popp, Richard. "Bub Meeks Was Tough Luck Member of the Wild Bunch." *NOLA Quarterly,* Vol. II, No. 2, Spring 1975, p. 8.

Meldrum, Robert D. "Bob"

Carson, John. "The Middle Years of Bob Meldrum." *Old West,* Spring 1970, p. 36.

_____. "Wyoming's Mysterious Badman." *Frontier Times,* Winter 1961, p. 16.

Davidson, Carl. Letter. *Frontier Times,* Fall 1962, p. 56.

Martin, Andrew. "I Knew Bob Meldrum." *Old West,* Spring 1970, p. 39.

Quinlan, Morris. "Bob Meldrum: Last of the Money Killers." *Frontier West,* Feb. 1972, p. 42.

Mendenez, Katherine "Kitty Tango," "Chicago Joe"

Henry, R.C. "The Shebang of Kitty Tango." *Pioneer West,* April 1971, p. 46.

Menken, Adah ("Ada, the Body")

Maldone, George. "New Facts About Ada, the Body." *Western Frontier,* Special Issue, Dec. 1974, p. 20.

Mentzer, Gus

Gregg, Andrew. "How They Hung Indestructible Gus." *Real West,* May 1962, p. 8.

Holben, Dick. "The Day They Hanged Gus Mentzer." *Real West,* Aug. 1973, p. 26.

Hornung, Chuck. "The Lynching of Gus Mentzer." *Real West,* April 1985, p. 10. Rpt. *Real West,* Special Issue, Spring 1986, p. 31.

Mercer, Asa

Auer, L.C. "Westward, the Mercer Girls." *Golden West,* March 1974, p. 20.

Landes, Cheryl. "Asa Mercer: Washington Territory's Matchmaker. *True West,* May 1990, p. 46.

Shulsinger, Stephanie Cooper. "Asa Mercer and the Johnson County War." *Real West,* Jan. 1970, p. 20.

_____. "Asa Mercer, Pioneer Promoter." *Real West,* Oct. 1969, p. 23.

Merritt, Wesley
Fleek, Sherman L. "Race Against Deadly Odds." *Wild West,* Oct. 1989, p. 40.

Mershon, J.H.
Shirley, Glenn. "A Basket of Bones." *Real Western Adventures,* June 1961, p. 24.

_____. "Rape and Death of Ella Stephens." *Real West,* June 1970, p. 32.

_____. "We Ought to Have the Bones of the Woman." *True West,* March 1991, p. 14.

Middleton, Thomas "Doc"
Andre, Barbara E. "Doc Middleton: Horsethief or Lawman?" *Golden West,* May 1968, p. 15. Rpt. *Golden West,* Feb. 1973, p. 10; *Western Frontier,* Sept. 1976, p. 17; and *Western Frontier,* May 1985, p. 23.

DeMattos, Jack. "Doc Middleton" ("Gunfighters of the Real West" column). *Real West,* March 1980, p. 32.

Dodge, Matt. "The Pony Boys." *Real West,* Aug. 1986, p. 18.

Lewis, Emily H. "The Colorful Horse Thief." *True West,* Aug. 1963, p. 38.

Parsons, Chuck. "Doc Middleton" ("Answer Man" column). *True West,* May 1990, p. 12.

Swanson, Budington. "Death of a Pony Boy." *Real West,* April 1981, p. 20. Rpt. *Real West,* Annual, Spring 1982, p. 48.

Mier Expedition Members
Robinson, Max. "Bitter Christmas." *Great West,* June 1974, p. 22.

Milam, Benjamin "Ben"
Preece, Harold. "Ben Milam, Texas Hero." *Real West,* Sept. 1967, p. 30.

Miles, Nelson A.
Erlanson, Charles B. "Battle of the Butte." *Old West,* Summer 1965, p. 2.

Malsbary, George. "Colonel Miles: Compassionate and Resolute Commander." *Real West,* Nov. 1979, p. 28. Rpt. *Real West,* Yearbook 1980, p. 53.

Pinkerton, Robert F. "The Indian Who Beat the U.S. Army." *True Western Adventures,* June 1960, p. 38.

Reedstrom, E. Lisle. "General Miles' Secret Weapon." *True West,* Aug. 1988, p. 14.

Turpin, Bob. "The Fight at Muddy Creek." *Great West,* June 1974, p. 6. Rpt. *Authentic West,* Summer 1981, p. 50.

Werner, Fred H. "Decision at Battle Butte." *Real West,* Jan. 1979, p. 46.

Miller Brothers (Joseph C., Zack T., and George L.)

Katigan, Madelon B. "The Fabulous 101!" *True West,* Oct. 1960, p. 6.

Shirley, Glenn. "The Most Fantastic Ranch the West Ever Knew." *True Frontier,* Dec. 1974, p. 30.

Virgines, George E. "The Miller's Great 101 Ranch." *Golden West,* Sept. 1967, p. 38. Rpt. *Golden West,* Dec. 1972, p. 14.

Miller, Charley "Broncho Charley"

Henderson, Sam. "Broncho Charley Miller." *Golden West,* July 1966, p. 20. Rpt. *Golden West,* Dec. 1972, p. 34.

Miller, Clelland D. "Clell"

Eden, M.C. "Clell Miller and the Corydon Bank Robbery." *English Westerners Brand Book,* Vol. XX, No. 3, April 1978, and No. 4, July 1978 (combined issue).

Fitzgerald, Ruth Coder. "Clell and Ed Miller: Members of the James Gang." *NOLA Quarterly,* Vol. XV, No. 3, July-Sept. 1991, p. 29.

Rickards, Colin. "Bones of the Northfield Robbers." *Real West,* Jan. 1979, p. 28.

Miller, Edward T.

Fitzgerald, Ruth Coder. "Clell and Ed Miller: Members of the James Gang." *NOLA Quarterly,* Vol. XV, No. 3, July-Sept. 1991, p. 29.

Miller, Henry

Degman, James P. "Portrait for a Western Album." *American West,* Vol. XV, No. 6, Nov.-Dec. 1978, p. 30.

Freeman, Olga. "A Cattle Empire Is Born." *Real West,* April 1973, p. 8.

Hurdy, John Major. "Onassis of Cattle." *Pioneer West,* Sept. 1969, p. 36. Rpt. *Pioneer West,* June 1975, p. 52; and *Oldtimers Wild West,* April 1980, p. 34.

Sherrill, Mack. "Henry Miller: Cattle Baron of California." *Real West,* Feb. 1972, p. 16.

Miller, James P. "Killing Jim"

Breihan, Carl W. "How They Hanged Jim Miller." *Real West,* March 1960, p. 11.

_____. "Killing Jim Miller." *Real West,* July 1978, p. 50.

_____. "The Man Who Killed Pat Garrett." *Westerner,* Jan.-Feb. 1970, p. 24. Rpt. *Old Trails,* Spring 1978, p. 56.

DeMattos, Jack. "Jim Miller" ("Gunfighters of the Real West" column). *Real West,* April 1983, p. 42.

Freeman, Frank M. "Gun for Hire, Killer Miller." *Oldtimers Wild West,* April 1974, p. 56.

_____. "Killer Miller: Gun For Hire." *Wild West,* Sept. 1971, p. 48. Rpt. *Wild West,* Sept. 1972, p. 46; and *Pioneer West,* Nov. 1977, p. 20.

Holding, Vera. "Mad Dog for Hire." *Great West,* Oct. 1972, p. 16.

Hubbard, George V. "The Lynching of 'Killer Miller.'" *True Frontier,* March 1969, p. 12. Rpt. *True Frontier,* Special Issue No. 1, 1971, p. 46.

Katigan, Madelon B. "How the Beau Brummel Died." *Real West,* Sept. 1963, p. 36.

O'Neal, Bill. "Killing Jim Miller vs Sheriff Bud Frazer" ("Great Western Gunfighters" column). *True West,* May 1989, p. 60.

Parsons, Chuck. "Killing Jim Miller" ("Answer Man" column). *True West,* April 1988, p. 13.

Raymond, Charles. "The Man Who Killed the Man Who Killed Billy the Kid." *Real West,* March 1969, p. 48.

Rescorla, Richard. "'Killing Jim' Miller." *Golden West,* Nov. 1969, p. 16. Rpt. *The West,* Dec. 1971, p. 10; *Western Frontier,* Special Issue, Fall 1974, p. 32; and *Western Frontier,* Jan. 1983, p. 12.

Secrest, William B. "The Last Ride." *True West,* Feb. 1967, p. 6.

Miller, Joaquin

Fitzgerald, A. "The Incredible Joaquin Miller." *Real West,* Nov. 1964, p. 42.

Kimmel, Thelma. "My God, My Hero, My Ideal." *Frontier Times,* July 1971, p. 32.

Nolan, Paul T. "Joaquin Miller, Western Hero or Fraud?" *Real West,* Annual, Summer 1973, p. 35.

Waldron, Larry. "The Poet and the Murderer." *Real West,* Jan. 1977, p. 36. Rpt. *Real West,* Annual, Winter 1977-78, p. 12.

Miller, Mose

Forbes, Jack. "Mose Miller, Mad Killer of the Cookson Hills." *The West,* Sept. 1964, p. 10. Rpt. *Western Frontier,* May 1980, p. 10.

Poling, Frederick. "Mad Killer of the Cookson Hills." *Real West,* April 1958, p. 18.

Miller, Sebastian
Timmen, Fritz. "Take Her Down or Wreck Her." *The West,* Dec. 1966, p. 44.

Millett Brothers (Eugene, Alonzo, and Hiram)
DeArment, R.K. "Toughest Cow Outfit in Texas." Part I, *True West,* April 1991, p. 26; Part II, *True West,* May 1991, p. 22.

Mills, Anson
Barsness, John, and William Dickinson. "Fight or Die!" *Frontier Times,* Summer 1960, p. 26.

Werner, Fred H. "The Horse-Meat March." *Real West,* March 1982, p. 24. Rpt. *Real West,* Annual, Spring 1983, p. 48.

Milner, Moses Embree "California Joe"
Bundy, Rex. "California Joe." *The West,* March 1970, p. 30.

Reedstrom, Ernest Lisle. "California Joe: Custer's Scandalous Chief of Scouts." *True Frontier,* April 1972, p. 15. Rpt. *True Frontier,* Special Issue No. 15, Summer 1976, p. 21.

_____. "The Real California Joe." *Old West,* Fall, 1986, p. 50.

Milton, Jefferson Davis "Jeff"
DeMattos, Jack. "Jeff Milton" ("Gunfighters of the Real West" column). *Real West,* June 1981, p. 16.

Qualey, J.S. "Jeff Milton, Nemesis of Three Fingered Jack." *Real West,* March 1962, p. 38.

Ryan, Jack. "The Making of a Town Tamer." *True Western Adventures,* Feb. 1960, p. 24.

Mims, Henry
Repp, Ed Earl. "Too Tough to Kill." *The West,* Dec. 1969, p. 16.

Miner, William "Bill"
Boessenecker, John. "Buckshot for Bill Miner." *True West,* Aug. 1988, p. 20.

Kirby, Ed M. "Bill Miner, The Grey Fox: Outlaw for Fifty Years." *NOLA Quarterly,* Vol. X, No. 1, Summer 1985, p. 3.

Parsons, Chuck. "Hold-up King" ("Answer Man" column). *True West,* May 1990, p. 13.

Pawley, Eugene. "He Out-Robbed Jesse James." *Old West,* Winter 1964, p. 28. Rpt. *Badman,* Annual 1971, p. 18.

Rickards, Colin. "Bill Miner, Fifty Years a Holdup Man." Part I, *Real West,* Sept. 1970, p. 21; Part II, *Real West,* Oct. 1970, p. 50.

Tench, C.V. "The Gentle Bandit." *Real West,* March 1964, p. 9.

Von Kreisler, Max. "The Bad Man from the East Who Terrorized the West." *Frontier West,* April 1973, p. 20.

Wishart, Bruce. "Bill Miner: The Canadian Years." *True West,* June 1990, p. 28.

Mitchell, Luther

Carsten, Lyle. "The Nebraska Man Burner." *Pioneer West,* April 1972, p. 32.

Chrisman, Harry E. "When 'Slow Elk' Came High." *Old West,* Summer 1965, p. 46.

Preece, Harold. "Strange Truth About Print Olive." *Golden West,* June 1974, p. 38.

Swanson, Budington. "Death at Devil's Gap." *Great West,* Aug. 1973, p. 10. Rpt. *Great West,* Fall 1981, p. 10.

Yost, Nellie Snyder. "The Olive Story." *True West.* May 1990, p. 30.

Modena, Mariano "Mary Anne" (sometimes spelled Medina)

Hitt, Jim. "Mexican Mountain Man." *Real West,* Dec. 1983, p. 38. Rpt. *Real West,* Annual, Spring 1985, p. 33.

Huett, Wil. "A Man Called 'Mary Anne.'" *True West,* Nov. 1991, p. 42.

Jenkins, Nedra C. "Beau Brummel of the Big Thompson." *Old West,* Winter 1968, p. 12.

Trestle, Fred. Letter. *Old West,* Summer 1970, p. 2.

Moessner, Christian "Dutch Chris"

Rasch, Philip J. "'Dutch Chris' Moessner, New Mexico Outlaw." *NOLA Quarterly,* Vol. III, No. 4, Spring 1978, p. 9.

Molly B'Dam (Maggie Hall)

"Molly B'Dam and Murray." *True West,* April 1984, p. 53.

Monk, Hank

Cheney, Louise. "Hank Monk, King of the Stage Drivers." *Real West,* Jan. 1969, p. 32.

Grubb, R.L. "The Tragic Stage Coach Saga." *True Frontier,* Dec. 1976, p. 34.

Monoghan, "Little Joe"

Robbins, Lance. "Little Joe Monoghan." *Real West,* Nov. 1970, p. 67.

Monroe, George

McCollum, Berkely. "Yosemite Turnpike's Crack Reinsman." *True West,* Aug. 1975, p. 18.

Montez, Lola

Cheney, Louise. "Lola Montez: A Most Notorious Lady." *Golden West,* Sept. 1969, p. 18. Rpt. *The West,* Jan. 1973, p. 26.

Fleming, Gerry. "Lola Montez: The Scarlet Angel." *Wild West,* July 1972, p. 21.

Nester, W. William. "Lola Montez: Empress of Sin." *Real West,* Jan. 1958, p. 20.

Repp, Ed Earl. "Joaquin Murietta and Lola Montez." *Real West,* Nov. 1969, p. 40.

_____. "Lola Montez: Man Breaker." *Old West,* Summer 1969, p. 8.

_____. "Tinsel and Gold." *Golden West,* Oct. 1974, p. 38.

Rosenhouse, Leo. "Lola Montez: The Spider Lady." *True Frontier,* Sept. 1970, p. 20. Rpt. *True Frontier,* Special Issue No. 3, 1972, p. 33; and *True Frontier,* April 1976, p. 17.

Wingfield, William. "A Countess in Exile: Lola Montez in California." *Real West,* May 1974, p. 14.

Montezuma, Carlos

Hyatt, Robert M. "The Restless Ghost of Doctor Montezuma." *Frontier Times,* March 1964, p. 28.

Lakritz, Ester. "The Apache Horatio Alger." *Real West,* Dec. 1968, p. 54.

Unger, Henry F. "Out of the Wilds: A Medical Genius." *The West,* May 1970, p. 20.

Montgomery, James

Scullin, George. "A Time For Battle." *True Western Adventures,* Summer 1958, p. 20.

Mooar, J. Wright, and John W. Mooar

Blalock, Fred Frank. "J. Wright Mooar and the Decade of Destruction." *Real West,* Jan. 1974, p. 50.

Hunter, J. Marvin. "J. Wright Mooar and John W. Mooar." *Old West,* Spring 1967, p. 27.

Robinson, Charles M., III. "Buffalo Hunting at Fort Griffin." *True West,* March 1988, p. 20.

_____. "J. Wright Mooar and the Great Buffalo Hunt." *Old West,* Winter 1989, p. 48.

Moon, Catherine "Katie"
Gremel, Barry. "The Terrible Rangeland Vengeance of Katie Moon." *Frontier West*, June 1971, p. 46.

Moon, James "Jim"
Phillips, Helen S. "Death of the Meanest Man." *The West*, Oct. 1973, p. 14.

Mooney, Jesse
Messick, H.A. and M.A. "The Bloody Feud in Yellville." *The West*, April 1968, p. 10. Rpt. *Western Frontier*, May 1979, p. 26.

Moonlight, Thomas
Swanson, Budington. "When Colonel Moonlight's Cavalry Walked Back." *Golden West*, July 1968, p. 26. Rpt. *Golden West*, May 1972, p. 22.

Moore, Alonzo "Little Lonnie"
Preece, Harold. "Lonnie's Magic Gun." *Real West*, March 1964, p. 36.

Moore, Scott
Albertson, Peter. "The Fantastic Ride of Scott Moore." *Western Tales*, April 1960, p. 32.

Moreno, Andres
Kildare, Maurice. "Arizona's Tragic Hero." *Real West*, Feb. 1971, p. 13.

Morgan, Anna
Souder, Eunice. "Female Captive of the Kiowa." *Oldtimers Wild West*, Aug. 1975, p. 19.

Morley, Ray
Keezer, W.S. "Capt. Morley's War on the Rails." *Westerner*, June 1971, p. 46.

Morley, William Raymond
Holben, Richard E. "Rock Forts and Iron Men." *Great West*, June 1974, p. 10.

Morrell, Edward "Ed"
O'Neil, Harold. "The West's Greatest Escape." *Big West*, Dec. 1969, p. 38.

Morris, Esther

Best, J.C. "Mrs. Morris' Tea Party." *Real West,* Feb. 1984, p. 47.

Cheney, Louise. "Esther Morris' Monumental Tea Party." *Real West,* Jan. 1968, p. 42.

Hanley, Charles. "Heroines In Bloomers." *Real West,* May 1959, p. 42.

Mayberry, C.L. "The Amazing Esther Morris." *The West,* Aug. 1965, p. 30.

Vandervelde, Marjorie. "A Revolutionary Tea Party." *True West,* July 1986, p. 46.

West, Bertha. "Esther Morris: Liberator of Women." *Pioneer West,* April 1971,. p. 28. Rpt. *Oldtimers Wild West,* Oct. 1974, p. 28, and *Pioneer West,* Nov. 1976, p. 10.

Morris, Joseph

Spendlove, Earl. "Bloody Sunday at Kingston Fort." *The West,* Oct. 1974, p. 34.

Morris, Josie Bassett

Stewart, John. "Josie Bassett Morris: A Husband Killer?" *NOLA Quarterly,* Vol. IX, No. 1, Summer 1984, p. 9.

Morrison, Donald

Butts, Ed. "The Outlaw of Magantic." *Old West,* Winter 1981, p. 26.

Morrow, David "Prairie Dog Dave"

Roberts, Gary Leland. "Prairie Dog Dave." *Frontier Times,* Nov. 1963, p. 46.

Morse, Harry Nicholson

Boessenecker, John. "It Was More Than Luck That Gave Sheriff Harry Morse a Charmed Life." *Frontier West,* Aug. 1972, p. 40.

Brown, Joseph E. "Duel at Dusk." *Frontier Times,* Fall 1960, p. 18.

Coe, Clint. "The West's First Private Eye." *True Western Adventures,* Dec. 1960, p. 14.

Harrison, John M. "Harry Morse: A Symbol of Honesty, Courage and Dedication." *The West,* June 1973, p. 18. Rpt. *Western Frontier,* Nov. 1986, p. 18.

Malsbary, George. "The Bullet-Proof Sheriff." *True Frontier,* July 1977, p. 16.

Reed, Harry. "Soto's Shootout With Sheriff Morse." *The West,* April 1970, p. 14.

Repp, Ed Earl. "Harry Morse: Fighting Sheriff." *Westerner,* April 1973, p. 22.

Secrest, William B. "Manhunt." *Old West,* Spring 1986, p. 12.

Morton, Nancy
Knudsen, Dean. "The Captive Ordeal of Nancy Morton." *True West,* Sept. 1991, p. 28.

Moses, Samuel H. "Sam"
Koller, Joe. "The Man All Rustlers Hated." *Real West,* Sept. 1963, p. 22.

Moshoquop
Spendlove, Earl. "Moshoquop's Terrible Revenge." *The West,* April 1967, p. 10.

Mossman, Burton C.
Arthur, Jim. "The Incredible Saga of Burt Mossman, the First Arizona Ranger." *Frontier West,* June 1972, p. 24.

Breihan, Carl W. "Burt Mossman: Arizona Ranger." *Golden West,* Nov. 1967, p. 10. Rpt. *The West,* Nov. 1972, p. 10; and *Western Frontier,* May 1981, p. 10.

Hartley, William B. "Turncoat From Tombstone." *True Western Adventures,* Dec. 1959, p. 30.

Jones, Bradford D. "The Man Who Cleaned Up Arizona." *Western True Story,* Oct. 1971, p. 16. Rpt. *America's Frontier West,* Issue No. 1, n.d., p. 12.

Phillips, Chct. "Burt Mossman: Ranger With a Cause." *Frontier West,* Oct. 1971, p. 36.

Preece, Harold. "Twelve Against Five Thousand Killers." *Real West,* March 1963, p. 38.

"The Secret Arizona Rangers." *True Frontier,* Aug. 1976, p. 6.

Shirley, Glenn. "Cap Mossman and the Apache Devil." *True West,* Oct. 1957, p. 4.

Stanley, Samuel. "Burt Mossman: Arizona Ranger." *Real West,* June 1987, p. 27.

Waltrip, Lela and Rufus. "Top Man of the Fearless Thirteen." *True West,* Dec. 1970, p. 22.

"Mother Featherlegs" (Mrs. Shephard)
Riske, Milt C. "Monument for Featherlegs." *Frontier Times,* Sept. 1978, p. 27.

Mowry, Sylvester
Helfrick, Mary. "Sylvester Mowry: Scoundrel or Persecuted Crusader?" *Old West,* Fall 1989, p. 52.

Lake, Ivan Clyde. "Hard Luck Mowry." *Golden West,* Jan. 1967, p. 20. Rpt. *Golden West,* Feb. 1972, p. 38.

Love, Frank. "The Crime Against Sylvester Mowry." *Old West,* Fall 1973, p. 30.

Sacks, Benjamin H. "Sylvester Mowry: Artilleryman, Libertine, Entrepreneur."
  American West, Summer 1964, p. 14.

Muir, John

Betts, William J. "John Muir: Savior of America's Wilderness." *Oldtimers Wild
  West,* Feb. 1978, p. 10.

Martin, Cy. "John Muir: The Tramp Who Saved the Wilderness." *Golden West,*
  Dec. 1972, p. 38. Rpt. *Western Frontier,* Jan. 1979, p. 38.

Mullan, John

Miller, Don. "The Northwest's First Interstate Highway." *True West,* May 1983,
  p. 46.

Mullen, William

Neill, Jane. "The Horse-Taming Evangelist." *Old West,* Summer 1991, p. 62.

Mulvenon, William J. "Billy"

Barkdull, Tom. "The Axings at House Rock Springs." *True Frontier,* Aug. 1974,
  p. 8.

Cornish, Ken, and Bill McClure. "Hangman's Hand." *Real West,* Oct. 1968, p.
  18.

Kildare, Maurice. "Posse Bushwhack." *Great West,* July 1968, p. 40.

Murietta, Joaquin (also spelled "Murieta," "Murrieta," and "Murrietta")

Bailey, Tom. "The Scourge of El Dorado." *True West,* Aug. 1961, p. 6.

Breihan, Carl W. "Joaquin Murietta, Fact or Myth." *Real West,* Feb. 1970, p. 54.

Johnston, Langford, with Eve Ball. "The Murieta Legend Is Haunting." *Old West,*
  Fall 1981, p. 16.

Kearns, Edward J. "Legend of Murietta's Gold Mine." *The West,* June 1965, p.
  29.

Lee, Hector. "Joaquin Murietta." *NOLA Quarterly,* Vol. V, No. 4, April 1980, p.
  17.

Maracin, Paul R. "Gunfighters and Lawmen" column. *Wild West,* June 1989, p.
  12.

Martin, Cy. "Wild and Wicked Hornitos." *Great West,* Dec. 1972, p. 10.

Mendez, Al. "El Bandido Californio: Joaquin Murieta." *Great West,* May 1968,
  p. 30.

O'Neal, Harold. "A Tree and a Treasure." *Western Frontier,* Annual, Spring 1981,
  p. 5.

Olmstead, L.A. "Murrietta's Insane Hate." *Real West,* Nov. 1960, p. 23. Rpt. *Real West,* Annual, Spring 1978, p. 16.

Pearson, R.E. "The Man Who Invented Joaquin Murieta." *Real West,* Americana Series, Fall 1964, p. 7.

Reinstedt, Randall A. "The Horseback Gangsters." *Wild West,* Sept. 1971, p. 27. Rpt. *Oldtimers Wild West,* April 1974, p. 45.

Repp, Ed Earl. "Joaquin Murietta and Lola Montez." *Real West,* Nov. 1969, p. 40.

Rosenhouse, Leo. "Joaquin Murieta: Man of Hate." *True Frontier,* Special Issue No. 17, Winter 1976, p. 30.

Ryall, William. "Captain Love's Bounty." *True Western Adventures,* Feb. 1960, p. 28.

Secrest, William B. "Hell for Leather Rangers." *True West,* April 1968, p. 20.

_____. "Severed Head of Cantua Creek." *Pioneer West,* Sept. 1967, p. 38.

_____. "The Second Life of a Severed Head." *True Frontier,* Nov. 1968, p. 31.

_____. "Who Died at Cantua Creek?" *Real West,* April 1984, p. 36. Rpt. *Real West,* Special Issue, Spring 1985, p. 20.

Steiner, Stan. "In Search of the Legendary Joaquin Murieta." *NOLA Quarterly,* Vol. II, No. 3, Autumn 1976, p. 7.

Young, Bob. "They Hung Up Murietta's Head." *Real West,* March 1964, p. 34.

Murill, William Bartley
Passley, Susan. "Saga of a US Marshal." *True Frontier,* June 1967, p. 20.

Murphy-Dolan Faction
Mays, Carelton. "The Cattle Baron Who Wouldn't Fight." *Real West,* Aug. 1958, p. 6.

Murphy, Johnny
Lamb, L.M. "Johnny Murphy: All Guts and Gumption." *Westerner,* July-Aug. 1970, p. 20.

Murray, George Fred
Hornung, Chuck. "Incident at San Rafael." *Real West,* Sept. 1980, p. 22.

Murrell, John A.
Galey, John. "Gunfighters and Lawman" column. *Wild West,* June 1988, p. 8.

"John Murrell, Master Mind: Conspiracy of Ten Thousand." *Gunslingers of the West,* Winter 1966, p. 46.

Musgraves, George

Ball, Eve. "Lawman of the Pecos." *True West,* June 1967, p. 20.

Parsons, Chuck. "Blackjack Christian and the High Five Gang" ("Answer Man" column). *True West,* May 1989, p. 12.

————. "Elusive Badman" ("Answer Man" column). *True West,* Nov. 1989, p. 12.

Musgrove, L.H.

Cook, D.J. "Hang Musgrove." *Westerner,* March-April 1974, p. 34.

————. "When Outlaws Organized the West." *Westerner,* March-April 1974, p. 26.

Jessen, Kenneth. "End of the Musgrove Gang in Colorado." *WOLA Journal,* Vol. I, No. 2, Fall-Winter 1991, p. 25.

Nachez (also spelled "Naiche" and "Natchez")

Ball, Eve. "Search for a Family." *True West,* May 1984, p. 52.

Gale, Jack C. "An Ambush for Nachez." *True West,* Aug. 1980, p. 32.

Nana

Kaywaykla, James. "Nana's People." *True West,* Aug. 1963, p. 20.

Qualey, J. "Nana, the Ancient One: Last of the Warrior Chiefs." *Real West,* Special Issue, Winter 1963, p. 50.

Qualey, Jake. "Nana: The Desert Fox." *Real West,* July 1960, p. 40.

Sanchez, Lynda A. "Nana's Legacy Beyond Tres Castillo." *Real West,* Oct. 1982, p. 45.

Wade, Kit. "Bloody Orgy at Dog Canyon." *Pioneer West,* Feb. 1972, p. 54. Rpt. *Real West,* Special Issue, Spring 1985, p. 58.

Ward, John K. "Ancient Warrior's Revenge." *Wild West,* Oct. 1989, p. 18.

Wiltsey, Norman B. "Hawks of the Desert." *True West,* Dec. 1955, p. 19.

Nance, Tom

Rasch, Philip J. "Tom Nance: A Dangerous Man." *Real West,* March 1979, p. 25.

Nation, Carry

Belton, George. "Carry Nation: Crusading Sinner." *Real West,* July 1960, p. 36.

Brown, Carl N. "Carry, the Barroom Smasher." *The West,* Oct. 1964, p. 18. Rpt. *The West,* Annual 1971, p. 18; and *Western Frontier,* Special Issue, Dec. 1974, p. 10.

Coburn, Walt. "Carry Nation Spooks a Montana Cowtown." *Frontier Times,* May 1975, p. 8.

Holding, Vera. "Carry Nation: Hellion With a Hatchet." *Great West,* July 1968, p. 18.

Hood, James G.H., and Evangeline Ames Hood. "Carry Nation's Other Side." *Frontier Times,* Nov. 1968, p. 26.

Nation, Earl F. "Carry A. Nation." *Los Angeles Westerners' Branding Iron,* No. 145, Dec. 1981, p. 1.

Nolan, Paul T. "Carry Nation: The One Woman Riot." Part I, *Real West,* March 1971, p. 22; Part II, *Real West,* April 1971, p. 52; Part III, *Real West,* May 1971, p. 52.

Neagle, David "Dave"

Osgood, Stacy. "The Life and Times of Dave Neagle." *Chicago Westerners Brand Book,* Vol. XIX, April 1962.

Neal, Edgar

Hancock, William CX, and Mrs. Edgar Thomas Neal. "Not a Single Notch." *True West,* Dec. 1959, p. 10.

Neighbors, Robert Simpson

Enright, Carl. "Robert Neighbors, Martyr to Indian Justice." *The West,* Nov. 1965, p. 30. Rpt. *Golden West,* Aug. 1972, p. 30.

Robinson, Charles M., III. "Life and Death of an Indian Lover." *True West,* Oct. 1991, p. 14.

Neiman, Willis

Neiman, Willis. "I Captured Harry Tracy." *Westerner,* July-Aug. 1972, p. 22.

Neis, Tony

McCubbin, Robert G. "Long Lost Photograph of Tony Neis and Bob Olinger is Found." *NOLA Quarterly,* Vol. XIV, Nos. 3 and 4 (combined issue), 1990, p. 3.

Nelson, "Black Jack"
Simmonds, A.J. "A Legend Named 'Black Jack.'" *Real West*, Annual, Summer 1973, p. 14.

Nelson, John
Secrest, William B. "'Indian' John Nelson." *Old West*, Spring 1969, p. 24.

Nephews, Rufus "Climax Jim" (alias Jim Thomas)
Kildare, Maurice. "The Outlaw Houdini of the West." *Pioneer West*, March 1968, p. 30. Rpt. *Pioneer West*, Collector's Annual, 1971, p. 42.

Waltrip, Charles. "Climax Jim." *Westerner*, Jan.-Feb. 1975, p. 14.

Waltrip, Rufus. "Climax Jim." *Old West*, Spring 1968, p. 30.

Nesmith, James Willis
Ankeny, Levi. "Treaty on the Rock." *True West*, Oct. 1962, p. 44.

Nevada, Emma (Emma Wilson)
Cheney, Louise. "Emma Nevada: The Comstock Nightingale." *Golden West*, Jan. 1965, p. 18. Rpt. *The West*, Dec. 1973, p. 16; *Western Frontier*, Special Issue, Dec. 1974, p. 6; and *Western Frontier*, Annual No. 4, 1976, p. 28.

Newcomb George "Bitter Creek" (sometimes spelled "Newcombe")
Bird, Roy. "The Wild Bunch Robbed the Spearville Bank." *Real West*, April 1987, p. 14.

McBee, G. Fred. "Don't Wake the Neighbors!" *Golden West*, March 1971, p. 20. Rpt. *Western Frontier*, Special Issue, Fall 1974, p. 38.

Parsons, Chuck. "Bitter Creek" ("Answer Man" column). *True West*, May 1991, p. 13.

Nickell Family (Willie, Kels Powers, and Mary)
Nickell, Phillip G. "The Family Tom Horn Destroyed." *Real West*, Dec. 1986, p. 23.

Nite Brothers (Jim and "Big Asa")
O'Neal, Bill. "First National Bank Robbery" ("Great Western Gunfights" column). *True West*, Oct. 1991, p. 58.

Nolan, Nicholas
Robb, Berniece. "Parched Horror on the Staked Plains." *Golden West*, March 1965, p. 22. Rpt. *Golden West*, April 1974, p. 40.

Nolan, Philip
Carson, Xanthus. "The Saga of the Frontier's 'Man Without a Country.'" *Frontier West,* Aug. 1972, p. 26.
Yarbrough, C.L. "Philip Nolan's Last Expedition." *Vanishing Texas,* March 1981, p. 13.

Nolin, Charles "Red"
Ewing, William E. "Mail Carrier's Last Ride." *Old West,* Fall 1988, p. 62.

Norfleet, J. Frank
Allen, Stookie. "Five Swindlers Caught Triple Trouble." *The West,* Feb. 1970, p. 34.

North, Frank
Judge, Bill. "Pawnee Scouts." *True West,* Feb. 1965, p. 18.
Manley, George. "A Battle for the Squaws." *The West,* July 1964, p. 22.
Tassen, Ray. "Greatest of the Plainsmen." *Frontier Times,* June-July 1963, p. 24.

North, Luther
North, Luther. "Last of the Great Scouts." *Golden West,* March 1969, p. 22. Rpt. *Golden West,* March 1973, p. 14.

North, Robert
Austerman, Wayne R. "North the Renegade." *True West,* Dec. 1986, p. 14.

Northrup, George W.
Eggleston, Edward. "The Strange Saga of George Northrup." *The West,* Jan. 1965, p. 10.

Norton, Joshua A. "Emperor Norton I"
Cheney, Louise. "Emperor Norton of San Francisco." *Golden West,* Jan. 1967, p. 32. Rpt. *Golden West,* May 1974, p. 18.
Lucia, Ellis. "The Emperor of San Francisco." *True Western Adventures,* June 1961, p. 15.
Rickards, Colin. "Emperor of the United States." *Western Round-Up,* Aug. 1970, p. 49. Rpt. *Wild West,* May 1972, p. 57; and *Oldtimers Wild West,* April 1974, p. 38.
Roper, William L. "The Emperor Who Fired President Lincoln." *True Frontier,* April 1973, p. 8.

Rosenhouse, Leo. "Emperor Norton." *Great West,* June 1973, p. 10. Rpt. *Great West,* Summer 1981, p. 10.

_____. "I Am the Emperor of the United States." *Frontier West,* Oct. 1975, p. 10.

_____. "When the United States Had a Mad Emperor." *True Frontier,* Special Issue No. 3, 1972, p. 9. Rpt. *True Frontier,* Dec. 1975, p. 14.

Smith, Barry D. "Emperor Norton I of the United States." *True West,* December 1988, p. 42.

Young, Jan. "His Majesty, Emperor Norton I." *Real West,* Jan. 1962, p. 30.

Oakes, Daniel C.
House, C.B. "Oakes Rhymes With Hoax." *Old West,* Spring 1968, p. 38.

Oakley, Annie
Breihan, Carl W. "Annie Oakley: 'Little Sure Shot.'" *Oldtimers Wild West,* Oct. 1979, p. 16.

Cheney, Louise. "Annie Oakley, Little Miss Sureshot." *Real West,* Nov. 1967, p. 20. Rpt. *Real West,* Annual, Summer 1971, p. 28.

Hurt, R. Douglas. "Annie Oakley: An Enduring Western Legend." *True West,* July 1989, p. 14.

Jones, Rebecca. "When Annie Oakley Was Accused of Theft." *Old West,* Spring 1977, p. 16.

Mendez, Al. "Annie Oakley." *Great West,* May 1969, p. 12.

Murray, Tom G. "Annie Oakley Memorabilia." *True West,* June 1981, p. 20.

O'Brien, Gressley. "Why Annie Oakley Hated Guns." *The West,* Nov. 1965, p. 38. Rpt. *Golden West,* Feb. 1972, p. 8.

Qualey, Jake. "Annie Oakley's Strange Secret." *Real West,* Sept. 1960, p. 12.

Seiler, Toni. Letter. *True West,* Nov. 1981, p. 8.

"True Western Hall of Fame" column. *True Western Adventures,* Dec. 1959, p. 59.

Weddon, Willah. "Remembering Annie Oakley." *Frontier Times,* Oct. 1984, p. 50.

Oatman Family

Cortesi, Lawrence J. "Massacre On Oatman Flats." *Oldtimers Wild West,* Dec. 1979, p. 22.

Turner, Alford E. "The Oatman Massacre." *Real West,* Oct. 1982, p. 25. Rpt. *Real West,* Special Issue, Spring 1983, p. 13.

Oatman, Lorenzo

Cortesi, Lawrence. "Tracking Down the Club-Wielding Tonto Tribe Had a Special Meaning for Lorenzo Oatman." *Frontier West,* Oct. 1975, p. 36.

Oatman, Olive

Cheney, Louise. "Olive Oatman, Mohave Captive." *Real West,* Nov. 1968, p. 13.

Dunn, Jacob Platt, Jr. "The Terrifying Ordeal of Olive Oatman." *The West,* March 1964, p. 16. Rpt. *The West,* Annual 1971, p. 31.

Hubbard, Freeman H. "Wife of the Chief." *True West,* Dec. 1958, p. 16.

O'Day, Tom

Engebretson, Doug. "The Belle Fourche Bank Robbery." *Real West,* Dec. 1981, p. 22. Rpt. *Real West,* Special Issue, Spring 1985, p. 54.

Kirby, Edward M. "The Sundance Kid and the Belle Fourche Bank Robbery." *True West,* Jan. 1983, p. 10.

O'Folliard, Tom

Rasch, Philip J. "The Short Life of Tom O'Folliard." *Potomac Westerners Corral Dust,* Vol. V, July 1960, p. 20.

Ogden, Peter Skene

Decker, Peter. "Peter Skene Ogden." *New York Westerners Brand Book* , Vol. XIII, No. 1, 1966, p. 4.

Ogilvy, Lyulph "Lord"

Freeman, Frank M. "Lord Ogilvy: Imperious Maverick." *True Frontier,* Special Issue No. 3, 1972, p. 14.

O'Kelly, Edward "Ed" (sometimes given as Ed O. Kelly)

Breihan, Carl W. "The Man Who Shot Bob Ford." *Pioneer West,* May 1980, p. 17.

Henderson, Sam. "The Saga of Big Anne." *Golden West,* May 1969, p. 26.

Huston, Fred. "Death of the Coward Killer." *Real Frontier,* Aug. 1971, p. 19. Rpt. *True Frontier,* Special Issue No. 9, 1974, p. 17.

Jessen, Kenneth. "Chain of Death Ends in Creede." *NOLA Quarterly,* Vol. XI, No. 3, Winter 1987, p. 16.

Nestor, William. "What Secret Died With Ed O'Kelly?" *Real West,* April 1958, p. 10.

Olinger, Robert "Bob"

Cline, Donald. "Bob Olinger: Killer Deputy." *Golden West,* Jan. 1967, p. 44. Rpt. *Golden West,* Feb. 1972, p. 41; *Western Frontier,* Annual, Winter 1977, p. 6; and *Western Frontier,* Special Issue, Sept. 1975, p. 14.

Hines, James. "Death of Bob Ollinger [sic], Sadistic Jailer." *Real West,* July 1966, p. 40.

Klasner, Lily Casey. "Bob Olinger—As I Knew Him." Ed. Eve Ball. *True West,* April 1970, p. 10.

McCubbin, Robert G. "Long Lost Photograph of Tony Neis and Bob Olinger Is Found." *NOLA Quarterly,* Vol. XIV, Nos. 3 and 4 (combined issue), 1990, p. 3.

Rasch, Philip J. "The Olingers, Known Yet Forgotten." *Potomac Westerners Corral Dust,* Vol. VIII, No. 1, Feb. 1963.

Shirley, Glenn. "The Coyote Badman." *Westerner,* Dec. 1970, p. 36.

Olive, Print

Carsten, Lyle. "The Nebraska Man Burner." *Pioneer West,* April 1972, p. 32.

Carter, James L. "Who Killed Print Olive?" *Real West,* March 1990, p. 23.

Chrisman, Harry E. "When 'Slow Elk' Came High." *True West,* Winter 1953, p. 26. Rpt. *Old West,* Summer 1965, p. 46.

DeMattos, Jack. "Print Olive" ("Gunfighters of the Real West" column). *Real West,* May 1978, p. 36.

Huston, Fred. "Good Things to Say About Print Olive Were Scarce Items." *Frontier West,* Aug. 1973, p. 12.

————. "Man Burner From Texas." *Real Frontier,* March 1970, p. 32. Rpt. *True Frontier,* Special Issue No. 9, 1974, p. 34.

Preece, Harold. "Strange Truth About Print Olive." *The West,* May 1964, p. 18. Rpt. *Golden West,* June 1974, p. 38.

Tilford, Van W. "Print Olive's Special Ticket to Hell." *Frontier Times,* Winter 1960, p. 20.

Yost, Nellie Snyder. "The Olive Story." *True West,* May 1990, p. 30.

Olney, Joseph Graves "Joe" (alias Joe Hill)

Parsons, Chuck. "Witness Against Wyatt" ("Answer Man" column). *True West,* Feb. 1990, p. 13.

Olquin Family

Rosson, Mary'n. "How Four Texas Rangers Declared War on the Frontier's 100 Worst Desperadoes." *Frontier West,* Dec. 1973, p. 8.

Omohundro, John B. "Texas Jack"

Bloom, S. "Texas Jack." *Great West,* Sept. 1974, p. 20. Rpt. *Authentic West,* Summer 1981, p. 20.

Cheney, Louise. "Texas Jack, Gallant Westerner." *Real West,* Aug. 1968, p. 36.

Hart, George. "How the Wild West Went East." *Real West,* June 1970, p. 16.

Long, Paul F. "Texas Jack Omohundro: Prairie Scout and Showman." *Real West,* Oct. 1988, p. 23.

Oñate, Juan de

Carson, Xanthus. "The Obsessed." *Real Frontier,* April 1971, p. 33. Rpt. *True Frontier,* Special Issue No. 16, Fall 1976, p. 19.

O'Neil, Lewis

Meier, Gary. "Bizarre Case of the Church Street Murder." *Old West,* Summer 1991, p. 42.

O'Neill, Buckey

Arnold, Oren. "The Train Robbers Forty-Thousand-Dollar Bride." *True Western Adventures,* Feb. 1961, p. 28.

Hartley, William B. "The Great Big World of Bucky [sic] O'Neill." *True Western Adventures,* Oct. 1959, p. 9.

Kildare, Maurice. "Arizona's Great Train Robbery." *Real West,* Sept. 1968, p. 15.

Lipton, Dean. "The Quiet Lawman." *True West,* April 1964, p. 32.

Stanley, Samuel. "The Many-Sided Life of Arizona Pioneer Buckey O'Neill." *True West,* June. 1984, p. 32.

Walker, Dale L. "Buckey O'Neill and the Holdup at Diablo Canyon." *Real West,* Nov. 1978, p. 40.

Opothle-yoholo "Hopo"

Katigan, Madelon. "Creek Martyrs of Round Mountains." *The West,* May 1964, p. 24.

Zoltan, E.L. "The Exodus of the Creeks." *True Frontier,* May 1969, p. 30. Rpt. *True Frontier,* Special Issue No. 2, 1972, p. 6.

Orchard, Harry

Grimmett, R.G. "The Regeneration of Harry Orchard." *The West,* Oct. 1969, p. 28.

Grover, David H. "The Disappearing Dynamiter." *True West,* July 1988, p. 28.

Kutac, C. "The Calm and Cold-Blooded Murderer." *Real West,* Nov. 1977, p. 36. Rpt. *Real West,* Annual, Winter 1979, p. 52.

Orchard, Sadie

Cheney, Louise. "The Cockney Madam Queen of New Mexico." *Pioneer West,* Nov. 1967, p. 32.

Rosson, Mary'n. "The Puzzle of Sadie Orchard: Frontier Saint or Wanton Hoax?" *Frontier West,* June 1972, p. 32.

O'Riley, Peter

DeNevi, Don. "How a Frog Helped Discover the Comstock Vein." *Real West,* Dec. 1980, p. 22.

Ormsby, William

Cerveri, Doris. "Paiute Battle at Pyramid Lake." *Real West,* Special Issue, Winter 1970, p. 24.

Moreson, Albert J. "They Died at Pyramid." *The West,* July 1965, p. 32. Rpt. *The West,* Nov. 1973, p. 30.

Noren, Evelyn. "Vengeance in Blood." *Old West,* Spring 1982, p. 58.

Roe, Kenn Sherwood. "Paiute Ambush." *Westerner,* Oct. 1970, p. 14.

Roe, Kenneth. "Slaughter at Pyramid Lake." *Real West,* July 1962, p. 12.

O'Rourke, Michael "Johnny-Behind-the-Deuce"

Reiss, Malcom. "Johnny-Behind-the-Deuce." *True Western Adventures,* Feb. 1961, p. 14.

Searles, Lin. "The Short Unhappy Life of Johnny-Behind-the-Deuce." *Frontier Times,* Jan. 1966, p. 22.

Traywick, Ben T. "Johnny-Behind-the-Deuce." *The West,* March 1971, p. 42. Rpt. *Western Frontier,* Special Issue, Fall 1974, p. 19; and *Western Frontier,* Jan. 1983, p. 34.

Orrum, Eilley

Bloom, Sam. "The Early Days of Eilley Orrum." *Golden West,* July 1971, p. 24.

Rutledge, William III. "Eilley Orrum: Queen of Hard Luck." *True West,* Feb. 1975, p. 39.

Otero, Miguel
Galbraith, Den. "The Lost Ledge of Governor Otero." *True West,* April 1964, p. 45.

Otherday, John
Webb, Wayne E. "Noble John Otherday." *Western Frontier,* Special Issue, March 1975, p. 6.

Otter Family
Farner, Thomas E. "Christopher Trimble and the Otter Massacre." *True West,* March 1991, p. 42.

Kliewer, Dorothy. "The Sinker Creek Massacre." *Real West,* Annual, Summer 1986, p. 68.

Ouray
Hurt, Amy Passmore. "Ouray, the Arrow." *Real West,* Nov. 1968, p. 21. Rpt. *Real West,* Special Issue, Spring 1972, p. 51.

Meketa, Jackie. "Kit Carson and Chief Ouray: Partners in Crime." *Real West,* Dec. 1986, p. 18.

Stanley, Samuel. "Chief Ouray, Warrior and Statesman." *Wild West,* March 1972, p. 25. Rpt. *Pioneer West,* Sept. 1975, p. 11.

Outlaw, Bass (sometimes spelled Baz)
Cunningham, Eugene. "Bass Outlaw: The Little Wolf." *True West,* Sept. 1954, p. 20. Rpt. *Old West,* Fall 1965, p. 28; and *Badman,* Summer 1971, p. 44.

Majors, Fredrick. "Bass Outlaw Was a Texas Riddle." *The West,* Oct. 1965, p. 20. Rpt. *Western Frontier,* May 1985, p. 31; and *Golden West,* Aug. 1974, p. 19.

O'Neal, Bill. "Baz Outlaw vs. John Selman and Joe McKidrict" ("Great Western Gunfights" column). *True West,* Oct. 1988, p. 68.

————. "The Latest on 'Bass' Outlaw." *Real West,* Aug. 1982, p. 40.

Rasch, Philip J. "Bass Outlaw: Myth and Man." *Real West,* July 1979, p. 13.

Rosson, Mary'n. "The Day Bass Outlaw Tried to Drink Up the Town." *Frontier West,* Dec. 1974, p. 18.

Shirley, Glenn. "A Ranger Named Outlaw." *True Frontier,* Nov. 1968, p. 8. Rpt. *True Frontier,* Special Issue No. 7, Fall 1972, p. 38.

Wayne, W.T. "The Fast Guns of Bass Outlaw." *Great West,* June 1972, p. 12. Rpt. *Authentic West,* Fall 1981, p. 12.

Walker, Wayne T. "Bass Outlaw: Renegade Ranger." *Oldtimers Wild West,* Aug. 1979, p. 26.

Owens, Commodore Perry

Bloom, Sam. "Shootout In Apache County's Hell Town." *Frontier West,* Dec. 1974, p. 34.

Boyer, Glenn G. "Commodore Perry Owens Revisited." *Real West,* Oct. 1982, p. 12. Rpt. *Real West,* Yearbook, Fall 1983, p. 6.

Breihan, Carl W. "C.P. Owens: Marshal Without a Town." *Westerner,* Nov.-Dec. 1972, p. 30.

————. "Sheriff Commodore Perry Owens, Savior of Arizona." *Real West,* May 1970, p. 30.

Compagnon, Frank D. "The Beautiful Sheriff." *True Western Adventures,* Oct. 1960, p. 19.

DeMattos, Jack. "Commodore Perry Owens" ("Gunfighters of the Real West" column). *Real West,* July 1978, p. 36.

O'Neal, Bill. "Commodore Perry Owens vs The Blevins Clan" ("Great Western Gunfights" column). *True West,* Oct. 1989, p. 60.

Preece, Harold. "Commodore Owens, Paid Killer or Hero?" *The West,* Jan. 1965, p. 40. Rpt. *Western Frontier,* March 1980, p. 26.

Wellman, Paul I. "A Rifle and Four Six-Guns." *True Western Adventures,* Spring 1958, p. 32.

Whipple, George T. "Commodore P. Owens Was a Tough Sheriff." *NOLA Quarterly,* Vol. VIII, No. 2, Fall 1983, p. 1.

Wilkes, Homer. "Lawman from Arizona." *Frontier Times,* Jan. 1965, p. 30.

Owens, John "Johnny"

Griffith, Elizabeth. "Johnny Owens: Gambler, Whoremaster, Rancher, Killer." *WOLA Journal,* Vol. I, No. 1, Spring-Summer 1991, p. 7.

Spring, Agnes Wright. "Twenty Notches on His Gun." *True West,* April 1970, p. 34.

Thorpe, E.J. "The Gambling Sheriff." *True West,* Aug. 1967, p. 34.

Packard, Jeff
Edwards, Harold L. "California's Ruthless Outlaw." *Old West,* Summer 1985, p. 52.

Packer, Alferd (also spelled "Alfred")
"Alfred Packer, Cannibal." *Great West,* Feb. 1970, p. 50.

Bentz, Donald V. "Al Packer: America's Frontier Cannibal." *Golden West,* Oct. 1972, p. 38. Rpt. *Western Frontier,* Jan. 1978, p. 34.

Bloom, Sam. "And Then There Were None." *Great West,* Dec. 1973, p. 14. Rpt. *Authentic West,* Spring 1981, p. 14.

Brown, Alma Margaret. "High Country Cannibal." *Real West,* April 1968, p. 14. Rpt. *Real West,* Annual, Summer 1970, p. 27.

Carson, Xanthus. "The Fantastic Saga of the Colorado Cannibal." *Frontier West,* Feb. 1973, p. 12.

"Feast of Flesh." *Great West,* June 1967, p. 17.

Gillette, Ethel. "The Grisly Tale of Alferd Packer, a Colorado Cannibal." *Frontier Times,* Oct. 1984, p. 25.

Hayden, Peter V. "The Incredible Polly Pry." *Frontier Times,* Jan. 1977, p. 16.

McClusky, Thorp. "The Colorado Cannibal." *True Western Adventures,* Feb. 1959, p. 34.

McCray, E. Ward. "Man-Eater of Powderhorn Creek." *Old West,* Winter 1964, p. 39. Rpt. *Badman,* Summer 1971, p. 15.

Spendlove, Earl. "Cannibals Leave Only Bones." *Real West,* Sept. 1964, p. 24.

Toal, Patricia K. "The Cannibal of Slumgullion Pass." *Real West,* March 1978, p. 46.

Triem, Frank. "The Shadow of Cannibal Plateau." *Golden West,* March 1965, p. 25. Rpt. *Western Frontier,* May 1979, p. 9.

Web, Edgar. "Feud With the Cannibal." *Westerner,* Nov.-Dec. 1974, p. 34.

Padilla, Juan de
Dorcey, Allen. "A Cross to Courage." *The West,* May 1964, p. 33.

Paget, Nellie

Kildare, Maurice. "Nellie Paget: Bannack's Tragic Belle." *Real West,* Sept. 1970, p. 38.

Palmer, William Jackson

Harvey, Fred. "King of the Narrow Gauge." *True West,* Feb. 1960, p. 24.

Johnson, Dennis A. "Palmer's Happy Little Railroad." *The West,* Oct. 1970, p. 26. Rpt. *Western Frontier,* Special Issue, Oct. 1983, p. 28.

Koller, Joe. "The Battling Quaker." *Golden West,* Sept. 1967, p. 34.

Sutton, Leo. "The Incredible Iron Horse War at Colorado's Royal Gorge." *Frontier West,* Oct. 1971, p. 26.

Parberry, Jack L.

Parberry, Jack. "Lawman of the Old Northwest." *The West,* Nov. 1968, p. 24. Rpt. *Western Frontier,* Aug. 1981, p. 24; and *Western Frontier,* Nov. 1986, p. 24.

Parker, Cynthia Ann

Andre, Barbara E. "The Fighting White Squaw." *The West,* May 1968, p. 14.

Andrews, Harry. "The Parker Story." *True West,* Sept. 1954, p. 24.

Breashers, Claudia. "White Mother of a Red Chief." *Big West,* Feb. 1968, p. 12. Rpt. *Pioneer West,* Collector's Annual, 1971, p. 70.

Holding, Vera. "The Last Fighting Comanche." *Westerner,* Nov.-Dec. 1969, p. 20.

Rozar, Lily-B. "Sooner Sanctuary." *Wild West,* Sept. 1971, p. 44.

Parker, Ely S. (Donehogawa)

Thomas, Mark. "Ely S. Parker, Indian." *Great West,* Sept. 1974, p. 14. Rpt. *Authentic West,* Summer 1981, p. 14.

Wingo, Ella Mae. "Ely Samuel Parker: Little Father of the Indians." *Pioneer West,* April 1972, p. 48.

Parker Family (Cynthia Ann Parker)

Flanagan, Betty. "Comanche Reunion." *True West,* Dec. 1962, p. 17.

Perkins, Mrs. Lewis. Letter. *True West,* Oct. 1981, p. 8.

Parker, Fleming

Rasch, Philip J. "Fleming Jim Parker, Arizona Desperado." *NOLA Quarterly,* Vol. VII, No. 1, Summer 1982, p. 1.

Secrest, William B. "Tell the Boys I Died Game." *True West*, Feb. 1980, p. 28.

Stano, Mary G. "The Lawless Trail of Fleming Parker." *True West*, Dec. 1990, p. 42.

Parker, Isaac Charles

Croy, Homer. "He Hanged Them High." *True Western Adventures*, April 1960, p. 36.

Dahl, Peter. "Judge Isaac Parker." *Real West*, Americana Series, Fall 1965, p. 30.

Dahl, Peter Andrew. "Hangman's Half Dozen." *Real West*, May 1959, p. 24.

Hill, O.E. "The Man Who Was Crushed by Success." *Golden West*, May 1971, p. 24.

Kelley, Charles. "New Facts About Judge Parker." *The West*, March 1966, p. 44.

Kelsey, Frederick W. "Judge Parker's Last Hanging." *The West*, March 1964, p. 23. Rpt. *The West*, June 1974, p. 23.

Levine, David. "The Gates of Hell." *Great West*, April 1967, p. 22.

Metcalf, Arthur. "Judge Parker's Game of Death." *The West*, Feb. 1966, p. 29. Rpt. *Western Frontier*, Annual, Fall 1980, p. 8.

Shirley, Glenn. "No God West of Fort Smith." *NOLA Quarterly*, Vol. XIII, No. 4, 1989, p. 1.

_____. "No God West of Fort Smith." *True West*, Feb. 1957, p. 14.

Spann, W.O. "Judge Parker's Laughing Ghost." *Real West*, May 1963, p. 18.

Stegmaier, R.M. "Jurisdiction of the Hanging Judge." *Golden West*, Sept. 1970, p. 26. Rpt. *The West*, Sept. 1973, p. 18; *Western Frontier*, Jan. 1977, p. 26; and *Western Frontier*, May 1985, p. 16.

Storm, Syd. "Hanging Judge Parker." *NOLA Quarterly*, Vol. VIII, No. 3, Winter, 1983-84, p. 1.

Wilson, William R. "Justice on the Sooner Border." *Golden West*, Sept. 1967, p. 12.

Parker, Jim

Dodge, Matt. "Jim Parker: Good Cowboy Gone Bad." *Real West*, July 1980, p. 8. Rpt. *Real West*, Yearbook 1981, p. 8.

Parker, Quanah

Andrews, Harry. "The Parker Story." *True West*, Sept. 1954, p. 24.

Ballenger, Dean W. "The Comanche Massacre That Turned Bad Water Red With Blood." *Frontier West*, June 1972, p. 28.

Bardon, Oscar C. "Quanah Parker's Famous Ride." *The West*, May 1964, p. 22. Rpt. *The West*, May 1972, p. 12.

Bennett, Wylie W. "I Knew Quanah Parker." *Frontier Times,* Spring 1960, p. 26. Rpt. *Old West,* Summer 1980, p. 20.

Deac, Wilfred P. "Victory by a Long Shot." *Wild West,* Dec. 1989, p. 35.

Fisher, Robert I. "Quanah Parker, Indian Judge, Chief of the Comanches." *NOLA Quarterly,* Vol. VI, No. 1, Summer 1982, p. 4.

Gilles, Albert S. "A Horse for Quanah Parker." *Frontier Times,* May 1966, p. 34.

Guttman, Jon. "Lord of Two Worlds." *Wild West,* Aug. 1989, p. 34.

Hart, George. "Quanah Parker's Last Days." *Real West,* May 1971, p. 23. Rpt. *Real West,* Special Issue, Spring 1972, p. 6.

Holding, Vera. "The Last Fighting Comanche." *Westerner,* Nov.-Dec. 1969, p. 20.

Lehman, Leola. "Quanah: Last Great Comanche Chief." *True Frontier,* May 1969, p. 12. Rpt. *True Frontier,* Special Issue No. 6, 1973, p. 34.

Neil, Wilfred T. "Quanah Parker's Magic Buttons." *The West,* June 1968, p. 26. Rpt. *Golden West,* April 1973, p. 38.

O'Quinn, Eugene G. Letter. *Real West,* May 1965, p. 8.

Orlov, Janice Wilks, with Olive Wilks Horton and Claude Wilks. "'Chief Casuse' and Quanah Parker." *Frontier Times,* Nov. 1977, p. 15.

Rozar, Lily-B. "Sooner Sanctuary." *Wild West,* Sept. 1971, p. 44.

Smith, Harley. Letter. *The West,* March 1969, p. 66.

Staley, J. Allen. "Quanah Parker and Adobe Walls." *Real West,* Jan. 1958, p. 22.

Swanson, Budington. "The Tragedy and Triumph of Quanah Parker." *Great West,* Feb. 1973, p. 6.

Tilghman, Zoe A. "Comanche Chief." *True West,* June 1955, p. 31.

Vanderwerth, W.C. "The Lord of the Plains." *True Frontier,* March 1971, p. 27. Rpt. *True Frontier,* Special Issue No. 10, 1974, p. 6.

Parker, Robert Leroy "Butch Cassidy"

Berk, Lee. "Butch Cassidy Didn't Do It—Winnemucca." *Old West,* Fall 1983, p. 22.

Betensen, Lula Parker, and Bill Kelly. "Butch Cassidy and When He Came Home." *Real West,* Sept. 1977, p. 14. Rpt. *Real West,* Annual, Winter 1979, p. 12.

Conway, Cliff. "Oldtimer Remembers Cassidy, Tracy, Lant, Warner." *NOLA Quarterly,* Vol. III, No. 1, Summer 1977, p. 9.

Boren, Kerry Ross. "Boren Says Butch Cassidy Did Not Die in Bolivia." *NOLA Quarterly,* Vol. I, No. 1, 1975, p. 8.

_____. "Butch's Outlaw Trail Ran from Canada to Mexico." *NOLA Quarterly,* Vol. I, No. 3, 1975, p. 3.

_____. "Proof: Butch Cassidy Came Back." *Westerner,* May-June 1973, p. 38.

Breihan, Carl W. "Butch Cassidy and Company: Long Riders of the Outlaw Trail." Part I, *Real West,* May 1971, p. 6; Part II, *Real West,* June 1971, p. 46.

Buck, Daniel, and Anne Meadows. "Closing in on the Bank Robbers." *WOLA Journal* Vol. I, No. 2, Fall-Winter 1991, p. 19.

_____. "The Many Deaths of Butch Cassidy." *Pacific Northwest,* July 1987, p. 26.

_____. "Where Lies Butch Cassidy?" *Old West,* Fall 1991, p. 29.

_____. "Wild Bunch Bank Holdup in Argentina: Banco de Londres y Tarapaca." *NOLA Quarterly,* Vol. XII, No. 3, Winter 1988, p. 4.

Button, I. Victor. "Butch Cassidy Gave Getaway Horse to Ten-Year-Old Boy." *NOLA Quarterly,* Vol. I, No. 2, 1975, p. 3.

Carson, John. "Butch Cassidy." *True West,* Dec. 1962, p. 45.

Conant, Lora M. "Butch Tangled With the Pinkertons." *Wild West,* Sept. 1970, p. 26. Rpt. *Pioneer West,* Aug. 1972, p. 50; and *Oldtimers Wild West,* May 1975, p. 26.

Dullenty, Jim. "Butch Cassidy's Revealing Letters." *NOLA Quarterly,* Vol. IX, No. 1, Summer 1984, p. 10.

_____. "Dullenty Says Butch Cassidy Was William T. Phillips." *NOLA Quarterly,* Vol. II, No. 2, 1976, p. 11.

_____. "He Was a Stranger in Globe, Arizona." *True West,* Sept. 1983, p. 36.

_____. "Wagner Train Robbery." *Old West,* Spring 1983, p. 40.

Flack, Dora D. "Butch Cassidy: The Living Dead." *Frontier Times,* Jan. 1981, p. 20.

Glen, Calvin. "Top Man of the Wild Bunch." *Frontier Times,* Winter 1960, p. 7. Rpt. *Badman,* Annual , 1971, p. 12.

Harris, Fredie Steve. "Butch Cassidy's Outlaw Horseman." *Golden West,* May 1969, p. 18. Rpt. *Western Frontier,* Annual No. 3, 1976, p. 34; and *Western Frontier,* Oct. 1984, p. 34.

Hartley, William B. "Swashbuckler in the Saddle." *True Western Adventures,* Feb. 1959, p. 36.

Horan, James D. "Butch Cassidy's Last Stand." *True Western Adventures,* April 1961, p. 14.

Johnson, D.R. "Pinkerton's and the Hold-In-The-Wall Gang." *Chicago Westerners Brand Book,* Vol. XV, No. 9, Nov. 1958, p. 1.

Johnston, Richard E. "The Robbery That Was to Have Been." *NOLA Quarterly,* Vol. IV, No. 4, June 1979, p. 9.

_____. "Who Robbed the Pleasant Valley Coal Company?" *NOLA Quarterly,* Vol. V, No. 4, July 1980, p. 13.

Kelly, Charles. "The Man Who Impersonated Butch Cassidy." *True West,* Dec. 1969, p. 38.

Kirby, Ed. "Butch, Etta and Sundance In the Big Apple." *Real West,* Jan. 1978, p. 46.

Kirby, Ed M. "Butch, Sundance, Etta Frolicked in Fun City." *NOLA Quarterly,* Vol. I, No. 4, Winter 1975-76, p. 5.

Kirby, Edward M. "Butch Cassidy and the Sundance Kid: An Historical Essay." *The Outlaw Trail Journal,* Vol. I, No. 1, Summer 1991, p. 23.

Kirkpatrick, J.R. "Butch Cassidy and the McCarty Gang." *Westerner,* Feb. 1971, p. 44.

Kyle, Thomas G. "Did Butch Cassidy Die in Spokane? Phillips Photo Fails." *Old West,* Fall 1991, p. 26.

Lacy, Steve, and Jim Dullenty. "Revealing Letters of Outlaw Butch Cassidy." *Old West,* Winter 1984, p. 10.

"Lula Parker Betensen Writes Biography of Her Brother, Butch Cassidy." *NOLA Quarterly,* Vol. I, No. 1, 1975, p. 7.

Majors, F. "The Strange Death of Butch Cassidy." *Real West,* Americana Series, Fall 1964, p. 48.

Majors, Frank. "Strange Death of Butch Cassidy." *Real West,* Sept. 1961, p. 8.

Meadows, Anne, and Daniel Buck. "Running Down a Legend." *Americas,* Vol. XLII, No. 6, 1990-91, p. 21.

"Monument Erected to Cassidy's Horse." *NOLA Quarterly,* Vol. I, No. 3, 1975, p. 10.

Pointer, Larry. "In Search of Butch Cassidy Switches: Cassidy to Phillips." *NOLA Quarterly,* Vol. III, No. 3, Winter 1978, p. 9.

Rabinowitz, Ilene. "Butch Cassidy and the Wild Bunch." *Great West,* May 1968, p. 4.

Rhoades, Gale R. "Butch Cassidy Didn't Die in an Ambush in South America." *The West,* Jan. 1974, p. 34.

Rile, Charlie. "The Trap Didn't Spring on Butch Cassidy." *True West,* Feb. 1969, p. 40.

Robinson, Howard. "The Day the American West Died." *America's Frontier West,* Issue No. 1, n.d., p. 30.

Schoenberger, Dale T. "Butch Was No Train Robber." *NOLA Quarterly,* Vol. V, No. 3, April 1980, p. 15.

Stewart, Arden. "Dad Nearly Rode With Butch." *The Outlaw Trail Journal,* Vol. I, No. 1, Summer 1991, p. 45.

Wiltsey, T.J. "When Butch Cassidy Returned for His Buried Coins." *Westerner,* Summer 1975, p. 20.

Parkhurst, Charles Darkey "Charlie"

Auer, L.C. "Mystery Whip of the West." *The West,* April 1966, p. 32. Rpt. *Western Frontier,* Jan. 1983, p. 40; and *Western Frontier,* July 1984, p. 5.

Fleming, Gerry. "The Astounding Secret of Charlie Parkhurst." *Pioneer West,* April 1972, p. 36.

Grubb, R.L. "The Strange Case of Old Charlie." *True Frontier,* Dec. 1972, p. 28. Rpt. *True Frontier,* Special Issue No. 11, Winter 1974-75, p. 4.

Lee, Hector. "The Legend of Charlie Parkhurst." *NOLA Quarterly,* Vol. VI, No. 1, 1981, p. 20.

McKelvey, Nat W. "Charlie the Whip." *True Western Adventures,* Summer 1958, p. 33.

Reinstedt, Randall "The West's Greatest Stage Driver Was a Gal!" *The West,* Nov. 1973, p. 26. Rpt. *Western Frontier,* Sept. 1977, p. 18.

Richeson, Cena Golder. "The Woman In Charles Parkhurst." *True West,* Aug. 1983, p. 39.

Wiltsey, Norman B. "Death Called Charlie's Bluff." *Real West,* Dec. 1968, p. 17.

_____ , "Mystery Driver of the Sierras." *True West,* Jan. 1955, p. 27. Rpt. *Old West,* Winter 1965, p. 51.

Parkman, Francis

Hilton, Joseph. "The Man Who Broke the Oregon Trail." *Real West,* Oct. 1957, p. 17.

"True Western Hall of Fame" column. *True Western Adventures,* April 1961, p. 48.

Parmer, Allen

Breihan, Carl W. "Allen Parmer: Quantrill Guerrilla." *Real West,* Sept. 1970, p. 10.

_____ . "The Charmed Life of Allen Parmer." *Pioneer West,* Jan. 1978, p. 8.

Parrish, Hank

Lewis, George. "Hank Parrish: Nevada's Worst Killer." *The West,* Sept. 1969, p. 30. Rpt. *Western Frontier,* Jan. 1978, p. 4; and *Western Frontier,* Nov. 1980, p. 16.

Parrott, George "Big Nose George"

Arlandson, Lee. "When 'Big Nose' George Parrott Was Hung." *Pioneer West,* June 1972, p. 40.

"Big Nose George." *Great West,* May 1969, p. 6.

Breihan, Carl W. "Big Nose George Parrott." *Real West*, Sept. 1968, p. 26. Rpt. *Real West*, Dec. 1974, p. 46.

_____. "The Outlaw Who Became a Pair of Shoes." *Oldtimers Wild West*, Oct. 1978, p. 24. Rpt. *True West*, Jan. 1983, p. 44.

Carson, John. "Frank James in Wyoming." *Real West*, March 1967, p. 50.

Engebretson, Doug. Letter. *True West*, March 1983, p. 8.

Hartley, William B. "The Man From North of Hell." *True Western Adventures*, Spring 1958, p. 12.

Holben, Richard. "Pickling Outlaws Was a Form of Lynch Law Vengeance." *Frontier West*, Dec. 1974, p. 22.

Kildare, Maurice. "Big Nose George Died the Hard Way." *Frontier West*, Oct. 1973, p. 42.

Mason, John. "Hanging of Big Nose George." *Real West*, Jan. 1960, p. 17.

Pearce, Bennett R. "No Grave for Big Nose George." *The West*, May 1969, p. 22. Rpt. *Western Frontier*, Jan. 1983, p. 20.

Wolfe, George D. "Curtains for Big Nose George." *True West*, April 1961, p. 18.

Patron, Juan B.
Edwards, Harold L. "The Short and Violent Life of Juan Patron." *True West*, March 1991, p. 28.

Kildare, Maurice. "New Mexico's Patron Killing." *Real West*, June 1973, p. 56.

Patterson, Ferd
Ankeny, Levi. "The Enigmatic Ferd Patterson." *The West*, Oct. 1965, p. 18. Rpt. *Golden West*, Oct. 1972, p. 26.

Kildare, Maurice. "The Patterson-Pinkham Feud." *Great West*, June 1970, p. 32.

Ryker, Lois. "The Man Who Killed Sheriff Pinkham." *Real West*, Sept. 1968, p. 10.

Shirley, Glenn. "Tennessee Hell Raiser. *Old West*, Summer 1968, p. 12.

Pattie, James Ohio
Molthan, Ruth. "The Perils of James Ohio Pattie." *Golden West*, March 1971, p. 22.

Young, Bob. "Curse of the Broken Totem." *Real West*, May 1962, p. 20.

Paul, Robert "Bob"
Kildare, Maurice. "The Mysterious Gunman." *The West*, Dec. 1966, p. 20.

_____. "The Youngest Stage Robber in Arizona." *Real West*, Jan. 1971, p. 34.

Long, J.A. "How Red Jack Almer Died." *The West,* Oct. 1964, p. 46.

Long, James. "Bob Paul: Shotgun Marshal." *Real West,* May 1965, p. 20.

Paulina

Corless, Hank. "Oregon's Bullet Proof Indian." *True West,* Sept. 1986, p. 36.

Fraser, B. Kay. "The Last Raid of Chief Paulina." *Real West,* Aug. 1970, p. 30.

Lyon, Howard E. "Paulina: Deadly Raider." *True West,* Oct. 1966, p. 6.

Payne, David

Mahalon, John. "When the Boomers Boomed." *Real West,* March 1960, p. 14.

Majors, John J. "The Man Who Stole Oklahoma." *Real West,* July 1965, p. 42.

Peacock, James

Hale, Donald R. "James Chiles: A Missouri Badman." *The West,* Oct. 1968, p. 14. Rpt. *Golden West,* April 1972, p. 6.

Thorp, Raymond W. "How 'Jim Crow' Chiles Died!" *Real West,* Jan. 1962, p. 32.

Peacock, Lewis

Jones, Nick. "The Lee-Peacock Feud." *Real West,* Jan. 1979, p. 12. Rpt. *Real West,* Annual, Winter 1980, p. 20.

Peavy, John R.

Edwards, Harold L. "He Policed the Rio Grande." *NOLA Quarterly,* Vol. XV, No. 4, Oct.-Dec. 1991, p. 1.

Peel, Langford "Farmer"

Greenfield, Charles D. "There Was Something About Him." *The West,* Feb. 1967, p. 30. Rpt. *Golden West,* April 1974, p. 28.

DeArment, Robert K. "John Bull: Gunman, Gambler—a Frontier Odyssey." *True West,* March 1986, p. 32.

Peeler, Thomas "Tom"

DeArment, R.K. "The Toughest Cow Outfit in Texas." *True West,* April 1991, p. 26.

Pelton, Clark

Carroll, Murray L. "Clark Pelton: The Stage Robbing Kid." *True West,* Aug. 1990, p. 16.

Penn, Charley
Marquiss, F.C. "Twice Punished: Was It Deserved?" *True West*, Feb. 1972, p. 28.

Pennington Family
Long, James A. "The Penningtons of Arizona." *Golden West*, Nov. 1964, p. 34.

Perret, Johnnie "Potato Creek Johnnie"
Miller, Lois. "Potato Creek Johnnie's Big Find." *True West*, June 1957, p. 4.

Perry, Charles C. "Charley"
DeArment, R.K. "The Fatal Defect of Charley Perry." *Old West*, Winter 1991, p. 24.

Perry, Howard
Carson, Xanthus. "Terlingua: Ghost Town of Hell." *Wild West*, March 1972, p. 11. Rpt. *Oldtimers Wild West*, Aug. 1975, p. 5.

Pershing, John Joseph
Murphy, John F., Jr. "Raiders Rapidly Pursued." *Wild West*, Aug. 1990, p. 42.
Smith, Burton K. "Pershing's First Adventure With Death." *The West*, June 1965, p. 16. Rpt. *The West*, Sept. 1974, p. 26.

Pfeiffer, Albert H.
Freeman, Frank M. "'And I Fed Them Well.'" *Real West*, April 1983, p. 20.
_____. "Albert H. Pfeiffer: Scourge of the Apaches." *The West*, Feb. 1967, p. 21. Rpt. *The West*, Jan. 1972, p. 6; *Western Frontier*, Annual No. 1, 1975, p. 2; and *Western Frontier*, May 1984, p. 14.
Jenkins, Nedra C. "Tata Pfeiffer: Nemesis of the Apaches." *Real Frontier*, June 1970, p. 40.
Meketa, Jacqueline Dorgan. "Personality" column. *Wild West*, Aug. 1991, p. 8.
Norwood, John. "War of Ballots in Archuleta County." *Real West*, Oct. 1983, p. 32. Rpt. *Real West*, Annual, Spring 1985, p. 12.
Settle, Raymond W., and Mary Lund Settle. "He Struck Terror to Apache Hearts." *True Frontier*, March 1968, p. 36.
Spendlove, Earl. "The Monument Valley Slaughter." *Great West*, Oct. 1973, p. 26.

Philip, James "Scotty"
Blasingame, C.M. "Scotty Philip, Man of the Plains." *Frontier Times*, Sept. 1966, p. 13.

Koller, Joe. "Scotty Philip: Living Legend." *Golden West,* Nov. 1968, p. 12. Rpt. *Golden West,* Oct. 1974, p. 16.

Robinson, James M. "Ghost Rider on the Prairie." *Frontier Times,* Sept. 1976, p. 6.

Voynick, Stephen M. "Bringing Back the Buffalo." *True West,* Feb. 1988, p. 52.

Phillips, John "Portugee"

Boucher, Leonard H. "Man of Iron, Horse of Steel." *Real Frontier,* March 1970, p. 18.

Brooks, Bill. "The Suicide Ride That Saved Ft. Kearney [sic]." *Western Action,* Dec. 1960, p. 18.

Day, DeWitt F. "Massacre and Rescue at Fort Phil Kearney [sic]." *America's Frontier West,* Issue No. 1, n.d., p. 32.

Harrison, Fred. "Portugee Phillips' Incredible Midnight Ride." *Golden West,* Nov. 1964, p. 42. Rpt. *The West,* Feb. 1972, p. 23.

Lutske, H. "Ride for Help." *Westerner,* Dec. 1970, p. 31.

McCready, Valdon. "Truth About Portugee Philip's [sic] Ride." *Real West,* Jan. 1961, p. 26.

Minton, Robert. "Three Thousand Sioux Barred His Way." *True Western Adventures,* Feb. 1961, p. 25.

Murray, Robert A. "'Portugee' Phillips Got Through." *True West,* July 1984, p. 59.

Sufrin, Mark. "Two Hundred Thirty-Six Miles of Frozen Hell." *Frontier West,* Oct. 1971, p. 8.

Swanson, Budington. "The Christmas Ride of Portugee Phillips." *True Frontier,* April 1978, p. 18.

Wiltsey, Norman B. "Message to Fort Laramie." *True West,* Winter 1953, p. 32.

_____. "Ordeal by Blizzard." *Real West,* Jan. 1969, p. 48. Rpt. *Real West,* Annual, Summer 1970, p. 34.

Phillips, Ora

Ballenger, Dean W. "The Blood-Bunch: Killers With a Cause." *Frontier West,* June 1975, p. 22.

Phillips, William T.

Dullenty, Jim. "Dullenty Says Butch Cassidy Was William T. Phillips." *NOLA Quarterly,* Vol. II, No. 2, 1976, p. 11.

_____. "Who Really Was William T. Phillips?" *WOLA Journal,* Vol. I, No. 2, Fall-Winter 1991, p. 10.

Kyle, Thomas G. "Did Butch Cassidy Die in Spokane? Phillips Photo Fails." *Old West,* Fall 1991, p. 26.

Pointer, Larry. "In Search of Butch Cassidy Switches: Cassidy to Phillips." *NOLA Quarterly,* Vol. III, No. 3, Winter 1978, p. 9.

Phy, Joseph "Joe"

Auer, L.C. "Gun Grudge in Florence." *Pioneer West,* July 1967, p. 24.

Ford, I.M. "Shoot-Out on Gunman's Walk." *The West,* June 1966, p. 24. Rpt. *Golden West,* Oct. 1973, p. 32; *Western Frontier,* Sept. 1977, p. 6; and *Western Frontier,* July 1983, p. 6.

McKelvey, Nat. "Death of an Angry Gun." *True Western Adventures,* June 1959, p. 28.

Rickards, Colin. "Sheriff Pete Gabriel and Deputy Phy." *Golden West,* Sept. 1970, p. 32.

Wilkes, Homer. "Joe Phy, Deputy." *Frontier Times,* May 1966, p. 47.

_____. "Justice and Joe." *Old West,* Winter 1968, p. 31.

Pickett, Bill

Dodge, Matt. "Bill Pickett in Arizona." *Real West,* Oct. 1983, p. 10. Rpt. *Real West,* Yearbook, Fall 1984, p. 53.

Hinkle, Milt. "The Dusky Demon." *True West,* Aug. 1961, p. 30.

Holding, Vera, and Will Seig. "Bill Pickett: The Choctaw-Negro Who Invented Bull Dogging." *Great West,* Feb. 1973, p. 20.

Judd, B. Ira, and John Matthews. "Bill Pickett: The Black Cowboy Who Invented Bulldogging." *Pioneer West,* Jan. 1978, p. 24.

Sawicki, Judy Sanders. "Bill Pickett: Brazen Bulldogger." *True Frontier,* Jan. 1974, p. 6. Rpt. *True Frontier,* Special Issue No. 19, Fall 1977, p. 26.

Shirley, Glenn D. "Bill Pickett: The Man Who Developed Bulldogging." *Golden West,* Nov. 1964, p. 10.

_____. "The First Bulldogger." *Westerner,* Nov.-Dec. 1969, p. 8.

Walker, Wayne T. "Bill Pickett, Bulldogger." *Great West,* Dec. 1969, p. 22.

Pickett, Nelly "Nell"

Mays, Carelton. "Angel From Hell." *Real West,* Annual, Spring 1968, p. 34.

Rasch, Philip J. "Was Nelly Pickett For Real or Just Imagined?" *NOLA Quarterly,* Vol. II, No. 2, Autumn 1975, p. 7.

Pickett, Thomas "Tom"
Parsons, Chuck. "Tom Pickett and Billy the Kid" ("Answer Man" column). *True West,* Jan. 1989, p. 12.

Rasch, Philip J. "He Rode With the Kid: The Life of Tom Pickett." *English Westerners' Brand Book,* Tenth Anniversary Publication, 1964, p. 11.

Pico, Pio
Cannon, Marian G. "Pio Pico: California's Last Mexican Governor." *True West,* Oct. 1982, p. 28.

Kennelly, Joseph. "Saga of Pio Pico." *Golden West,* March 1965, p. 14.

Kessinger, Dennis. "Kearny and Pico: The Battle of San Pasqual." *Old West,* Winter 1991, p. 20.

Pierce, Abel Head "Shanghai"
Blakely, Mike. "Shanghai's Legacy." *True West,* Jan. 1986, p. 48.

Frazier, Thomas A. "Shanghai Pierce." *Real West,* Jan. 1975, p. 38.

Nolen, Oran Warder. "Texas Cowman 'Shanghai' Pierce." *The West,* July 1967, p. 32. Rpt. *The West,* Oct. 1973, p. 18.

Pattie, J.R. "Shanghai Pierce: Webster on Cattle!" *True West,* April 1965, p. 12.

Pierce, Charley
McBee, G. Fred. "Don't Wake the Neighbors!" *Golden West,* March 1971, p. 20. Rpt. *Western Frontier,* Special Issue, Fall 1974, p. 38.

Preece, Harold. "The Sorry Saga of Charley Pierce." *Real West,* Nov. 1967, p. 18.

Pigeon, William "Bill"
Turpin, Robert F. "Cherokee Bill Pigeon." *Great West,* June 1971, p. 20.

Pike, George W.
Jones, Gene. "Wildest of the Wayward West." *The West,* March 1964, p. 26.

Pearce, Bennett R. "The Legend of George W. Pike." *Golden West,* May 1973, p. 32.

Riske, Milt. "Cow Country Lawyer." *Oldtimers Wild West,* Oct. 1978, p. 28.

Shirley, Glenn. "No Man Like Cowboy Pike." *Westerner,* March 1971, p. 36.

_____. "That Remarkable Horse Thief Pike." *True West,* Sept. 1986, p. 16.

Pike, James
Phares, Ross. "Hell-for-Leather Pike." *True West,* June 1955, p. 27. Rpt. *Badman,* Fall 1972, p. 11.

Pike, Zebulon

Majors, John. "Stockade of the Dead." *Real West,* May 1962, p. 18.

Murphy, John F., Jr. "West's Intrepid Pathfinder." *Wild West,* Aug. 1991, p. 18.

Stowell, H.W. "'Marco Polo' of Colorado." *Pioneer West,* Nov. 1969, p. 20. Rpt. *Wild West,* Sept. 1972, p. 14.

Sufrin, Mike. "The Desperate Sixteen Who Opened the West." *Frontier West,* June 1973, p. 24.

Pine Leaf

Wingo, Ella Mae. "Pine Leaf: Avenging Angel of Death." *True Frontier,* Aug. 1972, p. 34.

Pinkerton, Allan

Parsons, Chuck. "Allen Pinkerton: Outlaw Hunter" ("Answer Man" column). *True West,* May 1991, p. 12.

Underwood, Larry D. "Allan Pinkerton: Taming of the West." *True West,* July 1984, p. 18.

Pinkerton Family

Bourke, Charles Francis. "The Pinkertons Were Great." *Golden West,* July 1965, p. 25. Rpt. *Western Frontier,* Special Issue, April 1983, p. 30.

Gubitz, Myron B. "Those Hard Ridin' Pinkertons." *True Western Adventures,* Aug. 1961, p. 22.

Vail, Jason. "The Eye That Never Sleeps." *Wild West,* June 1991, p. 20.

Pinkham, Sumner

Ankeny, Levi. "The Enigmatic Ferd Patterson." *Golden West,* Oct. 1972, p. 26.

Kildare, Maurice. "The Patterson-Pinkham Feud." *Great West,* June 1970, p. 32.

Ryker, Lois. "The Man Who Killed Sheriff Pinkham." *Real West,* Sept. 1968, p. 10.

Shirley, Glenn. "Tennessee Hell Raiser." *Old West,* Summer 1968 p.12.

Pitts, Charlie

Giffen, Guy. "Charlie Pitts—RIP" *True West,* April 1963, p. 42.

Rickards, Colin. "Bones of the Northfield Robbers." *Real West,* Jan. 1979, p. 28.

Pizanthia, Joe

Kildare, Maurice. "The Man They Killed Three Times." *Big West,* Feb. 1968, p. 32.

_____. "Night of the Bloody Butcher." *Wild West*, Jan. 1972, p. 59.

Place, Etta
Grant, Maxwell. "Whatever Happened to Beautiful Etta?" *Westerner*, June 1971, p. 41.

Kirby, Ed M. "Butch, Sundance and Etta Place Frolicked in 'Fun City.'" *NOLA Quarterly*, Vol. I, No. 4, Winter 1975-76, p. 5.

Lodefink, John. "Was Etta Place Butch Cassidy's Cousin?" *NOLA Quarterly*, Vol. II, No. 2, Summer 1976, p. 9.

Masters, George. "She Devil of the Wild Bunch." *Real West*, Aug. 1959, p. 8.

Sparks, N. "The Mysterious Etta Place." *The West*, Dec. 1965, p. 36. Rpt. *The West*, Feb. 1973, p. 20; and *Western Frontier*, Sept. 1975, p. 22.

Von Kreisler, Max. "Etta Place: 'Associate of Outlaws.'" *Pioneer West*, March 1979, p. 30.

Plenty Coups
Czech, Kenneth P. "Warriors and Chiefs" column. *Wild West*, Oct. 1990, p. 8.

Wiltsey, Norman B. "Chief Plenty Coups: Savior of the Crows." Part I, *Real West*, Aug. 1968, p. 33; Part II, *Real West*, Sept. 1968, p. 32. Rpt. as one-part article, *Real West*, Special Issue, Winter 1970, p. 21.

_____. "Children of the Raven." Part I, *True West*, April 1955, p. 6; Part II, *True West*, June 1955, p. 18.

Plummer, Electa (Electa Maxwell)
Cunningham, Reba Pierce. "The Wife of a Philandering Outlaw Sheriff." *True West*, June 1982, p. 28.

Parsons, Chuck. "Mourning Becomes Electa" ("Answer Man" column). *True West*, May 1989, p. 12.

Plummer, Henry
Breihan, Carl W. "The Bannack Stage Robbery." *Real West*, May 1976, p. 46.

_____. "Henry Plummer's Horrendous Masquerade." *Golden West*, March 1968, p. 22.

_____. "The Vigilante Sheriff." *Westerner*, Oct. 1971, p. 48.

Cunningham, Reba Pierce. "The Wife of a Philandering Outlaw Sheriff." *True West*, June 1982, p. 28.

DeMattos, Jack. "Henry Plummer." *Real West*, Annual, Summer 1986, p. 10.

_____. "Henry Plummer" ("Gunfighters of the Real West" column). *Real*

West, Aug. 1985, p. 42.

Hartley, William B. "Outlaw Sheriff." *True Western Adventures,* June 1959, p. 38.

Kildare, Maurice. "Henry Plummer's Golden Loot." *Frontier Times,* May 1965, p. 6.

————. "Sheriff Crawford Bushwhacked Henry Plummer." *Great West,* Oct. 1970, p. 26.

————. "Vigilante's Doublecross." *Westerner,* March-April 1969, p. 44.

Lorenzi, Robert. "The Hanging of Henry Plummer." *Oldtimers Wild West,* April 1978, p. 8.

Mac, 'Tana. "Gold on the Grasshopper." *True West,* Dec. 1960, p. 23.

Mather, R.E. "Gold Camp Mother Who Brought Down the Marshal." *True West,* Nov. 1987, p. 14.

McKinnon, L.C. "The Devil's Sanctuary." *Real West,* Annual, Spring 1984, p. 34.

Moore, Jean Michael. "Henry Plummer's Promise." *The West,* March 1966, p. 25.

Stanley, Samuel. "The Renegade Sheriff Who Made the Idaho Territory His Own Poaching Ground." *Frontier West,* Dec. 1974, p. 6.

"They Hung Henry Plummer." *Great West,* Dec. 1968, p. 14.

Trapp, Bob. "They Hanged Henry Plummer High." *Real West,* Sept. 1960, p. 34.

Plummer, Rachel

Auer, L. "Horror of Rachel Plummer." *Real West,* May 1962, p. 44.

Webster, Carl. "Captured." *Great West,* April 1967, p. 20.

Yarbrough, C.L. "The Search for Rachel Plummer." *Vanishing Texas,* Oct.-Nov. 1980, p. 16.

Pocatello

Allen, Patricia A. "Warriors and Chiefs" column. *Wild West,* Dec. 1991, p. 16.

Poe, John William

Poe, John W. "Death of Billy the Kid." Rpt. *True West,* June 1962, p. 6.

Whitehead, Ruth W. "John Poe: Square Shooter With a Six Shooter." *Real West,* Nov. 1971, p. 30.

"Poker Alice" (see Tubbs, Alice)

Pollock, William "Pawnee"

Shirley, Glenn. "Pawnee Pollock: Indian Hero and Genius." *Real West,* Feb. 1969, p. 40.

Wilson, Roger. "William Pollock: The Fighting Pawnee Artist." *Great West*, Dec. 1974, p. 22.

"Polly Pry" (see Anthony, Leonel Ross)

Pomeroy, Mark M. "Brick"
Malocsay, Zoltan. "'Brick Head' Pomeroy and His Tunnel to the Pacific." *Westerner*, March-April 1972, p. 50.

Pomeroy, Reed
Gunther, Ralph. "'Hanging' Pomeroy Had the Fastest Noose in the West." *Frontier West*, June 1971, p. 20.

Ponting, Tom "Candy"
Long, Gordon. "The Most Bizarre Cattle Drive of Them All." *The West*, Feb. 1965, p. 38.

Pony Express Riders
Helfer, Harold. "Death Rides the Pony Express." *Western True Story*, Oct. 1971, p. 23.

Poole, Thomas
Archer, Myrtle. "California Stagecoach Skirmish." *True West*, May 1988, p. 44.

Popé
Duncan, Gra'Delle. "El Popé: The Pueblo Revolt." *Real West*, Americana Series, Winter 1964, p. 10.
Conant, Lora M. "The Fighting Priest of the Kiva." *Golden West*, May 1969, p. 16.
Hill, E.M. "Popé and the Pueblo Rebels." *Pioneer West*, April 1970, p. 44;. Rpt. *Pioneer West*, June 1974, p. 38.

Pope, Edmund Mann
Parsons, Chuck. "In Pursuit of the Northfield Robbers." *NOLA Quarterly*, Vol IV, No. 4, June 1979, p. 14.

Pope, John Theodore
Burton, Doris Karren. "Sheriff John Theodore Pope." *The Outlaw Trail Journal*, Vol. I, No. 1, Summer 1991, p. 3.

Porter, Benjamin
Rasch, Philip J. "One Killed, One Wounded." *NOLA Quarterly*, Vol. IV, No. 2, Autumn 1978, p. 11.

Porter, Fannie (or Fanny)
Hummel, John H. "Queen of Sin and Death." *Real West*, May 1960, p. 40.

Morris, Grant. "Kid Curry's Girl." *Westerner*, May-June 1972, p. 45.

Posey, William "Bill"
Kildare, Maurice M. "Piute [sic] Battle Cry." *Westerner*, May-June 1969, p. 24.

Reedstrom, Ernest Lisle. "Badman Bill Posey." *True West*, Jan. 1988, p. 22.

Stanley, Samuel. "Old Posey and the Last Indian Uprising." *Real West*, May 1973, p. 22.

Syndergaard, Iris. "Old Posey: Renegade Paiute." *True Frontier*, Jan. 1978, p. 18.

Will, Ed. "The Last Warrior." *Real West*, Americana Series, Winter 1964, p. 54.

Winslowe, John R. "Call of the Raider." *Westerner*, Sept.-Oct. 1973, p. 40.

Poston, Charles Debrille
Griffith, A. Kinney. "Charles Debrille Poston: The Father of Arizona." *The West*, July 1969, p. 32. Rpt. *The West*, Feb. 1973, p. 32.

Harrison, John H. "Lost Loot in Cerro Colorado." *True Frontier*, Special Issue No. 20, Winter 1977, p. 6.

Kelly, Joseph F. "Secret Silver Cache at Cerro Colorado." *True West*, Dec. 1982, p. 20.

Potter, Charles S.
Cline, Don. "Colonel Potter's Last Ride." *NOLA Quarterly*, Vol. XIV, No. 2, Summer 1990, p. 9.

Potter, Jack
Preece, Harold. "Jack Potter, Fighting Parson of Texas." *The West*, March 1964, p. 28.

Potter, Robert "Bob"
Jarrett, Calvin. "The Enigma of Texas Bob Potter." *Real West*, May 1966, p. 27.

Potts, Josiah and Elizabeth
Myles, Myrtle T. "When Nevada Hung a Woman." *Golden West*, Nov. 1964, p. 22. Rpt. *Golden West*, April 1974, p. 16.

Pourier, John Baptiste "Big Bat"
Lincoln, Lewis A. "The Day Old Bat Stood Off Fifty Sioux." *Frontier Times,* Spring 1962, p. 41.

Powell, James W.
Copeman, L. Berger. "Fight for Your Lives." *The West,* Feb. 1973, p. 28.
Westel, Freeman. "Powell's Fortress." *Big West,* Oct. 1968, p. 46.

Powell, John Wesley
Bellin, John E. "Conqueror of the Colorado." *Pioneer West,* Jan. 1971, p. 52. Rpt. *Oldtimers Wild West,* Aug. 1975, p. 38.
Spendlove, Earl. "Black River of the Dead." *The West,* May 1964, p. 10.

Power, John A.
Secrest, William B. "A Lion Walking Among Rats." *True West,* Feb. 1968, p. 16.

Power Brothers (Tom and John)
Long, James A. "Tragedy Stalked the Powers [sic] Family." *The West,* April 1970, p. 32. Rpt. *Golden West,* June 1973, p. 14.

Powers, Tom
Rosson, Mary'n. "The Gun That Killed Billy the Kid." *Old West,* Winter 1977, p. 6.

Powers, William St. (Bill Powers, Tom Evans)
Parsons, Chuck. "Answer Man" column. *Frontier Times,* Oct. 1984, p. 41.

Pratt, Richard Henry
Irons, Angie. "Richard Henry Pratt: That Indian Loving Pest." *True West,* Dec. 1988, p. 28.
Kyllo, Joan. "Blankets and Chains." *The West,* Nov. 1973, p. 16.
Nehoc, Chet. "The Warriors and Lt. Pratt." *Great West,* Oct. 1968, p. 34.

Preece, Richard Lincoln "Dick"
Preece, Harold. "My Grandfather, Dick Preece." *Real West,* Nov. 1964, p. 22.
————. "Real Grit in the West." *Real West,* Special Issue, Summer 1973, p. 46.

Preece, Thomas William "Billy"

Kirby, Ed, and Mary Preece. "Billy Preece, Frontier Lawman." *NOLA Quarterly,* Vol. IV, No. 3, March 1979, p. 11.

_____. "Billy Preece, Frontier Lawman." *Real West,* July 1979, p. 8.

Pridgen, Oscar Fitzgerald

Parsons, Chuck. "Feuds and a Texas Ranger." *Old West,* Winter 1983, p. 49.

Proctor, Zeke

Brewington, E.H. "Cherokee." *Great West,* July 1968, p. 30.

Myers, Olevia E. "Zeke Proctor: Outlaw or Hero?" *The West,* May 1966, p. 30. Rpt. *Golden West,* Nov. 1971, p. 14.

Payne, Ruth Holt. "One Man Peace Treaty" ("Nuggets" column). *Frontier Times,* Sept. 1965, p. 39.

Pruiett, Moman

Dana, Charles. "Moman Pruiett: Genius of Hate." *The West,* July 1965, p. 28. Rpt. *The West,* June 1972, p. 14.

Hayes, Frederick. "Frontier Lawyer." *Real West,* Aug. 1959, p. 14.

Kildare, Maurice. "Frontier Lawyer's Revenge." *Real West,* Jan. 1974, p. 46.

Pry, Polly (see Anthony, Leonel Ross)

Pryor, Nathaniel Hale

Shoemaker, Arthur. "The Many Faces of Nathaniel Pryor." *True West,* Sept. 1988, p. 48.

Puget, Peter

Herberg, Ruth. "Peter Puget: Navigator, Surveyor." *Golden West,* March 1971, p. 27.

Punteney, Walter "Walt"

Engebretson, Doug. "The Belle Fourche Bank Robbery." *Real West,* Dec. 1981, p. 22. Rpt. *Real West,* Special Issue, Spring 1985, p. 54.

Kirby, Ed. "The Sundance Kid and the Belle Fourche Robbery." *NOLA Quarterly,* Vol. VII, No. 2, Summer 1982, p. 5.

Kirby, Edward M. "The Sundance Kid and the Belle Fourche Bank Robbery." *True West,* Jan. 1983, p. 10.

Pushmataha

Hanna, Wilma Colson. "Great Chief of the Choctaws." *Golden West,* March 1971, p. 40. Rpt. *The West,* Feb. 1974, p. 14; and *Western Frontier,* Special Issue, Nov. 1985, p. 14.

Quantrill, Kate King

Breihan, Carl W. "Kate King Quantrill." *Real West,* Sept. 1977, p. 40.

Quantrill, William Clark

Breihan, Carl W. "The Day Quantrill Burned Lawrence." *The West,* Jan. 1967, p. 14. Rpt. *The West,* Jan. 1972, p. 14; *Western Frontier,* Sept. 1976, p. 34, *Western Frontier,* May 1979, p. 34; and *Western Frontier,* Aug. 1985, p. 34.

_____. "Quantrill at Richmond." *The West,* Nov. 1970, p. 26. Rpt. *Western Frontier,* Sept. 1979, p. 26.

_____. "Quantrill in Texas." *Real West,* July 1974, p. 26.

_____. "Quantrill's Bones Are Moving." *Westerner,* Jan.-Feb. 1973, p. 40.

_____. "The Sacking of Lawrence." *Real West,* Annual, Summer 1966, p. 10.

_____. "Truth About Sacking of Lawrence." *Real West,* Sept. 1960, p. 40.

_____. "William Clark Quantrill and His Lieutenants." *The West,* May 1969, p. 10. Rpt. *Western Frontier,* Nov. 1977, p. 34; and *Western Frontier,* Nov. 1982, p. 40.

Giles, Kenneth. "Quantrill's Blood Vengeance Against the Kansas Jayhawkers." *Frontier West,* Oct. 1971, p. 44.

Hart, George. "The Day They Shot Quantrill." *Real West,* May 1973, p. 24.

_____. "The Quest for Quantrill's Bones." *Real West,* May 1972, p. 24.

Hines, James. "Gunfighters and Lawmen" column. *Wild West,* Oct. 1991, p. 16.

_____. "When Death Came to Quantrill." *Real West,* March 1961, p. 42.

Holding, Vera. "Quantrill's Raiders." *Westerner,* Sept.-Oct. 1969, p. 30.

Karpisek, Marian E., and Samuel C. Ream. "Quantrill's Skull." *Old West,* Summer 1981, p. 36.

Knowles, Edward. "The Bartered Bones of William Quantrill." *True West,* Oct. 1967, p. 20.

Lebrow, Allen. "Quantrill's Killers." *Man's Western,* Jan. 1960, p. 12.

Moore, David K. "Raiders' Savage Attack." *Wild West,* Dec. 1988, p. 35.

Morando, B. "Quantrill's Guerrillas." *Real West,* Special Issue, Fall 1964, p. 16.

Mosny, Roy. "The Bloody Border War." *Great West,* April 1967, p. 4.

Rozar, Lily-B. "Quantrill's Bloody Trail." *Western Round-up,* May 1970, p. 16. Rpt. *Pioneer West,* March 1974, p. 38; and *Oldtimers Wild West,* April 1977, p. 12.

Settle, Raymond W. "An Eye for an Eye Was Not Enough." *Old West,* Spring 1968, p. 44.

Walker, Wayne T. "Give Them Hell." *Great West,* Feb. 1969, p. 6.

_____. "Massacre at Baxter Springs." *Old West,* Spring 1983, p. 18.

Watson, Thomas Shelby "Bob." "A Bloodstained Sword." *Real West,* May 1974, p. 9.

Quick, Florence "Flora"

Lehman, Leola. "Flora Quick, Alias Tom King." *Golden West,* Nov. 1966, p. 20. Rpt. *The West,* Oct. 1974, p. 32.

Lehman, M.P. "The Outlaw Was No Lady." *Real West,* Oct. 1972, p. 65.

Preece, Harold. "Bob Dalton's Bandit Bride." *Real West,* March 1965, p. 10.

Shirley, Glenn. "She Was the Jailor's Killer Sweetheart." *Westerner,* March-April 1974, p. 46.

Turpin, Robert F. "The Making of an Outlaw Queen." *Real Frontier,* March 1970, p. 26.

R

Rain-In-The-Face

Chatfield, Harry E. "When Rain-in-the-Face Saved Buffalo Bill." *Real West,* March 1970, p. 26.

Malsbary, George. "Revenge of Rain-in-the-Face." *Wild West,* Sept. 1971, p. 12.

Swanson, Budington. "Warriors and Chiefs" column. *Wild West,* April 1990, p. 12.

Ramsey, Alexander
"Ellis County Sheriff Killed by Thief." *Frontier Times,* June-July 1980, p. 36.

Rankin, Joseph F. "Joe"
Boucher, Leonard H. "The Battle at Milk Creek." *Real West,* Oct. 1970, p. 8.
Shafer, A.L. "Joe Rankin's Ride." *True West,* Oct. 1966, p. 27.

Rapelje, Hiram
Secrest, William B. "The Gunfight at Stone Corral." *True Frontier,* June 1973, p. 26.
_____. "A Man Called Hi: Gunfighter of the Old San Joaquin." *Old West,* Fall 1991, p 14.

Rash, Matt
Richards, T.J. "Matt Rash's Cabin." *True West,* Oct. 1989, p. 52.

"Rattlesnake Dick" (see Barter, Dick)

Ravalli, Anthony
Clark, Helen. "The Battle of the Big Hole." *Pioneer West,* March 1969, p. 36.

Rawleigh, D.C.
Mather, R.E. "Last Lynching at Bannack, Montana." *True West,* April 1991, p. 14.

Ray, Nick
Kelly, Bill. "The Death of Nate Champion and Nick Ray." *Real West,* Sept. 1979, p. 24.

Rayner, Hamilton Polk
Roberts, Gary L. "Hamilton Rayner and the Shootout at Pat Hanly's Saloon." *Real West,* Oct. 1985, p. 19.

Raynolds, William Franklin
Engebretson, Doug. "The Raynolds Expedition: 1859-1860." *Real West,* Feb. 1984, p. 40. Rpt. *Real West,* Annual, Spring 1985, p. 23.

Reading, Pierson B.
Malsbary, George. "Frontier Promoter." *Great West,* Dec. 1973, p. 32. Rpt. *Authentic West,* Spring 1981, p. 32.

Reavis, James Addison

Bailey, Tom. "The Baron of Arizona." *True Western Adventures,* Oct. 1958, p. 16.

Brown, Florence. "The Barony of Arizona." *Great West,* Sept. 1967, p. 30.

LeBaron, A.D. "He Stole Arizona." *Real West,* Aug. 1959, p. 28.

Meisse, William K. "The Biggest Outlaw of All." *Western True Story,* Oct. 1971, p. 28. Rpt. *America's Frontier West,* Issue No. 1, n.d., p. 28.

Metz, Leon C. "The Great Arizona Land Fraud." *Frontier Times,* Fall 1960, p. 28.

Pope, Norman J. "The Frontier's Biggest Swindle: How James Addison Reavis Stole Arizona." *Frontier West,* Feb. 1974, p. 12.

Price, Carter. "The Man Who Would Be Baron of Arizona." *Westerner,* Feb. 1971, p. 40.

Red Cloud

Beardsley, J.L. "A Good Day to Die." *Real West,* Special Issue, Winter 1963, p. 19.

Bennett, C.O. Letter. *Real West,* Jan. 1969, p. 9.

Deac, Wilfred P. "Bloody Assault Repelled." *Wild West,* April 1990, p. 19.

Holding, Vera. "Red Cloud: Napleon of the Sioux." *True Frontier,* Nov. 1968, p. 38. Rpt. *True Frontier,* Aug. 1972, p. 24. Rpt. *True Frontier,* Special Issue No. 6, 1973, p. 6; and *True Frontier,* Summer 1977, p. 4.

Jones, Gene. "Blood in the Hay Field." *Western Frontier,* May 1984, p. 24.

Mays, Carelton. "Red Cloud: White Man's Nemesis." *Real West,* Nov. 1958, p. 14. Rpt. credited to Philip Rand, *Real West,* Annual, Spring 1968, p. 38.

Shutt, Timothy Baker. "Warriors and Chiefs" column. *Wild West,* June 1988, p. 12.

Swanson, Budington. "How Little Big Man Tried to Save the Black Hills." *Western Frontier,* Special Issue, March 1975, p. 34.

Yarbrough, Leroy. "Red Cloud." *Real West,* Sept. 1968, p. 23. Rpt. *Real West,* Special Issue, Spring 1972, p. 46.

"Red Curly" (Andrew King)

Qualey, Jake. "Red Curly, Bloody Brigand of the Southwest." *Real West,* Sept. 1961, p. 23.

Redmon, J.M.

Parsons, Chuck. "Texas State Policeman Redmon in Lampasas." *English Westerners Brand Book,* Vol. XXIII, No. 1, Winter 1984, p. 11.

Reed, James Edward "Eddie"

Mooney, Charles W. "The Secret Belle Starr Took to Her Grave." *The West,* Nov. 1969, p. 28. Rpt. *Western Frontier,* Annual No. 1, 1975, p. 6.

Reed, J. Warren

Hill, O.E. "The Man Who Was Crushed by Success." *Golden West,* May 1971, p. 24.

Sherwood, Don. "J. Warren Reed, Nemesis of the Hanging Judge." *The West,* Jan. 1965, p. 30. Rpt. *The West,* Annual 1971, p. 34.

Reed, James C. "Jim"

Parsons, Chuck. "Jim Reed and Belle Starr" ("Answer Man" column). *True West,* March 1988, p. 12.

Steele, Phillip W. "Jim Reed, Outlaw." *NOLA Quarterly,* Vol. XIV, Nos. 3 and 4 (combined issue), 1990, p. 4.

_____. "The Shannon-Fisher War." *Old West,* Fall 1985, p. 44.

Reed, Nathaniel "Texas Jack" (also spelled "Reid")

Reed, Nathaniel. "Train Holdup at Blackstone Switch." *The West,* May 1964, p. 16. Rpt. *Western Frontier,* July 1980, p. 12.

Shirley, Glenn. "The Bungled Job at Blackstone Switch." *True West,* June 1966, p. 40.

Reed, Virginia

Mays, Carelton. "Cannibals in the Sierras." *Real West,* May 1960, p. 8.

Reeder, Andrew

Knellton, Ives. "When Rebellious Kansans Tried to Kill Their Governor." *True Frontier,* Special Issue No. 7, Fall 1978, p. 6.

Reeves, Bass

Burton, Art T. "Bass Reeves: Deputy U.S. Marshal." *True West,* Dec. 1991, p. 40.

McCollum, Berkley. "Bass Reeves, Black Scourge of Oklahoma Outlaws." *Pioneer West,* July 1977, p. 10.

Mooney, Charles W. "Bass Reeves: Black Deputy U.S. Marshal." *Real West,* July 1976, p. 48.

Reid, Frank

Martin, Cy. "He Died to Save Skagway." Part I, *Real West,* Jan 1968, p. 16; Part II, *Real West,* April 1968, p. 38.

Martin, Jeannie. "The Slickest of the Badmen." *Real West,* July 1975, p. 20.

Reilly, James
Palmquist, Bob. "Tombstone's Dogberry." *True West,* April 1987, p. 20.

Reno Brothers (John, William Frank, and Simeon)
Bourke, Charles Francis. "The Pinkertons Were Great." *Golden West,* July 1965, p. 24. Rpt. *Western Frontier,* April 1983, p. 30.

Breihan, Carl W. "America's First Train Robberies." *Frontier Times,* Summer 1960, p. 20.

_____. "The First Train Robbers." *Oldtimers Wild West,* June 1977, p. 6.

_____. "The Terrible Renos." *Real West,* Jan. 1961, p. 30. Rpt. *Real West,* Special Issue, Fall 1964, p. 10.

Cortesi, Lawrence. "The Reno Gang: Rangeland Heroes or Desperate Renegades?" *Frontier West,* Feb. 1973, p. 22.

Drake, John. "First Train Robbery." *Real West,* Nov. 1958, p. 28.

Eagan, Tom. "April Fools: The Reno Gang's Iowa Raid." *NOLA Quarterly,* Vol. XIII, No. 3, Winter 1989, p. 11.

Hines, James. "The First Train Robbery." *Great West,* June 1973, p. 24. Rpt. *Great West,* Summer 1981, p. 26.

Kildare, Maurice. "The Elkhorn Falls Loot." *Westerner,* May-June 1970, p. 20. Rpt. *Old Trails,* Spring 1978, p. 28.

Martin, Jeannie. "When the Reno Gang Rode the Rails." *True Frontier,* Oct. 1977, p. 12.

Mote, Wayne D. "The Reno Brothers' Night of Blood." *True Western Adventures,* Aug. 1959, p. 18.

"Still Wanted." *Man's Western,* Aug.-Sept. 1959, p. 12.

Von Kreisler, Max. "The Reno Brothers." *Real West,* Nov. 1977, p. 26.

Reno, John
Eagan, Thomas F. "John Reno: The First Train Robber." *Old West,* Summer 1988, p. 30.

_____. "Who Really Kidnapped John Reno?" *NOLA Quarterly,* Vol. XII, No. 2, Fall 1987, p. 9.

Lorentz, James. Letter. *Frontier Times,* Summer 1960, p. 56.

Miller, Brandon Marie. "Personality" column. *Wild West,* April 1989, p. 12.

Robbins, Lance. "On the Outlaw Trail at Age Eleven." *Real West,* Jan. 1969, p. 34.

Reno, Marcus A.

Brininstool, E.A. "Reno Was No Coward." *True West,* Feb. 1968, p. 38.

Mulhair, Charles. "Fatal Beauty: Major Reno and the Colonel's Daughter." *True West,* Dec. 1989, p. 44.

Paul, J.S. "If Reno Had Attacked." *True Frontier,* Jan. 1971, p. 8.

Rector, William G. "Was Reno Drunk at Little Bighorn?" *The West,* Nov. 1967, p. 8. Rpt. *Western Frontier,* Sept. 1980, p. 5.

Thane, Eric. "The Man Who Didn't Kill Custer." *True Frontier,* March 1969, p. 54.

Reynolds, Charles "Lonesome Charley"

Harrison, Fred. "Strange Death of 'Lonesome Charley' Reynolds." *Golden West,* Nov. 1968, p. 16. Rpt. *Golden West,* Jan. 1973, p. 26; and *Western Frontier,* Annual No. 3, 1976, p. 20.

Kildare, Maurice. "The Mystery of Lonesome Charley." *Westerner,* Jan.-Feb. 1972, p. 52.

Parsons, Chuck. "Custer's Lonesome Scout" ("Answer Man" column). *True West,* Oct. 1990, p. 12.

Price, Will. "Lonesome Charley." *True West,* June 1961, p. 16.

Underwood, Larry. "Lonesome Charley's Last Fight." *True West,* Nov. 1985, p. 12.

Walker, Wayne T. "Fighting Army Scouts of the Indian Wars." *Great West,* June 1972, p. 14. Rpt. *Authentic West,* Fall 1981, p. 16.

Reynolds Gang (Jim Reynolds)

Huston, Fred. "Fifty Thousand Dollars In Rebel Treasure Awaits You in the Colorado Wilds." *Frontier West,* April 1972, p. 16.

Kildare, Maurice. "Colorado's Guerrilla Loot." *Real West,* Nov. 1972, p. 26.

Shaw, Luella. "Jim Reynolds and His Gang." *Frontier Times,* June-July 1963, p. 15.

Reynolds, Glenn

Hayes, Jess G. "Apache Vengeance." *Frontier Times,* Sept. 1969, p. 6.

Reynolds, Joseph

Austerman, Wayne R. "Debacle on Powder River." *Wild West,* Dec. 1991, p. 22.

Reynolds, N.O.

Walker, Wayne T. "N.O. Reynolds: The Intrepid Ranger." *Real West,* Nov. 1976, p. 20.

Rhodes, John
Porter, Willard H. "Rhodes Was One of a Kind." *True West,* Sept. 1991, p. 44.

Rhodes, William B. "Billy"
Lebec, Ralph. "Lone Stand of Billy Rhodes." *The West,* Oct. 1973, p. 10. Rpt. *Western Frontier,* Annual No. 4, 1976, p. 10.

Richards, Samuel D.
Lee, Wayne C. "The Badman of Kearney." *True West,* Feb. 1990, p. 28.

Richardson, Levy (Levi)
O'Neal, Bill. "Cockeyed Frank Loving vs Levi Richardson" ("Great Western Gunfights" column). *True West,* June 1991, p. 62.

Wadley, Jerome. "The Gunfighters' Ladies." *Westerner,* July-Aug. 1973, p. 48.

Rickard, George Lewis "Tex"
Green, Julian R. "Tex Rickard, The West's Incredible Promoter." *The West,* April 1965, p. 14. Rpt. *Western Frontier,* Annual, Winter 1977, p. 40.

Ridge, John
Feder, Bernard. "The Ridge Family and the Death of a Nation." *The American West,* Sept.-Oct. 1978, p. 28.

Lehman, Leola. "Cherokee Blood Feud on the Trail of Tears." *True Frontier,* Oct. 1967, p. 34. Rpt. *True Frontier,* Special Issue No. 2, 1972, p. 28.

Riel, Louis
Chapin, Earl V. "The Northwest Rebellion." *The West,* Oct. 1974, p. 24.

Graf, E.A. "Louis Riel: Patriot or Traitor?" Part I, *Real West,* Aug. 1970, p. 26; Part II *Real West,* Sept. 1970, p. 50.

Guttman, Jon. "Revolt of the Metís." *Wild West,* June 1991, p. 34.

Preece, Harold. "Dream of Madness." *Real West,* Americana Series, Fall 1966, p. 34.

Riggs, Barney
Carson, Xanthus. "Shoot-Out in No. 11 Saloon." *Pioneer West,* April 1971, p. 32. Rpt. *Oldtimers Wild West,* Aug. 1973, p. 24; and *Pioneer West,* July 1976, p. 24.

Dearen, Patrick. "The Ghost of Fort Stockton Sutlery." *Old West,* Winter 1989, p. 54.

DeArment, Robert K. "Barney Riggs: Man of Violence." *Old West,* Fall 1983, p. 15.

O'Neal, Bill. "Barney Riggs vs Bill Earhart and John Denson" ("Great Western Gunfights" column). *True West,* Oct. 1990, p. 60.

Rasch, Philip J. "The Saga of Barney Riggs." *Real West,* June 1983, p. 38. Rpt. *Real West,* Annual, Spring 1984, p. 39.

Rickards, Colin. "Attempted Break at Yuma Pen." *True West,* June 1973, p. 28.

Riley, James "Jim"

Arango, Douglas. "The Deepest Pit of Hell." *Great West,* June 1967, p. 22.

Compagnon, Frank D. "Mike's Mad Shadow." *True Western Adventures,* Issue No. 1, 1957, p. 23.

Coulter, Eugene. "The Bloody Newton Shoot-Out." *Frontier West,* April 1971, p. 24.

Crane, Ray. "Shoot-Out at Newton." *Great West,* Oct. 1968, p. 4.

Holding, Vera. "Bloodiest Night in Kansas History." *True Frontier,* March 1970, p. 30.

O'Neal, Bill. "The Newton General Massacre" ("Great Western Gunfights" column). *True West,* Jan. 1988, p. 47.

Wiltsey, Norman B. "Thundering Guns at Tuttle's Dancehall." *Golden West,* Nov. 1966, p. 8.

Rinehart, Isaac

Horning, Chuck. "The Other Davy Crockett." *Western Frontier,* Jan. 1978, p. 24.

Ringo Family

Brant, Marley. "Outlaws' Inlaws in California." *Frontier Times,* Feb. 1985, p. 18.

Ringo, John "Johnny"

Ault, Phillip H. Letter, "John Ringo." *True West,* Jan. 1988, p. 7.

Burrows, Jack. "Fact and Fiction and John Ringo." *NOLA Quarterly,* Vol. XII, No. 1, Summer 1987, p. 4.

DeMattos, Jack. "Johnny Ringo: The Elusive Man Behind the Myth." *NOLA Quarterly,* Vol. III, No. 2, Autumn 1977, p. 1.

_____. "Johnny Ringo" ("Gunfighters of the Real West" column). *Real West,* April 1985, p. 38.

Dickey, Edward M. ("Nevada Dick"). "The Mysterious John Ringo." *Old West,* Spring 1965, p. 45. Rpt. *Badman,* Summer 1971, p. 7.

Earp, Josephine. "Who Killed John Ringo?" Ed. Glenn G. Boyer. *Real West,* Feb. 1987, p. 14.

Fallon, Clay. "Johnny Ringo: The Man Behind the Myth." *Real West,* March 1980, p. 6. Rpt. *Real West,* Special 1981, p. 25.

Freeman, Frank M. "Gentleman Johnny Ringo: Melancholy Man of Mystery." *True Frontier,* May 1970, p. 18. Rpt. *True Frontier,* Special Issue No. 3, 1972, p. 36.

Holman, Cole. "Johnny Ringold [sic]: the Deadliest Gunfighter." *Westerner,* Jan.-Feb. 1973, p. 26.

Horton, Harvey R. "Horton Favors Homicide Theory for Ringo." *NOLA Quarterly,* Vol. III, No. 4, Spring 1978, p. 8.

Huff, Era Fay. Letter. *True West,* July 1988, p. 6.

"Johnny Ringo: He Died With His Boots Missing." *Gunslingers of the West,* Winter 1966, p. 9.

Johnson, Dave. "Revenge in Mason County, Texas." *NOLA Quarterly,* Vol. X, No. 1, Summer 1985, p. 7.

Markson, Dave. "Johnny Ringo: Loner With a Six-Gun." *Western Action,* Dec. 1960, p. 24.

Millard, Joseph. "Johnny Ringo: Cultured Killer." *True Western Adventures,* Aug. 1960, p. 35.

Molthan, Ruth. "Johnny Ringo Gunslinger." *Great West,* July 1969, p. 20.

Parsons, Chuck. "John Ringo Before Tombstone" ("Answer Man" column). *True West,* Oct. 1987, p. 12.

Thomas, Robert L. "I Think Earp Took Johnny Ringo." *Old West,* Fall 1972, p. 13.

Traywick, Ben T. "Johnny Ringo, Gunslinger." *Great West,* June 1971, p. 32.

Riordan, Arch
Kildare, Maurice. "Arch Riordan: Buffalo Gap's Killer Marshal." *The West,* May 1971, p. 34. Rpt. *Western Frontier,* Sept. 1975, p. 34; *Western Frontier,* Annual, Winter 1977, p. 34; and *Western Frontier,* May 1986, p. 28.

Roberts, Andrew L. "Buckshot"
Adams, Jeff. "The Quality of Courage." *Real West,* July 1968, p. 10. Rpt. credited to Norman B. Wiltsey, *Real West,* Annual, Summer 1970, p. 40.

Harrison, John H. "Last Stand of 'Buckshot Billy.'" *Wild West,* March 1972, p. 8. Rpt. *Oldtimers Wild West,* Aug. 1975, p. 34.

Marsten, Russell. "Death of Buckshot Roberts." *Real West,* May 1960, p. 44.

O'Neal, Bill. "Buckshot Roberts vs The Regulators" ("Great Western Gunfights" column). *True West,* June 1990, p. 60.

Parsons, Chuck. "Buckshot Roberts" ("Answer Man" column). *True West,* Dec. 1988, p. 12.

Pauley, Eugene. "Buckshot Roberts, Fighting Man." *True West,* Sept. 1954, p. 16. Rpt. *Badman,* Summer 1971, p. 48.

Rasch, Philip J. "A Second Look at the Blazer's Mill Affair." *Frontier Times,* Jan. 1969, p. 30.

_____. Letter. *True West,* April 1955.

Roberts, Daniel Webster "Dan"

Gillespie, Thomas P. "Fight on the Concho Plains." *True West,* June 1963, p. 32.

Malocsay, Philip. "Captain Dan Roberts, Last of the Texas Rangers." *True Frontier,* Sept. 1968, p. 44.

_____. "Captain Dan Roberts of the Texas Rangers." *True Frontier,* June 1976, p. 10.

Malocsay, Zoltan. "Dan Roberts' Indian Killer Battalion." *Westerner,* Jan. 1971, p. 26.

Roberts, James "Jim"

Arlandson, R. "Frontier Marshal vs Modern Hoods." *Real West,* Jan. 1963, p. 42.

Burke, J.F. "Jim Roberts: Old Man With a Gun." *Frontier Times,* July 1980, p. 12.

Dodge, Matt. "Grandpa Gunfighter." *Real West,* March 1980, p. 16. Rpt. *Real West,* Special Issue, 1981, p. 33.

Long, James. "Jim Roberts, Last of the Six-Gun Marshals." *Real West,* Jan. 1966, p. 48.

Young, Herbert Vernon. "Who Shot the Bank Robber?" *Old West,* Fall 1982, p. 20.

Roberts, Ollie

Anderson, Pete. "A Damn Good Joke on the Bandits." *True Western Adventures,* Feb. 1961, p. 8.

Robertson, John "Uncle Jack"

Mathisen, Jean A. "Uncle Jack Robertson: A Natural Gentleman" ("Wild Old Days" column). *True West,* April 1991, p. 60.

Robidoux Brothers
Thompson, George A. "Old Fort Robidoux." *Old West,* Summer 1974, p. 28.

Robidoux, Joseph
Grenier, M.B. "Joseph Robidoux, Father of St. Joseph." *True West,* Dec. 1985, p. 52.

Robot, Dom Isadore
Brewington, E.H. "Sacred Heart: Outpost of Religion." *Golden West,* Aug. 1974, p. 28.

Rochas, Francois Jean "Frenchy"
Carpenter, Roy F. "Death at Christmas." *Old West,* Fall 1966, p. 50.

Carson, Kit. "Bloody Saga of Dog Canyon." *Real West,* Sept. 1963, p. 20.

Rasch, Philip J. "The Murder of Frank Rochas and Its Aftermath." *NOLA Quarterly,* Vol. V, No. 2, Jan. 1980, p. 2.

Wade, Kit. "Bloody Orgy at Dog Canyon." *Pioneer West,* Feb. 1972, p. 54.

Rock, George T.
Silva, Lee. "The Bullets That Wouldn't Kill." *Westerner,* Spring 1975, p. 34.

Rockwell, Kathleen Eloisa "Klondike Kate"
Howard, D.H. "The Truth About Klondike Kate." *Westerner,* May-June 1972, p. 34.

Kildare, Maurice. "Klondike Strumpet." *Westerner,* Dec. 1970, p. 20.

Martin, Jeannie. "The Incredible Story of Klondike Kate." *Golden West,* May 1973, p. 34. Rpt. *Western Frontier,* Nov. 1976, p. 6.

Stevenson, John. "Queen of the Klondike." *True West,* Feb. 1990, p. 22.

Rockwell, Orrin Porter
Fleek, Sherman L. "Gunfighters and Lawmen" column. *Wild West,* April 1989, p. 8.

Spendlove, Earl. "Four Men Rode South." *Golden West,* May 1969, p. 34. Rpt. *Golden West,* May 1972, p. 32; and *Western Frontier,* Nov. 1976, p. 6.

————. "The Shifting Sands of Jericho." *The West,* April 1970, p. 16.

Roden, William D.
Jones, Calico. "Grab Your Guns, Boys." *Real West,* Jan. 1968, p. 30.

Rodriquez, Chipita
Bair, Everett. "Queen of the Utes." *True West,* April 1956, p. 19.
Harrison, Fred. "They Hung Her on Friday the 13th." *Great West,* Feb. 1968, p. 14.
Qualey, J.S. "Tragic Fame of Chipeta." *Real West,* July 1961, p. 8.

Roe, William M.
Chegwyn, Michael. "One Killing Too Many." *True West,* Nov. 1991, p. 25.

Rogers, Christopher Columbus "Chris"
Jones, Ernest. "Marshal of the Red Hills." *True West,* June 1961, p. 22.

Rogers, Ike
Etter, Jim. "Cherokee Bill's Brother." *True West,* Oct. 1974, p. 14.

Rogers, Jennie
Cheney, Louise. "Jennie Rogers vs Mattie Silks for Holladay Street." *Real West,* May 1974, p. 20.
Rozar, Lily-B. "Magnificent Harlots of the 1870s." *Pioneer West,* April 1972, p. 40.

Roman Nose
Copeman, L. Berger. "Massacre at Red Butte." *The West,* Sept. 1973, p. 32.
_____. "Terror at Platte Bridge Station." *Real West,* Americana Series, Fall 1966, p. 22.
Dahl, Peter. "Death of Roman Nose." *Real West,* Americana Series, Winter 1964, p. 26.
Judge, Bill. "Roman Nose." *Frontier Times,* May 1964, p. 12.
Keenan, Jerry. "Cheyenne Island Siege." *Wild West,* June 1988, p. 35.
Mays, Carelton. "Roman Nose's War Bonnet." *Real West,* Sept. 1960, p. 18.
Murach, I. "Chief Sante's Magic Bonnet." *True Frontier,* Aug. 1974, p. 30. Rpt. *True Frontier,* Dec. 1976, p. 38.
Turpin, Robert F. "The Death of Roman Nose." *Great West,* Aug. 1971, p. 14.

Romero Brothers (of Las Vegas, New Mexico)
Callon, Milton W. "The Sheriffs of San Miguel." *True West,* Aug. 1973, p. 6.

Rooke, Sarah J.
Kemper, Troy. "Wall of Water!" *True West,* Feb. 1960, p. 21.

Roosevelt, Theodore "Teddy"

Bruce, John A. "Teddy's Army of Broncho Busters." *Real West,* Jan. 1961, p. 40.

Clough, Bob. "Theodore Roosevelt's First Safari." *Real West,* Yearbook, Summer 1978, p. 46.

Gard, Wayne. "Teddy Roosevelt's Wolf Hunt." *True West,* Aug. 1962, p. 34.

Kirby, Ed. "Teddy Roosevelt: Cowboy, Deputy Sheriff." *NOLA Quarterly,* Vol. IX, No. 2, Autumn 1984, p. 9.

Lehman, L.C. "Teddy Roosevelt and the Three Thieves." *Real West,* May 1964, p. 26.

Scheussler, Raymond. "How Teddy Roosevelt Blew Fifty Thousand Dollars As a Cattleman." *Pioneer West,* Dec. 1971, p. 40.

Webb, Harry E. "My Day With Teddy Roosevelt." *Westerner,* March-April 1972, p. 14.

Winslowe, John R. "Charge of the Rough Riders." *Westerner,* March-April 1982, p. 16.

Wolfe, George D. "Boss of the Maltese Cross." *True West,* June 1961, p. 6.

Wolfgang, Otto. "Theodore Roosevelt, Cattleman." *Real West,* March 1969, p. 28. Rpt. *Real West,* Annual, Summer 1971, p. 36.

Wukovits, John F. "Dude Too Tough to Buffalo." *Wild West,* Aug. 1990, p. 27.

Rosa May (Rosa Elizabeth White)

Cerveri, Doris. "The Lady From Virgin Alley and Other Bodie Characters." *Great West,* Oct. 1968, p. 14.

Kaltenbach, Peter J. "The Highgrade: A Story of Rosa May." *Real West,* Sept. 1979, p. 22. Rpt. *Real West,* Special Issue, 1981, p. 30.

Hitt, Jim. "Madame May." *Real West,* June 1985, p. 32. Rpt. *Real West,* Annual, Summer 1986, p. 16.

Rose, Edward "Ed"

Chatfield, Harry E. "Ed Rose: Negro Trail Blazer." Part I, *Real West,* Sept. 1969, p. 24; Part II, *Real West,* Oct. 1969, p. 13.

Holding, Vera. "'Cut Nose': Black Trail Blazer." *Pioneer West,* Oct. 1970, p. 56.

Spencer, G. "The Exploits of Edward Rose." *Real West,* Oct. 1988, p. 38.

Rose, Louis Moses

Teer, L.P. "Was There a Coward in the Alamo?" *Frontier Times,* Nov. 1965, p. 14.

Rose, Noah H.
Nolen, Oran Warder. "Noah H. Rose: Frontier Cameraman." *Old West,* Spring 1968, p. 32.

Rose of Cimarron
King, Sterling Price. "More Rose of Cimarron." *True West,* June 1955, p. 22.
Lehman, Leola. "Rose of Cimarron." *True Frontier,* July 1970, p. 36.
Oldham, Maggie Rex. "Rose of Cimarron." *True West,* Sept. 1954, p. 6.
Shirley, Glenn. "The Rose of Cimarron Myth." *True West,* Sept. 1954, p. 8.

Rose, Thomas E.
Moran, Frank E. "Escape From Libby Prison." *Big West,* April 1970, p. 6.

Ross, John
Koller, Joe. "Trail to Cherokee West." *Western Frontier,* July 1978, p. 2.
Lehman, Leola. "Cherokee Blood Feud of the Trail of Tears." *True Frontier,* Oct. 1967, p. 34. Rpt. *True Frontier, Special Issue No. 2,* 1972, p. 28.
Preece, Harold. "The Desperate Cherokee Forced March Across the Trail of Tears." *Frontier West,* Dec. 1972, p. 12.

Ross, Tom
Fenton, James I. "Tom Ross: Ranger Nemesis." *NOLA Quarterly,* Vol. XIV, No. 2, Summer 1990, p. 4.

Rowe, Martin
Walker, Wayne T. "Gunsmoke at the Courthouse." *Golden West,* Aug. 1974, p. 22.

Rucker, A.W.
Stephenson, Peggy. "Those Busy Bogus Bond Boys." *True West,* May 1988, p. 40.

Rudabaugh, Dave
Callon, Milton W. "Billy the Kid's Last Christmas." *Frontier Times,* Jan. 1968, p. 34.
Holben, Dick. "Biography of a Lynching." *The West,* July 1973, p. 34. Rpt. *Western Frontier,* Annual No. 1, 1975, p. 28.
Holben, Richard. "When the Dodge City Gang Took Over Las Vegas." *Pioneer West,* May 1977, p. 12.

Rasch, Philip J. "Dave Rudabaugh, Gunman." *Real West,* Nov. 1979, p. 18. Rpt. *Real West,* Special Issue, 1981, p. 46.

Rudolph, William "Missouri Kid" (alias William Anderson)
Speer, Lonnie R. "The Missouri Kid." *True West,* Dec. 1988, p. 22.

Ruggles Brothers (John and Charles)
Boessenecker, John. "The Ruggles Boys' Death Treasure." *Westerner,* May-June 1973, p. 34.

Champion, Dale. "The Lynching of the Ruggles Brothers." *Frontier Times,* Summer 1961, p. 14.

Holben, Richard. "The Day the Redding Lynch Mob Carried Two Ropes." *Frontier West,* Oct. 1974, p. 22.

Meier, Gary. "Where Is the Ruggles' Gold?" *Old West,* Fall 1991, p. 54.

Repp, Ed Earl. "Lawdogs Bite Hard." *True Frontier,* Sept. 1969, p. 30. Rpt. *True Frontier,* Sept. 1973, p. 32.

Rumph, John
Zachry, J. "Old Frontier 'Doc' Rumph." *Westerner,* Sept.-Oct. 1973, p. 14.

Russell, "Baldy" (Bill Mitchell, John Davis)
Sonnichsen, C.L. "Long, Long Trail of Baldy Russell." *NOLA Quarterly,* Vol. XII, No. 1, Summer 1987, p. 17.

Russell, William H.
Hartley, William B. "The Fabulous Pony Express." *True Western Adventures,* June 1960, p. 12.

Mays, Carelton. "Tragedy of the Pony Express." *Real West,* Nov. 1960, p. 8. Rpt. *Real West,* Annual, Spring 1978, p. 18.

"Russian Bill" (see Tattenbaum, William)

Rutgers, Wade
Phelps, Roy. "The Buffalo Slaughter That Led to a Savage War." *Frontier West,* Feb. 1972, p. 30.

Rutherford, Morton
Walker Wayne T. "Fighting Lawyer of the Indian Territory." *Pioneer West,* March 1979, p. 22.

Wayne, Roger. "Morton Rutherford." *Great West,* Aug. 1973, p. 28. Rpt. *Great West,* Fall 1981, p. 30.

Ryan, Bill

Breihan, Carl W. "Bill Ryan, Worst of the James Gang." *Real West,* July 1967, p. 24.

_____. "Jesse's Trouble Maker." *Frontier Times,* Fall 1959, p. 24.

_____. "'Whiskey Head' Bill Ryan." *Pioneer West,* Sept. 1979, p. 22.

Yeatman, Ted. "Bill Ryan, Outlaw." *NOLA Quarterly,* Vol. V, No. 4, April 1980, p. 20.

Rynerson, William L.

Barker, Allen. "The Man Who Triggered the Lincoln County War." *WOLA Journal Quarterly,* Vol. I, No. 2, Fall-Winter 1991, p. 16.

_____. "William Rynerson, True Leader of the Murphies." *NOLA Quarterly,* Vol. XV, No. 4, Oct.-Dec. 1991, p. 18.

Rynning, Thomas H.

Kildare, Maurice. "Ranger Shoot-out at the Cowboy Saloon." *Golden West,* March 1969, p. 26. Rpt. *The West,* Jan. 1973, p. 24.

Shannon, Tex. "Rynning's Rough Riders." *Frontier Times,* Summer 1960, p. 18.

Saban, George

Nelson, Andre. "The Last Sheepman-Cattleman War." *True West,* May 1988, p. 14.

Sacajawea

Clark, Helen. "Where Is the Grave of Sacajawea?" *Real West,* May 1967, p. 21.

Holding, Vera. "Sacajawea: Shoshone Maiden Guide." *Real Frontier,* April 1970, p. 12. Rpt. *True Frontier,* June 1973, p. 38.

Karolevitz, R.F. "Sacajawea: Heroine of the Lewis and Clark Expedition." *True West,* Aug. 1958, p. 4. Rpt. *True West,* Special Issue, 1978, p. 48.

Martin, Denise. "Sacajawea, Lewis and Clark's Amazing Girl Guide." *True*

Frontier, Jan. 1969, p. 16. Rpt. *True Frontier,* Special Issue No. 10, Fall 1974, p. 34.

Neill, Wilfred T. "Bird Woman's Real Story." Part I, *The West,* July 1968, p. 10; Part II, *The West,* Aug. 1968, p. 20.

Sagel, Lee (alias John Smith, John Crackentaw, John Johns)
Smith, Joy McDougal. "Alias John Smith." *Old West,* Winter 1990, p. 30.

Sample, Comer W. "Red"
Carson, Xanthus. "The Bisbee Massacre." *Westerner,* Nov. 1970, p. 48.

Ormes, Carl. "Blood at Bisbee." *Real West,* May 1959, p. 23.

Roensch, Dell. "Bisbee's Bath of Blood." *True Western Adventure,* Dec. 1959, p. 38.

Samuel, Reuben
Steele, Phillip W. "The Truth About the Man Who Was Jesse James' Stepfather." *Frontier Times,* Dec. 1984, p. 24.

Sanders Family
Beller, J. "Sanders of Turkey Creek." *Old West,* Fall 1972, p. 14.

Sandoval, Jesus
Joyce, Lynn R.S. "Jesus Sandoval: Real-Life 'Lone Ranger' on the Rio Grande." *Real West,* June 1983, p. 32.

Santa Anna, Antonio Lopez de
Brown, Epp. "Santa Anna and Sam Houston" ("Wild Old Days" column). *True West,* May 1987, p. 60.

Hayes, Frederick. "Mexican File: What Happened at the Alamo?" *Real West,* July 1960, p. 28.

Satank (Sitting Bear)
Foster, Bill. "We-Ko-eet-Senko Must Die." *True Frontier,* June 1967, p. 22. Rpt. *True Frontier,* June 1972, p. 26; *True Frontier,* Special Issue No. 10, Fall 1974, p. 40; and *True Frontier,* Special Issue No. 18, Summer 1977, p. 41.

Grove, Fred. "The Chiefs Must Die!" *Golden West,* March 1970, p. 42.

Huston, Fred. "The Favorite Son of Sitting Bear." *True Frontier,* Special Issue No. 2, 1972, p. 9. Rpt. *True Frontier,* Jan. 1978, p. 9.

_____. "The Kiowa Chief Refused to Surrender to Death." *Frontier West,* Feb. 1975, p. 6.

Morgan, Ronald J. "The Warren Wagon Train Fight" ("The Indian Side" column). *The West,* Oct. 1974, p. 8.

Wiltsey, Norman B. "Death of a Demon." *Real West,* June 1975, p. 38.

_____. "Death of a Warrior." *Golden West,* May 1966, p. 8. Rpt. *Western Frontier,* March 1979, p. 37.

Satanta

Allen, Chester. "His Enemies Voted Him Death." *Westerner,* May-June 1969, p. 36.

Catlin, W.S. "Guilty." *Great West,* Dec. 1970, p. 30.

_____. "The Strange Plains War of the Boyhood Pals Turned Mortal Enemies." *Frontier West,* Feb. 1974, p. 32.

Echols, Lee E. "The Kiowa Raiders of Rainy Mountain." *True West,* April 1978, p. 6.

Grove, Fred. "The Chiefs Must Die!" *Golden West,* March 1970, p. 42.

Irons, Angie. "Set-Tainte and His Bugle of Death." *True West,* Oct. 1989, p. 38.

Katigan, Madelon B. "Chief Satanta Comes Home." *The West,* March 1964, p. 40. Rpt. *The West,* Annual, 1971, p. 50; and *Western Frontier,* May 1981, p. 9.

Lehman, L.C. "Satanta's Red Raiders." *Real West,* Americana Series, Winter 1964, p. 34.

Morgan, Ronald J. "The Warren Wagon Train Fight" ("The Indian Side" column). *The West,* Oct. 1974, p. 8.

Shelton, Stanley O. "Death on the Butterfield Trail." *Frontier West,* April 1972, p. 24.

Walker, Wayne T. "Satanta: Oracle of the Plains." *The West,* May 1973, p. 14. Rpt. *Western Frontier,* Nov. 1975, p. 46.

Savage, James "Big Jim"

Traywick, Ben T. "Big Jim Savage." *Frontier Times,* Sept. 1963, p. 6.

Winslowe, John R. "The Mariposa Slaughter." *Great West,* April 1971, p. 20.

Scales, Chut

Qualey, J.S. "Chut Scales, Midget Marshal." *Real West,* Jan. 1960, p. 14.

Scarborough, George Adolphus

DeArment, Robert K. "Manhunter George Scarborough." *True West,* April 1982, p. 42.

Kildare, Maurice. "Killer's Trail to Nowhere." *The West,* March 1973, p. 27.

Scarbreast

Jones, Calico. "Ute Against Navajo." *Real West,* Special Issue, Winter 1970, p. 18.

Kildare, Maurice. "Chief Scarbreast Raids Oraibi." *The West,* May 1974, p. 28.

_____. "Chief Scarbreast, Master Killer." *The West,* Nov. 1965, p. 20. Rpt. *The West,* Feb. 1973, p. 22.

_____. "The Marauders." *Real Frontier,* Nov. 1971, p. 8.

Schieffelin, Ed

Bailey, Tom. "The Man Who Found Eighty-Five Million Dollars!" *True West,* Oct. 1959, p. 6.

Champlin, Tim. "His Tombstone Was Made of Silver." *Great West,* April 1973, p. 34.

Christy, Kent. "Tombstone, Arizona." *True West,* April 1955, p. 18.

Dobie, J. Frank. "Schieffelin's Gold." *True West,* Oct. 1958, p. 13.

Fink, Clarence M. "From Frustration to Fortune." *Real West,* Sept. 1981, p. 26.

Minckler, Jess. "Tombstone Ed's Treasure." *True Western Adventures,* Issue No 1, 1957, p. 44.

Rosenhouse, Leo. "Tombstone: Too Tough To Die." *True Frontier,* May 1971, p. 21.

Summit, Roger. "The Silver Strike That Built Tombstone, Arizona." *True Frontier,* Nov. 1967, p. 19. Rpt. *True Frontier,* Oct. 1972, p. 31; and *True Frontier,* Aug. 1976, p. 13.

Traywick, Ben T. "Mountain of Silver." *Wild West,* Dec. 1970, p. 24.

"True Western Hall of Fame" column. *True Western Adventures,* June 1961, p. 41.

Schnyder, Leodegar

Collings, Kit. "Sergeant Leodegar Schnyder: Forty Years at Fort Laramie." *True West,* June 1986, p. 32.

Swain, George R. "Fort Laramie's Silent Soldier." *The West,* Feb. 1965, p. 36.

Schultz, James Willard (Apikuni)

Schultz, James Willard. "My Last Great Buffalo Hunt." *True Western Adventures,* June 1959, p. 32.

Schumacher, Charles J.

Speer, Lonnie R. "The Missouri Kid." *True West,* Dec. 1988, p. 22.

Scott, Abigail (see Duniway, Abigail Scott)

Scott, James "Jim"
Kildare, Maurice. "Take a Walk to Doom." *Real West,* April 1970, p. 38.

Scott, Walter E. "Death Valley Scotty"
Anderson, Bryce W. "Scotty's Coyote Special." *True West,* Dec. 1959, p. 9.

Burke, William. "Scotty's Hot-Shot." *True Western Adventures,* Summer 1958, p. 36.

Coleman, Tom L. "Recollections of Death Valley Scotty." *Real West,* March 1973, p. 8.

Crow, Peter. "Death Valley Scotty: A Man Obsessed." *Old West,* Winter 1986, p. 60.

Repp, Ed Earl. "The Mystery of Death Valley Scotty." *True Frontier,* Jan. 1971, p. 17. Rpt. *True Frontier,* Special Issue No. 16, Fall 1976, p. 13.

Roope, William A. "My Winter With Death Valley Scotty." *True West,* June 1967, p. 6.

Scurlock, Josiah Gordon "Doc"
Rasch, Philip J., Joseph E. Buckbee, and Karl K. Klein. "Man of Many Parts." *English Westerners' Brand Book,* Vol. V, No. 2, January 1963, p. 9.

Searles, John W.
Murray, Tom G. "Borax King, John W. Searles." *Frontier Times,* July 1975, p. 23.

Swanson, Budington. "The Earth Empire." *True Frontier,* Special Issue No. 8, 1973, p. 40.

Sears, William "Bill"
Kansas State Historical Society. "How a Political War Almost Wrecked Kansas." *Western Frontier,* July 1977, p. 3.

Seattle (Seathl)
Starnes, Luke. "The Saga of Seattle." *Golden West,* Jan. 1968, p. 34. Rpt. *The West,* Sept. 1972, p. 22; *Western Frontier,* Special Issue, March 1975, p. 18; and *Western Frontier,* Feb. 1985, p. 26.

_____. "The Story Behind the Statue." *Pioneer West,* March 1969, p. 18.

Seger, John
Lehman, Leola. "John Seger, Teacher-Student of Indians." *True Frontier,* March 1969, p. 44.

Sell, William "Willie"
Murach, I. "Surviving a Massacre Could Be the Worst Luck of All." *Frontier West,* June 1974, p. 26.

Selman, John
Breihan, Carl W. "John Selman, Lone Wolf." Part I, *Real West,* June 1969, p. 19; Part II, *Real West,* Aug. 1969, p. 16.

Conant, Lora M. "Hang Them High." *Great West,* Feb. 1969, p. 12.

DeMattos, Jack. "John Selman" ("Gunfighters of the Real West" column). *Real West,* Oct. 1982, p. 40.

Mallory,George. "He Killed Wes Hardin." *Real West,* Sept. 1960, p. 8.

Metz, Leon C. "Why Old John Selman Died." *Frontier Times,* Nov. 1965, p. 30.

O'Neal, Bill. "Baz Outlaw vs John Selman and Joe McKidrict" ("Great Western Gunfights" column). *True West,* Oct. 1988, p. 68.

Selman, John Marion, Jr.
Metz, Leon C. "Why Old John Selman Died." *Frontier Times,* Nov. 1965, p. 30.

Seminole-Negro Scouts
Robinson, Charles M., III. "The Whirlwind and His Scouts." *Old West,* Summer 1991, p. 28.

Sequoyah
Darrow, W. T. "Warriors and Chiefs" column. *Wild West,* Oct. 1988, p. 12.

Kilpatrick, Jack E. "A Cherokee Account of Sequoyah." *True West,* Aug. 1967, p. 13.

Lehman, Leola. "The Talking Leaf." *True Frontier,* Dec. 1971, p. 36. Rpt. *True Frontier,* Special Issue No. 10, Fall 1974, p. 37.

Mays, Carelton. "Did Sequoyah Invent the Cherokee Alphabet?" *Real West,* July 1966, p. 16.

Qualey, J. "Sequoyah and the Mystery of the Talking Leaves." *Real West,* Special Issue, Winter 1963, p. 11.

Qualey, Jake. "Mystery of the Talking Leaves." *Real West,* March 1961, p. 8.

Riotte, Louise. "The Man Who Taught the Cherokee Nation How to Read." *The West,* Aug. 1972, p. 20. Rpt. *Western Frontier,* Jan. 1981, p. 38.

Traywick, Ben T. "Sequoyah." *Great West,* Fall 1970, p. 40.

Serra, Junipero

Serra, H.H. "The Dedication of Father Junipero." Part I, *The West,* Sept. 1967, p. 20; Part II, *The West,* Oct. 1967, p. 22. Rpt. Part I, *Western Frontier,* May 1980, p. 20; Part II, *Western Frontier,* July 1980, p. 23.

Seymour, Richard "Bloody Dick"

Hoctor, Emmett C. "The Greatest Dime Novel Never Written, or The Sketchy Life of 'Bloody Dick' Seymour." *NOLA Quarterly,* Vol. XV, No. 1, 1991, p. 11.

Parsons, Chuck. "'Bloody Dick' Seymour" ("Answer Man" column). *True West,* Jan. 1990, p. 14.

Shadley, Lafe

"Bloody Ingalls Under Siege." *Western Frontier,* July 1976, p. 6.

Shannon Family

Steele, Phillip W. "The Shannon-Fisher War." *Old West,* Fall 1985, p. 44.

Shannon, Mary Eulalie

Reese, Richard. "The Poet and the Pirate." *Old West,* Spring 1982, p. 38.

Sharkovich, George "Austrian George"

Repp, Ed Earl. "The Love That Killed." *True Frontier,* Sept. 1970, p. 28. Rpt. *True Frontier, Special Issue No. 7, Fall 1973, p. 22.*

Sharon, William M.

Freeman, Frank M. "The Case of the Two Imperious Men." *Golden West,* Sept. 1968, p. 34.

Young, Jan. "Sharon's Rose of Death." *Real West,* March 1963, p. 32.

Sharp, Milton Anthony "Milt"

Cheshire, Giff. "Milton Sharp: Gentlest Scourge." *True Western Adventures,* June 1960, p. 24.

Harrison, John H. "Baddest Man From Bowie." *Golden West,* May 1974, p. 34. Rpt. *Western Frontier,* May 1986, p. 34.

Hines, James. "Master Bandit." *Real West,* Jan, 1960, p. 24.

Monman, James E. "Milton Sharp, Nevada's Elusive Bandit." *Real West,* May 1966, p. 41.

Taylor, Paul. "He Would Never Stoop to Burglary." *True West,* Nov. 1989, p. 62.

Shaw, M.T.
Young, Robert. "Train Robbers Mystify Sheriff and Posse." *NOLA Quarterly*, Vol. VII, No. 4, Winter 1982-83, p. 16.

Shea, Cornelius "Con"
Skaggs, Colleen. "Con Shea: Idaho Cattle Baron." *Old West*, Summer 1982, p. 24.

Shelby, Joseph Orville "Jo"
Johnson, Norman K. "General Shelby and the Trial of Frank James." *Real West*, Oct. 1988, p. 14.

Joseph, Robert. "Tramp General." *Old West*, Winter 1966, p. 20.

Shepherd, George
Breihan, Carl W. "George Shepherd: A Quantrill Guerilla." *The West*, May 1971, p. 40. Rpt. *Golden West*, Aug. 1974, p. 26; *Western Frontier*, March 1977, p. 26; and *Western Frontier*, May 1985, p. 42.

_____. "Outlaw George Shepherd." *Pioneer West*, March 1978, p. 20.

Shirley, James "Jim"
Kelly, Bill. "Jim Shirley's Last Goodbye." *Real West*, July 1976, p. 41. Rpt. *Real West*, Yearbook, Summer 1977, p. 28.

Rockwell, Nelson. "The Case of the Bungling Bank Robbers." *Frontier Times*, Fall 1960, p. 20.

Shonsey, Michael "Mike"
Trenholm, Virginia Cole. "Last of the Invaders." *True West*, Feb. 1962, p. 18.

Short, Edward "Ed"
Kildare, Maurice. "Bullet Swapout in Oklahoma." *Real West*, Feb. 1973, p. 48. Rpt. *Real West*, Annual, Fall 1974, p. 62.

Shirley, Glenn. "One Hell-Firin' Minute to Death." *Golden West*, Sept. 1967, p. 16. Rpt. *Golden West*, Feb. 1972, p. 46; and *Western Frontier*, Special Issue, Fall 1974, p. 34.

Short, Josiah Washington, Jr., "Joe"
Self, Florence Short. "Luke Short's Brother Joe." *Old West*, Summer 1976, p. 14.

Short, Luke
Bradford, John R. "Showdown for Luke Short." *Western Action*, Sept. 1960, p. 16.

Breihan, Carl W. "Luke Short's Mystery Gun Fight." *Real West,* March 1961, p. 32. Rpt. *Real West,* Annual, Spring 1968, p. 50.

Burton, Carl. "Shoot-Out That Shocked the West." *Westerner,* July-Aug. 1973, p. 18.

Cox, William R. "Luke Short" ("Backgrounds of Famous Western Badmen" column). *True West,* Oct. 1961, p. 25.

DeMattos, Jack. "Luke Short" ("Gunfighters of the Real West" column). *Real West,* Dec. 1982, p. 26.

Kay, Jay F. "The Prodigal Gambler." *Golden West,* Nov. 1965, p. 10. Rpt. *Golden West,* Feb. 1972, p. 28; and *Western Frontier,* July 1977, p. 40.

Norman, Robert W. "Luke Short: Gambling Gunman." *True Frontier,* Sept. 1968, p. 26. Rpt. *True Frontier,* Special Issue No. 5, 1973, p. 10; and *True Frontier,* Special Issue No. 13, 1975, p. 18.

O'Neal, Bill. "Luke Short vs Longhaired Jim Courtwright" ("Great Western Gunfights" column). *True West,* Sept. 1989, p. 58.

Ryall, William. "The Luck of Luke." *True Western Adventures,* April 1960, p. 18.

Walker, Wayne T. "Killer in Fancy Pants." *True West,* Oct. 1956, p. 14.

Short, Oliver
Swanson, Budington. "Massacre On Crooked Creek." *Real Frontier,* Aug. 1971, p. 38.

Shoshone Mike
Robertson, Dorothy. "Shoshone Mike's Last Warpath." *Real West,* Aug. 1973, p. 8.

Traywick, Ben T. "The Suicidal Raid of Shoshone Mike." *Wild West,* Oct. 1969, p. 42. Rpt. *Pioneer West,* Oct. 1974, p. 40.

Shoup, George L.
Kimball, Ethel. "Red Friends, White Graves." *The West,* Sept. 1968, p. 10.

Sibley, Henry Hastings
Czech, Kenneth P. "High Plains Rebellion Rekindled." *Wild West,* June 1990, p. 27.

Hively, Russ and Kay. "Sibley's Victorious Blunder." *Wild West,* Nov. 1971, p. 8. Rpt. *Oldtimers Wild West,* July 1974, p. 46.

Sibley, Henry Hopkins
Gregg, Andy. "Sibley's Army of the Dead." Part I, *Real West,* Nov. 1964, p. 26; Part II, *Real West,* Jan. 1965, p. 30.

Linscombe, Matt. "The Fantastic Alliance That Triggered the Civil War's Strangest Battle." *Frontier West,* June 1973, p. 30.

Niderost, Eric. "River Crossing Contested." *Wild West,* Oct. 1989, p. 35.

Sides, Johnson

Cerveri, Doris. "Paiute Leaders." *Real West,* Special Issue, Spring 1972, p. 14.

Sieber, Al

Dillon, Richard. "Al Seiber's War With the Apache Kid." *Westerner,* Sept.-Oct. 1974, p. 51.

Gaddis, Robert. "The Unluckiest Scout in the West." *True Frontier,* Nov. 1969, p. 32. Rpt. *True Frontier,* Special Issue No. 3, 1972, p. 24.

Griffith, A. Kinney. "Mickey Free, Manhunter." Part I, *Old West,* Summer 1968, p. 2; Part II, *Old West,* Fall 1968, p. 2.

Ryan, Jack. "Scout for the Apache Hunters." *True West,* Feb. 1962, p. 26.

Sandell, Jay. "Beet Juice Massacre on Greene Creek." *Real West,* July 1960, p. 24.

Thrapp, Dan L. "Battle of Big Dry Wash." *True West,* Aug. 1962, p. 40.

Sigler, Les

Riotte, Louise. "Shoot-Out at the California Cafe." *The West,* Jan. 1974, p. 32.

Silcott, Jane

Timmen, Fritz. "Jane Silcott, Trailblazer to Idaho's Gold." *The West,* Dec. 1967, p. 30. Rpt. *Golden West,* Feb. 1973, p. 24; and *Western Frontier,* Nov. 1976, p. 40.

Silks, Mattie (Mattie Thompson, Martha A. Ready)

Cheney, Louise. "Jennie Rogers vs Mattie Silks for Holladay Street." *Real West,* May 1974, p. 20.

_____. "The Life, Loves and Battles of Madam Mattie Silks." *The West,* Sept. 1968, p. 24. Rpt. *The West,* Dec. 1972, p. 10; and *Western Frontier,* Sept. 1976, p. 24.

Ferdom, John. "Street of a Thousand Sinners." *Real West,* Sept. 1962, p. 20.

Indrysek, Don. "Mattie Silks, Queen of the Tenderloin." *Old West,* Fall 1988, p. 20.

Rozar, Lily-B. "Magnificent Harlots of the 1870s." *Pioneer West,* April 1972, p. 40.

Silva, Vicente

Beimer, Dorothy S. "Gallardo: The Dog Who Helped Capture the Silva Gang." *True West,* March 1983, p. 22.

Jones, Calico. "New Mexico's Horrible Bandit Society." *Real West,* July 1967, p. 12.

Kutz, Jack. "Vicente Silva and the Nightriders." *Great West,* Dec. 1974, p. 12.

Sena, Mitchell C. "Third Rate Henchmen of a First Rate Terror." *True West,* Feb. 1970, p. 28.

"Silver Heels"

Edelhart, Mike. "The Legend of Mount Silverheels." *The West,* Oct. 1974, p. 38.

Hochmuth, Charles A. "The Agony of Silver Heels." *The West,* March 1969, p. 32. Rpt. *The West,* June 1973, p. 32.

Krepela, Rick. "Mystery of the Beautiful Silver Heels." *Real West,* March 1964, p. 33.

Martin, Mary Joy. "Silverheels: She Stole the Miners' Hearts." *True West,* January 1985, p. 30.

Smathers, Will. "The Saga of Colorado's Most Improbable Angel of Mercy." *Frontier West,* April 1971, p. 14.

Simmons, Philander

Galbraith, Den. "Mountain Man." *True West,* Oct. 1972, p. 8.

Simpkins, I. J.

Grover, David H. "The Disappearing Dynamiter." *True West,* July 1988, p. 28.

Simpson, Joseph "Joe," "Hootch"

Edwards, Harold L. "The Legend of Hootch Simpson's Head-Skidoo Lynching Made Headlines." *NOLA Quarterly,* Vol. XIII, No. 3, Winter 1989, p. 22.

Simpson, Smith

Meketa, Jacqueline Dorgan. "The Taos Ghost." *True West,* Dec. 1987, p. 24.

Sippy, Ben

Kelly, Bill. "Bill Kelly Says Ben Sippy Top Gun in Tombstone." *NOLA Quarterly,* Vol. II, No. 3, Autumn 1975, p. 15.

Siringo, Charles "Charley"

Adams, Clarence Siringo. "Fair Trial at Encinosa." *True West,* April 1966, p. 32.

Ball, Eve. "Charlie Siringo and 'Eat Em Up Jake.'" *True West*, June 1969, p. 36.

Ballard, Dave. "Miner's All-Out War." *Wild West*, Feb. 1991, p. 26.

Frazier, Thomas A. "Charles Siringo, a Texas Cowboy." *Real West*, Feb. 1975, p. 40.

Negel, Stony. "When Siringo Was Marked for Death." *True West*, Dec. 1970, p. 30.

Nolen, Oran Warder. "Charles Siringo: Cowboy Writer." *Real Frontier*, June 1970, p. 42.

Roberts, McLean. "Shamus in Spurs." *True Western Adventures*, June 1960, p. 19.

Stanley, Samuel. "Spy for the Pinkertons." *Westerner*, Nov.-Dec. 1969, p. 46.

Thorp, Raymond W. "Cowboy Charley Siringo." *True West*, Feb. 1965, p. 32.

Sitters, Joseph "Joe"

Michaels, Kevin. "Tracker." *Great West*, Sept. 1974, p. 22. Rpt. *Authentic West*, Summer 1981, p. 22.

Sitting Bull

"The Cavalry Troop Sitting Bull Couldn't Massacre." *Western Frontier*, Jan. 1977, p. 8.

Chatfield, Harry. "When the Piegans Captured Sitting Bull." *Real West*, Oct. 1969, p. 43.

Clayton, Juliana. "The Private War of White Hair McLaughlin." *True West*, Nov. 1989, p. 52.

Dickie, Francis. "A Test of Courage." *Frontier Times*, May 1971, p. 6.

Eherts, Walter. "Death of Sitting Bull." *Real West*, June 1987, p. 18.

Hammer, Kenneth M. "Sitting Bull's Bones." *English Westerners Brand Book*, Vol. XXIII, No. 1, Winter 1984, p. 1.

Handleman, Charles. "Was Mrs. Weldon Sitting Bull's White Squaw?" *The West*, Oct. 1964, p. 8.

Koller, Joe. "There Were 'TWO' Sitting Bulls." *Pioneer West*, Nov. 1969, p. 57. Rpt. *Pioneer West*, Collector's Annual, 1971, p. 11; and *Pioneer West*, July 1973, p. 55.

Lehman, L. "Sitting Bull's Squaw War." *Westerner*, April 1971, p. 40.

Lipton, Dean. "They Murdered Sitting Bull." *Great West*, Dec. 1972, p. 16.

Osborne, Donald L. "Sitting Bull's Boss." *Frontier Times*, Summer 1961, p. 16.

Pearman, Robert. "Sitting Bull Murdered." *Real West*, Special Issue, Winter 1963, p. 30.

Rexroth, Mary Collins. "Auntie May and Sitting Bull." *The West,* Feb. 1974, p. 32.

Wiltsey, Norman B. "Death on the North Plains." *True West,* June 1958, p. 24.

_____. "Sitting Bull: Artist." *Real West,* Oct. 1972, p. 43.

_____. "The Saga of Sitting Bull." Part I, *Real West,* June 1970, p. 6; Part II, *Real West,* Aug. 1970, p. 42. Rpt. as one-part article, *Real West,* Special Issue, Spring 1972, p. 38.

Wishart, Bruce. "Grandmother's Land—Sitting Bull in Canada." Part I, *True West,* May 1990, p. 14; Part II, *True West,* June 1990, p. 26; Part III, *True West,* July 1990, p. 20; Part IV, *True West,* Aug 1990, p. 28.

Yarbrough, Leroy. "Sitting Bull: The Truth and the Legend." *Real West,* July 1962, p. 16. Rpt. *Real West,* Special Issue, Winter 1963, p. 26.

Sitting Bull (the other "Sitting Bull")

Koller, Joe. "There Were 'TWO' Sitting Bulls." *Pioneer West,* Nov. 1969, p. 57. Rpt. *Pioneer West,* Collector's Annual 1971, p. 11; and *Pioneer West,* July 1973, p. 55.

Mays, Carelton. "Sitting Bull's Fantastic Death Club." *Real West,* May 1962, p. 24.

Sixkiller, Sam

Ernst, Robert R. "Sam Sixkiller: Tragic Life of an Indian Lawman." *Frontier Times,* Oct. 1984, p. 36.

Walker, Wayne T. "Captain Sam Sixkiller: Indian Policeman." *Golden West,* Nov. 1969, p. 22.

_____. "Sam Sixkiller, Chief of the Indian Police." *Real West,* July 1977, p. 24.

Skinner, Cyrus "Cy"

Kildare, Maurice. "Hell Gate Hanging Bee." *Real West,* March 1967, p. 27.

_____. "Outlaw Lost in Missoula." *Frontier Times,* Nov. 1971, p. 16.

Mather, R.E. "Cyrus and Nellie and the Vigilantes." *True West,* May 1987, p. 20.

Skokum Jim

Benedict, Verne. "Skokum Jim's Musical Load." *The West,* Jan. 1967, p. 34.

Skywalker (Mamanti or Do-Ha-Te)

Kildare, Maurice. "Chief Skywalker." *Great West,* June 1973, p. 20. Rpt. *Great West,* Summer 1981, p. 22.

_____. "Sky Walker: Mystery Chief." *Westerner,* July-Aug. 1970, p. 10.

Slack, John B.

Hill, Leonard. "The Great Diamond Hoax." *True Frontier,* Special Issue No. 12, Spring 1975, p. 38. Rpt. *True Frontier,* Special Issue No. 20, Winter 1977, p. 8.

Scullin, George. "They Salted the Desert With Diamonds." *True Western Adventures,* June 1960, p. 30.

Sufrin, Mark. "The Fantastic Table Rock Swindle." *Frontier West,* June 1972, p. 12.

Slade, Joseph Alfred "Jack"

Arthur, Jim. "The Saga of Montana's Most Feared Badman." *Frontier West,* June 1971, p. 32.

Boren, Kerry Ross. "Jack Slade's Grave Located." *Frontier Times,* May 1976, p. 24.

Breihan, Carl W. "Captain Joe Slade, the Big Wolf." *Real West,* June 1968, p. 46. Rpt. *Real West,* Annual, Fall 1974, p. 45.

_____. "Joe Slade: Gunfighter." *Westerner,* March-April 1972, p. 38.

_____. "The Day They Hung Joe Slade." *Pioneer West,* March 1979, p. 28.

Christy, Mort. "Capt. Slade and the Frenchman's Ear." *Real West,* Feb. 1959, p. 15.

Churchill, Richard. "Legendary Jack Slade." *True Frontier,* March 1974, p. 30. Rpt. *True Frontier,* Special Issue No. 13, 1975, p. 38.

Darwin, Wayne. "Who Really Condemned Slade to Hang?" *Golden West,* July 1969, p. 10. Rpt. *Golden West,* March 1973, p. 38; *Western Frontier,* Annual, Summer 1978, p. 38; and *Western Frontier,* May 1985, p. 38.

DeMattos, Jack. "Jack Slade" ("Gunfighters of the Real West" column). *Real West,* June 1985, p. 46.

Elliott, Susan. "Fill His Coffin With Whiskey." *Great West,* July 1968, p. 5.

Hanson, James E. "The Killer Who Called Himself the Law." *True Western Adventures,* April 1961, p. 34.

Hart, George. "Some Notes on the Early Life of Joseph A. Slade." *NOLA Quarterly,* Vol. V, No. 1, Oct. 1979, p. 19.

Henry, Edwin C. "More Than Mighty!" *Frontier Times,* Winter 1958-59, p. 18.

Huston, Fred. "They Hung Him as a Drunk." *Pioneer West,* May 1969, p. 22.

"Jack Slade: The Whiskey Crazed Killer." *Great West,* June 1971, p. 34.

Long, James A. "Old Julesburg, Wickedest City on the Plains." *Frontier Times,* March 1964, p. 24.

_____. "The Strange Truth About Jack Slade." *The West,* Feb. 1966, p. 26. Rpt. *Golden West,* Oct. 1974, p. 8.

O'Dell, Roy. "Did Jack Slade Really Have Four Ears?" *NOLA Quarterly,* Vol. IX, No. 4, Spring 1985, p. 16.

_____. "The Terror of the Overland." *True West,* March 1988, p. 14.

O'Dell, Roy P., and Kenneth Jessen. "The Hanging of Joseph A. Slade." *The WOLA Journal,* Vol. I, No. 1, Summer 1991, p. 12.

O'Neal, Bill. "Jack Slade vs Jules Reni" ("Great Western Gunfights" column). *True West,* Dec. 1991, p. 61.

Patterson, Richard. "Mark Twain Meets J. Slade." *NOLA Quarterly,* Vol. XI, No. 3, Winter 1987, p. 17.

Rybolt, Robert. "Was Jack Slade an Outlaw?" *NOLA Quarterly,* Vol. IX, No. 4, Spring 1985, p. 14.

Smith, Joe Heflin. "Slade of the Overland." *Golden West,* July 1967, p. 32.

Wigle, Charles. "Stagecoach Baron." *Real West,* Oct. 1957, p. 36.

Slaughter, Christopher Columbus

Bishop, Curtis. "Race for Half a Million." *True West,* Sept. 1954, p. 22.

Cheney, Louise. "Bobby Slaughter's Half Million Dollar Ride." *Real West,* Jan. 1962, p. 11.

Wallace, George A. "Cattle Kings." *True West,* Feb. 1964, p. 44.

Slaughter, George

Preece, Harold. "George Slaughter, Texas Pioneer." *The West,* Nov. 1964, p. 16. Rpt. *Western Frontier,* Sept. 1980, p. 48.

Slaughter, John Horton

Baird, Clayton R. "I Knew John Slaughter." *Real West,* Sept. 1972, p. 40. Rpt. *Real West,* Yearbook, Spring 1974, p. 38.

Breihan, Carl W. "Desperate Men, Desperate Guns." *Real West,* Annual, Winter 1977-78, p. 16.

DeMattos, Jack. "John Slaughter" ("Gunfighters of the Real West" column). *Real West,* March 1982, p. 22.

Farfan, G.B. "Patchy Slaughter." *Frontier Times,* Sept. 1963, p. 28.

Howard, Elton. "The Sheriff's Reward." *Frontier Times,* Fall 1959, p. 60.

"John Slaughter, Cattle King." *Great West,* June 1970, p. 24.

Pinkerton, Robert E. "The Toughest Man in Tombstone." *True Western Adventures,* Spring 1958, p. 8.

"True Western Hall of Fame" column. *True Western Adventures,* Oct. 1959, p. 59.

Small, John

Southworth, John. "An Unlikely Pair of Outlaws" ("Wild Old Days" column). *True West,* Feb. 1991, p. 60.

Smith, Badger

Bailey, Tom. "The Indestructible Man." *True Western Adventures,* April 1960, p. 21.

Smith, Charley

Cole, Joe A., and Terry Cole. "Charley Smith Still Wears His Six-Gun." *True West,* April 1978, p. 20.

Smith, Charlie "One-Armed Charlie" (see Ford, Charlie)

Smith, Erastus "Deaf"

Huston, Cleburne. "Deaf Smith versus Santa Anna." *Old West,* Summer, 1974, p. 35.

Kingstrom, Ebba M. "Erastus 'Deaf' Smith." *Old West,* Summer 1983, p. 50.

Preece, Harold. "Deaf Smith: Texas Spy." *Real West,* Fall Yearbook 1979, p. 34.

Smith, Henry Weston "Preacher Smith"

Craig, Josh. "Who Killed Preacher Smith?" *Golden West,* July 1966, p. 31. Rpt. *Golden West,* Oct. 1972, p. 17; and *Western Frontier,* Annual No. 2, 1976, p. 5.

Smith, Hyrum

Fleek, Sherman L. "Exodus Triggered by Assassins." *Wild West,* Oct. 1988, p. 26.

Smith, James L. "Whispering Smith"

Carroll, Murray L. "Whispering Smith's Hundred Dollar Hit." *NOLA Quarterly,* Vol. XII, No. 1, Summer 1987, p. 8.

Parsons, Chuck. "Whispering Smith" ("Answer Man" column). *True West,* Sept. 1985, p. 41.

Rasch, Philip J. "'Six Shooter' and 'Three Shooter' Smith." *NOLA Quarterly,* Vol. IX, No. 4, Spring 1985, p. 9.

Rybolt, Bob. "The Search for Whispering Smith." *NOLA Quarterly,* Vol. XI, No. 2, Fall 1986, p. 5.

_____. "Whispering Smith: The Man, the Myths and the Mystery." Part I, *NOLA Quarterly,* Vol. IX, No. 3, Winter 1985, p. 18; Part II, *NOLA Quarterly,* Vol. IX, No. 4, Spring 1985, p. 1.

Rybolt, Robert T. "Legend Becomes Reality: Whispering Smith Is Real." *True West,* Feb. 1984, p. 32.

Smith, Jedediah Strong "Jed"

Crowns, Jud. "A Bible, a Rifle, a Dream." *Pioneer West,* May 1967, p. 39.

Gardner, Robert. "The Greatest Mountain Man of Them All." *True West,* April 1961, p. 21.

Griffith, A. Kinney. "Caballero: Prince of Mountaineers." *The West,* May 1970, p. 22. Rpt. *Western Frontier,* Jan. 1980, p. 22.

Haycox, Ernest. "Captain With the Book and Gun." *True Western Adventures,* Summer 1958, p. 26.

Indrysck, Don. "Jedediah's Jinxed Journey." *The West,* Feb. 1970, p. 20. Rpt. *The West,* Aug. 1974, p. 20.

Legg, John. "Jed Smith In the Arms of Old Ephraim." *Old West,* Summer 1985, p. 40.

Lehman, Leola. "Jedediah Smith: Trail Blazer of the West." *Real West,* Aug. 1971, p. 23. Rpt. *Real West,* Annual 1972, p. 14.

Repp, Ed Earl. "Jededlah Smith: The Pathfinder." *Real Frontier,* Feb. 1971, p. 27.

Smith, Alson J. "The Ordeals of Old Smith." *Old West,* Winter 1970, p. 6.

Wert, Jeffry D. "Personality" column. *Wild West,* Aug. 1988, p. 12.

Young, Bob. "Melancholy Death of Jedediah Smith." *Real West,* March 1962, p. 18.

Smith, Jefferson "Soapy"

Bayworth, Jerome. "Creede, Sin City of Colorado." *The West,* Dec. 1971, p. 28.

Berton, Pierre. "Dictator of Skagway." *True Western Adventures,* Aug. 1960, p. 30.

Christian, Bill. "The One-Man Cowboy Mafia." *Oldtimers Wild West,* Oct. 1979, p. 47. Rpt. *Pioneer West,* Sept. 1969, p. 48; and *Oldtimers Wild West,* May 1975, p. 44.

Guttman, Jon. "Con Man's Empire." *Wild West,* Dec. 1990, p. 43.

Henderson, Grace G. "Soapy Smith's Least Favorite Cheechakos." *Frontier Times,* March 1975, p. 29.

Kelly, J.N. "Soapy Smith: Dirtiest Crook in Skagway." *The West,* Nov. 1966, p. 25.

Lynch, John T. "Devil's Grin." *True West,* April 1955, p. 16. Rpt. *Old West,* Spring 1966, p. 44; and *Badman,* Summer 1971, p. 40.

Majors, George Malcom. "Soapy Smith's Greatest Hoax." *Real West,* Nov. 1960, p. 14.

Martin, Cy. "He Died to Save Skagway." Part I, *Real West,* Jan. 1968, p . 16; Part II, *Real West,* April. 1968, p. 38.

————. "There Was No Night in Creede." *Real West,* Annual, Fall 1974, p. 14.

Martin, Jeannie. "The Slickest of the Bad Men." *Real West,* July 1975, p. 20.

O'Connor, Wilson. "Take Him to See the Eagle." *The West,* July 1964, p. 26. Rpt. *Golden West,* Jan. 1972, p. 16.

Qualey, J.S. "How Death Came to Soapy Smith." *Real West,* Jan. 1958, p. 8.

Smith, John ("Jimmy," "Six-Shooter")
Sandell, Jay. "'Six-Shooter' Smith Wouldn't Die." *Real West,* Nov. 1961, p. 12.

Smith, Joseph
Fleek, Sherman L. "Exodus Triggered by Assassins." *Wild West,* Oct. 1988, p. 26.

Hellman, Stan. "Mormon Prophet-General." *Wild West,* Dec. 1970, p. 44.

Swanson, Budington. "Young Joseph's Strange Dream." *The West,* July 1973, p. 20. Rpt. *Western Frontier,* Nov. 1976, p. 2.

Winski, Norman. "The Fugitive General-Prophet." *Big West,* Dec. 1967, p. 40.

Smith, Lillian
Shirley, Glenn. "Lillian Smith, Bill Cody's 'California Girl.'" *Real West,* April 1973, p. 46.

Smith, Scott Andrew "Coyote"
Montgomery, Wayne. "They Called Him Coyote." *Old West,* Spring 1968, p. 2.

Smith, Sylvester Samuel
Walker, Roger O. "One Tall Drink of Water." *Old West,* Fall 1990, p. 28.

Smith, Thomas "Bear River Tom"
Angle, Robert E. "The Marshal Who Wouldn't Kill." *Frontier Times,* Fall 1962, p. 12.

Archer, Jules. "Bare-Knuckled Marshal From Abilene." *Western Action,* Dec. 1960, p. 12.

Breihan, Carl W. "Lawman With Deadly Fists." *True Frontier,* June 1972, p. 8. Rpt. *True Frontier,* Special Issue No. 15, Summer 1976, p. 46.

Henry, T.C. "The Marshal Who Got His Head Shot Off." *Great West,* June 1967, p. 4.

Kennedy, Michael. "Bare Fists vs Six-Guns." *True West,* June 1955, p. 10. Rpt.

Badman, Fall 1972, p. 20.

Koller, Joe. "Bear River Smith: Two Fisted Lawman." *Golden West,* Nov. 1964, p. 26. Rpt. *The West,* Feb. 1974, p. 10.

Maxwell, George. "Tom Smith at Bear River." *Real West,* Annual, Spring 1968, p. 58. Rpt. "Tom Smith at Bear River." *Real West,* Jan. 1961, p. 34.

Moss, Jackson. "Tom Smith." *Real West,* Americana Series, Fall 1965, p. 46.

————. "Tom Smith: Hero Without a Gun." *Real West,* Jan. 1958, p. 32.

Rader, Con. "Iron Marshal of Abilene." *True Western Adventures,* Summer 1958, p. 16.

Stanley, Samuel. "The Marshal Who Used His Fists to Clean Up Abilene." *Oldtimers Wild West,* Oct. 1977, p. 6.

"True Western Hall of Fame" column. *True Western Adventures,* Feb. 1960, p. 59.

Walker, Wayne T. "Abilene's Bare Knuckle Marshal." *Westerner,* Oct. 1970, p. 10. Rpt. *Westerner,* Nov.-Dec. 1972, p. 46.

Wiltsey, Norman B. "Bare Fists and Six Guns." *Real West,* June 1973, p. 26.

Smith, Thomas G.

Hawthorne, Roger. "Conflict and Conspiracy." *True West,* June 1984, p. 12.

Smith, Thomas "Peg-Leg"

Parsons, Chuck. "Pegleg Smith" ("Answer Man" column). *True West,* July 1991, p. 12.

Smith, Alson J. "The Incorrigible Peg-Leg Smith." *Frontier Times,* Nov. 1964, p. 32.

Stuckie, J.U. "The Peg-Leg Smith Story." *Golden West,* May 1971, p. 16. Rpt. *Golden West,* Aug. 1974, p. 14; and *Western Frontier,* Annual 1977, p. 40.

Smith, Will

Edwards, Harold L. "Will Smith, a Study in Controversy." Part I, *NOLA Quarterly,* Vol. XII, No. 3, Winter 1988, p. 16; Part II, *NOLA Quarterly,* Vol. XII, No. 4, Spring 1989, p. 12.

Smith, William "Whispering Bill"

"Shootout at Abilene." *Man's Western,* Jan. 1960, p. 43.

Smith, William "Billy"

Walker, Wayne T. "How Billy Smith Brought a New Brand of Law and Order to Wichita." *Frontier West,* June 1975, p. 10.

Snipes, Ben

Koller, Joe. "Ben Snipes' Beef Bonanza." *Golden West,* May 1965, p. 16. Rpt. *The West,* June 1974, p. 40.

Snook, John Wilson

Kimball, Ethel. "John W. Snook, Pioneer Warden." *Real West,* April 1970, p. 24.

Snow, Erastus

Taylor, Paul. "A Cotton Mission." *True West,* June 1986, p. 46.

Somerby, Rufus

O'Neal, Bill. "A Cavalryman Who Didn't Want Rank." *Old West,* Summer 1981, p. 39.

Sontag, George (George C. Contant)

Boessenecker, John. "Red Shirt and Gatling Gun." *True West,* Jan. 1987, p. 14.

Edwards, Harold L. "Chris Evans: The Ready Killer." Part I, *NOLA Quarterly,* Vol. XI, No. 1, Summer 1986, p. 5; Part II, *NOLA Quarterly,* Vol. XI, No. 2, Fall 1986, p. 14.

————. "Odyssy of George C. Contant." *NOLA Quarterly,* Vol. X, No. 4, Spring 1986, p. 12.

Secrest, William B. "A Folsom Graduate." *True West,* Oct. 1979, p. 6.

Sontag, John (John Contant)

Boessenecker, John. "Buckshot for a Marshal." *Real West,* Feb. 1983, p. 35.

Edwards, Harold L. "Chris Evans: The Ready Killer." Part I, *NOLA Quarterly,* Vol. XI, No. 1, Summer 1986, p. 5; Part II, *NOLA Quarterly,* Vol. XI, No. 2, Fall 1986, p. 14.

————. "Hatred of Railroad Triggers Death." *NOLA Quarterly,* Vol. IX, No. 1, Summer 1984, p. 6.

Jackson, Fred. "Four Lawmen Ambush Two California Outlaws." *NOLA Quarterly,* Vol. III, No. 1, Winter 1975-76, p. 1.

O'Neal, Harold. "The San Joaquin Train Holdups. *Golden West,* March 1966, p. 44. Rpt. *Western Frontier,* Aug. 1981, p. 36.

Secrest, William B. "Death of an Outlaw." *True Frontier,* Nov. 1973, p. 12. Rpt. *True Frontier,* Special Issue No. 17, Winter 1976, p. 22.

————. "He Saw the Posse Die." *Frontier Times,* July 1966, p. 10.

————. "The Fantastic Train Robbery Drama." *True Frontier,* May 1970, p. 38. Rpt. *True Frontier,* Special Issue No. 5, 1973, p. 29.

_____. "The Gunfight at Stone Corral." *Real Frontier,* June 1970, p. 8. Rpt. *True Frontier,* Special Issue No. 1, 1971, p . 18; *True Frontier,* June 1973, p. 26; and *True Frontier,* Aug. 1975, p. 36.

Sullivan, Edward. "The Last of the West's Desperadoes." *Pioneer West,* May 1967, p. 11.

Young, Bob and Jan. "Tilt With the Iron Horse." *True West,* Dec. 1956, p. 18.

Sorbel, Asle Oscar
Parsons, Chuck. "In Pursuit of the Northfield Robbers." *NOLA Quarterly,* Vol. IV, No. 4, June 1979, p. 14.

Soto, Juan
Ripple, Samuel. "Juan Soto: He Murdered With His Bare Hands." *Westerner,* Jan.-Feb. 1973, p. 32.

Spalding, Henry H. (and Eliza)
Lavender, David. "Sky of Brass, Earth of Iron." Rpt. *Old West,* Fall 1966, p. 2.
Pratt, Grace Raffey. "Black Robes and Circuit Riders." *Old West,* Fall 1972, p. 28.

Sparks, Elijah "Lige"
Sparks, John E. "Lige Sparks, Texas Deputy." *True West,* July 1988, p. 40.

Speed, Richard "Dick"
Koller, Joe. "Bloody Ingalls Under Siege." *Western Frontier,* July 1976, p. 6.

Spencer, Pete M. (Pete Spence, real name Elliot Larkin Ferguson, "Lark")
Parsons, Chuck. "Little Known Badman" ("Answer Man" column). *True West,* May 1989, p. 11.
Winslowe, John R. "Murdering Outlaw's Revenge." *Westerner,* May-June 1969, p. 29. Rpt. *Westerner,* July-Aug. 1974, p. 26.

Spencer, Ethan Allen "Al"
Shoemaker, Arthur. "Al Spencer: Transition Outlaw." *True West,* March 1987, p. 24.

Spiers, William H. "Bill"
Chegwyn, Michael. "Finest Kind." *Old West,* Summer 1991, p. 21.

Spikes, John Wesley

Bedingfield, John "Dub." "The Spikes-Gholson Feud." *Real West,* Dec. 1985, p. 18. Rpt. *Real West,* Annual, Summer 1986, p. 24.

Splitlog, Matthias

Brewington, E.H. "Phantom Message From Cayuga Springs." *True West,* Dec. 1968, p. 22.

Nieberding, Velma. "Matthias Splitlog's Salted Mine." *The West,* July 1965, p. 22. Rpt. *The West,* Dec. 1971, p. 33.

Walker, Wayne T. "Matthias Splitlog: Millionaire Indian." *Pioneer West,* Feb. 1972, p. 9. Rpt. *Pioneer West,* June 1975, p. 8.

Spotted Tail

Spencer, G. "Murder Among the Sioux." *Real West,* Jan. 1988, p. 18.

Swanson, Budington. "How Little Big Man Tried to Save the Black Hills." *Western Frontier,* Special Issue, March 1975, p. 34.

Spradley, A. John.

Lansdale, Joe R. "Piney Woods Lawman." *Frontier Times,* Jan. 1978, p. 20.

Spurgeon, Elizabeth "Lizzie," "Cock-Eyed Liz"

Cheney, Louise. "The Madam Who Switched." *Great West,* Feb. 1969, p. 18.

Spurrier, John Ray

Henderson, Sam. "The Incredible Saga of the West's Worst Badman Who Wasn't What He Seemed." *Frontier West,* June 1974, p. 28.

"Squirrel Tooth" Alice

Bird, Roy. "'Squirrel Tooth' Alice, or the Sporting Women of Dodge City." *Real West,* Feb. 1984, p. 26. Rpt. *Real West,* Annual, Spring 1985, p. 62.

Standifer, William "Billy"

Dodge, Matt. "Shootout in Standifer Thicket." *Oldtimers Wild West,* Dec. 1978, p. 20.

DeArment, R.K. "The Protection Man." *Old West,* Spring 1991, p. 20.

Standing Bear

Holding, Vera. "Standing Bear's Contribution to Justice for All American Indians." *True Frontier,* Sept. 1973, p. 29.

Neill, Wilfred T. "The Bloodless War of Chief Standing Bear." *The West,* Feb. 1969, p. 38.

Uhlarick, Carl. "Standing Bear: Eloquent Advocate." *Real Frontier,* Aug. 1971, p. 26.

Stanley, David

Stanley, Samuel. "General David Stanley: Frontier Soldier." *Real West,* Year-book, Summer 1978, p. 56.

Stanley, Richard "Dick"

Carlson, Chip. "An Outlaw on Outlaw Horses." *True West,* July 1991, p. 23.

Stanton, Charles

Barkdull, Tom. "The Defrocked Tyrant-Priest of Antelope Station." *Big West,* Feb. 1968, p. 38.

_____. "Stanton's Most Notorious Citizen." *The West,* Dec. 1966, p. 22.

Kutac, C. "The Curse of Stanton." *True West,* July 1981, p. 25.

Staples, Joseph M.

Archer, Myrtle. "California Stagecoach Skirmish." *True West,* May 1988, p. 44.

Starr, Belle

Boswell, Charles. "Belle of the Six-Gun." *True Western Adventures,* Aug. 1961, p. 16.

Breihan, Carl W. "Belle Starr: Oklahoma Whirlwind." *The West,* March 1967, p. 30. Rpt. *The West,* Aug. 1972, p. 28; and *Western Frontier,* July 1977, p. 28.

Breshears, Claudia. "The Outlaw Was a Lady." *Big West,* Aug. 1967, p. 22.

Brown, Florence V. "The Legend of Belle Starr, Courtesan." *Great West,* April 1967, p. 26.

Denton, Cyclone. "I Danced With Belle Starr." *True West,* Aug. 1970, p. 18.

Flynn, Claire. "The Children of Belle Starr." *True Frontier,* Aug. 1975, p. 6. Rpt. *True Frontier,* Oct. 1977, p. 30.

Hardcastle, Stoney. "Belle Starr's Piano." *True West,* June 1977, p. 22.

Helms, Jo Rheta Shirley. Letter. *True West,* June 1969, p. 4.

Holding, Vera. "Belle Starr: Queen Bandit." *True Frontier,* Nov. 1969, p. 20. Rpt. *True Frontier,* Dec. 1972, p. 12; and *True Frontier,* Special Issue No. 9, Summer 1974, p. 10.

Kilpatrick, Jack F. "Belle Starr's Medicine Man Boyfriend." *Real West,* March 1967, p. 38.

Mason, John. "Belle Starr, Bandit Queen." *Real West,* Annual, Summer 1966, p. 22.

_____. "Belle Starr, Sister of Sin." *Real West,* Feb. 1959, p. 38.

Mooney, C.W. "Belle Starr As Her Doctor Knew Her." *True Frontier,* April 1973, p. 12. Rpt. *True Frontier,* April 1976, p. 38.

_____. "Belle Starr's Killer Revealed." *True West,* Feb. 1969, p. 12.

_____. "The Secret Belle Starr Took to Her Grave." *Western Frontier,* Annual No. 1, 1975, p. 6.

Nieberding, Velma, and Harold Preece. "The West's Outlaws Found No Peace Even in Death." *Frontier West,* Dec. 1971, p. 42.

Qualey, J.S. "The Legend of Belle Starr: Outlaw Queen." *Real West,* Special Issue, Fall 1964, p. 34.

Repp, Ed Earl. "Belle Starr Saved My Life." *Real West,* Feb. 1970, p. 23.

_____. "Gun-Toting Female Killer." *Pioneer West,* April 1971, p. 36. Rpt. *Oldtimers Wild West,* Aug. 1973, p. 46; and *Pioneer West,* July 1976, p. 16.

Shirley, Glenn. "How Belle Starr Got to Be a 'Desperate Woman.'" *True West,* Sept. 1982, p. 10.

_____. "Outlaw Queen." *Old West,* Spring 1965, p. 26. Rpt. *Badman,* Summer 1971, p. 8.

Steele, Phillip W. "Belle Starr Museum Dedicated." *True West,* Nov. 1991, p. 9.

Towns, Leroy. "Was Belle Starr Killed by Mistake?" *True West,* April 1971, p. 20.

Walker, Wayne T. "To Hell in a Tumble Weed Wagon." *Oldtimers Wild West,* Oct. 1979, p. 22.

Starr, Henry

Allen, F.M. Letter. *True West,* Dec. 1956, p. 46.

Black, J. Dickson. "The Day Henry Starr Robbed Our Bank." *Frontier Times,* Summer 1962, p. 20.

Breihan, Carl W. "Close the Banks, Henry Starr's Coming." *Westerner,* June 1971, p. 36.

_____. "Henry Starr: Bank Robber Extraordinary." *The West,* Jan. 1968, p. 10. Rpt. *Golden West,* Dec. 1972, p. 10; *Western Frontier,* Sept. 1975, p. 44; and *Western Frontier,* Nov. 1982, p. 10.

_____. "The Incredible Career of 'Bearcat' Starr." *Oldtimers Wild West,* Dec. 1977, p. 23.

_____. "King of the Bank Robbers." *Frontier Times,* May 1964, p. 24.

DeMattos, Jack. "Henry Starr" ("Gunfighters of the Real West" column). *Real*

West, June 1982, p. 38. Rpt. *Real West,* Yearbook, Fall 1983, p. 32.

Hinkle, Milt. "Henry Starr and the Rough Ones." *The West,* May 1966, p. 12. Rpt. *Golden West,* March 1974, p. 10; *Western Frontier,* Annual 1977, p. 22; and *Western Frontier,* Feb. 1985, p. 34.

Hurst, Irvin. "Robbingest Robber." *Frontier Times,* Spring 1960, p. 16.

Mason, John. "The Miracle Bank Robber." *Real West,* Feb. 1959, p. 34.

Proctor, Charles. Letter. *True West,* Feb. 1981, p. 6.

Raymond, Jack. "Henry Starr: The Articulate Bandit." *Great West,* May 1968, p. 24.

Scott, Jay. "Henry Starr: Natural Born Bank Robber." *True Western Adventures,* Dec. 1960, p. 17.

Shirley, Glenn. "He Outrobbed Them All." *True West,* Dec. 1955, p. 16. Rpt. *Badman,* Fall 1972, p. 28.

————. "Train Robbery That Fizzled." *Old West,* Winter 1986, p. 12.

Sufrin, Mark. "Half Genius, Half Madman: The Saga of the Wildest Gunslinger of Them All." *Frontier West,* Dec. 1971, p. 8.

Walker, Wayne T. "The King of the Bank Robbers." *Real Frontier,* June 1971, p. 8. Rpt. *True Frontier,* Special Issue No. 13, 1975, p. 32.

Starr, Rose Pearl (Pearl Younger, Pearl Reed)
Kelly, Bill. "Pearl Younger and the Falling Starrs." *Real West,* Nov. 1976, p. 36.

Starr, Sam
Bruner, James. "Gunfighters and Lawmen" column. *Wild West,* Oct. 1989, p. 8.

Starr, Tom
Eagles, Don. "Bill West's Head." *Real West,* May 1961, p. 15.

Thrasher, Helen Starr. "The Blood of a Hundred Men!" *True West,* June 1972, p. 22.

St. Helen, John
McKee, S.J. "Who Was John St. Helen?" *Real West,* April 1987, p. 20.

Steele, James H. (real name John B. Goodwin)
Kildare, Maurice. "The Kibbe-Hillpot Murders." *Real West,* Feb. 1970, p. 28.

Stephens, Jarvis "Red"
Holmes, Lee. "Red Stephens Was the Most Unlikely Horse Thief of Them All." *Frontier West,* April 1972, p. 34.

Steptoe, Edward J.
Ballard, David M. "War of Extermination Backfired." *Wild West,* June 1989, p. 43.
Price, Will. "Battle on the Ingossomen." *Frontier Times,* Fall 1958, p. 12.
Ryker, Lois. "Spokan Garry: Peaceful Indian Chief of the Northwest." *Real West,* Feb. 1974, p . 24.

Sternberg, Sigismund
Bundy, Rex. "Sigismund Sternberg: Professional Soldier." *Real West,* April 1972, p. 15. Rpt. *Real West,* Annual, Summer 1973, p. 58.

Stevens, Isaac Ingall "Ike'
Koller, Joe. "Ike Stevens: Rambunctious Governor." *The West,* March 1974, p. 30.

Stewart, Henri
Wilson, Roger. "Owlhoot Medico." *Great West,* Dec. 1973, p. 28. Rpt. *Authentic West,* Spring 1981, p. 28.

Stewart, William
Kildare, Maurice. "The Kibbe-Hillpot Murders." *Real West,* Feb. 1970, p. 28.

Stewart, William Drummond
Arthur, Alton. "Personality" column. *Wild West,* June 1988, p. 10.

Stewart, William Morris "Bill"
Koller, Joe. "Bill Stewart, Nevada's Silver Chief." *Golden West,* May 1969, p. 12.

Stiles, William "Billy" (of Arizona)
Hartley, William B. "Turncoat From Tombstone." *True Western Adventures,* Nov. 1959, p. 30.
Repp, Ed Earl. "Loot the Village, Kill the Males." *True Frontier,* Nov. 1969, p. 38. Rpt. *True Frontier,* Special Issue No. 5, 1973, p. 38.

Stiles, William "Billy," "Bill Chadwell" (of Missouri)
Repp, Ed Earl. "Last of the Oldtime Outlaws." *True Frontier,* Special Issue No. 17, Winter 1976, p. 6.
Stiles, Bill. "I Was Hanged by Jesse James." *The West,* Nov. 1973, p. 34.
_____. "I Was the Last of the James Gang." *True Frontier,* June 1972, p. 18.

Stillwell, Frank
Parsons, Chuck. "Answer Man" column. *True West,* Oct. 1983, p. 43.

Stillwell, Simpson Everett "Comanche Jack"
Harrison, Fred. "Comanche Jack Stillwell: Hero of the Arikaree." *True Frontier,* Jan. 1970, p. 16. Rpt. *True Frontier,* Oct. 1974, p. 33; and *True Frontier,* Oct. 1977, p. 33.

Turpin, Robert F. "Comanche Jack Stillwell" ("Nuggets" column). *Frontier Times,* Jan. 1977, p. 41.

Walker, Wayne T. "Fighting Army Scouts of the Indian Wars." *Great West,* June 1972, p. 14. Rpt. *Authentic West,* Fall 1981, p. 16.

Stinson, Joseph "Joe"
Holben, Richard E. "Badman Saloonkeeper." *Pioneer West,* Feb. 1972, p. 14. Rpt. *Pioneer West,* June 1975, p. 14; and *Oldtimers Wild West,* Oct. 1979, p. 40.

St. John, Silas.
Boyer, Glenn G. "The Murders at Dragoon Springs." *Real West,* Feb. 1983, p. 25; and *Real West,* Annual, Spring 1984, p. 28.

Lebec, Ralph. "Mercy Express to Dragoon Springs." *True West,* Aug. 1970, p. 8.

Stockton Brothers (Ike and Port)
Holben, Dick. "The Vengeance Vendetta of the Stockton Terror." *Frontier West,* Aug. 1973, p. 26.

Jones, Calico. "New Mexico's Stockton Gang." *Real West,* July 1973, p. 38.

Stockton, Ike
Holben, Richard E. "Ike Stockton's Revenge." *Westerner,* March 1971, p. 44.

Johnson, Fred M. "Gunman of Durango." *True West,* May 1984, p. 54.

Stockton, Porter "Port"
Hawk, G.K. "He Lived by the Sword." *Western Frontier,* Special Issue, Fall 1974, p. 3. Rpt. *Western Frontier,* Jan. 1978, p. 44.

Rasch, Philip J. "Sudden Death in Cimarron." *NOLA Quarterly,* Vol. X, No. 4, Spring 1986, p. 7.

Stockton, Robert F.
Kells, Robert E., Jr. "Farthest Western Victory." *Wild West,* Aug. 1988, p. 18.

Stokes, Elta
Edwards, Harold L. "No Monument for Elta Stokes." *Real West,* Feb. 1987, p. 37.

Stokes, Joe
Secrest, William B. "Fast Guns in Old California." *Real West,* June 1980, p. 10.

Shirley, Glenn. "Monument to a Badman." *Old Trails,* Winter 1977, p. 40.

Stoner, Clarence A.
Stoner, Mary E. "My Father Was a Train Robber." *True West,* Aug. 1983, p. 14.

Story Brothers (Eugene and Brooks)
O'Dell, Roy. "A Story of Crime: The Notorious Story Brothers." *NOLA Quarterly,* Vol. XI, No. 2, Summer 1986, p. 12.

Story, Nelson
Beardsley, J.L. "Nelson Story Out-Fought Crazy Horse." *The West,* April 1970, p. 34. Rpt. *The West,* April 1974, p. 28.

Harrison, John. "Montana's Horse Thief War." *Great West,* Oct. 1973, p . 16.

Hart, Ernest H. "First Trail Drive to Montana Territory." *Real West,* Oct. 1974, p. 22.

Koller, Joe. "Nelson Story Was Montana's First Drover." *Golden West,* July 1965, p. 20. Rpt. *Golden West,* Aug. 1974, p. 40.

Pinkerton, Robert E. "Nelson Story Was a Fighting Man." *True Western Adventures,* June 1959, p. 12.

Shirley, Glenn. "Nelson Story and His Cattle Drive Through Hell." *Real West,* Aug. 1969, p. 32.

Wiltsey, Norman B. "Mean As Hell, Tough As Rawhide." *Real West,* Jan. 1975, p. 44.

Stott, James "Jim"
Kildare, Maurice. "Take a Walk to Doom." *Real West,* April 1970, p. 38.

Wilkes, Homer. "The Stott Hangings" ("Nuggets" column). *Frontier Times,* May 1964, p. 70.

Stoudenmire, Dallas
Barstow, Bob. "The Patch-Pocket Marshal Took to Drink." *America's Frontier West,* Issue No. 1, n.d., p. 42.

Bristow, Bob. "Patch Pocket Gunman." *True Western Adventures,* April 1959, p. 8.

Cunningham, Eugene. "Two-Gun Marshal." *Old West,* Winter 1965, p. 40. Rpt. *Badman,* Annual 1971, p. 42.

DeMattos, Jack. "Dallas Stoudenmire" ("Gunfighters of the Real West" column). *Real West,* April 1982, p. 32.

Dial, Scott. "Dallas Stoudenmire and the El Paso Saloon War." *Westerner,* Spring 1975, p. 26.

Metz, Leon C. "Four Dead in Ten Seconds." *Real West,* Nov. 1972, p. 32. Rpt. *Real West,* Annual, Summer 1973, p. 46.

_____. "The Death of Dallas Stoudenmire." *Real West,* Feb. 1973, p. 38.

Nolen, Oran Warder. "Gunfire In El Paso." *True Frontier,* Jan. 1969, p. 42.

O'Neal, Bill. "Dallas Stoudenmire in El Paso" ("Great Western Gunfights" column). *True West,* April 1988, p. 58.

Rosson, Mary'n. "How the Three-Gun Marshal Brought Law and Order to El Paso." *Frontier West,* Jan. 1976, p. 22.

Shirley, Glenn. "Death in His Hip Pockets." *The West,* Aug. 1967, p. 26. Rpt. *The West,* Oct. 1971, p. 30; and *Western Frontier,* Annual, Summer 1979, p. 30.

Wolfgang, Otto. "Hell Town of Texas." *Pioneer West,* May 1969, p. 54. Rpt. *Pioneer West,* Collector's Annual 1971, p. 4; *Pioneer West,* July 1973, p. 36; *Pioneer West,* Jan. 1976, p. 50; and *Oldtimers Wild West,* June 1976, p. 50.

Stuart, Granville

Abbott, Mary Stuart. "Child of the Open Range." *Frontier Times,* Jan. 1964, p. 20.

Clark, Helen. "Mr. Montana." *Pioneer West,* Jan. 1970, p. 24. Rpt. *Pioneer West,* July 1973, p. 38; and *Pioneer West,* Bicentennial Souvenir Edition, 1976, p. 37.

Harrison, John. "Montana's Horse Thief War." *Great West,* Oct. 1973, p. 16. Rpt. *Authentic West,* Spring 1981, p. 50.

McCray, E. Ward. "Stuart's Stranglers." *True Western Adventures,* Feb. 1961, p. 10.

Morando, B. "Montana's Stranglers." *Real West,* July 1974, p. 36.

Studebaker, John Mohler

Hill, Carson. "Hangtown Blacksmith to Auto King: The Studebaker Story." *True Frontier,* Jan. 1970, p. 29.

Rosenhouse, Leo. "Wheelbarrow Johnny." *Great West,* Dec. 1968, p. 38. Rpt. *Pioneer West,* Nov. 1972, p. 20; *Pioneer West,* Jan. 1976, p. 42; and *Oldtimers Wild West,* June 1976, p. 6.

Thomas, Diane. "John Studebaker: Wagon Maker, Gold Camp Worker, and Motorcar Magnate." *Real West,* Annual, Winter 1977-78, p. 66.

St. Vrain, Ceran

Densmore, Lee. "The One Man Bushwhack of Ceran St. Vrain." *Frontier West,* Oct. 1971, p. 18.

Sublette, Milton

Franks, George. "Milton Sublette: Thunderbolt of the Rockies." *The West,* May 1965, p. 14.

Sublette, Pinckney W.

Spring, Agnes Wright. "The Bones of Pinckney W. Sublette." *True West,* Oct. 1972, p. 63.

Sughrue Brothers, Michael and Patrick

Snell, Joseph W. "Sheriffs Pat and Mike Sughrue." *Frontier Times,* Jan. 1976, p. 8.

Walker, Wayne T. "Pat and Mike Sughrue: Double Trouble for Lawbreakers." *Real West,* Feb. 1983, p. 9. Rpt. *Real West,* Yearbook, Fall 1983, p. 14.

_____. "The Twin Sheriffs of Western Kansas." *The West,* April 1969, p. 28. Rpt. *Golden West,* April 1973, p. 28; and *Western Frontier,* Annual No. 2, 1976, p. 6.

Sullivan, W.J.

Sullivan, W.J.L. "Twelve Years in the Saddle for Law and Order on the Frontiers of Texas." Rpt. *Old West,* Spring 1967, p. 57.

Sully, Alfred

Czech, Kenneth P. "High Plains Rebellion Rekindled." *Wild West,* June 1990, p. 27.

Eagen, William. "General Sully and That Other Seventh Cavalry." *True West,* Sept. 1990, p. 30.

Young, Jan. "General Sully's Strange Indian Campaign." Part I, *The West,* March 1965, p. 36; Part II, *The West,* April 1965, p. 42 Rpt. as one-part article *Western Frontier,* Sept. 1979, p. 6.

Sumner, Edwin V.

James, Louise Boyd. "Classic Confrontation on the Soloman." *True West,* March 1986, p. 40.

"Sundance Kid" (see Longabaugh, Harry)

Sunday, Jesse

Kildare, Maurice. "The Senseless Killing of Sheriff Sunday." *Real West*, May 1971, p. 28.

Walker, Wayne T. "Gunsmoke at the Courthouse." *Golden West*, Aug. 1974, p. 22.

Sutro, Adolph

Martin, Cy. "Crazy Sutro and His Tunnel That Went Up To Hell." *Westerner*, July-Aug. 1970, p. 46.

————. "Sutro's 'Coyote Hole' to the Comstock." *Golden West*, March 1965, p. 30. Rpt. *The West*, April 1972, p. 40.

Sutter, Johann Augustus, Jr.

Barrows, Wray. "A Gold Watch: Sutter's Legacy." *The West*, July 1971, p. 10. Rpt. *Western Frontier*, Feb. 1984, p. 6.

Holyer, Ernie. "Sins of the Father." *True West*, July 1982, p. 42.

Young, Bob. "The Tragic Riddle of Sutter's Gold." *Real West*, Sept. 1965, p. 54.

Sutter, John Augustus, Sr.

Barrows, Wray. "A Gold Watch: Sutter's Legacy." *The West*, July 1971, p. 10. Rpt. *Western Frontier*, Feb. 1984, p. 6.

Bloom, Sam. "John Sutter Was a Born Loser." *Frontier West*, Dec. 1972, p. 36.

Jones, George E. "Under the Heel of the Argonauts." *Frontier Times*, Dec.-Jan. 1963, p. 6.

Peterson, Richard. "John Sutter and the California Indians." *True West*, Feb. 1991, p. 42.

Rosenhouse, Leo. "El Dorado at the Sawmill." *Pioneer West*, April 1970, p. 16. Rpt. *Pioneer West*, Aug. 1972, p. 40; and *Pioneer West*, June 1974, p. 28.

Unger, Abraham. "Personality" column. *Wild West*, June 1989, p. 10.

Young, Bob. "The Tragic Riddle of Sutter's Gold." *Real West*, Sept. 1965, p. 54.

Sutton Clan

Browning, Dwain. "Texas' Bloody Taylor-Sutton Feud." *The West*, June 1969, p. 10.

Nolen, Oran Warder. "The Most Murderous Feud in Texas History." *True Frontier*, Sept. 1969, p. 14. Rpt. *True Frontier*, June 1976, p. 22.

Parsons, Chuck. "Treaties of Peace, Acts of War." *Real West*, Yearbook, Fall 1982, p. 50.

Sutton, Raymond, Sr., "Ray"
Hornung, Chuck. "The Mystery Death of Federal Prohibition Officer Ray Sutton." *NOLA Quarterly,* Vol. XV, No. 2, April-June 1991, p. 3.

Sutton, William "Bill"
Parsons, Chuck. "Bill Sutton Avenged: The Death of Jim Taylor." *NOLA Quarterly,* Vol. IV, No. 3, March 1979, p. 3.

Swain, John (Southwest cowboy)
Bentz, Donald N. "John Swain and Tombstone's Boothill." *Frontier Times,* Nov. 1975, p. 24.

Swain, John (Deputy U.S. Marshal)
Holding, Vera, and Bill Burchardt. "The 'Dead or Alive' Marshal." *Wild West,* Sept. 1971, p. 16.

Swazer, Sam
Leyden, Gary. "The Law Made Sam a Bad Man." *Frontier West,* April 1975, p. 22.

Swenson, Jack.
McBee, Fred. "The Gunslingers." *Great West,* Oct. 1972, p. 8.

Swenson, S.M.
Wallis, George A. "Cattle Kings." Part I, *True West,* April 1964, p. 8.

Swilling, Jack
Barkdull, Tom. "Gillette's Most Legendary Citizen." *Frontier Times,* May 1966, p. 30.
Olson, James R. "Jack Swilling: Father of the Salt Water." *True Frontier,* March 1970, p. 36. Rpt. *True Frontier,* Aug. 1976, p. 26.
West, Elliott. "The Impossible Jack Swilling." *The West,* Dec. 1966, p. 25.

Swingle, G.S. "Kid" ("Montana Kid," Claude Preston, C.W. Johnson)
Rasch, Philip J. "Kid Swingle: A Forgotten Highwayman." *NOLA Quarterly,* Vol. IX, No. 3, Winter 1985, p. 6.

Tabor, Elizabeth McCourt "Baby Doe"

Auer, Louise. "Colorado Remembers Baby Doe." *The West,* June 1966, p. 30. Rpt. *Western Frontier,* May 1980, p. 30.

Durning, Albert L. "A Ton of Coal for Baby Doe." *True West,* April 1970, p. 12.

Mac, 'Tana. "The Belle From Oshkosh." *Wild West,* Oct. 1969, p. 12. Rpt. *Pioneer West,* Dec. 1974, p. 10; and *Pioneer West,* Sept. 1976, p. 29.

McDearmon, Kay. "Silver Queen." *True West,* April 1959, p. 18. Rpt. *Frontier Times,* Spring 1962, p. 9.

Tabor, Horace A.W.

Auer, Louise. "Colorado Remembers Baby Doe." *The West,* June 1966, p. 30. Rpt. *Western Frontier,* May 1980, p. 30.

Cheney, Louise. "The Fourteen-Karat Loves of a Silver King." *The West,* Oct. 1970, p. 16. Rpt. *The West,* Oct. 1973, p. 38, and *Western Frontier,* Nov. 1976, p. 26.

Freeman, Frank M. "With Egg on His Chin." *Real West,* Feb. 1983, p. 44. Rpt. *Real West,* Special Issue, Spring 1985, p. 26.

Mabry, Charles. "Silver King." *Frontier Times,* Spring 1962, p. 6.

Mac, 'Tana. "The Belle From Oshkosh." *Wild West,* Oct. 1969, p. 12. Rpt. *Pioneer West,* Dec. 1974, p. 10; and *Pioneer West,* Sept. 1976, p. 29.

Secrest, Clark. "HAW Tabor's Silver Touch." *Real West,* Sept. 1966, p. 39.

Shulsinger, Stephanie Cooper. "Horace Tabor: The Silver King With Two Queens." *Real West,* March 1971, p. 27.

Sooner, Paul. "Crazy Tabor and His Silver Tunnel." *Westerner,* May-June 1973, p. 50.

Tabor, Rose Mary Echo Honeymoon "Silver Dollar"

Pharo, Agnes M. "Silver Princess." *Frontier Times,* Spring 1962, p. 11.

Tachee

Walker, Wayne T. "Cherokee Warhawk." *Great West,* Oct. 1973, p. 6.

Talbot, James "Jim"

DeArment, R.K. "Toughest Cow Outfit in Texas." Part II, *True West,* May 1991, p. 22.

Talbotte, Henry J. "Cherokee Bob"
Corless, Hank. "Cherokee Bob's Last Gunfight." *Old West,* Spring 1988, p. 26.

Peltier, Jerome. "Gold Camp Ruffian." *Frontier Times,* Nov. 1964, p. 28.

Timmen, Fritz. "Deadly Belle of the Ball." *True Frontier,* May 1970, p. 36. Rpt. *True Frontier,* April 1975, p. 40.

Tall Bull
Beardsley, J.L. "The Fight at Fossil Creek." *Western Frontier,* Special Issue, Summer 1974, p. 16.

James, Stuart. "Death of a Dog Soldier." *Real West,* Oct. 1957, p. 10.

Tascosa Gunfighters
Bundy, Rex. "Tascosa: Notorious Town of the Texas Panhandle." *Real West,* Oct. 1971, p. 25.

Kildare, Maurice. "The Gut Fighters Who Made 'Hell Town' the Bloodiest Place in Texas." *Frontier West,* Dec. 1972, p. 28.

Tattenbaum, William "Russian Bill"
Cheney, Louise. "Russian Bill: Aspiring Badman." *The West,* Nov. 1968, p. 36. Rpt. *Golden West,* June 1972, p. 18; and *Western Frontier,* July 1977, p. 38.

Gray, Morton. "Russian Bill." *Western Tales,* April 1960, p. 18.

Howe, Ted. "The Counterfeit Gunman of Tombstone." *Frontier Times,* Summer 1958, p. 24. Rpt. *Old West,* Winter 1978, p. 14.

Rasch, Philip J. "AKA Russian Bill." *Los Angeles Westerners Brand Book,* No. 86, March 1968, p. 12.

Youngs, C. Daniel. "The Strange Case of Russian Bill." *Real West,* Aug. 1958, p. 22.

Tatum, Lawrie
Grove, Fred. "Quaker Agent to the Kiowas." *The West,* March 1974, p. 42.

Taylor Clan
Browning, Dwain. "Texas' Bloody Taylor-Sutton Feud." *The West,* June 1969, p. 10. Rpt. *Western Frontier,* July 1983, p. 8.

Nolen, Oran Warder. "The Most Murderous Feud in Texas History." *True Frontier,* Sept. 1969, p. 14. Rpt. *True Frontier,* June 1976, p. 22.

Parsons, Chuck. "Treaties of Peace, Acts of War." *Real West,* Yearbook, Fall 1982, p. 50.

Taylor, Garrett
Taylor, Paul. "Visions of Wealth." *True West*, Sept. 1989, p. 42.

Taylor, James "Jim"
Parsons, Chuck. "Bill Sutton Avenged: The Death of Jim Taylor." *NOLA Quarterly*, Vol. IV, No. 3, March 1979, p. 3.

Taylor, John Henry
Parsons, Chuck. "Destroying the Hardin Gang." *NOLA Quarterly*, Vol. V, No. 4, April 1980, p. 1.

Taylor, Tillman D. "Till"
Patch, Charles C. "Bars Instead of Bullets." *Old West*, Spring 1969, p. 22.

Temple, Sam
Ramsey, A.L. "Sam Temple, the Villain Who Wanted to Be a Hero." *Real West*, Nov. 1967, p. 31.

Tempter, Matt
Kildare, Maurice. "Pedro's Lost Silver." *Oldtimers Wild West*, Aug. 1975, p. 14.

Tendoy
Kimball, Ethel. "Red Friends, White Graves." *The West*, Sept. 1968, p. 10. Rpt. *Golden West*, Jan. 1974, p. 28.

————. "Tendoy: The Indian Chief Who Fought for Peace." Part I, *Real West*, March 1969, p. 16; Part II, *Real West*, April 1969, p. 44.

Lashbrook, Mary Pease. "Chief Tendoy and His Band." *True West*, April 1962, p. 20.

Tennille, George Culver
Parsons, Chuck. "Doc Bockius Survived Civil War, Texas Feud." *NOLA Quarterly*, Vol. II, No. 4, Fall 1976, p. 9.

————. "Forgotten Feudist." *Frontier Times*, Jan. 1976, p. 28.

Ten Sleep Assassins
Bryan, LaMar. "Nowood's Night Riders." *Wild West*, Dec. 1990, p. 19.

Terry, Alfred
Swanson, Budington. "How Little Big Man Tried to Save the Black Hills." *Western Frontier*, Special Issue, March 1975, p. 34.

Terry, David Smith

Cox, Dick. "Duel At Dawn." *Real West*, Nov. 1968, p. 23.

Freeman, Frank M. "The Case of the Two Imperious Men." *Golden West*, Sept. 1968, p. 34.

McGuckin, Andrew J. "San Francisco's Vigilantes versus the U.S. Navy." *The West*, Oct. 1974, p. 28.

Malsbary, George. "Guns, Gold and Politics." *Great West*, April 1973, p. 28.

Peterson, Marc. "California's Wildest Judge." *Frontier Times*, May 1964, p. 45.

Phipps, B.L. "The Last Great Duel." *Frontier Times*, Dec.-Jan. 1963, p. 44.

Rosenhouse, Leo. "The Duel That Rocked the Gold Coast." *Frontier West*, Oct. 1971, p. 30.

————. "The Duel That Rocked the West." *True Frontier*, Oct. 1976, p. 16.

Ross, David R. "California's Gun-Toting Chief Justice." *Old West*, Summer 1989, p. 48.

Von Kreisler, Max. "Death in the Morning." *True Frontier*, July 1971, p. 8.

Young, Bob. "Terry, the Terrible." *Real West*, May 1961, p. 42.

Young, Jan. "Sharon's Rose of Death." *Real West*, March 1963, p. 32.

Tevis, James H.

Tevis, James H. "Arizona in the Fifties." Part I, *True West*, June 1968, p. 6; Part II, *True West*, Aug. 1968, p. 6.

Tewksbury Clan

Breihan, Carl W. "Death in Pleasant Valley." *The West*, Feb. 1970, p. 14.

Bruce, John. "When Death Came to Tonto Basin." *Real West*, Nov. 1960, p. 38.

Combs, Richard. "War in the Tonto." *Real West*, Oct. 1986, p. 5.

Forrest, Earle R. "The Old West's Bloodiest Feud." *NOLA Quarterly*, Vol. IX, No. 2, Autumn 1984, p. 1.

Guttman, Jon. "Unpleasant Valley War." *Wild West*, Oct. 1990, p. 19.

Kildare, Maurice. "Cabin Bushwhack." *Real West*, Jan. 1969, p. 17.

————. "The Horrible Graham-Tewksbury Feud." *Real West*, Nov. 1967, p. 14.

Millard, Joseph. "Valley of Blood." *True Western Adventures*, Dec. 1959, p. 8.

O'Neal, Bill. "Graham War Party vs Tewksburys" ("Great Western Gunfights" column). *True West*, May 1990, p. 54.

Peterson, Marc. "The Tonto Basin War." *Old West*, Summer 1965, p. 38.

Smith, Richard C. "Arizona's Bloodiest Feud." *Pioneer West*, May 1968, p. 20.

Stanley, Samuel. "The Pleasant Valley War in Arizona." *Oldtimers Wild West,* Aug. 1977, p. 23.

Texas Rangers
Chambers, Howard V. "The Texas Rangers." *Pioneer West,* Aug. 1972, p. 14.

Mendell, Ann. "The Texas Rangers." *Great West,* July 1969, p. 6.

Preston, N.E. "The Texian Devils." *Great West,* Dec. 1969, p. 42.

Thacker, Jonathan N. "John"
Boessenecker, John. "John Thacker: Train Robbers' Nemesis." *Real West,* Sept. 1976, p. 14.

Thomas, Henry Andrew "Heck"
DeMattos, Jack. "Heck Thomas" ("Gunfighters of the Real West" column). *Real West,* Jan. 1980, p. 16.

Lehman, M.P. "Terror of the Territorial Outlaws." *Golden West,* Jan. 1966, p. 42. Rpt. *The West,* March 1972, p. 34; and *Western Frontier,* May 1980, p. 46.

Millard, J M. "Heck Thomas: Lawman Who Tamed the 'Most Wanted.'" *True Frontier,* Sept. 1969, p. 8.

O'Neal, Bill. "Bill Doolin vs Heck Thomas" ("Great Western Gunfights" column). *True West,* Sept. 1991, p. 60.

Parsons, Chuck. "The Three Guardsmen" ("Answer Man" column). *True West,* March 1990, p. 12.

Shirley, Glenn. "How Heck Thomas Outwitted Sam Bass." *Real West,* Sept 1968, p. 42.

Smith, Robert Barr. "No God West of Fort Smith." *Wild West,* Oct. 1991, p. 46.

Thomas, Lovick O. Letter. *Real West,* Jan. 1964, p. 76.

Turpin, Robert F. "Wanted Dead or Alive: The Lee Brothers." *Great West,* Feb. 1970, p. 12.

Upchurch, C. Winn. "Heck Thomas Started Fighting At Age Twelve." *True West,* Oct. 1980, p. 17.

Thompson, Benjamin "Ben"
"Ben Thompson: The Gambling Gunslinger." *Great West,* Aug. 1971, p. 24.

"Ben Thompson: The Silk Hat Six Shooter." *Gunslingers of the West,* Winter 1966, p. 14.

Breihan, Carl W. "Ben Thompson: The Reluctant Killer." *Golden West,* Nov. 1969, p. 30. Rpt. *The West,* July 1973, p. 16; and *Western Frontier,* May 1986, p. 16.

_____. "The Day King Fisher and Ben Thompson Were Killed." *Oldtimers Wild West,* April 1977, p. 6.

Burkholder, Edwin V. "King of the Gamblers." *True Western Adventures,* Oct. 1959, p. 32.

DeMattos, Jack. "Ben Thompson." *Real West,* Annual, Summer 1986, p. 38.

_____. "Ben Thompson" ("Gunfighters of the Real West" column). *Real West,* Oct. 1985, p. 32.

"From Marshal to Gambler." *Great West,* Sept. 1967, p. 8.

"Gunslinger From Texas: Ben Thompson." *Great West,* Dec. 1969, p. 26. Rpt. *Great West,* Feb. 1973, p. 35.

Harrison, Fred. "San Antonio's Greatest Murder Enigma." *Golden West,* May 1965, p. 34. Rpt. *Golden West,* Oct. 1972, p. 32.

Heath, Charles G. "The Thompsons of Knottingly." *NOLA Quarterly,* Vol. XIV, No. 1, 1990, p. 4.

Hunter, J. Marvin. "Ben Thompson: Killer of Men." *Frontier Times,* Nov. 1978, p. 10.

Lafferty, Jack. "The Fabulous Ben Thompson." *True West,* Oct. 1959, p. 22.

Malocsay, Zoltan. "Five Cards and Six-Shooter." *Westerner,* March-April 1970, p. 38. Rpt. *Old Trails,* Spring 1978, p. 16.

Norman, Robert. "The Deadly Gun of Ben Thompson." *True Frontier,* Nov. 1968, p. 45. Rpt. *True Frontier,* Special Issue No. 5, 1973, p. 4.

O'Neal, Bill. "Ben Thompson and King Fisher" ("Great Western Gunfights" column). *True West,* April 1990, p. 60.

_____. "Ben Thompson vs Mark Wilson and Charles Mathews" ("Great Western Gunfights" column). *True West,* March 1990, p. 58.

Panfeld, Peter M. "Sensational Feud Between Two Cities." *Real West,* March 1974, p. 36.

Parsons, Chuck. "Man Without a Past" ("Answer Man" column). *True West,* May 1990, p. 12.

Rickards, Colin. "Gunfighter from Yorkshire." *Frontier Times,* Nov. 1963, p. 22.

Sandell, Jay. "Five Hours of Hell in Ellsworth." *Real West,* Jan. 1960, p. 8.

Sherman, Jory. "Whiskey Guns." *Pioneer West,* March 1968, p. 40. Rpt. *Wild West,* May 1972, p. 40.

Smith, Lew. "Take Your Time—And Aim." *True West,* Oct. 1958, p. 17.

Thorpe, John. "Ben and Billy Thompson." *English Westerners Brand Book,* Vol. XXIII, No. 1, Winter 1984, p. 9.

Thompson, J.H.
Kildare, Maurice. "The Kibbe-Hillpot Murders." *Real West,* Feb. 1970, p. 28.

Thompson, John "Snowshoe Thompson"
Cheney, Louise. "Snowshoe Thompson's Mountain Mail Run." *Real West,* May 1965, p. 27.

Edring, Rupert. "The Race Thompson Had to Win." *The West,* April 1971, p. 40.

Friedman, Ralph. "A Bible for Snowshoe." *Real West,* Jan. 1961, p. 37.

Heald, Weldon F. "Snowshoe Thompson." *True West,* Spring 1954, p. 9.

Scott, Jim. "Snowshoe!" *Frontier Times,* Fall 1962, p. 39.

"Snowshoe Thompson." *Great West,* Dec. 1968, p. 10.

Wagner, Marjorie. "A Man to Match the Mountains." *Frontier Times,* July 1977, p. 14.

Thompson, William "Billy"
DeArment, Robert K. "Bat Masterson's Rescue of Bully Bill." *True West,* Oct. 1979, p. 10.

Heath, Charles G. "The Thompsons of Knottingly." *NOLA Quarterly,* Vol. XIV, No. 1, 1990, p. 4.

Sandell, Jay. "Five Hours of Hell in Ellsworth." *Real West,* Jan. 1960, p. 8.

Schoenberger, Dale T. "Texas Billy Thompson." *Real West,* Spring Special 1985, p. 61.

_____. "Whatever Happened to Texas Billy Thompson?" *Real West,* March 1982, p. 6.

Sherman, Jory. "Whiskey Guns." *Pioneer West,* March 1968, p. 40. Rpt. *Wild West,* May 1972, p. 40.

Thorpe, John. "Ben and Billy Thompson." *English Westerners' Brand Book,* Vol. XXIII, No. 1, Winter 1984, p. 9.

Thompson, William
Carson, Kit. "The Scalping of William Thompson." *The West,* April 1974, p. 32.

Thompson, William Haven "Kid"
Edwards, Harold L. "Kid Thompson and the Roscoe Train Robberies." *True West,* Jan. 1988, p. 48.

Kildare, Maurice. "Kid Thompson's Silver Pesos." *Westerner,* March-April 1970, p. 10.

Thorn, Benjamin "Ben" (also spelled "Thorne")

Greco, David. "Gunfighters and Lawmen" column. *Wild West*, Aug. 1991, p. 12.

Stanley, Samuel. "Ben Thorn: California Lawman." *Real West*, Sept. 1980, p. 36. Rpt. *Real West*, Annual 1981, p. 46.

Traywick, Ben T. "How to Tweak a Killer's Nose." *Golden West*, Jan. 1968, p. 14. Rpt. *Golden West*, Nov. 1973, p. 20; *Western Frontier*, Annual No. 5, 1977, p. 2; and *Western Frontier*, Jan. 1983, p. 2.

Wood, R. Coke. "Ben Thorn, Brave Sheriff." *NOLA Quarterly*, Vol. IV, No. 4, June 1979, p. 6.

Young, Jan. "Killers and Kings at Murphy's" *Real West*, Jan. 1965, p. 42.

Thorn Family (Thomas, Mary, David "Shar," T.J.)

Lehman, Leola. "The Thorns: A New Breed of Men." *Wild West*, March 1971, p. 43. Rpt. *Oldtimers Wild West*, Aug. 1973, p. 54.

Thornburgh, Thomas Tipton

Bloom, Sam. "Crossing the Milk Creek Line." *Real West*, July 1979, p. 32.

Boucher, Leonard H. "The Battle at Milk Creek." *Real West*, Oct. 1970, p. 8.

Clatworthy, Alan. "The Black Private Whose Battle Plan Smashed the Utes." *Frontier West*, Feb. 1972., p. 38.

Fleek, Sherman L. "Race Against Deadly Odds." *Wild West*, Oct. 1989, p. 40.

Greene, Lewis Douglass. "The White River Campaign." *True West*, July 1991, p. 24.

Kirkpatrick, J.R. "The Ambush at Milk Creek." *True West*, July 1991, p. 24.

Malsbary, George. "Massacre at the Agency." *Pioneer West*, Dec. 1971, p. 12.

Tibbets, Robin. "The White River Massacre." *True West*, June 1961, p. 30.

Werner, Fred H. "Ute Fury at Milk Creek." *Real West*, Aug. 1985, p. 32. Rpt. *Real West*, Yearbook, Winter 1986, p. 51.

Thumm, Christopher Fritz

Fitterer, Gary P. "F. Thumm, der Revolverheld von Deutschland." Part I, *NOLA Quarterly*, Vol. XIV, Nos. 3 and 4 (combined issue), 1990, p. 23; Part II, *NOLA Quarterly*, Vol. XV, No. 1, 1991, p. 25; Part III, *NOLA Quarterly*, Vol. XV, No. 2, April-June 1991, p. 16; Part IV, *NOLA Quarterly*, Vol. XV, No. 3, July-Sept. 1991, p. 8.

Thurmond, Charlotte "Lottie Deno"

Cheney, Louise. "The Frozen Heart of Fort Griffin." *Real West*, Sept. 1973, p. 42. Rpt. *Real West*, Annual, Fall 1974, p. 72.

Lewis, Preston. "Lottie Deno, Gambler." *True West,* Sept. 1987, p. 16.

Rainman, Philip. "The Legend of Lottie Deno." *The West,* Dec. 1965, p. 18. Rpt. *The West,* Feb. 1972, p. 10.

Tibbet, William

Edwards, Harold L. "California's Ruthless Outlaw." *Old West,* Summer 1985, p. 52.

————. "Who Killed William Tibbet?" *Real West,* June 1987, p. 23.

Tibbles, Thomas

Stanley, Samuel. "The Saga of Thomas Tibbles: First Fighter for Indian Rights." *Frontier West,* Dec. 1973, p. 38.

Tichenor, William

Fitzgerald, Arlene. "Siege at Battle Rock." *The West,* Sept. 1965, p. 34.

Tilghman, William Matthew "Bill"

Bird, Roy. "Bill Tilghman's Day in Jail." *True West,* Nov. 1991, p. 46.

Breihan, Carl W. "Bill Tilghman: Last of the Old-Style Lawmen." *Oldtimers Wild West,* June 1978, p. 14.

Brock, Paul. "Smash 'Em Down Tilghman." *Western Tales,* April 1960, p. 10.

Burchardt, Bill. "Who Was the Greatest Lawman?" *True West,* Feb. 1957, p. 12.

Craighead, David G. "How a Great Lawman Died." *True West,* Dec. 1967, p. 30.

Croy, Homer. "Bill Tilghman's Prairie Queen." *True West,* June 1960, p. 25.

Dahl, Peter. "Bill Tilghman." *Real West,* Americana Series, Fall 1965, p. 38.

Dahl, Peter Andrew. "He Was the Greatest of Us All." *Real West,* Nov. 1958, p. 36.

DeMattos, Jack. "Bill Tilghman" ("Gunfighters of the Real West" column). *Real West,* Nov. 1979, p. 22.

Gaddis, Bob. "Bill Tilghman, Frontier Lawman." *True Frontier,* Nov. 1968, p. 18.

Holding, Vera. "Bill Tilghman: Frontier Lawman Supreme." *Real Frontier,* March 1970, p. 14.

Malocsay, Zoltan. "Defiance in the Street." *Westerner,* Sept.-Oct. 1972, p. 28.

Morton, Gregory. "Bill Tilghman: Buffalo Hunter Supreme." *Real West,* Jan. 1963, p. 38.

Parsons, Chuck. "James Elder Was Close Friend of Bill Tilghman." *NOLA Quarterly,* Vol. III, No. 1, Summer 1977, p. 11.

————. "The Three Guardsmen" ("Answer Man" column). *True West,* March 1990, p. 12.

Shirley, Glenn. "Guthrie: High, Wide, and Handsome." Rpt. *True West*, April 1989, p. 14.

Stanley, Samuel. "Bill Tilghman Was the Toughest Lawman of Them All." *Frontier West*, Oct. 1973, p. 14.

"True Western Hall of Fame" column. *True Western Adventures*, Dec. 1960, p. 56.

Winfield, Craig. "Tilghman From Dodge City." *Westerner*, Oct. 1971, p. 28.

Wukovitz, John F. "Gunfighters and Lawmen" column. *Wild West*, Aug. 1988, p. 10.

Timothy

Alcorn, Rowena L., and Gordon D. Alcorn. "The Chief Whose Hands Were Never Red." *Old West*, Fall 1967, p. 8.

Price, Will. "Battle on the Ingossomen." *Frontier Times*, Fall 1958, p. 12.

Tobin, Thomas "Tom"

Burke, William. "Vendetta." *True Western Adventures*, Spring 1958, p. 40.

Carson, Kit. "Reward for Juan Espinosa's Head." *Real West*, Sept. 1962, p. 30.

Carson, Xanthus. "Rampage of the Espinosas." *Pioneer West*, July 1969, p. 12.

Churchill, E. Richard. "Tom Tobin: Sack Full of Heads." *True Frontier*, Feb. 1973, p. 19. Rpt. *True Frontier*, Special Issue No. 9, Summer 1974, p. 25; and *True Frontier*, Special Issue No. 19, Fall 1977, p. 17.

Hoskins, James H. "Kit Carson, III, Relates How Tobin Killed Espinosa" ("Wild Old Days" column). *True West*, Dec. 1960, p. 32.

Kildare, Maurice. "The Killers." *Great West*, Dec. 1972, p. 20. Rpt. *Great West*, Summer 1981, p. 56; and *Authentic West*, Fall 1981, p. 61.

Tobin, Harold. "The Most Unforgettable Character I Never Met: Tom Tobin Mountain Man." *Real West*, July 1977, p. 46. Rpt. *Real West*, Yearbook, Summer 1978, p. 36.

Watson, Editha L. "Tom Tobin, Reluctant Hero." *The West*, Dec. 1966, p. 10. Rpt. *Golden West*, April 1974, p. 10.

Todd, George

Breihan, Carl W. "The Battle of Centralia." *Real West*, Dec. 1980, p. 28. Rpt. *Real West*, Annual 1981, p. 54.

Hart, George. "Irvin Walley: The Murderer of Cole Younger's Father." *NOLA Quarterly*, Vol. XV, No. 1, 1991, p. 4.

Tolby, F.J.
Kildare, Maurice. "The Assassination of Parson Tolby." *Golden West,* Sept. 1967, p. 24. Rpt. *The West,* March 1972, p. 20.

Tom, John
Reed, Mrs. Terry J. Letter. *True West,* Oct. 1979, p. 5.

Tombstone Gunfighters
Barkdull, Tom. "There Never Was a Gunfight at the O.K. Corral." *Wild West,* July 1972, p. 8.
Deac, Wilfred P. "Two Minutes in Tombstone." *Wild West,* Aug. 1991, p. 42.
Wasserman, Murray. "Another View of the OK Corral Shoot Out." *Great West,* April 1967, p. 17.

Tompkins, Selah R.J. "Tommy"
Meed, Douglas V. "Attack Pancho Villa!" *Old West,* Fall 1991, p. 40.

Tompkins, William O. "Bill"
Stevens, Robert W. "Ambush in the Chaparral." *Frontier Times,* May 1967, p. 30.

Topperwein, Adolph "Ad"
Wiltsey, Norman B. "The West's Greatest Marksman." *Real West,* Nov. 1968, p. 15.

Toppy Johnson Gang
Rasch, Philip J. "Train Robbery Times Four." *Real West,* Special Issue, Spring 1983, p. 51.

Torrey, Jay L.
Mathisen, Jean A. "Rocky Mountain Riders: Wyoming's Volunteer Cavalry." *True West,* Nov. 1991, p. 30.

Tosah, Jim
Kelly, Bill. "In Pursuit of Jim Tosah." *Real West,* Nov. 1977, p. 22.

Tough, William Sloan
Hale, Donald. "William Sloan Tough: Federal Guerrilla." *True Frontier,* Sept. 1969, p. 24. Rpt. *True Frontier,* Special Issue No. 15, Summer 1976, p. 18.
Snell, Joseph W. "Captain Tough and His Buckskin Scouts." *True West,* April 1970, p. 28.

Walker, Wayne T. "A Man Called Tough." *Real West,* Sept. 1980, p. 6. Rpt. *Real West,* Special Issue, Spring 1982, p. 48.

_____. "Captain Tough: Buckskin Patriot." *The West,* March 1969, p. 24. Rpt. *Western Frontier,* May 1978, p. 16; and *Western Frontier,* Oct. 1984, p. 16.

Tovey, Michael "Mike"

Harrison, John H. "Baddest Man From Bowie [sic]." *Golden West,* May 1974, p. 34. Rpt. *Western Frontier,* May 1986, p. 34.

Ware, Melvin H. "Mike Tovey Rode Shotgun for Twenty Years." *Frontier Times,* July 1978, p. 6.

Tracy, Harry (Harry Severns)

Blankenship, J.W. "Oldtimer Remembers Cassidy, Tracy, Lant, Warner." *NOLA Quarterly,* Vol. III, No. 1, Summer 1977, p. 9.

Breihan, Carl W. "Hank Tracy, the West's Mad Killer." *Real West,* Nov. 1960, p. 32.

_____. "Harry Tracy's Murderous Escape." *Real West,* Jan. 1982, p. 38. Rpt. *Real West,* Yearbook, Fall 1982, p. 46.

Cheney, Louise. "Jail Breaking Cowgirl." *Pioneer West,* Jan. 1968, p. 12.

Cody, John. "Gunsmoke Payoff." *True Frontier,* Feb. 1975, p. 42.

DeMattos, Jack. "Harry Tracy" ("Gunfighters of the Real West" column). *Real West,* Dec. 1985, p. 38.

Dullenty, Jim. "Bad Blood: The True Story of Harry Tracy." *Old West,* Summer 1983, p. 38.

_____. "Bad Man's Death Mask." *True West,* Nov. 1987, p. 37.

_____. "The Many Strange Loves of the Notorious Outlaw Harry Tracy." *NOLA Quarterly,* Vol. XIII, No. 3, Winter 1989, p. 6.

_____. "Plaster Cast of Tracy Found." *NOLA Quarterly,* Vol. XI, No. 3, Winter 1987, p. 3.

_____. "The Tragedy of Harry Tracy." *NOLA Quarterly,* Vol. IV, No. 2, Autumn 1978, p. 10.

Ellison, Douglas W. "Tracy and Lant Escape from Aspen Jail." *The WOLA Journal,* Vol. I, No. 1, Summer 1991, p. 17.

"Harry Tracy: The Man They Couldn't Kill." *Great West,* Dec. 1968, p. 24.

Horan, James. "The Greatest Manhunt in the West." *True Western Adventures,* Issue No. 1, 1957, p. 20.

Johnston, Richard. "Who Robbed the Pleasant Valley Coal Company?" *NOLA Quarterly,* Vol. V, No. 4, April 1980, p. 13.

Norwood, John. "Brown's Hole: Historic Border Hideout." *Frontier Times,* Feb. 1985, p. 43.

Oldham, Maggie Red. "Tragedy Trail of Harry Tracy." *True West,* June 1957, p. 24.

Osgood, Stacy W. "Harry Tracy: Meanest Man Alive or Dead." *Chicago Westerners Brand Book,* Vol. XVI, No. 6, August 1959, p. 1.

Parberry, Jack. Letter. *True West,* Oct. 1957, p. 3.

Repp, Ed Earl. "Oregon Death Dealer." *Westerner,* Jan.-Feb. 1970, p. 48. Rpt. *Westerner,* July-Aug. 1974, p. 18.

Roberts, S.E. Letter, "Old-Timers Corral." *True West,* Oct. 1957, p. 3.

Sanderson, Sandy. "Last of the Great Desperadoes." *True Western Adventures,* Dec. 1960, p. 8.

Webb, Harry. "I Helped Harry Tracy Escape." *Westerner,* April 1971, p. 36.

Williams, Gary. "Harry Tracy, the West's Mad Killer." *Real West,* May 1964, p. 10.

_____. "Mad Dog Killer of the West." *Real West,* Special Issue, Fall 1964, p. 54.

Winfield, Craig. "Harry Tracy's Most Fiendish Act." *Westerner,* Nov.-Dec. 1973, p. 25.

Trafton, Edward "Ed"

Rice, E.R. "The Last of the Stage Coach Robbers." *The West,* Dec. 1965, p. 13. Rpt. *The West,* Jan. 1973, p. 13.

Scott, Jay. "The Friendly Bandit of Yellowstone Park." *True Western Adventures,* Aug. 1960, p. 29.

Watson, John. "A Most Unusual Rustler." *True West,* Sept. 1985, p. 46.

Travis, William Barret

Hayes, Frederick. "Mexican File: What Happened at the Alamo?" *Real West,* July 1960, p. 28.

Traynor, William S. "Bill"

Rickards, Colin. "There Were All Kinds of Gunfighters." *Old West,* Fall 1969, p. 22.

Trevitt, Victor

Holden, Jan. "Victor Trevitt's Last Wish" ("Wild Old Days" column). *True West,* Nov. 1991, p. 62.

Tribolet, Robert
Long, James A. "Bloody Crimes of Robert Tribolet." *The West,* Aug. 1965, p. 34.

Trimble, Christopher
Farner, Thomas E. "Christopher Trimble and the Otter Massacre." *True West,* March 1991, p. 42.

Trousdale, David Andred
Carson, Xanthus. "Gunfight on the Sunset Limited." *Real Frontier,* Aug. 1971, p. 14. Rpt. *True Frontier,* Feb. 1975, p. 8.

Troutman, Joanna
Cheney, Louise. "The Lady and the Flag." *Real West,* Jan. 1967, p. 46.

Truckee
Cerveri, Doris. "Paiute Leaders." *Real West,* Special Issue, Spring 1972, p. 14.

Truesdale, David "Dave"
Mallory, Burr H. "The Jest That Backfired." *True West,* Aug. 1957, p. 22.

Tubbs, Alice "Poker Alice" (Alice Ivers)
Ballenger, Dean W. "Poker Alice Was Too Much for the West's Slickest Card Sharps." *Frontier West,* Oct. 1972, p. 26.

Breihan, Carl W. "Poker Alice: The West's First Woman Gambler." *The West,* June 1972, p. 38.

Cheney, Louise. "Poker Alice." *Pioneer West,* July 1967, p. 11.

Darby, Ray. "Poker Alice: Queen of Gamblers." *True Western Adventures,* June 1961, p. 18.

Drake, John. "Poker Alice: Queen of Gamblers." *Real West,* Aug. 1958, p. 32.

Fielder, Mildred. "Deadwood's Lady of Cards." *Old West,* Fall 1969, p. 32.

LoBello, Nino. "Poker Alice." *True West,* Oct. 1956, p. 47.

Martin, Jeannie. "Poker Alice: Fabulous Lady Gambler." *Real West,* Nov. 1970, p. 10. Rpt. *Real West,* Annual 1972, p. 35.

Miller, James F. "The Greatest Woman Gambler In the West." *True Frontier,* March 1968, p. 14. Rpt. *True Frontier,* Special Issue No. 3, 1972, p. 20.

Nolen, Richard. "Poker Alice: A Woman Given Up." *Westerner,* May-June 1972, p. 44.

Robbins, Lance. "Poker Alice." *Real West,* Jan. 1967, p. 48.

Trendall, Norm. "Poker Alice." *Westerner,* Sept.-Oct. 1969, p. 46.

Tucker, Daniel "Dan"
DeArment, R.K. "Deadly Deputy." *True West*, Nov. 1991, p. 14.

Tucker, David G. "Dave"
Meier, Gary. "The Fall and Rise of Dave Tucker." *True West*, April 1990, p. 52.

Tumlinson Family
White, Lucille Latham. "Tumlinsons: Texas Rangers." *Old West*, Winter 1981, p. 14.

Tunstall, John Henry
Rasch, Philip J. "How the Lincoln County War Started." *True West*, April 1962, p. 30.

Tunstall, Thomas Todd
Rains, Ray D. "The Remarkable Thomas T. Tunstall." *Real West*, Yearbook, Fall 1979, p. 38.

Turkey Leg
Ballenger, Dean W. "How the Cheyennes Bushwhacked An Iron Horse." *Frontier West*, Dec. 1974, p. 10.

Manly, George. "A Battle for the Squaws." *The West*, July 1964, p. 22. Rpt. *The West*, June 1974, p. 26.

O'Donnell, Jeffrey P. "Turkey Leg Raid." *Real West*, Jan. 1988, p. 27.

Uhlarik, Carl. "Scalped by Chief Turkey Leg." *Western Frontier*, Special Issue, Summer 1974, p. 24.

Turner, Clarence
Hoover, Lee. "Clarence Turner, Oklahoma Pioneer." *Real West*, April 1972, p. 24.

Turnow, John
Bush, D.R. Letter. *True West*, April 1969, p. 72.

Henderson, Harley. "Six Notches on Turnow's Gun." *Pioneer West*, March 1968, p. 16.

Lind, C.J. "Oxbow Manhunt." *True Frontier*, Jan. 1971, p. 33. Rpt. *True Frontier*, Special Issue No. 9, 1974, p. 4; and *True Frontier*, Special Issue No. 17, Winter 1976, p. 4.

Kelly, Bill. "I Hunted John Turnow." *Real West*, March 1976, p. 42.

Shields, Mike. "Terror in the Mist." *True West,* Feb. 1967, p. 25.

Tutt, Davis K. "Dave"
Clark, J.B. "The Hickok-Tutt Duel." *Frontier Times,* Spring 1962, p. 45.

Hart, George. "Davis K. Tutt of Yellville." *NOLA Quarterly,* Vol. VIII, No. 1, Summer 1983, p. 8.

Two Moon
Garland, Hamlin. "Chief Two Moon Tells About Custer." *Golden West,* May 1965, p. 43. Rpt. *The West,* July 1972, p. 35; *Western Frontier,* March 1976, p. 34; and *Western Frontier,* Jan. 1981, p. 42.

Werner, Fred H. "The Attack on Two Moons' [sic] Village." *Real West,* Sept. 1979, p. 40.

Wright, Kathryn. "The Mystery of Custer's Lost Gold." *True West,* March 1983, p. 12.

Two Red Tails
Ballenger, Dean W. "How Chief Two Red Tails Won the Rotgut Whiskey War." *Frontier West,* June 1974, p. 22.

Tyson, Mary Ann "Bareback Billie"
Jones, Calico. "The Female Rowdy of the Mother Lode, Bareback Billie." *Real West,* Yearbook, Spring 1974, p. 32.

Underwood, Henry "Dad" (Dr. Henry "Henri" Stewart)
Repp, Ed Earl. "The Mystery of Dad Underwood." *Real Frontier,* April 1970, p. 28. Rpt. *True Frontier,* June 1972, p. 30.

Walker, Wayne T. "The Doctor Who Rode With Sam Bass." *True West,* April 1983, p. 12.

Upson, Marshall Ashmun "Ash"
Henderson, Sam. "Ash Upson: Pat Garrett's Sidekick—and Ghost Writer." *Golden West,* March 1974, p. 26.

Uzzell, Thomas A.
Freeman, Frank M. "He Did His Level Best." *Golden West,* May 1968, p. 14.

Vail, L.B.
Cerveri, Doris. "Nevada's Killer With a Queer Quirk." *True Frontier,* June 1972, p. 24. Rpt. *True Frontier,* Special Issue No. 17, Winter 1976, p. 16.

Vallejo, Mariano Guadalupe
Andrews, Drew. "The Rebel Autocrat of Northern California." *Pioneer West,* May 1967, p. 20.
Malsbary, George. "Comandante Mariano Vallejo." *Great West,* Aug. 1973, p. 24. Rpt. *Great West,* Fall 1981, p. 26.

Vance, Robert Frank
Hornung, Chuck. "Frank Vance, Lawman." *Real West,* April 1980, p. 16. Rpt. *Real West,* Special Issue, 1981, p. 57.

Van Dorn, Earl
"Action at Rush Springs." *Authentic West,* Summer 1981, p. 6.
Edwards, Charles M. "Battle at Crooked Creek." *The West,* July 1964, p. 34.
Lehman, Leola. "Camp on Otter Creek." *The West,* Sept. 1966, p. 28.

Van Orsdel, William Wesley "Brother Van"
Clarke, H. McDonald. "Brother Van Goes West." *The West,* Feb. 1965, p. 8.
Fugleberg, Paul. "Brother Van: A Diamond in the Rough." *True West,* Aug. 1989, p. 40.
Mac, 'Tana. "The Cowboy's Skypilot." *True West,* Oct. 1960, p. 20.
Vander Horck, John. "Blood Bath at Red River." *Real West,* Americana Series, Fall 1966, p. 18.
Webb, Grayce R. "The Friends of Brother Van." *Golden West,* Nov. 1970, p. 30.

Varnum, Charles A.

Shelton, Vern E. "Personality" column. *Wild West,* Dec. 1988, p. 8.

Vasquez, Tiburcio

Bradley, J.R. "The Legend That Was Vasquez." *True West,* Aug. 1962, p. 32.

Coletti, Bruno. "Tiburcio Vasquez, Bandit King." *The West,* Jan. 1967, p. 30. Rpt. *Golden West,* Dec. 1972, p. 22.

Conway, Lenore. "Tiburcio Vasquez: Long Career for Notorious California Bandit." *NOLA Quarterly,* Vol. XII, No. 4, Spring 1988, p. 4.

Cox, Dick. "Tiburcio Vasquez: Lover Bandit." *Real West,* Nov. 1965, p. 34.

DeMattos, Jack. "Tiburcio Vasquez" ("Gunfighters of the Real West" column). *Real West,* July 1981, p. 18.

Kennelly, Joseph. "When Bandit Vasquez Met His Match." *Golden West,* May 1965, p. 20. Rpt. *Golden West,* Feb. 1972, p. 22; and *Western Frontier,* May 1976, p. 12.

Mendoza, Robert. "Bandido, Tiburcio Vasquez." *Great West,* June 1972, p. 34.

Millard, Joseph. "California's Loving Bandit." *True Western Adventures,* Dec. 1960, p. 22.

Noblitt, Jim. "California's Last Outlaw Gang." *Wild West,* Sept. 1970, p. 56. Rpt. *Pioneer West,* Jan. 1977, p. 24; and *Authentic West,* Fall 1981, p. 40.

Reinstedt, Randall A. "The Horseback Gangsters." *Wild West,* Sept. 1971, p. 27. Rpt. *Wild West,* Sept. 1972, p. 19; *Oldtimers Wild West,* April 1974, p. 44; and *Oldtimers Wild West,* Oct. 1974, p. 52.

Rosenhouse, Leo. "The Wild Killer." *Westerner,* July-Aug. 1974, p. 34.

Secrest, William B. "Kingston Raid." *NOLA Quarterly,* Vol. V, No. 1, Oct. 1979, p. 12.

_____. "Riders With Vasquez." *Real West,* Oct. 1986, p. 20.

Vaughn, Hank

Edgerton, Ralph P. "Hank Vaughn, Terror of the Northwest." *NOLA Quarterly,* Vol. IX, No. 2, Autumn 1984, p. 19.

Grant, Robert W. "Hank Vaughn: The Happy Killer." *Westerner,* Nov.-Dec. 1974, p. 32.

Meier, Gary. "Hank Vaughn: Oregon's Native Son-With-A-Gun." *True West,* Aug. 1990, p. 22.

Venard, Steve

Boessenecker, John. "Steve Venard: Wells Fargo's Ace Troubleshooter." *Golden West,* Sept. 1972, p. 10. Rpt. *Western Frontier,* Nov. 1976, p. 12.

Hammond, Vern. "The Bloody Trial [sic, Trail] of Steve Venard." *Real West,* Feb. 1969, p. 24.

Repp, Ed Earl. "Lynch Fever." *Pioneer West,* Oct. 1971, p. 39. Rpt. *Pioneer West,* March 1974, p. 31.

Secrest, William B. "When the Ghosts Met Steve Venard." *Old West,* Fall 1968, p. 20.

Vernon, Tom Averill
Breihan, Carl W. "Tragedy on the Sweetwater." *Golden West,* July 1967, p. 10. Rpt. *The West,* June 1972, p. 20; and *Western Frontier,* Nov. 1978, p. 32.

Victorio
Aranda, Daniel. "An Episode from Victorio's War." *Real West,* Feb. 1984, p. 14. Rpt. *Real West,* Yearbook, Fall 1984, p. 26.

Ball, Eve. "The Fight for Ojo Caliente." *Frontier Times,* Spring 1962, p. 22.

Harnin, William. "Apache Siege at Alma." *True West,* June 1956, p. 8.

Jameson, W.C. "Victorio's Lost Gold." *Old West,* Spring 1989, p. 51.

Jones, Calico. "Victorio's Vengeance Raid." *Real West,* April 1970, p. 31.

Lehman, Leola. "The Day the Tinde Became Apaches." *True Frontier,* Special Issue No. 2, 1972, p. 8.

Rosson, Mary'n. "The Pursuit of Victorio." *Real West,* March 1980, p. 26. Rpt. *Real West,* Special Issue, 1981, p. 14

Tarin, Don Jesus. "Who Was Victorio?" *Frontier Times,* Sept. 1963, p. 24.

Webb, Walter Prescott. "Last War Trail of Victorio." *True West,* April 1957, p. 20. Rpt. *Old West,* Fall 1964, p. 30.

Wiltsey, Norman B. "Hawks of the Desert." *True West,* Dec. 1955, p. 19.

Yarbrough, Leroy. "Victorio, The Desert Fox." *Real West,* June 1969, p. 10. Rpt. *Real West,* Special Issue, Spring 1972, p. 8.

Vigil, Juan
McAdams, Charles. "Sheep Camp Murders." *Frontier Times,* July 1970, p. 6.

Villa, Pancho
Boucher, Leonard H. "Pancho Villa's Revenge." *True Frontier,* May 1971, p. 8. Rpt. *True Frontier,* Special Issue No. 9, Summer 1974, p. 20.

Carson, Xanthus. "How Pancho Villa Groomed General Pershing for World War I." *Wild West,* Nov. 1971, p. 12. Rpt. *Oldtimers Wild West,* July 1974, p. 16; and *Pioneer West,* March 1976, p. 6.

Cole, Martin. "Pancho Villa's Columbus Raid." *Old West,* Fall 1989, p. 46.

Edwards, Harold L. "Rio Grande Valley Scene of Depredations." *NOLA Quarterly,* Vol. IX, No. 3, Winter 1985, p. 11.

Flores, Juan. "Pancho Villa's Benevolent Side." *Old West,* Spring 1982, p. 34.

Fox, Dorothea Magdalene. "A Former Dorado Looks at Villa." *Old West,* Summer 1968, p. 24.

Hunter, J. Marvin. "Pancho Villa's Assassination." Rpt. *Frontier Times,* March 1979, p. 25.

Judia, Bert. "Viva Villa!" *Frontier Times,* Fall 1961, p. 20.

King, Richard A. "Viva Villa: A Meeting With an Old Foe." *Wild West,* March 1970, p. 8.

Klohr, James E. "Chasing the Greatest Bandido of All." *Old West,* Spring 1971, p. 6.

Knoles-Peterson. "Scarlet Finale: The Death of Pancho Villa." *The West,* Feb. 1967, p. 10. Rpt. *The West,* Sept. 1973, p. 28.

Meed, Douglas V. "Attack Pancho Villa!" *Old West,* Fall 1991, p. 40.

Molthan, Ruth. "Pancho Villa's Columbus Raid." *The West,* March 1973, p. 34. Rpt. *Western Frontier,* Sept. 1975, p. 28.

Morrison, William V., and C.L. Sonnichsen. "They Killed Pancho Villa." *Frontier Times,* Winter 1959-60, p. 6.

Murphy, John F., Jr. "Raiders Rapidly Pursued." *Wild West,* Aug. 1990, p. 42.

Rossen [sic, Rosson], M.N. "The Life After Death of Pancho Villa." *Westerner,* Spring 1975, p. 8.

Rosson, Mary'n. "El Paso Kibitzes a Revolution." *Pioneer West,* June 1972, p. 30.

————. "Pancho Villa Didn't Spend All His Time Fighting." *Frontier West,* Oct. 1974, p. 10.

Valdner, Robert. "I Fought Pancho Villa." *True West,* Nov. 1982, p. 24.

Violet, James Ruben
Kelly, Bill. "The Vendetta Against Violets." *Real West,* July 1978, p. 38.

Vizcarra, Jose Antonio
Kildare, Maurice. "El Toro, Toro!" *Great West,* Aug. 1973, p. 32. Rpt. *Great West,* Fall 1981, p. 36.

Voigt, Andrew
Koller, Joe. "Andrew Voigt: Cow Country Stalwart." *Golden West,* July 1966, p. 14.

Von Berg, Charles L.

Steele, Phillip. "Captain Charles Louis Von Berg." *True Frontier*, March 1970, p. 26.

Waddell, William

Hartley, William B. "The Fabulous Pony Express." *True Western Adventures*, Jan. 1960, p. 12.

Mays, Carelton. "Tragedy of the Pony Express." *Real West*, Nov. 1960, p. 8. Rpt. *Real West*, Annual, Spring 1968, p. 18.

Wade, William Albert "Kid"

Dodge, Matt. "Kid Wade: Youngest of Nebraska's Pony Boys." *Old West*, Fall 1984, p. 20.

Swanson, Budington. "Death of a Pony Boy." *Real West*, Annual, Spring 1982, p. 48.

Waggoner, Daniel "Dan," and William Thomas "Tom"

Allen, Stookie. "The Richest Rancho In Texas." *The West*, March 1969, p. 16.

Hancock, Wm. CX, and Wylie W. Bennett, Sr. "Ranchero Grande." *Frontier Times*, March 1964, p. 14.

Waggoner, Thomas J. "Tom"

Hancock, Wm. CX, and Wylie W. Bennett, Sr. "Ranchero Grande." *Frontier Times*, March 1964, p. 14.

Hawthorne, Roger. "Conflict and Conspiracy." *True West*, June 1984, p. 12.

Waightman, George "Red Buck"

Beutler, Randy L. "'Red Buck': An Unknown Oklahoma Outlaw." *NOLA Quarterly*, Vol. VII, No. 1, Spring 1982, p. 4.

Bowen, Sanford. "End of the Trail for Red Buck." *Frontier Times*, July 1970, p. 26.

Steele, Phillip. "The Woman Red Buck Couldn't Scare." *The West*, April 1971, p. 20. Rpt. *Western Frontier*, Special Issue, Fall 1974, p. 12.

Wakara (Walkara) (see Walker)

Walker

Fleek, Sherman L. "Warriors and Chiefs" column. *Wild West,* Feb. 1990, p. 12.

Kildare, Maurice. "Chief Walker's War!" *True Frontier,* July 1971, p. 8.

Spendlove, Earl. "Wakara, the Mormon Menace." *The West,* Dec. 1966, p. 26.

Young, Bob and Jan. "Wakara: Napoleon of the Desert." *Real West,* Dec. 1968, p. 14.

Walker Brothers (Newt, Thomas, James, and Phillip)

Edwards, Harold L. "The Deadly Walkers." *True West,* July 1991, p. 37.

Walker, Joe

Kelly, Bill. "The Extermination of Joe Walker." *Real West,* May 1979, p. 38.

Parsons, Chuck. "Walker of the Wild Bunch" ("Answer Man" column). *True West,* Nov. 1991, p. 12.

Walker, Joseph Reddeford

Booth, Percy H. "West Wind: The Life of Joseph Reddeford Walker." *Old West,* Winter 1966, p. 72.

Cherry, Neeli. "Tough Trailblazer." *Western Round-up,* Aug. 1970, p. 58. Rpt. *Oldtimers Wild West,* April 1974, p. 34; and *Pioneer West,* May 1976, p. 6.

_____. "The Tremendous Feat of Trailblazer Joe Walker." *Pioneer West,* May 1968, p. 36.

Walker, Samuel "Sam"

Bishop, Curtis. "He Made the Colt Pistol Work." *Frontier Times,* Summer 1961, p. 4.

Bloom, Sam. "How the Revolver Blasted the Hell Trails Open." *Frontier West,* April 1975, p. 30.

Walker, Thomas Ira

Parsons, Chuck. "Wanted for Murder" ("Answer Man" column). *True West,* Dec. 1989, p. 12.

Walker, William

Repp, Ed Earl. "Legion of the Damned." *Pioneer West,* Feb. 1972, p. 32. Rpt. *Pioneer West,* June 1975, p. 34.

Roper, William L. "The Man Who Took Over Nicaragua." *True Frontier,* May

1971, p. 26. Rpt. *True Frontier,* Special Issue No. 7, Fall 1973, p. 32.

Young, Bob and Jan. "William Walker: King of the Filibusters." *True West,* Winter 1953, p. 30. Rpt. *Old West,* Summer 1965, p. 50.

Walla Tonka (William Going)

Secrest, William B. "Walla Tonka's Way." *Real West,* March 1982, p. 18. Rpt. *Real West,* Special Issue, Spring 1983, p. 30.

Wallace, Jake

Carmody, Lee. "Whiskey Vengeance of the Outraged Sioux." *Frontier West,* June 1975, p. 18.

Wallace, James "Jim"

O'Neal, Bill. "First National Bank Robbery" ("Great Western Gunfights" column). *True West,* Oct. 1991, p. 58.

Wallace, Lew

Carson, Kit. "Ben Hur and Billy the Kid." *Real West,* Jan. 1965, p. 16.

Cheney, Louise. "The Saga of Governor Lew Wallace." *The West,* Feb. 1970, p. 16. Rpt. *Golden West,* July 1973, p. 40.

Shulsinger, Stephanie Cooper. "'Ben Hur' Wallace Out West." *Real West,* Jan. 1975, p. 49.

Wallace, William Alexander Anderson "Big-Foot"

Gipson, Tommie. "Big Foot Wallace and the Little Author." *True West,* June 1958, p. 4.

Howard, Glenn T. "Exhuming Big Foot in Texas." *True West,* Sept. 1984, p. 23.

Powers, Mark. "Big Foot Wallace: A Legend in His Own Time." *Real West,* Feb. 1974, p. 10.

———. "Legendary Texan: Big Foot Wallace." *True Frontier,* Nov. 1967, p. 28. Rpt. *True Frontier,* Special Issue No. 3, 1972, p. 16; and *True Frontier,* June 1976, p. 16.

Reed, James. "Giant Killer Wallace." *Real West,* Feb. 1959, p. 24.

Sowell, A.J. "The Life of Big Foot Wallace." *Old West,* Fall 1964, p. 68.

Whittlesey, Dorothy. "Big Foot Wallace: The Texas Daniel Boone." *True Frontier,* Jan. 1970, p. 8. Rpt. *True Frontier,* Special Issue No. 7, Fall 1973, p. 16.

Zoltan, E.L. "Big Foot Wallace of Texas." *Golden West,* May 1968, p. 22.

Walley, Irvin

Hart, George. "Irvin Walley: The Murderer of Cole Younger's Father." *NOLA Quarterly,* Vol. XV, No. 1, 1991, p. 4.

Walsh, Molly

Robertson, Dorothy. "Molly Walsh." *True Frontier,* April 1973, p. 39.

Walters, William "Broncho Bill"

Boessenecker, John. "I Shot Broncho Bill." *Real West,* Feb. 1986, p. 24.

Cox, "Salty John," transcribed by Eve Ball. "Salty John Cox and Broncho Bill." *True West,* June 1977, p. 24.

Rasch, Philip J. "An Incomplete Account of 'Broncho Bill' Walters." *English Westerners Brand Book,* Vol. IXX, No. 2, Jan. 1977.

Winfield, Craig. "Broncho Bill Walters: Last of the Old Time Train Robbers." *Oldtimers Wild West,* Dec. 1977, p. 8.

_____. "Broncho Bill Walters: Texas Badman." *Real West,* Oct. 1969, p. 10.

Walzer, Jacob

Morando, B. "The Murderous Lost Dutchman Mine." *Real West,* Summer 1964, p. 54.

Spanish, Johnny. "The Cave of Gold." *True Frontier,* Special Issue No. 8, Winter 1973, p. 26.

Ward Family (massacre victims)

Underwood, Larry. "The Ward Massacre." *True West,* May 1988, p. 54.

Ward, Molly

Crosby, Harold. "The Bloody Revenge of Molly Ward." *Frontier West,* Feb. 1972, p. 14.

Ware, Richard C. "Dick"

Baum, Jim. "Colorado City Killings." *Old West,* Winter 1988, p. 26.

Hamm, Michael. Letter. *The West,* June 1973, p. 6.

Warner, Willard Erastus Christianson "Matt"

Blankenship, J.W. "Oldtimer Remembers Cassidy, Tracy, Lant, Warner." *NOLA Quarterly,* Vol. III, No. 1, Summer 1977, p. 9.

Hardy, Harvey. "A Long Ride With Matt Warner." *Frontier Times,* Nov. 1964, p. 34.

Lacy, Steve. "Matt Warner's Daughter Meets Butch Cassidy." *NOLA Quarterly,* Vol. VII, No. 1, Summer 1981, p. 17.

Rhoades, Gale R. "The Different Worlds of Matt Warner." *The West,* June 1971, p. 24. Rpt. *Western Frontier,* Special Issue, Fall 1974, p. 24; and *Western Frontier,* May 1985, p. 24.

Sheller, Roscoe. "The Sheriff Was in Trouble." *Golden West,* April 1974, p. 26. Rpt. *Western Frontier,* Jan. 1978, p. 22.

Skovlin, John. "The McCarty Gang." *NOLA Quarterly,* Vol. V, No. 3, April 1980, p. 16.

Stewart, Robert Haslam. "Young Bob Stewart Recalls Meeting Matt Warner." *NOLA Quarterly,* Vol. VII, No. 1, Summer 1981, p. 19.

Warner, Joyce. "I Remember My Father, Matt Warner." *NOLA Quarterly,* Vol. XIII, No. 3, Winter 1989, p. 19.

Warren, George

Stevens, Peter F. "The Man Who Threw Away Twenty Million Dollars" ("Wild Old Days" column). *True West,* June 1989, p. 60.

Underwood, Dale T. "Bisbee: The Queen of Copper." *Frontier Times,* Jan. 1975, p. 6.

Washakie

Clack, Jeff. "Chief Washakie: Some Personal Recollections." *Golden West,* July 1973, p. 34. Rpt. *Western Frontier,* Sept. 1976, p. 40; and *Western Frontier,* April 1982, p. 12.

Clark, Helen. "Saga of Chief Washakie." *Real West,* Sept. 1965, p. 22.

Delo, David M. "The Battle of Snake Mountain." *The West,* Nov. 1987, p. 26.

Judge, Bill. "Chief Washakie's Sack of Scalps." *True West,* April 1963, p. 19.

Slantey, Samuel. "Washakie: Shoshone Chief." *Real West,* Nov. 1987, p. 25.

Walker, Wayne T. "Chief Washakie." *Great West,* June 1972, p. 6. Rpt. *Authentic West,* Fall 1981, p. 6.

————. "Chief Washakie of the Shoshone." *Pioneer West,* Nov. 1978, p. 22.

Washington, William "Bill"

Lehman, Leola. "Cattle King of Mud Creek." *The West,* April 1974, p. 26. Rpt. *Western Frontier,* Jan. 1977, p. 18.

Wassaja (see Montezuma, Carlos)

Waters, James

Silva, Lee A. "James Waters: Mountain Man." *True West,* May 1988, p. 30.

Watie, Stand

Brewington, E.H. "River Full of Whiskey." *The West,* Aug. 1969, p. 14.

Gaines, W. Craig. "The Great Wagon Train Raid." *Wild West,* Dec. 1991, p. 30.

Gilstrap, Lou. "Cherokee General." *Frontier Times,* Summer 1961, p. 8.

Johnson, Norman K. "General Stand Watie and the Indians' Confederacy." *True West,* Sept. 1985, p. 18.

Lehman, Leola. "Cherokee Blood Feud On the Trail of Tears." *True Frontier,* Special Issue No. 2, 1972, p. 28.

Stanley, Samuel. "The Rebel Cherokee General Who Refused to Sound Retreat." *Frontier West,* June 1975, p. 32.

Walker, Wayne T. "Soldiers in War Paint." *The West,* March 1967, p. 22.

Watkins, Solomon

Kildare, Maurice. "Master Trapper, Indian Fighter and Squaw-Man." *Wild West,* Oct. 1969, p. 19. Rpt. *Pioneer West,* Dec. 1974, p. 17.

Watson, Edgar J. "Ed"

Caruso, Cecelia. "Emperor Watson: Belle Starr's Killer Had Secret Career As Murderer." *True West,* Jan. 1983, p. 38.

Kelly, Bill. "Pearl Younger and the Falling Starrs." *Real West,* Nov. 1976, p. 36.

Watson, Ella "Cattle Kate"

Anderson, Pete. "The Hanging of Cattle Kate." *True Western Adventures,* Dec. 1960, p. 28.

Beachy, E.B. Dykes. "The Saga of Cattle Kate." *Frontier Times,* March 1964, p. 22.

Boucher, Leonard H. "The Wyoming Invaders." *Great West,* Sept. 1969, p. 16.

Dickson, Ruth. "The Terrible Fate of Cattle Kate." *Big West,* Aug. 1967, p. 11.

Hines, Lawrence. "Horror Lynching of the Petticoat Rustler." *Frontier West,* Feb. 1973, p. 36.

Holding, Vera. "Cattle Kate, Queen of the Rustlers." *True Frontier,* Sept. 1969, p. 42.

Mumey, Nolie. "Behind a Woman's Skirt: The Saga of 'Cattle Kate.'" *Denver Westerners' Brand Book,* Vol. VI, No. 12, Dec. 1950, p. 1.

Pons, A.C. "The Lynching of Cattle Kate." *The West,* March 1964, p. 34. Rpt. *The West,* Annual 1971, p. 25.

"The Sweetwater Rustlers." *Great West,* Aug. 1970, p. 29.

Webb, Harry E. "With a Noose Around Her Neck." *Westerner,* May-June 1972, p. 14.

Wattron, Frank J.
Secrest, William B. "Nobody Laughed When Smiley Died." *True West,* Oct. 1967, p. 24.

Weaver Brothers (Phillip, Henry, and Oliver)
Pfalser, Ivan L. "Schoolhouse Lynching." *True West,* April 1969, p. 37.

Weaver, Powell "Pauline"
Cheney, Louise. "Powell Weaver: Arizona Pioneer." *The West,* Jan. 1967, p. 29.

Webb, John Joshua
DeMattos, Jack. "John Joshua Webb" ("Gunfighters of the Real West" column). *Real West,* April 1981, p. 32.

Holben, Dick. "Biography of a Lynching." *The West,* July 1973, p. 34. Rpt. *Western Frontier,* Annual No. 1, 1975, p. 28.

_____. "Playing Both Sides of the Law Was a Desperate Game." *Frontier West,* June 1974, p. 18.

Holben, Richard. "When the Dodge City Gang Took Over Las Vegas." *Pioneer West,* May 1977, p. 12.

Robbins, Lance. "The Respectable Mr. Webb." *Real West,* July 1968, p. 35.

Snell, Joseph W. "'Wretched Webb.'" *Frontier Times,* March 1973, p. 26.

Webb, William W.
Kildare, Maurice. "Ranger Shoot-Out at the Cowboy Saloon." *The West,* Jan. 1973, p. 24.

O'Neal, Bill. "Arizona Rangers vs Lon Bass" ("Great Western Gunfights" column). *True West,* Nov. 1990, p. 58.

Webster, A.B.
Madden, Bill. "Dodge City's Wildest Day." *Real West,* Oct. 1957, p. 50.

Wells, Charles Knox Polk
Breihan, Carl W. "The Fieldon Bank Robbery." *Real West,* Nov. 1977, p. 18. Rpt. *Real West,* Yearbook, Fall 1979, p. 12.

_____. Letter. *Real West,* Sept. 1971, p. 59.

Wells, Henry

Coonfield, Ed. "The West's Last Successful Outlaw." *Westerner,* April 1971, p. 58.

Shoemaker, Arthur. "Henry Wells Outlived Them All." *True West,* Feb. 1990, p. 42.

Turpin, Robert F. "The Nitro Gang." *Great West,* April 1971, p. 18.

Wells, Samuel (Charlie Pitts)

Hart, George. "Irvin Walley: The Murderer of Cole Younger's Father." *NOLA Quarterly,* Vol. XV, No. 1, 1991, p. 4.

Wells, William

Boessenecker, John. "William Wells' Bloody Escape." *True West,* Sept. 1986, p. 44.

West, Richard "Little Dick"

Parsons, Chuck. "Doolin Gang Lookout" ("Answer Man" column). *True West,* July 1984, p. 38.

Qualey, Jake. "Little Dick, the Terrible." *Real West,* Nov. 1960, p. 24.

Westfall, Jasper

Meier, Gary. "Last Gunfight in Westfall." *True West,* Jan. 1991, p. 26.

Westfall, William

Winfield, Craig. "Jesse James and the 1881Winston Train Robbery." *Oldtimers Wild West,* Aug. 1977, p. 14.

Wetzel, Lew

Wiltsey, Norman B. "Frontier Guardian." *Frontier Times,* Winter 1958-59, p. 14.

Wheeler, Benjamin F. "Ben"

Breihan, Carl W. "Desperate Men, Desperate Guns." *Real West,* Annual, Winter 1977-78, p. 16.

Wheeler, Grant

Kildare, Maurice. "The Wilcox Double Robbery." *Real West,* June 1968, p. 31.

Wheeler, Harry C.

O'Neal, Bill. "Arizona Lawmen vs Rustlers" ("Great Western Gunfights" column). *True West,* Nov 1988, p. 60.

_____. "Harry Wheeler, Captain of the Arizona Rangers." *Real West,* Dec. 1983, p. 20. Rpt. *Real West,* Yearbook, Fall 1984, p. 58.

_____. "Harry Wheeler vs J.A. Tracy" ("Great Western Gunfights" column). *True West,* July 1988, p. 54.

_____. "Harry Wheeler vs Joe Bostwick" ("Great Western Gunfights" column). *True West,* Nov 1989, p. 60.

Wheeler, Henry H.

Bender, William, Jr. "'You Shot Him, He's Yours.'" *True Western Adventures,* April 1960, p. 10.

Rickards, Colin. "Bones of the Northfield Robbers." *Real West,* Jan. 1979, p. 28.

Wheeler, John W.

Froman, Robert. "The Giant and the Gunslinger." *True Western Adventures,* Oct. 1960, p. 23.

"Was 'Big Foot' Only a Legend?" *Western Frontier,* Nov. 1976, p. 5.

Wheeler, Oliver W

Shirley, Glenn. "Col. Oliver W. Wheeler: He Broke the Chisholm Trail." *True West,* Oct. 1988, p. 22.

_____. "First Up the Chisholm." *Real West,* Oct. 1968, p. 39.

Whicher, John

Fitzgerald, Ruth Coder. "John Whicher: Fallen Pinkerton." *NOLA Quarterly,* Vol. XIV, No. 1, 1990, p. 6.

White, Gideon Shields "Cap"

McKennon, C.H. "'Cap' White Followed the Book." *Old West,* Fall 1973, p. 16.

White, James "Jim"

DeArment, Robert K. "Boss Hunter." *True West,* April 1989, p. 20.

Shull, Hella I. "Jim White: 'Boss Hunter.'" *Old West,* Fall 1983, p. 61.

White, Jonathan ("Buffalo Chip"; "Jim" White, "Charlie" White)

"Buffalo Bill's Shadow." *Great West,* Dec. 1968, p. 20.

Koller, Joe. "How Death Came to Buffalo Bill's Shadow." *The West,* May 1964, p. 14.

White Bull

Turpin, Bob. "The Fight at Muddy Creek." *Great West,* June 1974, p. 6.

Whitehill, Harvey H.

Caldwell, George A. "New Mexico's First Train Robbery." *NOLA Quarterly,* Vol. XIII, No. 3, Winter 1989, p. 14.

Cline, Don. "Strange Fate for the Bloody Benders." *NOLA Quarterly,* Vol. XI, No. 4, Spring 1987, p. 15.

Kildare, Maurice. "Saga of the Gallant Sheriff." *The West,* Aug. 1968, p. 26. Rpt. *Western Frontier,* April 1983, p. 22.

White Horse

Huston, Fred. "White Horse Was a Special Kind of Frontier Terrorist." *Frontier West,* April 1975, p. 26.

Whitley, William "Bill"

Burton, Jeff. "The Most Surprised Man in Texas." *Frontier Times,* March 1973, p. 18.

Whitman, Marcus and Narcissa

Bishop, Jack. "The Whitman Misson Horror." *The West,* Sept. 1964, p. 40.

Cheney, Louise. "The Cayuse Massacre." *Pioneer West,* Nov. 1969, p. 22.

Fleming, Gerry. "Narcissa Whitman: First Woman to Cross the Rockies." *True Frontier,* Dec. 1971, p. 20.

Frazier, Thomas A. "Over the Rockies." *Real West,* June 1975, p. 42.

Kirkpatrick, J.R. "The Incredible Journey of Marcus Whitman." *Real West,* June 1986, p. 42.

Larson, Jack. "The Devil Half Breed and the Columbia River Massacre." *Frontier West,* June 1975, p. 40.

Lavender, David. "Sky of Brass, Earth of Iron." Rpt. *Old West,* Fall 1966, p. 2.

Malsbary, George. "The Oregon Missionary Massacre." *True Frontier,* April 1978, p. 6.

Pratt, Grace Raffey. "Black Robes and Circuit Riders." *Old West,* Fall 1972, p. 28.

Schurmacher, Emile C. "The Four-Thousand-Mile Survival Ordeal of Long-Chance Marcus Whitman." *Western Action,* Sept. 1960, p. 36.

Scott, Paul T. "Day of Massacre." *Frontier Times,* Winter 1958-59, p. 4.

Whitney Brothers

Bradak, Gary S. Letter. *True West,* April 1980, p. 5.

Hadley, Mary Stoner. "Cokeville, a Rough Town in the Old West." *NOLA Quarterly,* Vol. VII, No. 1, Spring 1982, p. 9.

Stoner, Mary E. "My Father Was a Train Robber." *True West,* Aug. 1983, p. 14.

Whitney, Chauncey B.

Kansas State Historical Society. "Ellsworth County Sheriff Murdered." *Frontier Times,* March 1974, p. 40.

Sherman, Jory. "Whiskey Guns." *Pioneer West,* March 1968, p. 40. Rpt. *Wild West,* May 1972, p. 40.

Whitney, Hugh

Thompson, George A. "How Come They Never Caught Hugh Whitney?" *True West,* Oct. 1979, p. 25.

Whittlesey, Elston C.

Whittlesey, D.H. "He Said 'Hell No' to the Daltons." *Golden West,* May 1974, p. 38.

Wickenburg, Henry

Goff, Carolyn. "RIP Henry Wickenburg." *True West,* June 1976, p. 28.

Keller, Kent J., and Smoki Wolfe. "The Vulture Mine: Arizona's Comstock Lode." *True West,* Oct. 1991, p. 50.

Warner, Fred E. "Henry Wickenburg's Old Colt." *Frontier Times,* Sept. 1972, p 30.

Wilbarger, Josiah

Auer, Louise Cheney. "Miracle of Josiah Wilbarger." *Real West,* Sept. 1965, p. 51.

Blakely, Mike. "A Ghost of a Chance." *True West,* Oct. 1987, p. 52.

Dobie, J. Frank. "The Dream That Saved Wilbarger." *True West,* Aug. 1955, p. 14.

Howard, Robert E. "Apparition of Josiah Wilbarger." *The West,* Sept. 1967, p. 40.

Wilbur, James H.

Sheller, Roscoe. "James H. Wilbur, Indian Agent." *Golden West,* July 1967, p. 22. Rpt. *The West,* Aug. 1974, p. 28.

Wild Bunch

Barton, John D. "Outlaws, Lawmen, Law-Abiding Citizens, and Mormons." *The Outlaw Trail Journal,* Vol. I, No. 1, Summer 1991, p. 15.

Beasley, Phillip. "The Wild Bunch's $137,000 Buried Fortune Is Waiting for You." *Frontier West,* Oct. 1971, p. 48.

Borger, Ed. "Attack at Wilcox." *Westerner,* Nov.-Dec. 1973, p. 29.

Breihan, Carl W. "Butch Cassidy and Company: Riders of the Outlaw Trail." Part I, *Real West,* May 1971, p. 6; Part II, *Real West,* June 1971, p. 46.

Buck, Dan, and Anne Meadows. "What the Wild Bunch Did in South America." *The WOLA Journal,* Vol. I, No. 1, Spring-Summer 1991, p. 3.

Chambers, Howard V. "The Wild Bunch." *Pioneer West,* May 1969, p. 6. Rpt. *Pioneer West,* Collector's Annual 1971, p. 58.

Masters, George. "She Devil of the Wild Bunch." *Real West,* Aug. 1959, p. 8.

Pointer, Larry. "Probable Photo of Wild Bunch Discovered." *NOLA Quarterly,* Vol. II, No. 3, 1976-77, p. 9.

Wilford, Lem

Mitchell, George. "The Day the Town Was Forced to Mourn Its Most Notorious Harlot." *Frontier West,* Feb. 1975, p. 14.

Willard, Marshal "Cap"

Koller, Joe. "Montana's Bloodiest Day." *The West,* Oct. 1964, p. 24. Rpt. *Golden West,* June 1974, p. 9.

Williams, Ben

Henderson, Sam. "Ben Williams: The Fighting Quaker." *The West,* March 1974, p. 22.

Shirley, Glenn. "Ben Williams, Quaker Marshal." *Real West,* Jan. 1969, p. 10. Rpt. *Real West,* Special Issue, Fall 1973, p. 18.

Williams Brothers (Ed and Lon, real names Ed and Lon Maxwell)

Chapin, Earl V. "The Day They Hanged Ed Williams." *Real West,* Nov. 1971, p. 33.

Williams, Frank

Lawson, George. "Death Drove the Last Chance Stage." *Frontier West,* Dec. 1971, p. 24.

Williams Gang
Repp, Ed Earl. "Lynch Fever." *Pioneer West,* Oct. 1971, p. 39. Rpt. *Pioneer West,* March 1974, p. 31.

Williams, George
Ernst, Robert R. "Gunfire in Bartlesville." *NOLA Quarterly,* Vol. XV, No. 4, Oct.-Dec. 1991, p. 26.

Williams, James
Kildare, Maurice. "Hell Gate Hanging Bee." *Real West,* March 1967, p. 27.

Williams, Joe
Rasch, Philip J. "Two Diamonds Bid, Two Diamonds Down." *NOLA Quarterly,* Vol. IX, No. 2, Autumn 1984, p. 8.

Williams, Loren L.
Collins, Orpha. "Ambush on the Coquille." *True West,* Aug. 1963, p. 44.

Wylie, Howard. "An Incredible Journey to Save a Friend." *Golden West,* Aug. 1974, p. 34.

Williams, Moses
Meketa, Jacqueline Dorgan. "With Unflinching Devotion to Duty." *True West,* March 1991, p. 18.

Williams, William Sherley "Old Bill"
Burke, James. "Savage With a Bible." *Great West,* June 1967, p. 9.

Griffith, A. Kinney. "Old Solitaire: Bill Williams." *True West,* Oct. 1969, p. 6.

Williamson, Robert McAlpin "Three-Legged Willie"
Cheney, Louise. "Fabulous 'Three-Legged Willie' of Texas." *Real West,* April 1973, p. 18.

Goff, Dot Smollen. "Three-Legged Willie." *Frontier Times,* July 1975, p. 19.

Shanklin, John M. "'Three-Legged Willie' Williamson." *The West,* Jan. 1966, p. 8.

Willie Boy (Swift Fox)
Quinn, Jay. "Marathon of Death." *True Western Adventures,* June 1959, p. 22.

Young, Bob. "They'll Kill You, Willie Boy!" *Real West,* July 1966, p. 26.

Willingham, Caleb Berg "Cape"

Kildare, Maurice. "The Gut Fighters Who Made 'Hell Town' the Bloodiest Place in Texas." *Frontier West,* Dec. 1972, p. 28.

Walker, Wayne T. "Cape Willingham: Panhandle Legend." *Real West,* March 1977, p. 18. Rpt. *Real West,* Annual, Winter 1979, p. 28.

_____. "Lawman Willingham and the Taming of the Panhandle." *The West,* Dec. 1969, p. 30. Rpt. *Western Frontier,* Winter 1978, p . 6.

Willow, Edward

Edwards, Harold L. "The Unpleasant Task." *True West,* March 1990, p. 20.

Wilson, Charley

Holt, Roy D. "Feuding With the Southern Pacific." *Frontier Times,* May 1975, p. 14.

Wilson, Clay

Pharo, Agnes M. "The Intellectual Con-Man." *Frontier Times,* Sept. 1965, p. 25.

Wilson, Samuel A. "Sam"

Murray, David. "Sam Wilson: Single-Handed Train Robber." *Old West,* Summer 1984, p. 38.

Wilson, Vernon "Vic"

Boessenecker, John. "Buckshot for a Marshal." *Real West,* Feb. 1983, p. 35. Rpt. *Real West,* Annual, Spring 1984, p. 59.

Secrest, William B. "He Saw the Posse Die." *Frontier Times,* July 1966, p. 10.

Wilson, William "Billy"

Kildare, Maurice. "Take a Walk to Doom." *Real West,* April 1970, p. 38.

Wilson, William "Billy" (David L. Anderson)

Browning, Jim. "Who Was Billy Wilson?" *NOLA Quarterly,* Vol. XIV, No. 2, Summer 1990, p. 25.

Wilson, William

Klasner, Lily Casey. "Double Hanging at Lincoln." *Frontier Times,* Sept. 1972, p. 10.

Wilson, William J. "One-Armed Billy"

Garner, E.L. "Bill Wilson's Getaway." *Frontier Times,* March 1968, p. 21.

Windolf, Charles W.
Ross, Raymond J. "He Rode to the Little Big Horn." *Real West,* Sept. 1970, p. 46.

Winema (Toby Riddle)
Cheney, Louise. "Winema, Heroine of the Modoc War." *Real West,* Oct. 1970, p. 56.

Jan, Bob. "Pocahontas of the Far West." *The West,* May 1964, p. 21. Rpt. *Western Frontier,* Special Issue, Dec. 1974, p. 13.

Wiltsey, Norman B. "Winema: Indian Heroine of the West." *Real West,* April 1973, p. 31.

Wingart, George
Neilson, Lawrence. "The Bloody Showdown at Jacob's Well." *Frontier West,* Aug. 1971, p. 28.

Winn, "Big Anne"
Henderson, Sam. "The Sad Saga of Big Anne." *Golden West,* May 1969, p. 26.

Winnemucca
Cerveri, Doris. "Paiute Battle at Pyramid Lake." *Real West,* Special Issue, Winter 1970, p . 24.

Snipes, Earl. "Strange Sacrifice of Winnemucca's Young Wife." *The West,* March 1972, p. 18.

Swanson, Burlington. "Paiute Poison." *The West,* June 1973, p. 16.

Winnemucca, Sarah
Canfield, Gae Whitney. "Sarah Winnemucca and the War in the West." *True West,* Nov. 1983, p. 34.

Cerveri, Mrs. John. "Sarah Winnemucca." *True West,* Aug. 1964, p. 41.

Stewart, Patricia. "Sarah Winnemucca: Paiute Princess." *Real Frontier,* Oct. 1970, p. 12. Rpt. *True Frontier,* Special Issue No. 2, 1972, p. 34; and *True Frontier,* Special Issue No. 14, Spring 1976, p. 46.

Winters, Jim
Coburn, Walt. "No Re-Ride." *True West,* Sept. 1954, p. 11.

Wise, Eugene B.
Dorry, Jack. "The Boomerang Necktie Party." *Wild West,* May 1972, p. 44.

Wister, Owen
Kimmel, Thelma. "The Virginian." *True West,* Dec. 1970, p . 32.

Wöhrle, John Anton (also spelled Whorlie, Whorle, Worley)
Johnson, Dave. "Revenge in Mason County, Texas." *NOLA Quarterly,* Vol. X, No. 1, Summer 1985, p. 2.

Wolcott, Frank
Cortesi, Lawrence J. "The Johnson County War." *Pioneer West,* March 1979, p. 6.

Walker, Wayne T. "Johnson County War: Final Test of Cattleman Supremacy." *Real West,* Annual 1981, p. 42.

Womack, Robert "Crazy Bob"
Gaddis, P.W. "The Cripple Creek Mines." *Westerner,* May-June 1970, p. 38.

Lanza, Ruth Willett. "'Crazy Bob' Womack: Cripple Creek Prospector." *True West,* Dec. 1991, p. 35.

Wood, George
O'Neal, Bill. "George Flatt vs. George Wood and Jake Adams" ("Great Western Gunfights" column). *True West,* May 1988, p. 59.

Woods, Zadock
Howell, Montie. "The Woods Clan and the Dawson Massacre." *True West,* June 1988, p. 52.

Woolsey, King Sam
Cortesi, Lawrence. "The Apache Peace Conference That Set the Southwest Aflame." *Frontier West,* April 1975, p. 14.

Dillon, Richard. "King Sam Woolsey and the Bloody Tanks Expedition." *Frontier Times,* Nov. 1978, p. 20.

Long, James. "Saga of King Sam Woolsey." *The West,* Jan. 1966, p. 30. Rpt. *Golden West,* Feb. 1972, p. 5; and *Western Frontier,* May 1976, p. 5.

Wooten, Richens Lacy "Uncle Dick"
Huston, Fred. "Mountain Man Capitalist." *The West,* Feb. 1970, p. 28.

————. "Uncle Dick Wooten: the Mountain Man's Locomotive." *Western Frontier,* Special Issue, Oct. 1983, p. 34.

Martin, Bernice. "Uncle Dick." *Frontier Times,* Fall 1961, p. 30.

Martin, Cy. "It Took a Special Brand of Courage to Be a Rangeland Tycoon." *Frontier West,* April 1973, p. 34.

Millard, Joseph. "Cut Hand, the Mountain Man." *True Western Adventures,* April 1961, p. 28.

Tidwell, Dewey. "Uncle Dick Wooten, Trailblazer." *Real West,* Dec. 1981, p. 18. Rpt. *Real West,* Annual, Spring 1983, p. 28.

Worcester, Samuel Austin

Koller, Joe. "Trail to Cherokee West." *Golden West,* Sept. 1968, p. 14.

Worden, Salter "Limp Foot"

DeNevi, Don. "The San Joaquin Bandit King." *Real West,* Yearbook, Fall 1984, p. 66.

Workman, William

Kennelley, Joe. "Life and Death of a Pioneer Family." *Golden West,* Aug. 1972, p. 18.

Wovoka (Jack Wilson)

"Great Ghost Dance of the Western Plains." *Western Frontier,* Nov. 1976, p. 16.

Guttman, John. "Warriors and Chiefs" column. *Wild West,* April 1989, p. 10.

Johnson, Dorothy M. "Wovoka: The Indian Christ." *True Western Adventures,* Oct. 1960, p. 16.

Lehman, Leola. "The Ghost Dancers." *Real Frontier,* Aug. 1971, p. 16.

Meyers, John Frederick. "Where the Ghosts Danced in Blood." *Real West,* July 1961, p. 20. Rpt. *Real West,* Special Issue, Winter 1963, p. 38.

Noren, Evelyn. "Wovoka: Messiah or Fraud?" *Frontier Times,* Dec. 1984, p. 11.

Wratten, George Medhurst

Ball, Eve. "Interpreter for the Apaches." *True West,* Dec. 1971, p. 26.

Henderson, Sam. "George Wratten: Interpreter to Geronimo." *Pioneer West,* Jan. 1979, p. 22.

Reis, Judy R. "An Unlikely Power Struggle." *True West,* Feb. 1991, p. 26.

Wright, Cooper

Timmons, Herbert M. "When Cooper Wright Met the Mob." *Old West,* Fall 1964, p. 26.

Wright, Lawerence Baker
Parsons, Chuck. "A Pair of Texas Rangers: The Wright Brothers." *Old West,*
Winter 1986, p. 24.

Wright, Linton Lafayette
Parsons, Chuck. "A Pair of Texas Rangers: The Wright Brothers." *Old West,*
Winter 1986, p. 24.

Wyatt, Nelson "Zip" (see Yeager, Dick)

Wyeth, Nathaniel
Allen, Paul G. "The Bitter Trip Back." *True West,* Dec. 1967, p . 22.
Grimmett, Robert G. "Wyeth Believed in Himself." *Golden West,* March 1971,
p. 14.

Wynkoop, Ned
Kraft, Louis. "Shoot Them on Sight." *Wild West,* Oct. 1988, p. 43.

Yaholo
Malocsay, Zoltan. "Yaholo: The Yankee Indian General." *Westerner,* Aug. 1971,
p. 29.

Yantis, Oliver "Ol"
Bird, Roy. "The Wild Bunch Robbed the Spearville Bank." *Real West,* April 1987,
p. 14.
Holt, Daniel D., and Joseph W. Snell. "Who Killed Oliver Yantis?" *True West,*
Feb. 1966, p. 24.

Yarberry, Milton J.
Cline, Donald. "City Constable Hanged for Murder." *NOLA Quarterly,* Vol. IX,
No. 2, Autumn 1984, p. 13.
DeArment, Robert K. "The Blood-Spattered Trail of Milton J. Yarberry." *Old
West,* Fall 1985, p. 8.

Gregg, Andy. "The Day They Hung Marshal Yarbery [sic]." *Real West*, Nov. 1961, p. 8. Rpt. *Real West*, Annual, Spring 1968, p. 24.

Robbins, Lance. "The Killer Who Succeeded at Dying." *Real West*, Americana Series, Fall 1965, p. 59.

Yeager, "Dick" (Nelson "Zip" Wyatt)

Harrison, Fred. "The Desperado With Nine Lives." *The West*, Oct. 1965, p. 28. Rpt. *Western Frontier*, Annual, Spring 1981, p. 8.

Hughes, F. Horace. "Outlaws Black and Yeager." *Frontier Times*, July 1969, p. 38.

McBee, G. Fred. "Zip Wyatt's Winchester for Killing." *Great West*, Oct. 1970, p. 6.

Morton, Ross. "Outlaw from Cowboy Flat." *Real West*, May 1960, p. 16.

Schott, Joseph. "Zip Wyatt: Fadeout Bandit." *True Western Adventures*, April 1961, p. 8.

Yeager, Sam

Dallenger, Dean. "The Old West's Incredible Counterfeiter." *True Western Adventures*, June 1961, p. 8.

_____. "They Hanged the Fabulous Little Sam." *Real West*, Nov. 1963, p. 22.

Garvin, Fred L. "Sam Yeager Was a Counterfeiter." *Golden West*, July 1965, p. 8.

McCammon, Warren. "They Hung Sam Yeager." *Great West*, Aug. 1971, p. 6.

Yellow Wolf

Ballard, David M. "Yellow Wolf, Loner in the Nez Percé War." *Frontier Times*, April 1985, p. 38.

Ege, Robert J. "The Escape of Yellow Wolf." *Real West*, Jan. 1971, p. 6.

"Yellowstone Kelly" (see Kelly, Luther Sage)

York, William H.

Holding, Vera. "The Goings On At the Bender Place." *Golden West*, June 1972, p. 32.

Yoscolo

Cox, Dick. "Yoscolo, Fighting Alcalde of the Digger Indians." *Real West*, Special Issue, Spring 1972, p. 34.

Young, Brigham
Evans, Mark. "Brigham Young and the Saints Went Marching." *True West*, Dec. 1961, p. 20.

Pierce, Norman C. "Brigham Young's Fabulous Lost Gold Mine." *Real West*, Special Issue, Summer 1964, p. 22.

Swanson, Budington. "The Glory Vision." *Real Frontier*, June 1971, p. 14.

Young, Cole
Cline, Donald. "Cole Young, Train Robber." *Old West*, Summer 1985, p. 10.

Kelly, Bill. "Cole Young and Friends." *Real West*, May 1977, p. 36.

Young, Emma
Jones, Calico. "Wild Horse Mary." *Pioneer West*, Jan. 1968, p. 30.

Young, Ewing
Friedman, Ralph. "West's Wildest Cattle Drive." *Real West*, March 1965, p. 23.

Hicks, Flora Weed. "Ewing Young: Pathfinder and Pioneer." *Golden West*, Jan. 1969, p. 28.

Meier, Gary. "The West's First Cattle Drive." *True West*, Feb. 1990, p. 37.

Young-Man-Afraid-of-His-Horses
Swanson, Budington. "How Little Big Man Tried to Save the Black Hills." *Western Frontier*, Special Issue, March 1975, p . 34.

Younger Brothers (Cole, Jim, and Bob)
Brant, Marley. "Outlaws' Inlaws in California." *Frontier Times*, Feb. 1985, p. 18.

_____. "Whatever Happened to the Russellville Bank?" *True West*, March 1987, p . 42.

Breihan, Carl W. "The Northfield Raid." *The West*, Nov. 1966, p. 10. Rpt. *The West*, June 1972, p. 26; and *Western Frontier*, Sept. 1980, p. 34.

Elliott, Susan. "Sixguns at Northfield." *Great West*, May 1968, p. 16.

Gaddis, Robert W. "They Headed North to Death." *True Frontier*, June 1967, p. 32.

Linn, William C. "The James-Younger Gang: Murderers." *NOLA Quarterly*, Vol. III, No. 4, Spring 1977, p. 7.

Mallory, Charles. "Younger Family Reunion." *Frontier Times*, Feb. 1985, p. 54.

McLeod, Norman. "The Northfield Raid and Whiskey." *NOLA Quarterly*, Vol. XIII, No. 3, Winter 1989, p. 25.

Parsons, Chuck. "The Boy Who Turned in the Younger Gang." *True West,* Jan. 1984, p. 24.

_____. "In Pursuit of the Northfield Robbers." *NOLA Quarterly,* Vol. IV, No. 4, June 1979, p. 14.

Reedstrom, E. Lisle. "Free the Youngers!" *True West,* Feb. 1991, p. 14.

Thomas, Leva L. "A Family Letter Regarding the Youngers." *True West,* Oct. 1972, p. 34.

Turner, Brian P. "The James-Younger Gang in Kentucky." *Real West,* Special Issue, Spring 1985, p. 8.

_____. "The James-Younger Gang: Some Profitable Time Spent in Kentucky." *Real West,* Dec. 1982, p. 41.

Wukovits, John F. "Raiders Repulsed by Fire." *Wild West,* Oct. 1988, p. 18.

Younger, Bruce

Brant, Marley. "Bruce Younger: The Man, the Myth, the Mummy." *True West,* March 1989, p. 37.

Younger, Coleman "Cole"

Breihan, Carl W. "Cole Younger of Lee's Summit." *Real West,* Dec. 1973, p. 14.

_____. "Did Cole Younger Rob the Bank at Corinth?" *Real West,* Nov. 1971, p. 17.

Croy, Homer. "Last of the Great Outlaws." *America's Frontier West,* Issue No. 1, n.d., p. 44.

Huntley, A. "Cole Younger." *Real West,* Special Issue, Fall 1964, p. 26.

Nieberding, Velma, and Harold Preece. "The West's Outlaws Found No Peace Even in Death." *Frontier West,* Dec. 1971, p. 42.

O'Liam, Dugal. "Cole Younger: Outlaw King." *True Western Adventures,* Feb. 1960, p . 40.

Younger, Henry W.

Hart, George. "Irvin Walley: The Murderer of Cole Younger's Father." *NOLA Quarterly,* Vol. XV, No. 1, 1991, p. 4.

Younger, James "Jim"

Knowles, Edward. "The Lost Love of Jim Younger." *Old West,* Spring 1967, p. 18.

O'Neal, Bill. "John and Jim Younger vs Pinkertons" ("Great Western Gunfights" column). *True West,* Feb. 1991, p. 56.

Younger, John

Brant, Marley. "John Younger: James Gang Member?" *True West,* March 1987, p. 45.

Breihan, Carl W. "Death of John Younger." *Real West,* Sept. 1974, p. 36.

O'Neal, Bill. "John and Jim Younger vs Pinkertons" ("Great Western Gunfights" column). *True West,* Feb. 1991, p. 56.

Zink, Wilbur A. "Gun Battle at Roscoe." *Frontier Times,* March 1969, p. 6.

Yount, George C.

Parsons, Chuck. "Mountain Men" ("Answer Man" column). *True West,* Oct. 1989, p. 14.

Yuba

Kildare, Maurice. "Chief Yuba's Death Trail." *Westerner,* July-Aug. 1974, p. 50.

Yuma Prison Inmates

Carson, Xanthus. "Death Trek to Hell!" *True Frontier,* Aug. 1974, p. 16.

About the Author

Jim Browning was born in 1921 near Atlanta, Georgia. During World War II, he spent three and one-half years in the United States Army Air Corps. After completing his military service, he returned to the University of Georgia, where he earned his BS and MS degrees in chemistry and was elected to the Phi Beta Kappa Honor Society. He taught chemistry at the college level for forty years, the last thirty-six at The Citadel, The Military College of South Carolina. He retired from that institution in 1986.

Jim's interest in the Old West began more than fifty years ago. Since then he has traveled and done research extensively throughout the United States, Canada, Mexico, and Central America. He estimates that he has driven more than 300,000 miles and taken more than 34,000 color slides of old forts, ghost towns, gravesites, and weapons owned by famous outlaws and lawmen.